The History Detectives

Explore Lincoln's Letter, Parker's Sax and Mark Twain's Watch

And Many More Mysteries of America's Past

The history
Detectives

Explore Lincoln's Letter, Parker's Sax and Mark Twain's Watch

And Many More Mysteries of America's Past

BARB KARG

WILEY

John Wiley & Sons, Inc.

This book is dedicated to George and Trudi Karg, Chris Grant,
Piper Maru, and Rick Sutherland. All survivors. All my heroes.

And to every individual the world over who strives to shed light
on history, and in doing so makes his or her own history.

CONTENTS

Evelyn Nesbit,
page 41

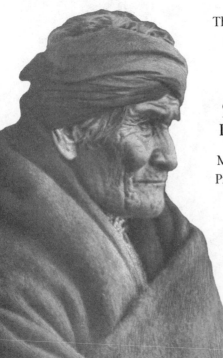

Crystal cross, page 278

John Brown, page 195

*World War II Pacific
Theater artifact,
page 343*

PREFACE

When you think of American history, what's the first thing that comes to mind? The birth of the United States? The fight against slavery or for women's suffrage? The Gold Rush? The successes and tragedies of wars? The study of history can be a passionate pursuit, whether it means learning more about local, national, or global events surrounding individuals or artifacts, or simply uncovering your own familial heritage. Many years ago, one of my best friends recited to me the words from a Leonard Cohen song: "There's a crack in everything. That's how the light gets in." Those words had a very profound and lasting impact on me. And while that concept applies to every aspect of life, it's especially true of historical investigations. History isn't made by just the movers and shakers, but by each one of us every minute of every day. Birth, death, marriage, career, art, entertainment, sports, blogs; everything we say and do is a record of our existence, and while not everything makes it into a book or newspaper or online, it marks a moment in history—a moment that may one day become part of an investigation by an intrepid professional or amateur historian searching for answers to complex questions.

Since 2002, hundreds of thousands of loyal viewers have journeyed through time, exploring a wide range of mysteries presented to them by the popular PBS series *History Detectives*. By examining simple objects, documents, and structures, the show has drawn us into major sagas of American history, offering a creative approach to television programming. Each *History Detectives* episode is told from many different angles as the intrepid investigators draw on a multiplicity of investigative strategies utilizing modern research techniques, scientific tools, library research, and interviews with some of the most talented scholars, scientists, historians,

History Detective
Gwendolyn Wright.

and experts in their field. As a joint production between Oregon Public Broadcasting and Lion Television, the series has showcased dozens of mysteries surrounding various homes, family genealogies, and artifacts ranging from letters, books, paintings, weapons, vehicles, rare documents, and musical instruments to war memorabilia and even a few skeletons. Each investigation is unique and in many cases highly personal in its research, analysis, procedure, and above all, its telling of a story that might never have seen the light of day. This book is a compilation of the journey *History Detectives* has taken, focusing on investigations prompted by viewers who sought help in solving a historical mystery. Also included are additional stories and background research associated with each investigation—information that adds even more breadth and scope to the journey taken by the History Detectives in their quest for answers.

What makes *History Detectives* so special is that it makes history fun and engaging, inspiring individuals of all ages to investigate American history through interesting artifacts, objects, and structures, many of which are close to home. The majority of investigations are begun as a result of viewer participation. As thousands of viewers' e-mails can attest, *History Detectives* is innovative in its approach to teaching all of us how we can unravel the secrets of bygone eras, starting with something we may have in our own homes. Over 150 investigations have resulted in amazing revelations that answer some baffling historical questions presented to us by a quartet of very special hosts.

Each of the four History Detectives approaches an investigation in his or her own way, and the journeys they take us on are fascinating no matter what the outcome may be. Exploring history is as close as we get to time travel, and *History Detectives* has taken viewers across the millennia from a 5,000-year-old bison skull to several present-day family reunions. Gwendolyn Wright, Elyse Luray, Tukufu Zuberi, and Wes Cowan know how to make history sing, and the heart and savvy they apply to solving the mysteries of history make them rock stars of their respective disciplines.

A renowned Columbia University professor of Architecture, Planning, and Preservation and a professor of history, Gwendolyn Wright is highly respected in several fields for a career that spans all kinds of buildings and places, showing how they connect with larger cultural histories. A well-known national and international lecturer, she is the author of six books, including *Building the Dream: A Social History of Housing in America*, now in its seventeenth printing. Her latest book, *USA: Modern Architectures in History*, has already been hailed as "the standard reference." Gwen holds a doctorate and a master's degree in architecture from the University of California, Berkeley. She has received numerous awards, including a prestigious Guggenheim Fellowship. Gwen brings a unique perspective, depth, and joie de vivre to each of her investigations, whether it's examining nuclear submarine documents, helping an adoptee find her birthplace and mother, or identifying an unusual concrete home. There's no stopping Gwen in her search for answers, a fact made all the more apparent by her breadth of experience and willingness to think outside the box—an invaluable asset for any historian, scholar, or professional history detective.

History Detective
Elyse Luray.

A former Christie's auction house appraiser and auctioneer for over a decade, Elyse Luray brings her own expertise, excitement, and heart to each investigation. Elyse's youthful exuberance and presence belies the critical eye and systematically analytic detecting skills she brings to the team. In her own words: "To be a successful detective you have to reason, dissect, and conclude," and that's exactly how she handles every case, whether it's an ancient bison skull, a presidential letter, or a pilfered Revolutionary War cannon. Shortly after graduating from Tulane University with a major in art history, Elyse gravitated to Christie's, where she became vice president of the Popular Arts Department, launching new markets in Western Memorabilia, Arms and Armour, and Native American Art. While at Christie's, Elyse appraised the archives of Lucasfilms, DreamWorks, Planet Hollywood, Warner Bros., Hanna-Barbera, and the personal collection of influential animator Chuck Jones. Among her many notable auction sales was a record-setting $690,000 garnered for one of the few pairs of Judy Garland's ruby slippers used in *The Wizard of Oz*.

A licensed auctioneer, Elyse spends a lot of her spare time lending her auctioneering skills to charities throughout the country to help raise money for many different causes. She is currently part of the Dean's Council of Tulane University, where she is involved in helping students and the university. Turning her unmistakable talents to the small screen, Elyse was an appraiser on the PBS production *Antiques Roadshow* and *The Early Morning Show* on CBS. In addition to participating in *History Detectives*, she is also an appraiser for the television programs *If Walls Could Talk* and is the host of *Treasure Seekers* on Rainbow Media's satellite service, VOOM.

By his own admission, History Detective Tukufu Zuberi has never been disappointed with any investigation, a fact clearly evidenced by the enthusiasm, determination, and emotion he puts into solving each and every mystery that comes his way. Since the beginning of the series, Tukufu has delved into everything from the poignant letters written by abolitionist John Brown to tracking down a Japanese internment camp survivor to racing around Death Valley in a 1932 Ford Roadster. No mystery is

History Detective
Tukufu Zuberi.

insignificant for Tukufu, who wears several hats at the University of Pennsylvania, serving as professor of sociology, Lasry Family Professor of Race Relations, and director of the Center of Africana Studies. In addition to being an author, Tukufu directs an international collaboration of thirty African nations known as the African Census Analysis Project (ACAP), and has served as visiting professor in Kampala, Uganda, at Mekerere University, and in Tanzania at the University of Dar es Salaam. Raised in the housing projects of Oakland, California, Tukufu was born Antonio McDaniel. His Swahili name translates to "beyond praise" and "strength," a tribute born of his desire to "make and have connection with an important period where people were challenging what it means to be a human being."

As a child, History Detective Wes Cowan had a love of antiques, which has served him well in his adult endeavors as both an appraiser and an auctioneer. Wes is the founder and owner of Cowan's Auctions, Incorporated, an internationally recognized Cincinnati-based auction house. Like his colleagues, Wes brings enormous depth, experience, and humor to his investigations, whether he's dressing up in a Civil War uniform, interviewing a survivor of the USS *Indianapolis*, or donning a ten-gallon hat for an investigative romp through the OK Corral. Interestingly, his scholastic pursuits originally took him down the academic path. With a B.A. and a master's degree in anthropology from the University of Kentucky, and a Ph.D. in anthropology from the University of Michigan, Wes taught at Ohio State University and served as Curator of Archaeology at the Cincinnati Museum of Natural History. He has also been widely published in the American archaeology and paleoethnobotany fields. But all that changed in 1995, when he departed from

History Detective
Wes Cowan.

the academic environment and returned to his love of antiques. To date, he's received international acclaim for his expertise in historic Americana and is an appraiser on the PBS series *Antiques Roadshow*.

As any historian, scholar, researcher, newshound, history buff, or average reader can attest, attempting to dive headfirst into historical research is not for the faint of heart. Save for a handful of major historical events, the names, dates, and especially accounts about any given historical era, figure, or event are always the subject of great debate. Just ask anyone for their opinion about who was on the grassy knoll or what occurred at Area 51 and you'll quickly experience the pride and pitfalls of compiling historical data. Whether you're a professional or an amateur history detective, it's certain that you can become frustrated by the alternate glut or apparent lack of information available on a subject, but remember that every historical hindrance may somehow lead you to the pot of gold at the end of the rainbow in one form or another. The thrill is in the chase, and that's part and parcel of what drives the History Detectives down steep slopes, scenic byways, and sometimes bumpy roads that lead them off the beaten path. Oftentimes, that's where they find the best information.

Whether you're an ardent fan of *History Detectives* or new to the series, you'll no doubt appreciate the research and presentation that goes into each episode, created by dozens of incredibly hard-working individuals who are passionate about uncovering a story and sharing with you the methods they utilized so that you can become your own history detective. Winston Churchill once wrote: "History with its flickering lamp stumbles along the trail of the past, trying to reconstruct its scenes, to revive its echoes, and kindle with pale gleams the passion of former days," a statement well suited to the embarkation of any investigative endeavor. It is my fondest hope, as well as that of everyone involved in *History Detectives*, that you enjoy the telling of these tales and revel in the light that exudes from the cracking of each mystery.

Looking forward to joining you on the next season of *History Detectives*!

ACKNOWLEDGMENTS

Creating a book from start to finish is never an easy endeavor, and it invariably requires the help and creative collaboration of many talented individuals. *The History Detectives Explore Lincoln's Letter, Parker's Sax, and Mark Twain's Watch: And Many More Mysteries of America's Past* is a labor of love that highlights the multi-faceted investigations of the highly popular and innovative PBS series *History Detectives*. Joining me on this remarkable adventure were crews of talented individuals who since the beginning of the series have worked tirelessly to create a show that provides hundreds of thousands of viewers a unique slant on history by investigating a wide range of objects, events, and individuals that have left an indelible mark on the intricate collage of our past.

For starters, I'd like to thank the amazing folks at Oregon Public Broadcasting, many of whom played invaluable roles in the making of this book. Co-executive producer David Davis has been deeply involved since the inception of the project, and his professionalism is unmatched. Thank you, Dave, for allowing me to run with this project, and for all the sound advice, patience, graciousness, and humor you've displayed, and for the long hours you put into every stage of production from start to finish. You are, quite simply, the best, and I couldn't have done this without you. To researcher Carol Sherman I also offer my highest accolades. My "soul sister" in the research realm, I can't tell you how much I appreciate all of your hard work and persistence in the search for photography and show participants, and above all, your lasting friendship, which means the world to me. You're the bomb! I'd also like to give a major shout to associate producer Larry Johnson for the excellent work he did in procuring and checking images with such professional aplomb. Thanks, Larry, your contributions to the book and your brilliant humor are priceless!

Several other outstanding individuals at OPB were invaluable in bringing this book to fruition. Many thanks to production management coordinator Susan Boyd, senior production manager Cheri Arbini, marketing associate Claire Adamsick, administrative ace Stacy Coonfield, and transcriber Trish Bunyard for their combined efforts in providing all of the show transcripts, episode dubs, Web access, and every other conceivable bit of information that was needed. A hearty thanks as well to OPB staff attorney Rebecca Morris for her help in finalizing all of the contracts and agreements necessary to make this book happen, and to illustrator Chris Gates, a talented artist with whom it has been my distinct pleasure to work. To all of you exceptional folks, I'd like you to know that you're the finest group of individuals I've ever worked with, and it has been my great pleasure and honor to have shared this journey with you.

I also offer my gratitude to *History Detectives* co-executive producer Nick Catliff, who continues his hard work on the series to this day, and co-executive producers Tony Tackaberry and Chris Bryson, whose diligence results in the ongoing excellence of *History Detectives*. Special thanks go out to John Wilson and his staff at PBS for supporting the series since its premiere in 2002, and to Jacoba Atlas, the former co-chief programming executive at PBS who was instrumental in supporting the series when it first began, and to a host of talented individuals, including Lyn Seymour, Sandy Heberer, Allison Winshel, and Shawn Halford. And a sincere round of applause must also go to all of the outstanding production teams who have worked tirelessly on the series over the past six years. Many thanks as well to the fine folks at Lion Television, co-producers and creators of the series, with a special shout to Kevin McLoughlin for his consistently Herculean efforts to make a lot from a little (money, that is).

In addition to all of these wonderful folks, I'd like to thank the four History Detectives: Elyse Luray, Wes Cowan, Tukufu Zuberi, and Gwen Wright. Their insight and dedication to the show have brought class, education, and intelligence to the series since its first episode. Thanks as well to all of the experts, historians, and scholars who gave their time and valuable advice to each investigation, and to the amazing audience and online visitors PBS and OPB are indebted to for making *History Detectives* the success that it is. On that note, ultimate thanks go to all of the individuals and families who have willingly and bravely shared with all of us their personal histories and objects and, above all, the stories of family members whose remarkable tales might never have been recognized. In particular, I'd like to thank Dodie Jacobi and George Tamura for their courage and their willingness to share their lives and photos with us for this book. Without all of you, quite simply, there would be no *History Detectives*.

At the production end of the spectrum, I'd like to thank John Wiley & Sons for working with OPB, PBS, and me to bring this book to life. Special thanks go to editor Stephen S. Power for all his help in making this book happen and for his great enthusiasm for *History Detectives*. Without his dogged determination, this book might never have seen the light of day. Also, to senior production manager Marcia Samuels for her tireless work toward making this project the best it could possibly be. I salute you both. I'd also like to give a shout out to Wiley editorial assistant Ellen Wright, and fellow Quark enthusiast Colleen Dunlap of Forty-Five Degree design for their kind assistance during the making of this book.

On a personal note, I have many amazing individuals to thank for their never-ending support and love, including my awesome parents, George and Trudi Karg, and my sister, Chris, the best family anyone could ever hope for. Also to Glen, Ellen and Jim, Jeannie and Jim, and the entire Spaite family, Paula Munier, Jim Van Over, Linda Bruno, Karla Edwards, Professor Jack Hicks, and my beloved Scribe Tribe. Above all, there are two individuals without whom I couldn't have written and produced this book. To Ellen Weider, my dear friend and colleague who has been with this project since day one through its planning, copyediting, researching, and fact checking. Words cannot express how much respect and admiration I have for you on all levels. You are astonishing, brilliant, and I love you to bits! And to Rick Sutherland, my partner in life and crime, I offer my highest regard and admiration for his skills as a writer, editor, researcher, artist, designer, printer, and hero in the face of overwhelming adversity. I love you with all my heart. And for always keeping me on the straight and narrow, my heart belongs to Piper, Jazz, Maya, Jinks, Scout, Sasha, Harley, and Mog. My love and gratitude to you all.

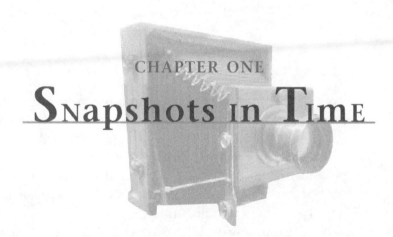

CHAPTER ONE

Snapshots in Time

Many of the investigations *History Detectives* tackles shed light on some of the darkest and most challenging incidents and artifacts that American history has to offer. Some of those mysteries focus on the life of a particular man or woman, while others center on the role a specific object played in a historic setting. The tales you're about to read are a perfect example of the many roles individuals have played in this nation's saga.

The name Robert Smith is very common, but chances are you won't recognize him as a prisoner of war. The same holds true for Adolf Fingrut, a man whose ingenuity kept him alive during the Holocaust, and John Thompson, whose work ethic and sheer bravery made him the most famous mail carrier in history. And then there's the formidable duo of Alice Paul and Lucy Burns, two women whose fearlessness and tenacity helped give American women the right to vote. All of these heroes left a mark on history, and while they aren't household names, they should be, because without their efforts—amid thousands of other individual efforts—our daily lives wouldn't be as rich with courage, wisdom, and the ability to perform honorably in the face of abominable circumstances.

1

The Haunting Portraits in the Attic

When Americans discuss historical atrocities of warfare, few may realize that terrible cruelties took place in the United States during the Civil War, when dozens of camps in the North and the South held Union and Confederate prisoners in deplorable conditions. Infamous prisons such as Andersonville, Johnson's Island, Fort Delaware, and Rock Island were sites of egregious abuse of Civil War POWs, an estimated 55,000 of whom lost their lives as a result of their incarceration.

This particularly disturbing aspect of American history was brought to the attention of *History Detectives* by Floridian Geoffrey Feazell, who was mystified by a set of old photographs, shown to him by his grandmother, that were allegedly taken by his great-great-grandfather, Robert M. Smith, who was a Confederate prisoner. Feazell's story caught the attention of History Detective Wes Cowan, who traveled to Daytona Beach to examine the photos firsthand and was amazed by the story told to him by Feazell.

According to family history, Smith was confined at Johnson's Island in Lake Erie, Ohio, where he is said to have taken portraits of fellow inmates with a very special camera of his own making and developed them using pilfered chemicals. Feazell showed Wes four photos inside a case bearing a label explaining that Smith secretly built his camera with salvaged materials and that the chemicals came from the camp's hospital. Feazell also produced several unusual jewelry pieces that the family was certain Smith had created.

time
TEASER Which Confederate general traveled with an unusual hen that each morning left a single egg under his cot?

Answer: Robert E. Lee.

The truly astonishing aspect to the mystery was that according to the label, Smith used a pocket knife to build his camera out of a tin can, a pine plank, and a spyglass lens. It also indicated that the photos Smith took were taken "in the gable of the garret, or attic of Cell Block Number Four." At the outset, the story seemed unbelievable—that a prisoner of war would have the wherewithal to actually pull off such a technically demanding endeavor. And that was precisely what Geoffrey Feazell wanted Wes to confirm.

Caustic Camps

In the scope of history, surprisingly little is written about the horror of Civil War prison camps and the brave souls who, no matter which side they fought for, were made to endure deplorable conditions during the four years that war raged, from 1861 to 1865. Without question one of the bloodiest conflicts the United States has ever fought, the Civil War is estimated to have caused at least one million casualties, including the injured, missing in action, and the 650,000 soldiers who perished. Statistics of several of the worst battles alone, such as Gettysburg, Shiloh, Antietam, and Stones River, account for tens of thousands of casualties.

The death tolls at over 150 Union and Confederate POW camps were just as horrifying. Estimates show that around 211,000 Union and over 620,000 Confederate soldiers wound up in a prison camp. Of those, it is said that over 55,000 men died while imprisoned. Georgia's Andersonville Prison had an astonishing death toll of almost 13,000, more than 40 percent of its 33,000 prisoners.

Incarceration in any one of these camps was a lesson in misery, primarily as a result of overcrowding, disease, improper sanitation, shortage of food, sparse medical care, and lack of clothing and proper shelter against bitter temperatures. Isolated from their families, prisoners did the best

Johnson's Island POW camp in Lake Erie's Sandusky Bay.

they could to pass the time, including plotting the most effective means of escaping what could only be described as hell. Considered at first to be one of the less brutal camps was Ohio's Johnson's Island, which primarily housed Confederate officers.

But all of that changed in early 1864 when rumors about atrocities occurring in Southern POW camps like Andersonville reached the North. Outraged by the treatment of their prisoners, Union officials returned the favor by cutting off supplies and basics to Confederate prisoners in an evil game of tit for tat. If Robert Smith was indeed at Johnson's Island as his family legend suggests, it's likely he would have had a hard time building a camera and procuring chemicals for his photo development process.

In order to establish Smith's incarceration, Wes did Internet searches on Civil War sites to find out more about Smith and two of the men he took portraits of: F. M. Jackson and James G. Rose. What he discovered was that Lieutenant Smith was indeed imprisoned on the 300-acre Johnson's Island, which was located in Lake Erie's Sandusky Bay and leased by the government for an annual fee of $500. Originally built to contain about 2,500 inmates, the sixteen-acre compound included over forty structures and about a dozen two-story cell blocks that confined more than 10,000 Confederate prisoners from 1862 to 1865.

Guarded by the 128th Ohio Volunteer Infantry, Johnson's Island was plagued by harsh winters, disease, and a continued lack of fuel and sustenance. No doubt Smith found the situation as deplorable as fellow inmates, Jackson and Rose, both of whom Wes was able to confirm as prisoners. Captain F. M. Jackson spent eighteen months on Johnson's Island after being apprehended at the Battle of Big Black River Bridge in the spring of 1863. Part of the 61st Tennessee Mounted Infantry, James G. Rose was captured near Bulls Gap, Tennessee. Upon closer inspection of the portraits of Jackson and Rose, Wes was baffled as to how a makeshift camera made of such unsophisticated materials could possibly have taken any picture, let alone portraits. Not having the original camera, he decided it was time for drastic experimentation.

DID YOU know

New York's Mathew B. Brady is often credited as the master photographic chronicler of the Civil War. Brady was a successful and well-established photographer before the advent of war and felt that his unique position gave him the responsibility for documenting the reality of the conflict. In truth, many photographs credited to Brady were actually taken by members of his staff, and the cost of financing his extensive operations severely drained his bank account by war's end. In 1875, Congress paid Brady $25,000 for full title to his images.

PHOTO FINISH

To confirm Robert Smith's masterful McGyveresque camera construction, Wes contacted Civil War photography expert Rob Gibson, who gathered up the same materials Smith allegedly used to build his camera. Gibson's analysis of the old portraits indicated that they were produced by means of *wet-plate photography*, which utilizes a glass or metal plate coated with light-sensitive chemicals that is placed into a camera for exposure, after which the plate negative is exposed to photographic paper for final developing. According to the label on Smith's box, he used a pine plank to create the camera's housing, a piece of soap-smeared glass for focusing, and a tin can as the lens tube, which held the lens from his spyglass. Is it possible that such a crude contraption could actually work?

If you think it's a ruse, guess again. Gibson built a camera using the same materials as Smith, surmising that to cap off his lens for exposure time, the inmate would likely have used a tin cup. Gibson then took a picture of Wes, who was aptly dressed in a Civil War uniform for his big close-up, complete with a revolver. After snapping the image, Gibson removed the plate and placed it in a potassium cyanide solution to fix the intrepid History Detective's warrior pose onto the plate. When the silver dissolved, so did all speculation as to whether or not Smith's camera worked. Looking every bit the investigative soldier that he is, the image of Wes appeared on the plate.

With his camera experiment a proven success, Wes was then faced with the question of whether or not Smith would really have had access to the prison hospital and its cache of chemicals. To learn more, Wes met with Ryan Rokicki, curator of the National Museum of Civil War Medicine in Frederick, Maryland, and presented him with a list of very harsh chemicals used at the Johnson's Island hospital. Given that bacteriology was as yet an unknown discipline, Rokicki explained that it was a commonly held belief that those types of chemicals helped dispel poisons from the body.

The chemicals that Smith required for photo development, including 190 proof alcohol, ether, ferrous sulfate, iodide, and silver nitrate, were typically available in Civil War–era hospitals. The only chemical in doubt was cyanide, but Rokicki found an equivalent—sodium thiosulphate—which was used as a laxative, and was cited in another reference guide as a photographic reduction agent.

With everything falling into place, there was but one burning question left to answer. Amid the strife and starvation of a high-security prison, how in the world was Smith able to not only build a camera and develop photos, but actually get away with shooting them without being caught and punished?

In full Civil War regalia, Wes poses for a photo taken using a re-creation of Lieutenant Robert Smith's amazing camera.

The handmade replica built for *History Detectives* by photography expert Rob Gibson.

More often than not, when it comes to solving an investigation, a dedicated detective needs to go straight to the source. Fortunately for Wes, teams of archaeologists led by Dr. David R. Bush have been excavating the site of Johnson's Island prison since 1989 and have turned up thousands of artifacts that helped piece together how the POWs lived and died and how they attempted escape via tunnels in their latrines. When Wes showed Bush the lockets, necklaces, and rings Robert Smith allegedly made, they matched the excavated hard-rubber trinkets that inmates created for money or trading or to give to their loved ones. When taking a tour of the site, Bush showed Wes where the hospital once stood, in a location known as Block Six. Directly next to it was Block Four, and it was at that point that Wes solved a crucial piece of the puzzle.

Dr. David Bush at the archaeological site of Johnson's Island.

To wrap up his investigation, Wes brought Geoffrey Feazell to the Johnson's Island dig site, to the very spot where Cell Block Four once stood, and where his great-great-grandfather was incarcerated in 1864. Even more amazing was what Wes revealed to Feazell about his ancestor's furtive prison career. When Wes met with David Bush, he asked him if he recognized Smith's name, after which Bush showed him a Confederate magazine published just after the war. In it was a picture of Smith with a description that read: "Picture made on oyster can while on Johnson's Island Prison. Lt. Smith, of Bristol, Tennessee, had his lens with him when captured and taken as prisoner to Johnson's Island, Ohio. By bribing a guard, he procured some chemicals, placed his lens in a tobacco box, and with this crude outfit, opened a gallery clandestinely in the garret of block number four of that prison."

To pull off his photographic ploy, Lt. Robert M. Smith no doubt possessed the talent of an artist, the knowledge of a chemist, and a brave

Lieutenant Robert M. Smith.

constitution. And lest anyone forget his achievements, one need only look at the powerful portraits he created of men who were fighting for their beliefs and their lives.

The Puzzle in the Painting

For historians, garage sales, flea markets, estate sales, and antique shops are virtual treasure troves. Whether you peruse a seller's goods for long hours or mere minutes, you never know what you'll find. It could be a first edition of Tolstoy's *War and Peace*. It could be a diamond brooch worn by Eleanor Roosevelt. It could even be a letter written by Abraham Lincoln (see chapter 4). It had been over twenty years since Laura Greiner of League City, Texas, went to a garage sale in Galveston at a house next door to her mother's. As with all garage sales, she didn't have an inkling of what she might find. What caught her eye was a beautifully colored painting depicting a woman in medieval costume sitting erect atop a white horse leading a procession of women marching toward the U.S. Capitol building. Clearly it was in support of a march for women's suffrage, but what was the event?

History Detective Gwen Wright took up Greiner's investigative cause and traveled to Texas to see the remarkable painting for herself. Upon examining it, she was struck by the strength and romantic imagery the artist portrayed, an artist whose signature simply read: "Dale." Having studied

Lost and Found

If you're searching for information about a family ancestor who served in the Civil War or just want to learn more about the brave soldiers who fought in the conflict, there are a number of Web sites you can access that offer Civil War records that can be searched by name, rank, regiment, and a host of additional options. Various regiments also have informational and family sites, as do some of the prison camps. Bear in mind that there are millions of documents concerning the Civil War, and many of those are incomplete. Records for the Confederate Army in particular may be sketchy because so many were lost during and after the war.

The Web site of the National Park Service provides an excellent jumping-off point for a Civil War search, along with links to many Internet resources. Check it out at: www.nps.gov/archive/vick/other/archives.htm

Benjamin Dale's watercolor for the famous 1913 suffrage march on Washington, D.C.

the women's rights movement for many years, Gwen surmised that Dale's image was a poster from a famous women's suffrage demonstration in Washington, D.C., on March 3, 1913. She was unable to determine if the image was a print or an original, but was excited about the find and learning more about the artist and women's suffrage.

The act of casting a vote for your favorite candidate during a political election is often taken for granted, but for women, gaining the right to vote has been a long and arduous fight, and in some countries it is yet to be won. Women's *suffrage*, meaning the right to vote, has been an issue since the 1600s and continues to be debated and fought to the present day. Prominent in the U.S. campaign were trailblazers Elizabeth Cady Stanton, Susan B. Anthony, Lucretia Mott, Lucy Stone, Sojourner Truth, Julia Ward Howe, and Carrie Chapman Catt. All of these women and many more were leaders who vehemently fought to receive and maintain voting rights equal to those of their male counterparts. They were often shunned, ostracized, and even arrested for their views, but that didn't stop any of them from campaigning for what they believed was right.

Gwen's first major break in her investigation was confirmation that the date on the poster did indeed correspond with a major protest march on Washington in 1913. Her next turning point came at the Library of Congress Manuscripts Department, when archivist Janice Ruth showed Gwen one of two programs in their collection. To Gwen's delight, the image on the cover was an exact match to Laura Greiner's painting. Not only did the date match, but the image itself served as the cover for a program created for the march. Ruth had never heard of the existence of the original painting, but she was able to shed light on the two visionary organizers of the 1913 march—Alice Paul and Lucy Burns.

Brought together while taking part in the suffrage campaign in Britain, Americans Alice Paul and Lucy Burns met in classic protest style—at a police station after they'd both been arrested for demonstrating. They were continuing a battle that had begun almost a century earlier. In 1840, the World Anti-Slavery Convention was held in London, but unfortunately, male-dominated ideals of the era prevented women from actively participating, going so far as to force them to sit behind partitions. Eight years later, on July 19 and 20, 1848, a group of American women led by Elizabeth Cady Stanton and Lucretia Mott, who had taken an affront to the World Convention, organized the historic Seneca Falls Convention, where over 300 attendees anxiously listened to Stanton's Declaration of Sentiments—similar in its construction to the Declaration of Independence—which sparked civil, social, and religious debate among the participants, who eventually approved a series of equality resolutions.

The conference was a bold move and not without its virulent critics, but the meeting set the wheels of American women's suffrage in motion. Inherent to the movement was the belief that women have the right to choose their own representation and are not simply physical and moral bystanders to the political choices in life. Of course this belief system made the male majority's blood run cold. After all, according to the dominant viewpoint, women were meant to be mothers and wives, and giving them power would gravely disrupt family dynamics. They were also considered ill-prepared on an emotional level, incapable of making sound and informed decisions.

PORTRAIT OF A REBELLION

The American women's suffrage movement was still local in the early twentieth century, with isolated groups focused on the regional and state level. Alice Paul and Lucy Burns were determined to effect change at a national level, so using their political and public relations savvy they planned an epic protest march on the eve of President Woodrow Wilson's inauguration. The program boldly announced that the march would be "the most conspicuous and important demonstration that has ever been attempted by suffragists in the country."

time TEASER

The Susan B. Anthony coin was worth fifty cents. True or false?

Answer: False. It was a one-dollar coin.

DID YOU know

After the 14th and 15th Amendments were passed during the Civil War, men of color were given the right to vote, but women were not. As a result, two rival women's suffrage groups were formed. In 1869, lifelong friends Elizabeth Stanton and Susan B. Anthony founded the National Woman Suffrage Association (NWSA). Lucy Stone and Julia Ward Howe represented a more conservative group of feminists and formed the American Woman's Suffrage Association (AWSA). By 1890, after little legal success, the two groups joined forces and formed the National American Woman Suffrage Association (NAWSA).

With a mere nine weeks to plan the event, Paul and Burns worked hard to present an image of female solidarity. Dale's art evoked the spirit of a crusade to unify men and women from around the country. If Laura Greiner's painting was indeed an original, it would be a valuable historical treasure, so to make that final determination, Gwen took the painting to Library of Congress conservators Diane van der Reyden and Dr. Nels Olson, who would be able to tell if the image was the original or merely a reproduction.

The first step was to examine it under ultraviolet light, also called *black light*, to ascertain if the materials used were aged or merely made to look old. In particular, they analyzed the work to search for brighteners that are found in modern papers. Over time, thick paints begin to crack, a function that serves to help authenticate and date a painting, and van der Reyden was able to see some graphite reflections under the paint, indicating that the image might have first been sketched in pencil. The two conservators then took a host of high-resolution images for further analysis.

Smoke and Mirrors

When U.S. serviceman Walter Ladziak plucked a few canisters of film from the bombed-out ruins in the vicinity of the opera house in Bayreuth, Germany, during the Allied advance into the country at the end of World War II, he had no idea of their historical significance. Ladziak sent the film reels back to his family in the States, and they remained stored away virtually untouched for decades until his niece's husband, Francis Caramone of Staten Island, New York, brought them to the attention of History Detective Gwen Wright.

With the aid of archivist Cooper Graham at the Library of Congress, Gwen determined that most of the films were displays of Nazi conquests and German industrialization propaganda, including industrialized gingerbread making. Ladziak was especially intriqued by the title of one reel, *Der Führer in Bayreuth Ein Akt*, which proved a remarkable discovery. The film featured candid footage of Adolf Hitler and high-ranking members of the Nazi elite, including Heinrich Himmler and Hermann Göering, attending the Wagner Festival at the opera house in a display of military power and affected sophistication.

Raye Farr, archivist at Washington's Holocaust Museum, provided evidence that the film was probably shot as a home movie by Hitler's personal chef and Nazi insider Arthur Kannenberg. Walter Ladziak had unknowingly salvaged never-before-seen footage of Adolf Hitler, and as Ladziak's young relative Francis Caramone perceptively noted: "This is a prime example that history happens to everybody."

While awaiting the results, Gwen met with Professor Nancy Cott at the Arthur and Elizabeth Schlesinger Library on the History of Women in America. Cott showed how much the image that Paul and Burns chose to promote their march was influenced by the more militant tactics of the British suffragists. Twenty-eight-year-old Alice Paul, in particular, was firm in her conviction that women shouldn't beg for the right to vote—they should *demand* it. Nancy Cott noted that the purple and gold colors used in the painting were intentional, gold (or yellow) being the color used by American suffragists since the 1860s, and purple by the British.

Unfortunately, the regal colors used in the image belied the disturbances that occurred during the protest. Cott shared with Gwen a newspaper article that read: "Women were insulted, kicked, and struck by ruffians, and many of the policemen on the spot made no effort to stop these outrages." Though the protest ultimately proved successful and the cause gained public sympathy, over 8,000 suffragists risked life and limb in front of 20,000 spectators to earn the right to vote, a battle that to this day continues to be fought. For example, it wasn't until 1971 that Swiss women were enfranchised. Samoan women only gained full voting rights in 1990, and Kuwaiti females weren't granted full suffrage until 2005.

time TEASER

Who was the first U.S. president photographed in office?

Answer: James Polk, in 1849.

Following her investigative instincts, Gwen had but one final mystery to solve—the artist with the last name of "Dale." Library research turned up a trio of artists by that name who were painting in 1913. Given that long-distance communication during that era was difficult, it seemed likely that Alice Paul and Lucy Burns would have chosen a local artist. Ellen Dale lived in Salem, Massachusetts, and Marguerite Dale was in Australia. Both were too far away. That left only one possible contender: Benjamin Moran Dale, a twenty-four-year-old artist who lived in Philadelphia. Further digging turned up Dale's wedding announcement in the *Washington Post* and a later obituary listing his magazine work. An examination of Dale's illustrations in several *Ladies Home Journal*s from 1929 proved frustrating, as Dale's signature on those works didn't match the signature on Laura Greiner's painting. Fortunately, Internet research yielded earlier illustrations that Dale had done for the *Philadelphia Public Ledger* in 1914—and those signatures matched.

Young artist Benjamin Dale must have been a suffrage sympathizer, and whether he knew it or not, his powerful imagery and rich colors contributed not only to the success of the 1913 protest, but to the eventual ratification of the 19th Amendment on August 18, 1920, which at long last granted women the right to vote. But was Laura Greiner's painting the real deal?

When returning for a second consultation with Library of Congress conservators Diane van der Reyden and Dr. Nels Olson, Gwen learned that further infrared analysis of the painting confirmed that the graphite markings under the paint were part of the artist's original sketch, which was probably done sometime between 1900 and 1913. Laura Greiner's Galveston garage-sale find wasn't a printed reproduction, it was Benjamin Dale's original painting, which he created for a pair of determined nineteenth-century women fighting for equality.

Time and Tide

So many of the mysteries *History Detectives* takes on have resulted in major twists and turns, especially when investigating the lives of individuals who more often than not have shown themselves to be remarkable human beings. For example, Tukufu Zuberi's queries into a box of letters written by renowned abolitionist John Brown revealed an extraordinary relationship between two progressive women (see chapter 12). Likewise, Gwen Wright's investigation into a tiny medallion pinned to the diaper of Dodie Jacobi when she was adopted helped Jacobi find her birth mother (see chapter 11).

History affects each of us, whether it's global or right in our own backyard, and as long as our curiosity outweighs our complacency, we'll always strive to uncover the truth. Such was the case with a trio of mysteries that on the surface couldn't be more different, but in the end gave the History Detectives and all of us a snapshot in time, framed by courage and forever displayed for posterity.

THE TRIUMPHANT TALE OF THE POLISH PHOTOGRAPHER

The first of these incredible tales was investigated by Wes Cowan, and it was a journey whose outcome no one could have predicted. At first glance it may be impossible to ascertain how a camera could save someone from one of the greatest atrocities of the twentieth century, but a humbling investigation into a man named Adolf Fingrut and his curious camera captured an image of enduring love amid the Holocaust of World War II.

As a Polish Jew in Poland during the 1939 German invasion, Fingrut was an inevitable candidate for imprisonment in one of Germany's horrific concentration camps. How he could have eluded the death that befell more than three million of his countrymen was precisely what his niece Sandra Gasson wanted to know about her late uncle, who had remained in Poland until 1961, when he im-

Holocaust survivor Adolf Fingrut and his beloved wife, Michelle.

migrated to America. A studio photographer by trade, Fingrut was married to a beautiful Christian woman named Michelle, whose picture was among several shown to Wes. On the back of one of the photos was stamped "A. Fingrut, Rembertow." Further investigation into the Nazi propaganda machine showed that unless their work was officially sanctioned, neither Jews nor Poles were allowed to own cameras, yet some Jewish photographers continued documenting what took place in the Jewish ghettos.

Analysis of Fingrut's camera, which he brought with him when he immigrated, showed that it was dated between 1910 and 1920 and was likely used for taking portraits. Wes also received information from a Polish researcher who indicated that he had found not only Fingrut's studio but also people in Rembertow who remembered the couple. One man recalled how his mother once hid Fingrut in her cellar, while another resident mentioned that Fingrut departed Rembertow in 1942 by using forged documents and eventually became a photographer of German soldiers. If true, how did he pull off the unbelievable ruse?

In the end, it was Fingrut's Christian wife, Michelle, who at enormous risk served as the forger of papers identifying her husband as Polish. Amazingly, her ploy was successful and she managed to get him out of the ghetto only a few hours before he was to be transported to a camp and face certain death. Fingrut subsequently traveled with Michelle to a town more

time
TEASER

What is the most expensive commercial camera ever sold at auction?

Answer: An 1839 German daguerreotype, which sold in 2007 for $792,000.

than a hundred miles away and, posing as a Christian, worked in a Nazi-controlled photo studio. Adolf Fingrut was a Polish Jew who beat the odds and survived the Holocaust with the help of his devoted wife *and* his trusty camera.

NEITHER RAIN NOR SLEET

Almost a century before Adolf and Michelle Fingrut survived the horrors of World War II, another luminary was delivering his own brand of heroism in a very different way. In 2000, Michael Trujillo purchased a curious leather satchel from a small antiques store, but the bag turned out to be an amazing treasure. Wes Cowan was intrigued by the satchel and its identifying tag, which read: "Shoe Thompson." What could be so interesting about an old leather pouch, you ask? The possibility that it was carried by one of the most famous postmen in history.

Traveling on homemade skis, Norwegian-born Jon Tostensen, better known as John "Snowshoe" Thompson, faithfully delivered mail to settlers isolated by the brutal snows and 7,500-foot-high passes of the Sierra Nevada Mountains. Thompson began his career in 1856 as a result of a newspaper advertisement in the *Sacramento Union*, which called for an individual to transport mail during the winter for some ninety miles over the Sierras to Carson Valley. It was an outrageous and dangerous proposition, and Thompson willingly embraced it by carving a ten-foot-long pair of oak skis weighing over twenty pounds, which he skillfully maneuvered with the use of only a single pole. He is said to have reached speeds of up to sixty miles per hour when skiing down the Sierra's precarious slopes.

Carrying over a hundred pounds on his back and traveling without a blanket, a gun, or camping equipment, Snowshoe made two

The "Father of California Skiing," John "Snowshoe" Thompson. At right, the leather satchel allegedly carried by Thompson.

to four monthly deliveries for two decades, and, remarkably, was never paid because he hadn't officially signed a contract with the postal service.

So resilient and unflinching was Snowshoe that in 1856 he rescued James Sisson, a prospector who had been stranded with badly frostbitten legs for almost two weeks. In total, Snowshoe traveled ten days and over 400 miles to procure medicine to save Sisson's life. So was Michael Trujillo's satchel the real thing? During his investigation, Wes uncovered strong evidence that the satchel was a saddlebag that did indeed belong to Snowshoe Thompson, who used it during his summertime deliveries when riding horseback, and who will forever be known as the "Father of California Skiing."

time TEASER

Who was the first U.S. Postmaster General?

Answer: Benjamin Franklin, named by the Continental Congress in 1775.

POWER TO THE PEOPLE

Courage in the face of adversity kept alive Adolf Fingrut's survival instinct. For Snowshoe Thompson, courage fueled his desire to battle Mother Nature in an effort to help individuals in extreme isolation. Lucy Parsons had a different type of courage, one that intensified her personal zeal for freedom in the form of anarchism. Lucy Ella Gonzales Parsons was born a slave in Texas around 1853. Her her role as a revolutionary is largely lost to time, but her efforts as an anarchist, labor activist, orator, and writer cannot be understated.

History Detective Elyse Luray's investigation into Lucy Parsons came as a result of a book found by Stephen Magro at the library of Wesleyan University in Connecticut. What made the book so special is that the cover is stamped as belonging to Lucy Parsons.

Written by August Spies, the 1887 book, which was published by his wife, Nina

The autobiography of August Spies, showing the address stamp of Lucy Parsons.

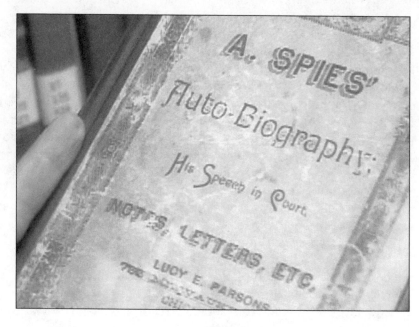

DIY DETECTIVE

Photography is one of our most enduring art forms, but photographs require special care and attention to maintain their lasting qualities. The first commercially viable photographs were *daguerreotypes*, perfected in 1839 by French chemist Louis Daguerre in a painstaking process that permitted a unique positive image to be captured on a polished metal plate coated with light-sensitive silver halide fumes.

The resulting images were artistically beautiful but susceptible to damage from handling and exposure. Since the silver image can tarnish when exposed to air, modern preservation techniques for daguerreotypes utilize sealed glass cases filled with inert nitrogen gas. *Ambrotypes* and *tintype* photographs, which were developed just prior to the Civil War era, must also be handled with care.

A rule of thumb for any early and irreplaceable photographs you happen to find is to never remove them from their cases. It's also wise to avoid direct sunlight completely and restrict exposure to artificial light for extended periods. Keeping rare photographs in acid-free containers or boxes designed specifically for photographs at a steady room temperature will extend their life indefinitely. If they do need attention, it's best to get them into the hands of an expert.

Although it may seem counterintuitive, it's generally safe to digitally scan daguerreotypes and tintypes as long as they're kept inside their cases and not overdone. The limited light exposure of one or two scans won't cause discernable damage, and once the scans are completed you can put the originals safely away and reproduce multiple copies of the scanned image.

If you don't have scanning equipment or are unsure of your expertise, contact local freelance professional graphic artists or a photography studio for help. Graphic artists invariably use good quality scanners and have a great deal of experience creating excellent digital images. Quite often, they can significantly enhance the quality of old photographs using digital graphics programs that are not commonly in use in the average home office.

Also, bear in mind that albums are equally important to the preservation process. For years, the "magnetic" type of photo album was considered a godsend to collectors because the tacky pages held pictures in place without tape or tabs. Unfortunately, the plastic pages can degrade over time and chemically react with photographic prints, causing irreparable harm, either through discoloration or by turning the photo surfaces into a sticky mess that is nearly impossible to remove.

Many inexpensive modern photo albums manufactured with limited quality control or concern for the consumer are also subject to degradation. Album pages and pockets made with polyester or polypropylene are chemically inert and when placed into archival-quality covers provide a safe, easily accessible, and long-term storage solution. As a general rule, scanning all of your beloved photos and tucking them safely away will guarantee the enjoyment of your priceless collection for generations. For more information, visit *History Detectives* at www.pbs.org.

Van Zandt, was his memoir, written during his incarceration and impending execution for his alleged participation in the infamous 1886 Chicago Haymarket bombing. At first a peaceful gathering as part of a campaign to regulate work hours, the meeting of labor activists and anarchists turned violent when close to 200 policemen raided the meeting.

The crowd was hit by a bomb tossed by an unknown individual, causing mass panic and police shooting that resulted in at least seven deaths and more than sixty civilian casualties. Albert Parsons, Lucy's husband, was one of the eight anarchist leaders who were arrested as a result of the Haymarket affair, although none actually had anything to do with the bombing. Four of the eight individuals, including Spies and Albert Parsons, were eventually hanged.

As a dissident, Lucy Parsons was fearless. With a mixed heritage of African American, Native American, and Mexican American ancestry, Parsons worked tirelessly as an activist, spearheading protests by tens of thousands of workers, especially on behalf of her husband after the Haymarket affair. Through expert analysis, Elyse was able to ascertain that the book was authentic and one of the few anarchist materials that wasn't destroyed by the Attorney General during the early 1920s.

Renowned activist Lucy Parsons.

Parson's stamp on the cover was a clear indicator of her desperate efforts to save her beloved husband from the gallows.

As a way to raise money for his defense, she sold copies of the Spies memoir, and, as with all anarchist material she disseminated, she stamped her contact information on the cover. For three decades as an internationally renowned labor activist, Lucy Parsons strove for equality for the working and poorer classes, and her compassion caused her to endure many arrests and police surveillance until her death as a result of her home catching fire in 1942.

CHAPTER TWO
Entertainment in the Shadows

Every culture has its distinctive skills and special forms of entertainment that set it apart from others, whether they be musical, artistic, literary, philosophical, or even athletic. African American artists, performers, and athletes may be integral players in the modern age, but that wasn't the case even as recently as the early 1900s. The entertainment industry, like most other industries, had a racial barrier that hadn't yet been negotiated, but with the help of some amazing individuals it was only a matter of time until scores of African American performers emerged from the shadows, made their presence known, and in doing so set the standard for all future generations.

John W. Cooper was one of those trailblazers, a man whose incredible ventriloquial gift made him one of the most engaging performers on the vaudeville stage. Musician Charlie "Bird" Parker was another pioneer who lived without boundaries; his prodigious talent set roots in the jazz music world that continue to grow as a result of his profound influence. When History Detectives Tukufu Zuberi, Gwen Wright, and

Wes Cowan delved into investigations surrounding these two men, they paid homage not only to their courage and talent, but also to all who have the tenacity to live their dreams.

The Tale of the Ventriloquist's Dummy

Over the centuries barriers encompassing just about every aspect of life have been broken by many notable individuals. In the modern era, we've had the distinct privilege of witnessing some of these astonishing feats, like Amelia Earhart's 1928 solo flight across the Atlantic Ocean, Roger Bannister's 1954 record of becoming the first human to break the four-minute mile, Jonas Salk's 1955 development of a polio vaccine, and Neil Armstrong's giant leap for mankind during his 1969 moon walk. You may not recognize the names John W. Cooper or Sam Jackson, but as an African American team they broke personal and professional barriers in their own dynamic way.

John W. Cooper was a supremely gifted ventriloquist who gave voice to his dummy, Sam Jackson, during an era when white entertainers blackened their faces in an effort to portray African Americans. Cooper's daughter, Joan Maynard, is now Sam's keeper and she had several important questions she wished to have answered in regard to the dummy's heritage and how her father was

Ventriloquist John W. Cooper and his legendary dummy, Sam Jackson.

able to get his first big break on the vaudeville stage. Throwing his voice and skills into the investigation was History Detective Tukufu Zuberi, who went to the Crown Heights neighborhood in Brooklyn, New York, to visit Maynard and meet the legendary Sam Jackson.

With his large, bright eyes and animated face, Sam was the ideal counterpart to his talented owner, John W. Cooper. Their spirited repartee and exceptional humor were in perfect harmony, a sharp contrast to the discrimination and segregation that continued to run rampant during the early twentieth century. After formally meeting Sam, Tukufu was asked by Maynard if he could establish whether Sam was created by Theodore Mack.

DID YOU know

Widely considered to be one of the world's greatest ventriloquists was The Great Lester, otherwise known as Harry Lester, who made history with his renowned dummy, Frank Byron Jr. Wildly popular during the vaudeville era, Lester and Frank astounded audiences with their flawless performances, which included Lester famously drinking a glass of water while Frank continued talking.

Dubbed the "Golden Boy of Ventriloquism," Lester was responsible for training a young boy named Edgar Bergen. It remains hotly debated as to whether Lester created Frank himself in Theodore Mack's shop under Mack's guidance or whether Mack himself built Frank.

A celebrated puppet master, Mack is credited with creating the world-famous dummy Charlie McCarthy, who for fifty years performed on stage, radio, and television with his owner, Edgar Bergen. Frank Marshall, who began working for Mack when he was fourteen, is alternately credited with McCarthy's creation, having built later versions of the dummy.

To begin his investigation, Tukufu first researched the history of vaudeville by meeting with theater historian Robert Snyder, who confirmed that during the vaudeville years African American performers were appreciated but often had to compete with and overcome the stereotyping of *blackface minstrelsy*. Minstrelsy was a form of entertainment that involved white actors, singers, dancers, and comics wearing blackface makeup, known simply as blackface. Popularized in the United States during the early- to mid-1800s, minstrel shows enhanced what they falsely believed were stereotypical characteristics of African Americans, often showing them as lazy, ignorant, and buffoonish. Jubilee groups, another popular form of entertainment, were often more faith-based but at the same time offered African Americans the chance to express cultural and even political beliefs. An African American who actually was a headline performer would have been very rare and *very* special.

THE REBEL MINSTREL

To learn more about Cooper, Tukufu went to the New York Public Library for the Performing Arts. His research there showed that Cooper was a talented and determined performer whose first venture into the entertainment world came in 1886 when he became part of the Southern Jubilee Singers. A mere thirteen years old at the time, Cooper traveled with the group for four years, after which he contracted with the Richards and Pringle's Georgia Minstrels for the 1900 to 1901 theater season. But

Cooper's act wasn't the old song and dance. Cooper was unique. His gift for ventriloquism set him apart from the rest of the performers, especially his act entitled "Fun in a Barber Shop," in which he would operate five different dummies and throw five different voices. The humorous act was made all the more astonishing by the fact that Cooper used his hands to cut hair during the performance—he operated all five of the dummies with his feet.

Cooper's innovative barbershop act was a hit with audiences of all races, but that didn't explain how he was able to make the huge leap from minstrel shows to the vaudeville stage. After all, by 1907 it was reported by *Variety* that vaudeville was raking in over $30 million a year, and performers had to be top notch. Continuing his research, Tukufu discovered that in the early 1900s, vaudeville succumbed to a strike at the hands of an up-and-coming union of white performers called the White Rats. As is traditional with strikes of any magnitude, one man's loss is another's gain. For African American performers it was the perfect avenue to gain entry through a door that might otherwise never have opened. John W. Cooper ignored the 1901 strike, and in doing so he made a name for himself on the vaudeville stage.

A newspaper promo for John W. Cooper and his act "Fun in a Barber Shop."

With that part of the mystery solved, Tukufu set out to determine if Sam Jackson was in any way related to Charlie McCarthy. His first lead was a 1939 newspaper article that reported on the repartee between Cooper and an annoying heckler, in which Sam mentioned that he and Charlie "came from the same wood pile." Of course Tukufu needed more than a "dummy's" word to verify that claim, so he traveled to Kentucky to visit one of the world's most unique museums. Located in Fort Mitchell, the Vent Haven Museum was founded by William Shakespeare Berger and is home to over 700 ventriloquial figures amid its extensive memorabilia collection spanning nearly two centuries.

The charismatic Sam Jackson.

Curator Lisa Sweasy showed Tukufu a Charlie McCarthy replica that clearly showed similarities in facial construction to Sam Jackson. She also shared with him a catalog published by Theodore Mack that contained several pictures of an unnamed figure that appeared to be Sam. Even more convincing was an interview filed amid correspondence between Berger and Cooper in which Cooper confirmed in 1953 that Sam

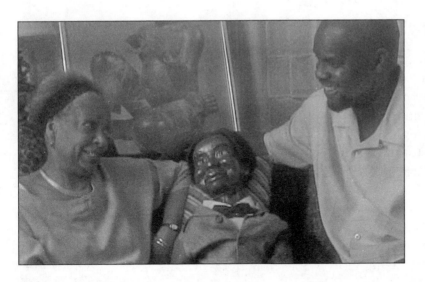

Tukufu with Sam
Jackson and John W.
Cooper's daughter,
Joan Maynard.

was created by Theodore Mack. The only problem was that it's common for ventriloquists to replace their partners over time as a result of wear. Could it be that the Sam Jackson dummy owned by Joan Maynard is a second-generation replacement?

FOREVER YOUNG

In order to determine with some measure of certainty that Sam was the brainchild of Theodore Mack, Tukufu took the figure to renowned "dummy doctor" Alan Semok, who has healed hundreds of ailing figures over the years, including the spectacularly freckled television marionette Howdy Doody. During his examination of Sam, Semok mentioned one particular commonality among puppets—the fact that a "family resemblance" is unavoidable when artists fashion dummies, no matter how hard they try to make them appear different.

The shape of a dummy's eyes is often a dead giveaway when it comes to identification, and in the case of Theodore Mack, the ears possessed a telltale shape. Semok determined that Sam was indeed carved of wood and that the area for his taxidermy eye was created with a countersink drill typically used during the early 1900s. In addition, Sam's mouth was attached with a door hinge, and the inside of his head showed marks of the wood having been scooped out—both telltale signs indicating Mack construction.

Upon meeting with Joan Maynard, Tukufu was able to relate to her how brave and tenacious her father was when he broke a vaudeville strike that ultimately gave him the exposure and respect he rightly deserved. Even more exciting was the news that Sam Jackson was indeed created by puppet master extraordinaire Theodore Mack, and not only was he Charlie McCarthy's brother—he was his *older* brother. Sam Jackson may have outlived his dear partner, John W. Cooper, but he has a lot to be proud of. Cooper was a performer unwilling to take a backseat to white per-

time
TEASER

Which famous ventriloquist of the 1950s, whose dummy was called Jerry Mahoney, patented an artificial heart?

Answer: Paul Winchell.

formers of the day, and his perseverance and graciousness paid off. Well into his eighties, he continued to teach his craft to others while simply performing for kids when visiting local parks. It was there that he taught a young girl named Shari Lewis how to throw her voice, a talent that enabled her to give life to her future ventriloquial partner Lambchop. In addition, Tukufu had a special surprise for Joan Maynard. He played for her an audio tape of one of her father's performances when he was eighty-six, a tape containing two voices from the past, eloquently spoken by one amazing man.

The Curious Case of the Broken Banjo

On the banks of the Ohio River, the tiny town of Bethel, Ohio, has always been a close-knit community; its present-day population has barely doubled since the early 1900s. For a community of just 2,600, Bethel has experienced its share of historical curiosities, such as hosting the only "witch trial" in Ohio's history in the early 1800s, which resulted in the "witch" being quickly acquitted by the general populace and the common sense of a judge. The town also elected Jesse Root Grant as the city's first mayor after the town incorporated in 1851, Grant being the father of Civil War hero and future U.S. president Ulysses S. Grant.

History Detectives was led to Bethel to investigate a slightly different historical mystery after being contacted by Dave Brown of Baltimore, Maryland, who'd purchased a battered banjo with an intriguing legacy. According to an old note attached to the instrument, the banjo had come from the son of a Civil War–era abolitionist who purchased it from a recently freed slave in the mid-1850s.

The find piqued the interest of heritage-conscious detectives Tukufu Zuberi and Wes Cowan, who quickly found themselves immersed in a remarkable music

Make 'Em Laugh!

One of the most popular forms of American entertainment in the early 1900s was vaudeville, which had originated in France decades earlier. Touted as "a show with something for everyone," vaudeville was a compilation of song and dance routines, comedy acts, burlesque, acrobats and jugglers, minstrels, theater acts, and a wide variety of performers like mind readers, regurgitators, high divers, and quick-change artists meant to wow audiences of all ages.

Dubbed the "Father of American Vaudeville" was Benjamin Franklin Keith, a former circus barker turned entrepreneur whose strict adherence to non-risqué performances and courteous audience decorum appealed to everyone. He and his partner, Edward F. Albee, set about defining the very nature of vaudeville in theaters across the nation.

It's estimated that during the fifty-some years of vaudeville, 25,000 individuals left their mark on it. Many of them, including Bob Hope, Milton Berle, Ethel Barrymore, George Burns and Gracie Allen, Jack Benny, Al Jolson, Kate Smith, and Eddie Cantor used the medium as a stepping-stone to ultimate stardom.

The very rare slave-owned banjo investigated by *History Detectives*. The close-up detail above shows the tattered documentation of the banjo's history.

investigation enveloped in social and cultural revelation. It was a tall order. Not only did they have to determine if the banjo was authentic, they had to figure out if it indeed belonged to an emancipated slave.

To begin his inquiries, Tukufu met with legendary musician Taj Mahal to discuss the profound effect blackfaced minstrels had on the distancing of African Americans from their instrumental heritage with the banjo. Although representations of banjo players are indelibly linked to modern bluegrass, country, and folk music, the most persistently disturbing visual images of banjoists depict the racism of blackface. Sociologists have long debated the outrageous characterizations of white performers pretending to be black, but unmistakably, the underlying fear that white America had of the slave-based black culture of the period most certainly played a significant part in popularizing the blackface music genre by buffering social alarm with ignorance, mimicry, and mockery.

When the predecessors of the modern banjo were first created by African slaves in America, the music they created became a cultural mainstay for a people denied other forms of expression. The co-opting of the instrument by white minstrels, and its subsequent gentrification into polite society, created a visual and viscerally emotional distaste that has taken generations to overcome. Further transitions of banjo musicality in the late 1800s and early 1900s shifted the instrument into common use in traditionally white bluegrass and country music genres that are far removed from the music first created by the victims of slavery.

SONG OF THE SOUTH

For years before the first Civil War battle on April 12, 1861, when Confederate forces fired on the U.S. military installation at South Carolina's Fort Sumter, America was torn by a nationwide ideological split that supported slavery in the Southern states and its expansion into the western territories, and a growing abhorrence of the institution of slavery in the North. An accident of geography and political boundaries, the Ohio River became a primary natural partition between the slave states and the free states, and the Holy Grail for slaves escaping the shackles of Southern bondage. On the free side of the river, the small Ohio town of Bethel was a destination that offered sanctuary, and through the efforts of a select few sympathetic townspeople, fleeing slaves were given their first taste of freedom.

time
TEASER

A degradingly racist black-face minstrel song was popularized in the late 1820s and titled "Zip Coon." What was its recognizable tune?

Answer: "Turkey in the Straw."

What set the tone for Wes and Tukufu's investigation was the note accompanying Dave Brown's banjo, which helped explain the phenomenal journey of the old instrument during the mid-1800s. The note claimed that the banjo was originally owned by a young mulatto slave named Christian Anderson who sold it to childhood friend and schoolmate John Rice, the son of Bethel abolitionist Benjamin Rice. From Underground Railroad historian Gary Knepp, Wes learned that Benjamin Rice was responsible for guiding over a hundred slaves into the free states. Even more intriguing, Wes discovered that the Anderson and Rice families became neighbors in Bethel, living only a few blocks apart in the tiny town.

To play the final note of this musical mystery, the History Detectives needed to determine the authenticity of the banjo, so Tukufu met with banjo expert and craftsman George Wunderlich, who was delighted to discover that the instrument's construction was absolutely legitimate for the period; the banjo was probably built between 1853 and 1860. Traced back to childhood friends Christian Anderson and John Rice, one a former slave, the other the son of an Underground Railroad conductor,

DID YOU know

Many early African instruments have functional similarities to the modern-day banjo, and several have recognizable names, such as the "banjar," "bangoe," and "banshaw." As early as 1620 in Africa, records of instruments created from gourds with long necks and strings for plucking notes illustrate forefathers of the banjo. In modern Senegal and Gambia, the *akonting* bears a remarkable resemblance to the modern banjo, with a drum-shaped gourd or wooden base covered by stretched animal hide, and a slender multi-stringed neck made of papyrus or bamboo. The notes from the akonting bear a striking and unmistakable resemblance to those of the banjo and can be seen and heard on home computers by searching for the word "akonting" on major Internet video Web sites.

Dave Brown's banjo was validated by Tukufu and Wes as one of the rarest examples of early banjos in existence, and a priceless link between two men who if they'd lived in a Southern state likely would never have become friends.

A saxophone allegedly owned by Charlie Parker.

The Bird Saxophone Mystery

It's no mystery that everyone on the planet has his or her own personal demons. For some, those demons are vanquished and bade never to return. For others, the demons linger, feeding upon the confidence and creativity that makes us human. Famed musician and composer Charlie Parker had his share of tumultuous times, which played in sharp contrast to the brilliance of his musical talent. As a quintessential example of "the light that burns twice as bright burns half as long," Parker left an indelible mark on music history that will continue to influence future generations. Parker once said: "Music is your own experience, your own thoughts, your wisdom. If you don't live it, it won't come out of your horn. They teach you there's a boundary line to music. But, man, there's no boundary line to art." And indeed there were no boundaries in Charlie Parker's life, as Gwen Wright and Wes Cowan learned when they investigated a saxophone that allegedly once belonged to the man simply known as "Bird."

Taxed into the Limelight

One of the unknown influences on the popular emergence of solo music and bebop virtuosos such as saxophonist Charlie Parker, pianist Art Tatum, drummer Max Roach, and trumpeter Dizzy Gillespie during the 1940s was the national 20 percent entertainment tax imposed by the federal government to help finance U.S. involvement in World War II.

Because of the tax, many clubs couldn't afford to hire big bands and opted for smaller combos with just a handful of players. What this meant to musicians was fewer jobs, and competition between them became fierce. During the era, mediocre musicians had a tough time making a living and only the best and most innovative were hired regularly, giving exposure to a relative handful of brilliant artists whose skillful mastery of their instruments continues to influence musicians and music lovers to this day.

The sax in question is now owned by Oakland, California, resident Jenifer Hood, whose father, jazz musician Bill Hood, performed with Frank Sinatra, Sarah Vaughan, and Quincy Jones, among others. So how did Parker's sax end up in the hands of Bill Hood? According to his daughter, Hood and Parker were in Portland, Oregon, working a gig when Bird showed up without his horn because he'd pawned it. Hood chided him for his action and was actually given the pawn ticket by Bird, who appeared unconcerned. Hood got the horn out of hock and kept it as a family heirloom.

Legendary jazz musician Charlie "Bird" Parker.

It was a baffling mystery for Gwen and Wes, who wondered why Parker would have pawned his sax, let alone given the ticket to a fellow musician. If the story was true, it would be an amazing find not only for its historical significance but for its financial value. In keeping with other Charlie Parker saxophones that have been auctioned, Wes estimated that Jenifer Hood's sax might be worth at least $20,000 to $30,000, if it had actually been owned by Parker. Market value for memorabilia is strongly dependent on *provenance*, the record of previous ownership. For instance, in 2005, a Charlie Parker saxophone with impeccable provenance was sold at auction for $225,000. Without the pawn ticket for Hood's sax there was little to go on, but fortunately there's less of a mystery when it comes to Parker's life and the history of jazz.

All That Jazz

While World War II raged overseas during the early 1940s, Parker, like many other musicians and artists of the day, left his Midwest Kansas City roots and headed for the Big Apple. Up until that time, big bands and their elaborate arrangements ruled the music world, and it's fair to say that no one connected to the business or

time TEASER

Which actor was originally intended to play the role of Charlie Parker in the 1988 film *Bird*?

Answer: Richard Pryor. Ultimately, the role went to Forest Whitaker.

music lovers themselves were prepared for the brilliance of Charlie Parker, one of the leaders of a new style of jazz called *bebop*, which evolved into modern jazz. Suffice to say, bebop was not for the faint of heart. Characterized by incredibly fast playing, difficult rhythms, and rapid chord changes, bebop's heart and soul was improvisation, and no one did it better than Charlie Parker.

At the renowned Blue Note nightclub in New York, Gwen met with Parker biographer and jazz critic Stanley Crouch, who characterized Bird as a phenomenon who could play at breakneck speed with sheer confidence and with a sound that came straight from the heart. And play he did, with the likes of Dizzy Gillespie, Thelonious Monk, and Miles Davis, among many other jazz superstars. In counterpoint to his generosity as an artist, however, were the personal demons Parker couldn't control. According to Crouch, Parker wasn't just a drug addict but a "drug fanatic" who found solace in heroin and alcohol. Sadly, Parker's addictions often got the best of him, contributing to several arrests, two suicide attempts, four marriages, and a nervous breakdown in 1946. But through it all, he never missed a beat when it came to performing, and never met a sax he couldn't make sing.

To establish the authenticity of Jenifer Hood's sax and ascertain if Bill Hood and Parker knew each other, Gwen and Wes traveled to Portland, Oregon, where Wes took the instrument to the Portland Music Company. Appraiser and dealer Doug Metzker noted that the E-flat alto sax is a Buescher Aristocrat, and that according to the serial number it was made in the early 1930s. He also confirmed that just because the sax isn't a snazzy gold-plated model doesn't mean a musician of Parker's caliber wouldn't play it. Further research at the Multnomah County Library produced an account by Jay McShann which stated that: "There were two horns that always had to be gotten out of hock. Bird's was one." McShann, an accomplished blues pianist and bandleader, played with Parker in the late 1930s and early 1940s. Further confirmation came from one of Parker's friends, alto saxophonist and vocalist Cliff Jetkins, who said: "He once handed me a $25 pawn ticket, which he told me to redeem and keep what I got. It was an expensive French Selmer tenor saxophone." Clearly, Charlie Parker had a habit of pawning his horns, but that didn't prove that Bill Hood was the recipient of a golden ticket.

time
TEASER   Which 1986 film starred a number of jazz greats in lead roles?

Answer: *Round Midnight*, with Dexter Gordon, Herbie Hancock, and Bobby Hutcherson.

DIY DETECTIVE

For many hardcore music fans, a collection of choice tunes just isn't complete without a companion collection of memorabilia that brings them a step closer to the inner sanctum of their favorite artists. The most accessible collections are autographs, out-of-print recordings, concert memorabilia such as tickets and posters, and more mundane items such as guitar picks and even novelty bubbleheads. More expensive items include rare autographs, one-of-a-kind pieces, artists' stage-worn apparel, and personally used instruments.

As with most collectibles, there's a plethora of music memorabilia for sale on Internet auction sites, and you'll want to do plenty of research and check the experience, return policies, and validity of any Web site before making an investment. Bear in mind that music memorabilia generates millions of dollars in annual sales, and a few dealers are aware of the inflated prices some items can bring. The most important indicator of authenticity is provenance, and reputable collectors and dealers should provide that information.

The need for clear provenance is illustrated by one gimmick used by unscrupulous sellers that involves gathering artists' signatures on guitar pick guards, which are inexpensive plastic plates designed to screw onto the body of a guitar to protect the surface from wear as the instrument is played. These signed pick guards can be attached to an inexpensive electric or acoustic guitar, and the entire item marketed as a genuine autographed instrument. Although the autograph may be authentic, the inflated value of the instrument is questionable and its association with the artist is zero.

Although CDs and digital recordings have long since replaced vinyl records, autographed albums continue to make up a large part of the memorabilia market. On the low end of the scale, it's possible to find autographed recordings from rock groups such as Aerosmith for less than $200. At the other end of the vinyl spectrum, an early record album signed by all four of the Beatles recently sold for $125,000.

From the bebop era, a music manuscript written by jazz legend John Coltrane and an autographed Miles Davis photograph sold in 2007 for just over $1,200 each. In a relative steal for one jazz buff, an autographed photo of jazz singer Josephine Baker was purchased for just under $300. It's important to remember that prices vary widely depending on condition, provenance, and demand. Virtually any item associated with music artists can be collectible for music buffs, and reputable dealers will work to earn your trust *and* your business. Don't be afraid to ask for references, and remember that the best dealers offer 100 percent lifetime guarantees of authenticity. For more advice on working with Internet auction sites, see chapter 15.

Wes continued to dig until he found a 1953 newspaper advertisement for Portland's Playhouse Theater announcing an engagement by the Charlie Parker Quintet. It was a long shot, but the information did lead Gwen to jazz historian Bob Dietsche, who was able to shed some light on Portland's swinging ways during the 1950s. Dietsche was familiar with Bill Hood, who was in his teens at the time and had a habit of showing up at jazz clubs in predominantly black north Portland neighborhoods, especially a club called Frat Hall. Parker was also known to frequent the same club when he was in town playing gigs. Much to Gwen's delight, Dietsche played a tantalizing audiotape, a radio show tribute to Bill Hood. On the program there was mention of a 1954 letter written by Hood to his brother in which he described a wild night in 1953 when he, Chet Baker, Jimmy Rowles, and Charlie Parker had a drunken jam session in which "Bird went to sleep in a chair and everyone draped him in Mexican garb with a sombrero over his face, and Bill said, 'He snores beautifully.'"

Before concluding the investigation, Wes had one final lead to explore, but the chances of success were slim. Studying the 1953 *Yellow Pages*, he set about finding local pawn shops and cross-checking them with current listings to see if any were still in business. His research paid off. Formerly known as the H&B Loan Office, the present-day H&B Jewelry and Loan Company was alive and kicking after sixty years. When meeting with owner Phil Tobin, Wes discovered that their records from the early 1950s no longer existed, but fortunately one of their former employees had a few tales to tell, one of which would prove very interesting to Jenifer Hood.

Tobin told Wes that he absolutely recalled the employee relaying to him that Charlie Parker showed up at H&B and pawned his alto sax. Not only was Hood's sax authentic to the era, it most likely belonged to one of the greatest jazz musicians ever to grace the stage. Sadly, two years after Parker and Bill Hood had their frivolous jam session in 1953, "Bird's" miraculous musical flight came to an end. On March 12, 1955, Charlie Parker passed away as a result of pneumonia, likely brought on by drug addiction. Jazz great Miles Davis was once asked to summarize the history of jazz, and his response was one that couldn't have been more plain and more appropriate. His response? "Louis Armstrong, Charlie Parker."

time
TEASER

What is the best selling jazz album of all time?

Answer: The 1959 album *Kind of Blue* by Miles Davis.

At left, Atlantic City Little League Commissioner Lamont Fauntleroy inside Pop Lloyd Stadium. Above, baseball great Pop Lloyd.

The Mysterious Affair of Pop Lloyd Stadium

Growing up just half a mile from Pop Lloyd Stadium in urban Atlantic City, New Jersey, Lamont Fauntleroy found in baseball a safe haven from inner-city drug and gang activity. After his playing days were over, Fauntleroy went on to become the Commissioner of Atlantic City's Little League program and an advocate for disadvantaged kids. He coaches at Pop Lloyd Stadium, a place that to this day still plays an important part of his lifelong passion.

But one of the venue's great mysteries continued to plague Fauntleroy. He wanted to know, in light of the segregation and racism so pervasive during the era, why this city built a stadium in an African American neighborhood in 1949 and how it came to be named after Henry "Pop" Lloyd, who played in the early Negro Leagues and became one of the greatest players professional baseball has ever known.

History Detectives Tukufu Zuberi and Gwen Wright discovered that part of the motivation for the creation of the stadium came as a result of the political dealings of Republican Senator Frank "Hap" Farley. As the new "boss" of Atlantic City, Farley wanted to impress the sizeable African American population because he wanted their votes.

Despite the political backstory of the construction of Pop Lloyd Stadium, the facility stands today as a landmark and tribute to one of baseball's true heroes, and it remains an inspiration to young athletes who discover Lloyd's legacy and who play ball in their own field of dreams.

CHAPTER THREE

Life Imitates Art

When it comes right down to it, most things in life are highly subjective, guided almost entirely by personal perspective, wants, and opinions. Art is perhaps one of the most hotly disputed, given that art means something different to each of us. But art can also be highly deceptive in a very elusive way—especially when it comes to an artist's authenticity. Over the years, the History Detectives have explored a colorful range of artful mysteries, several of which had more twists and turns than a Swiss mountain road.

One of those investigations involved George Washington and examined the work of one of America's most revered portrait artists. Another sent detectives on a journey to find the true identity of a beautiful and mysterious early twentieth-century supermodel, who became embroiled in the "trial of the century." A third investigation delved into the high-profile world of political satire during World War II, in a foray that yielded surprising results. All of these artistic mysteries proved that life most certainly imitates art, but the real conundrums are those individuals who imitate famous artists, such as renowned con man John Drewe and his partner in crime, John Myatt.

The Dilemma of the Dubious Drawing

George Washington was a man of pride, honor, and determination, and for most Americans he'll always be revered for being the "Father of His Country." That's an intimidating title for a mortal man, but in Washington's case it held true, as he became the first president of the United States and a permanent icon of a burgeoning nation. So how likely would it be that someone would come to own an authentic drawing of Washington created by one of the most famous portrait artists in history? That was the artistic mystery that History Detective Wes Cowan set out to unravel, but what he uncovered was much more than a simple sketch of a legendary politician.

Jim Colket of Frederick County, Maryland, inherited from his father a drawing of Washington signed by Gilbert Stuart, an artist who didn't simply capture an individual's likeness, but offered an uncanny glimpse of the subject's true personality. According to Wes, the drawing might be worth between $30,000 and $50,000 if proven authentic, but in order to reach that point the sketch would require expert analysis. The fact that it was done on handmade laid paper was a promising start, given that this kind of paper was commonly used in Stuart's era.

From 1775 until 1793, Stuart trained in the United Kingdom before returning to America. His reputation preceding him, he began painting influential individuals of the day, including several portraits of George Washington, the second of which he did in 1796 when Washington was sixty-four. Nicknamed the *Athenaeum Portrait*, it became the image we see today on the one-dollar bill.

In an attempt to authenticate the drawing allegedly done by Stuart, Wes first took it to be analyzed by Dr. Thomas Hoving, former director of New York's Metropolitan Museum of Art. Upon close scrutiny, Hoving noticed several inconsistencies, including Washington's attire and the lack of wear of the paper itself. There was a watermark, and there was a small tear in the

Gilbert Stuart's 1796 portrait of George Washington. This version, known as the *Lansdowne Portrait*, was commissioned for the Marquis of Lansdowne as a gift.

paper, which indicated age, but in general, a genuine drawing would likely have more indiscriminate wear or damage. He also observed that the drawing appeared to almost be split in half, with one half appearing more detailed than the other. Overall, Hoving felt that the authenticity of the drawing was somewhat weak.

Not fully convinced, Wes traveled to Delaware's Henry Francis DuPont Winterthur Museum and presented the drawing to art historian and Gilbert Stuart expert David Meschutt. Almost immediately, Meschutt was

The drawing of George Washington investigated by *History Detectives*.

suspicious, given the fact that Stuart rarely made drawings after 1780, instead painting straight to canvas. As with Hoving, a point of contention for Meschutt was Washington's attire. The drawing shows Washington wearing a uniform, but by 1795 he was already president and would've been wearing civilian clothing. Still another problem was Stuart's signature, which appears in the bottom left corner of the drawing. According to Meschutt, Stuart seldom signed his work, but when he did, he signed "G. Stuart." This drawing shows Stuart's full name. But it's what Meschutt said next that turned the investigation upside down. The drawing wasn't a Stuart original, it was the work of master forger Ferdinand Danton.

FORGING AHEAD

It's an utter tragedy that an artist who possesses extraordinary talents is destined to duplicate—with amazing precision—the work of a master artist. At best, it's a dose of karmic fate. At worst, it's a criminal act. In the case of Ferdinand Danton, it was both. In order to better understand the mindset of a forger, Wes met with John Myatt, who faked an estimated 200 paintings to the tune of almost $200,000 during a nine-year period ending in 1995. Myatt's forgery career came as a result of his association with Englishman John Drewe, a scheming, inveterate liar who'd already successfully passed himself off as an atomic physicist to the British

Energy Authority, where he worked for two years before being discovered and fired. Years later Drewe met Myatt, who at the time was a struggling artist, and convinced him that he was a high-level nuclear physicist with ties to British Intelligence. Succumbing to Drewe's pathological charms, Myatt painted forgeries for him before being arrested and cooperating in Drewe's prosecution. The twisted bit is that Drewe's real talent for passing off Myatt's forgeries was in gaining access to the archives of major galleries and museums.

As part of his con, he created false provenances with stolen stationery and inserted fake pages into archive catalogs to create documentation for artwork that had never before existed. Both Sotheby's and Christie's auction houses and a variety of respected galleries sold large numbers of faked artwork Drewe peddled, and made him a very wealthy man. Ironically, his endgame didn't come as a result of professional detection. Instead, he was done in by a woman scorned. In 1995, Drewe left his lover of fifteen years, Bat-Sheva Goudsmid, for another woman, leaving behind incriminating documents and letters. Goudsmid realized that he'd been conning her and the art world for years and turned the documents over to Scotland Yard, triggering the arrest of John Myatt and, in 1996, John Drewe himself. After a contentious court trial, during which Drewe concocted an elaborately idiotic and unprovable defense of an international frame-up, he was sentenced to six years in prison, of which he served only two.

Myatt was also convicted, and wound up serving just four months. He has continued working as an artist, painting admitted copies of masterworks and holding occasional exhibitions. Only seventy-three of the estimated 200 forgeries were ever recovered. The fact that during his interview with Wes, Myatt confirmed he'd never heard of Ferdinand Danton actually gave credence to Danton's ability, as the most successful forgers are the ones who go unnoticed.

> **time TEASER**
>
> George Washington's false teeth were made out of wood and porcelain. True or false?
>
> **Answer:** False. His faux choppers were made of carved ivory that was set in silver plate.

TIES THAT BIND

Taking a more direct approach, Wes did an Internet search and found a Web site explaining that Danton died in 1939. He had four brothers and a wife named Henrietta, and one of his several sons was named George Grieve. Wes met Grieve in Washington, D.C., where he learned that

George Grieve, son of infamous forger Ferdinand Danton, meeting with Wes Cowan in Washington, D.C.

Con artist and forger Ferdinand Danton.

Grieve was adopted at age two after being abandoned by his parents and left to roam the streets of Washington. Grieve showed Wes a picture of his father and mentioned that Danton spent two years in Virginia's Lorton Reformatory for forgery. Overwhelmed by the curiosity of Danton's duplicitous career, Wes contacted various galleries and museums in the faint hope of finding someone who had heard of Ferdinand Danton. Very quickly, he was contacted by the Historical Society of Delaware, whose historian Dr. Constance Cooper told Wes that in 1934 the society paid $1,500 for seven portraits of Delaware dignitaries painted by renowned artist Rembrandt Peale. Unfortunately, they weren't actually created by Peale, they were forged by Danton.

Over the years, the Historical Society collected significant information on Danton, and it was those documents that painted him as a very savvy and relentless con artist whose favorite ploy was fabricating sad stories in order to emotionally blackmail buyers into giving him money. In many of his scams he used his own children, claiming in one note that his son had passed away, and in another that his children had chicken pox and he was losing his home and needed money quickly. Ferdinand Danton was shameless. One document, dated December 26, 1935, from the Post Office Department detailed Danton's arrest the previous February for mail fraud in connection with his forgeries. That conviction resulted in a one- to two-year prison sentence. The second was a posthumous FBI report on Danton dated 1955 that named his wife and sons George and David Danton. But there was another name in the report that would take the investigation in an entirely new and exciting direction.

Back in Frederick County, Maryland, Wes informed Jim Colket that his father's drawing of George Washington was masterfully drawn by career forger Ferdinand Danton, who fooled loads of experts during his twenty-year con game. What truly made the revelation special was that Wes introduced Colket to George Grieve, Danton's abandoned son. But that wasn't the end of this artistically audacious adventure. What Wes found in Danton's FBI report was that forged art wasn't the only thing he was hiding. Among his many secrets was a man in San Francisco by the name of Clifton Danton who turned out to be a brother that George Grieve never knew he had.

Bait and Switch

Ferdinand Danton and John Myatt were brilliant artists who took the criminal path of intentionally misleading the world, but many of the earliest art duplicators in history were, in their own right, great artistic masters of their time. For centuries, copying the work of the Masters has been part of every serious art student's curriculum, and up until the Renaissance began in the fourteenth century most artwork was owned by the Church or the State and had little monetary value outside those institutions.

Hair-Raising History

Boston tailor Henry Price received a charter from the Grand Lodge of England in 1733 to establish what would become the third-oldest operating Masonic Lodge in the world. Since the inception of Freemasonry in the colonies, some of our most noteworthy founding fathers and revolutionary figures have been members, including John Hancock, John Adams, Benjamin Franklin, and George Washington.

The Masonic Lodge in Boston contains a priceless archive of treasures from the nation's earliest period, including the trowel used by the Marquis de Lafayette to lay the cornerstone of the Bunker Hill Monument, a pistol owned by Revolutionary War naval hero John Paul Jones, and a lock of Washington's hair given to the Freemasons by Martha Washington after the great man's death. The hairy heirloom is encased in a tiny gold urn cast by none other than silversmith and patriot messenger Paul Revere, who was also a Freemason.

During those eras, duplicating the work of another artist was considered nothing more than a display of respect and admiration. In fact, the cultural awakening of the Renaissance for a newly affluent merchant class created an explosive demand for artwork, and with it a lucrative market for unscrupulous art dealers and talented but struggling artists. Art experts with enough knowledge to spot forgeries were a rarity, and many forgeries went undetected for hundreds of years.

Modern scientific methods have been applied to the study of art work, with the result that hundreds of works that had been accepted as genuine were deemed questionable, if not outright fakes. Infrared and ultraviolet examinations (commonly referred to as "black light" examinations), x-rays, and photospectrography have provided techniques for scientists to view artwork—quite literally—in a new and revealing light. Some museums, such as the Victoria and Albert Museum in London, have even gone so far as to create separate galleries for forgeries of exceptional quality. It must be noted, however, that the best art forgers have fooled some pretty intimidating art buyers. When a previously unknown painting by the great master Johannes Vermeer was discovered in the possession of notorious Nazi chief Hermann Göering after World War II, the sale of the work was traced to Dutchman Han van Meegeren. Arrested as a Nazi collaborator and facing the death penalty, van Meegeren chose the lesser of ill fates and confessed to having painted the piece himself.

DID YOU know

According to international investigators, stealing artwork and antiquities is the third most lucrative criminal activity worldwide, behind drugs and arms trafficking, generating an estimated $2 billion to $6 billion a year. Expert opinion suggests that stolen art and ancient relics are used to fund terrorism and drug and arms trafficking, and serve as an alternative to traceable monetary transactions.

In an unusual defense strategy, van Meegeren demonstrated his skill by recreating another Vermeer in his prison cell. Ultimately, he was convicted only of fraud charges and sentenced to one year in prison, but van Meegeren suffered a heart attack and died before he could serve a day of his sentence. In total, fourteen masterpieces attributed to Vermeer and Pieter de Hooch were found to be the work of Han van Meegeren.

SNUBBING THE SNOBS

Like Han van Meegeren, Englishman Tom Keating pulled a similar ruse, only with a distinctly wicked twist. In the art world, one would hardly expect to find clues of fakery left intentionally by an art forger, but that's exactly what Keating did in an odd effort to expose what he considered to be a corrupt gallery system. Keating often wrote text in white paint on canvases before beginning his paintings, knowing it would be exposed under ultraviolet or x-ray examinations. He also purposely painted flaws into his works, or used pigments that would dissolve during an examination cleaning.

Wes Cowan meeting with renowned forger John Myatt.

Claude Manet, Rembrandt, Auguste Renoir, and Amedeo Modigliani were among the dozen or so masters whose styles and techniques Keating could replicate with apparent ease. He was eventually exposed in 1976 and confessed to putting an astonishing 2,000 forgeries into the art market. Three years later Keating was put on trial, but ill health preempted court proceedings. He later went on to develop a cottage industry out of his notoriety, even hosting a BBC television art series in the early 1980s in which he examined and recreated famous artworks for his viewers. Keating died at the age of sixty-five in 1984, after which his fraudulent artwork became—and remains—highly collectible. That wasn't the case, however, with a man called Otto Wacker, who painted the art world into a corner some fifty years earlier.

VAN GOGH'S WACKING

In the heady days of the late 1920s, several prominent Vincent van Gogh experts fell under the spell of German art dealer Otto Wacker until a 1925 Berlin exhibition unhinged the art world. Nearly thirty of what were believed to be van Gogh's works had already been displayed in anticipation of a showing at Paul Cassirer's

time TEASER

Painter Andrew Wyeth's brother, Nathaniel, is known for a famous invention. What is it and when did he patent it?

Answer: DuPont chemical engineer Nathaniel Wyeth invented the plastic soft drink bottle, which he patented in 1973.

Pillage and Plunder

The era of Adolf Hitler's Germany also encapsulated the days of the most egregious and systematic plundering of artwork in the twentieth century. Hitler fancied himself a connoisseur, and after becoming Chancellor of Germany in 1933 began making elaborate plans to transform the city of Linz, Austria, into the Third Reich's cultural center for fine arts. In the name of the Führer, specialized Nazi organizations looted hundreds of thousands of art objects frommuseums and private collections in every Nazi-occupied nation in Europe.

Although many of the most identifiable masterpieces were recovered by the Allies after the end of the war in 1945 and redistributed to their rightful owners, many thousands of significant art objects are still missing. Political and public pressure, along with advances in technological identification, have helped return a relative handful of artworks to their owners, but sadly, an incalculable number remain unaccounted for.

Berlin art gallery, with space reserved for four more that were late in delivery. When the final four paintings arrived the evening before the show, they were brought into the gallery and set on the floor in front of their assigned wall positions. Moments later, Grete Ring, co-manager of the gallery, walked past and froze. Even Ring's cursory inspection showed the quartet to be obvious fakes. The paintings were traced directly to art dealer Otto Wacker and immediately returned to him.

To make matters even worse, at least thirty more of the paintings for the exhibition had come from Wacker, and all fell under suspicion. It seems that the infamous Wacker had created a cat-and-mouse art provenance of political intrigue for the works, which allegedly moved the paintings through confidential Russian hands and eventually to a private Swiss collection. His entire trail of provenance, of course, proved to be poppycock, and the resulting uproar put van Gogh into the international spotlight and Otto Wacker into prison for eighteen months on fraud charges. To this day, no one knows with certainty who painted the fraudulent van Goghs, and no trace of any of them remains.

MILLION-DOLLAR MASTERPIECES

In today's marketplace, it's no secret that genuine masterpieces by known artists are hot commodities. In fact, the sales prices for their works can approach the gross national product of a small country. The top three sales price record holders were all sold in private sales in 2006. Jackson Pollock's *No. 5, 1948* sold for $140 million. Close on its heels is *Woman III*, a painting by Willem de Kooning that went for $137 million, and not far behind is *Portrait of Adele Bloch-Bauer I* by Gustav Klimt, which brought in a cool $135 million. In contrast to those sales is the revenue generated by sales of "original fakes," which has actually become a niche market in the art world. For example, recently produced fake masterpieces by John Myatt are sold for as much as $10,000.

The difference between these and Myatt's criminally produced artworks of the past is that the inscription "genuine fake" is written in indelible ink on the back of the canvas, which also holds an identifying computer chip. With clearly identifiable disclaimers, the production and sale of fake art in good faith is perfectly legitimate. Many art experts suspect that unidentified forged art masterpieces hang in museums and in private collections worldwide. As John Myatt himself said: "If someone came to me with one of my fakes now, I wouldn't let on . . . I'd be losing a perfectly innocent person money."

A Manhattan Murder Mystery

Picture, if you will, what it might have been like living in New York City at the start of the twentieth century. In a growing metropolis filled with culture and decadence, Gotham's rich and famous gorged themselves on lavish soirées and luxurious living. But even the "beautiful" people were unable to escape scandal, and in 1906 there was no more sordid affair than the murderous love triangle of Harry Thaw, Stanford White, and a stunning dark-haired beauty named Evelyn Nesbit.

Twentieth-century ingénue Evelyn Nesbit.

Today, a woman named Sarah Powell owns a 1921 portrait by renowned illustrator and artist Howard Chandler Christy that her family believes is of Evelyn Nesbit. Fueled by the lure of art and high-society mayhem, History Detectives Elyse Luray and Tukufu Zuberi traveled to New Jersey to meet Powell and check out the painting of an unknown woman casually posed in a chair. Could she indeed be trailblazing model turned celebrity socialite Evelyn Nesbit?

While Nesbit was still a young girl, her magnificent features turned the heads of dozens of artists and photographers. Shortly after moving with her family to New York, she caught the eye of renowned illustrator Charles Dana Gibson and became one of his famous "Gibson Girls," the iconic modern and elegant women of turn-of-the-century America. In 1901, at the tender age of sixteen, Nesbit met legendary architect Stanford White, a wealthy man with a penchant for underage girls. It was a fateful introduction that would forever change the young beauty's life.

Evelyn Nesbit, her husband, Harry Thaw, and the object of his aggression, Stanford White.

At age forty-eight, White seduced Nesbit and she became his mistress for a time, but White's behavior paled in comparison to that of Pittsburgh millionaire Harry Kendall Thaw, who became utterly obsessed with the hauntingly beautiful ingénue. Known for his various psychoses, extreme jealousy, and abusive nature, Thaw would become the undoing of this bizarre love triangle, especially after his marriage to Nesbit in 1905, and his seething over the fact that White was responsible for taking her virginity.

TRIAL AND ERROR

For a city hellbent on delicious scandal, the night of June 25, 1906, turned out to be a doozy. On that evening, Stanford White was taking in a show on the rooftop garden theater of Madison Square Garden when a deranged Harry Thaw pulled out a pistol and shot White several times in the face. It was an act that rattled the champagne corks of everyone in New York to such an extent that the sensationalized trial that followed was deemed the "trial of the century." Jam-packed with juicy details of Thaw's tumultuous marriage and Nesbit's sexual dalliances with White, the Big Apple's high society hung on every lurid scrap of information. Nesbit in particular gave explicit testimony that women of the era wouldn't have dreamed of uttering.

Avid readers hung on every word printed about Stanford White's murder and Harry Thaw's trial.

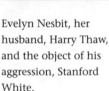

In the end, all three of the main actors in the Shakespearean-style encounter were dragged through the mud, with only Nesbit rising from the proceedings like a golden phoenix, despite the fact that her testimony on Thaw's behalf saved him from certain execution. Nesbit became the toast of the town after the trial, her subsequent life and legend proving that one can never truly know what lies beneath the surface of a seemingly crystal-clear pond.

If Tukufu and Elyse were to prove that the provocative painting was indeed Evelyn

Nesbit, they needed to focus on learning everything they could about both Nesbit and artist Howard Chandler Christy.

Elyse's first consultation was with Roger Reed, director of Illustration House in New York City, who relayed to her that Christy was a superstar among illustrators of the day, renowned for his aptly named "Christy Women." Analyzing the watercolor, the positioning of the model's hands and casual sitting position, and Christy's unique signature, Reed was able to quickly confirm that the painting was indeed authentic.

Elyse Luray and Roger Reed examining the Howard Chandler Christy painting believed to be of Evelyn Nesbit.

Visiting the Players Club in New York, a building remodeled by Stanford White in 1888, Tukufu met with Hofstra University English professor Dr. Paula Uruburu, who clarified Nesbit's status as the "first supermodel and the first sex goddess of the twentieth century." Upon viewing a famous photograph taken by White of Nesbit au naturel on a bearskin rug, it became apparent that while she did pose for Christy at some point, the woman in the portrait didn't resemble Nesbit. Meanwhile, Elyse went to the American Illustrators Gallery in New York to meet with Christy expert Judy Goffman Cutler. The year of the portrait, 1921, was enough to tell Cutler that the illustration was likely done for a magazine layout, and upon examining a World War I poster, the identity of Christy's model became immediately apparent.

PORTRAIT OF A LADY

It's no secret that throughout history, many of the world's greatest artists were inspired by women—but typically not their wives. Andrew Wyeth, for example, rocked the art world with his highly successful "Helga" series. Pablo Picasso's mistress was the subject of many of his paintings, including *Nude in a Black Armchair*, which sold for

time
TEASER

The 1955 film *The Girl in the Red Velvet Swing* was based on Evelyn Nesbit. Who was originally slated to play Nesbit and who ended up portraying her?

Answer: Marilyn Monroe was originally cast to play Nesbit, but ultimately she was portrayed by Joan Collins.

Howard Chandler Christy and his wife and muse, Nancy Palmer Christy.

$45 million in 1999 at Christie's. So who was it who served as Howard Chandler Christy's ultimate inspiration? With a solid identification of their mystery woman, and a hearty appreciation for turn-of-the-century illustrators and their models, Tukufu and Elyse returned to New Jersey to relate their findings to Sarah Powell. Without a doubt, the woman in the portrait was not infamous socialite Evelyn Nesbit, but it was someone nobody could have guessed. Christy had an obvious affection for this particular model—she was the face of the quintessential modern woman and was featured in all types of magazines and even recruitment posters. Powell's portrait itself illustrated a story in the 1922 issue of *McCall*'s magazine. Timeless in her beauty, the model was none other than Christy's wife, Nancy Palmer Christy.

DID YOU know

Before the advent of film and television, people focused on reading anything they could get their hands on, and because of this, artists and illustrators of the early 1900s were the rock stars of their day. Joining Howard Chandler Christy in the limelight were A. B. Wenzell, Arthur Keller, Henry Hutt, Daniel Carter Beard, and Harrison Fisher, whose "Fisher Girls" became competitors of the "Christy Girls" and Charles Dana Gibson's "Gibson Girls."

One-Man Army

Have you ever seen an object that you knew you just had to have? Did you purchase it because you felt it had a story to tell? No doubt this overwhelming urge has happened to many of us at one time or another, but in the case of Adam Lubas, he needed help uncovering what could prove to be a fascinating tale. As a result of an Internet auction purchase, Polish American collector Adam Lubas came into possession of four illustrations of armed soldiers, signed by an artist named "Szyk." Suspecting these might have been the original works of

DIY DETECTIVE

In today's market, identifying art can be an intimidating ordeal, especially given the daunting process of deciphering original works from forgeries. So what do you do if you think you've got a valuable piece of art or you just want to find out if your painting is authentic? The first step is careful analysis of the painting's size, color, and frame, as well as the signature, imprint, or title, if they exist.

Second, start a search for the provenance of the work. If it's been in your family for years, see if you can find out the date and purchase price, along with any information or tall tales anyone has about the painting and its artist. If your painting was done by a famous artist, chances are good that you'll need expert opinions and scientific testing and evaluation by a professional appraiser.

Qualified appraisers often begin their work with historical research to determine if the artist actually painted the piece and if the subject matter is consistent with a particular artist's work. Appraisers also study the stylistic elements of artwork, including composition, color combinations, and brushstrokes, to match known traits of particular artists. If these combined research elements indicate that your painting may be a highly valuable masterpiece, a laboratory analysis can determine if the paint and canvas are consistent with the artist. Lab analyses can reveal the actual age of a canvas, the type of paints used, and the wood in a stretched canvas, and above all, verify an artist's signature. A fascinating cutting-edge development in painting appraisal is the use of DNA to identify plant and animal material used in known paintings by particular artists and compare them to those used in unknown works.

When searching for a competent art appraiser, bear in mind that ethical appraisers will usually first examine photographs of your work before offering to conduct a full appraisal, and most won't charge for that service. If your painting is worth less than around $5,000, you may not need to go any further. Basic appraisals can cost a few hundred dollars, with high-tech appraisals running as much as $2,500 or more. A good place to start looking for a qualified art appraiser is the American Society of Appraisers or the Appraisers Association of America.

Above all, if you're buying a work of art, be sure to check for comparable prices, use only reputable dealers, and always ask for the work's provenance and certificates of authenticity. For more information about art analysis, visit *History Detectives* at www.pbs.org.

Close-ups of three of the four 1914 Arthur Szyk works investigated by *History Detectives*.

famed political cartoonist Arthur Szyk but not knowing how to confirm his purchase, Lubas called upon History Detective Elyse Luray to establish authenticity and learn more about the artist.

With no known history behind the illustrations, all Elyse had to work with was the information on the pieces themselves: four slightly different signatures, the dates 1914 and 1915, and the Polish city Lodz, correctly pronounced "wooch." With the illustrations in hand, Elyse first needed to research Arthur Szyk to try to authenticate what could prove to be an extraordinary find. Her research showed that Szyk was Jewish, born in Poland, and had lived in the city of Lodz. Although his birthdate remains unclear, Szyk studied art in Paris in 1909 and in Krakow in 1913, after which he made a name for himself illustrating books and manuscripts. After moving to Paris in 1921, he continued to build a career illustrating children's books and religious publications, and his reputation garnered him commissions from the French government and an invitation from the League of Nations to illustrate the organization's charter, called the League Covenant.

In 1937, Szyk relocated to London and began focusing on drawing political satires, caricatures, and anti-Fascism cartoons, especially after the German Army invaded Poland in 1939. At the suggestion of influential political figures in Poland and Great Britain, he came to the United States to tour his works in order to heighten public awareness of the tragedy Nazi Germany was inflicting upon Europe, and his work was soon featured on the covers of major American magazines such as *Time* and *Collier's*. So renowned was Szyk that Eleanor Roosevelt herself made the observation that: "This is a personal war of Szyk against Hitler, and I do not think Mr. Szyk will lose."

time
TEASER

Many artists practice anthropomorphism. What does it mean?

Answer: It means applying human behaviors or traits to animals, deities, or inanimate objects.

After taking the illustrations to Debra Evans, director of the Western Regional Paper Conservation Laboratory at the California Palace of the Legion of Honor in San Francisco, Elyse was able to establish that the paper, framing, and level of deterioration of the works were all authentic to the time period. With that crucial information confirmed, she then traveled to the United States Holocaust Memorial Museum in Washington, D.C., where permanent exhibitions at the museum illustrate the suffering, torture, and deaths of the estimated eleven million Jews, Gypsies, homosexuals, and other targets of Nazi Germany during the Holocaust.

Dr. Steven Luckert, curator of the Arthur Szyk exhibition, possessed a wealth of knowledge about the famous illustrator. Upon examining the illustrations, Luckert corroborated Szyk's presence in the city of Lodz in 1915, and he allayed Elyse's concerns about the varying signatures on the works by showing her examples of the artist's work as his career evolved and the range of signatures he used. In addition, Luckert had another convincing detail about Arthur Szyk.

In 1914, Szyk enlisted in the Russian Army and remained in Russian service until 1915. In an amazing turn of events, the museum exhibition had a postcard that Szyk illustrated of a Russian soldier that was nearly a dead ringer for the illustrations now belonging to Adam Lubas. The hats, uniforms, weapons, and the soldier's poses were clearly the same subject material rendered by the same artist. From every aspect, Adam Lubas possessed four of the earliest known works by illustrator Arthur Szyk, a talented and determined artist who served as a one-man army against Hitler.

One-man army and illustrator Arthur Szyk takes on the Axis powers in this 1946 self-portrait.

CHAPTER FOUR
AN UNCIVIL WAR

Winston Churchill once said: "In war, as in life, it is often necessary, when some cherished scheme has failed, to take up the best alternative open, and if so, it is folly not to work for it with all your might." In its timelessness, that's a pearl of wisdom that holds true for all wars and for the soldiers who fight for their nations, their families, and their beliefs. The American Civil War was the bloodiest conflict ever fought on American soil, and it remains a constant reminder of our racial past underlying a fierce loyalty to a stagnant belief system that to this day makes its presence known.

The History Detectives are no strangers to the Civil War, as over the years many artifacts have come to their attention, each one bringing us a small step closer to understanding why the conflict occurred and how it affected every American citizen. For centuries battles have been won and lost, and no doubt they will continue to be fought. But in the end, one sees the true story of war not just in newspapers or on television, but in the faces of those who've seen battle firsthand and lived to tell the tale.

The Riddle of the Old GAR Photo

Every now and again you see a photograph that takes you by surprise, one that's so mesmerizing you can't take your eyes off it. Perhaps it's the way the photo is taken, its scenery, or the way it's lit. And sometimes . . . it's the look on a person's face. Wartime photographs are arguably some of the most powerful images in the world, as the faces of soldiers before, during, and after battle tell an unspoken tale of the horrors and depravity of conflicts that no individual should ever endure. Such is the case with a photograph owned by Etters, Pennsylvania, collector Angelo Scarlato, an image of a group of Civil War veterans in full military dress, whose intense and timeless gazes are moving in a way that belies the obvious toll their battles have taken. Just one look and you can almost smell the burnt gunpowder.

Now, you might wonder what makes this particular group photo so special. After all, it's not uncommon to see companies of soldiers posing for a photograph. But this image is unique, for amid this group of sea-soned vets are two African Americans, one of whom is holding a flag. In a world that was rife with racial segregation, one can't help but wonder why these two soldiers were included in the photo. Needless to say, that

The Grand Army of the Republic Knowl-ton Post No. 160 of Cazenovia, New York.

was the task for Elyse Luray, a challenge that could well be akin to finding a needle in a haystack, given the amount of incomplete Civil War records available today. But regardless of whether or not any of the veterans could be identified, the photograph must be admired for its stoic strength.

Elyse estimated that the large photograph was taken in the early 1900s, and the occasion appears to have been a celebration or even a reunion, as each man is in formal dress and wearing a flower on his uniform. Upon each of their hats is the acronym "GAR," which signifies the Grand Army of the Republic, America's first significant veterans organization. On April 6, 1866, a year after the end of the Civil War, infantry surgeon Dr. Benjamin F. Stephenson founded the GAR in Decatur, Illinois, for Union Army, Navy, and Marine Corps troops who'd received honorable discharges.

DID YOU know

At age seventeen, Albert Woolson was a bugler and drummer in the Civil War. What sets Woolson apart from all other veterans of America's bloodiest conflict? When he died on August 2, 1956, he was 109 and the last survivor of both the Union Army and the GAR.

A carpenter by trade with a penchant for storytelling, he was reportedly receiving a pension of $135 a month. A bust of Woolson is on display at the Grand Army of the Republic Civil War Museum and Library in Philadelphia.

As an organization, the GAR set up community "posts," or outposts, and worked tirelessly at the community and governmental levels, providing soldiers' homes, relief work, and future legislation for military pensions. By 1890, it was estimated that the GAR boasted a membership of almost 410,000 former soldiers, an astonishing brotherhood, considering that the casualties of the Civil War numbered over one million (see chapter 1).

The fact that there was no mention of race in the GAR membership requirements proved intriguing. When researching GAR history, Elyse learned that after the war, contingents of Northern veterans formed posts in the Southern states, and their groups did split along racial lines. Elyse found a score of accounts listing complaints about the admission of African Americans into GAR groups, some whites even threatening to leave if their group was integrated. Given the racial climate of the era and that soldiers who fought in the war were usually segregated, Angelo Scarlato's photograph became all the more mysterious.

By scanning the image and increasing its size, Elyse was able to discern some of the photo's text, which read: "Knowlton Post No. 160, Cazenovia, New York." Following the trail, she visited the Cazenovia Public Library and met with local historian Sue Greenhagen, who revealed that about 387 local men enlisted in the army, fifty-six of whom never returned home. At the time, the population of Cazenovia, a liberal antislavery town, was around 4,000, a mere forty of whom were African American.

A search of records from the town clerk listed vital information of the town's soldiers, including their race. Only two men of color were on record—Joseph Brown and John Stevenson. But it didn't end there. The neighboring town of Smithfield lacked a GAR post, and a search of their records turned up a third GAR member: Alberta Leroy Robbins.

With three men, and only two in the photograph, Elyse needed to dig deeper, so she requested all of their military and pension records from Washington's National Archives. But while the records might explain who these men were, it wouldn't solve the issue of what they were doing in the photo or the special occasion it represented.

time TEASER

How many soldiers constitute a company and how many companies constitute a regiment?

Answer: There are ten companies in a regiment, with a hundred men in each company.

BROTHERS IN ARMS

A visit to the African American Civil War Museum in Washington gave Elyse further background on the GAR and its members, notably that outposts such as Cazenovia's hold great historical significance as being among the first organizations in the United States to be racially integrated. For these veterans, whose bonds were cemented in the heat of battle, there was no difference between black and white. According to historian Barbara Gannon, it was comradeship under fire that enhanced the group's desegregation, a concept supported by a senior GAR official's own words: "A man good enough to stand between the flag and those who would destroy it is good enough to be a comrade of the Grand Army of the Republic."

George Geder and his great-great-grandfather, GAR member John Stevenson.

Veterans best understand the plight of their fellow veterans, a concept reinforced by the wearing of flowers on their lapels in Angelo Scarlato's photo. The occasion was most likely Memorial Day at a gathering to honor their fallen brethren. Gannon also believed that the fact that one of the African American vets is holding the flag is a sure sign of the respect and honor his peers bestowed upon him. As luck would have it, Char McCargo Bah, a historian and genealogist whom Elyse contacted early on in the investigation, made several remarkable discoveries, the first of which was an obituary mentioning "our faithful and esteemed color bearer." Alberta Robbins was indeed the flag bearer in the photograph. According to military records, he enlisted in the military in 1863 just after President Abraham Lincoln's Emancipation Proclamation granted slaves their freedom.

As for the second veteran, McCargo Bah gave Elyse a substantial lead that took her to Santa Fe, New Mexico, to the home of George Geder, the great-great-grandson of John Stevenson. What Geder shared with Elyse was a remarkable family photo of his father as a youngster sitting on the lap of his great-grandfather. A close inspection of that photo against the GAR reunion photo showed that it was indeed John Stevenson, a fact Elyse confirmed when the two images were analyzed by a New York State Police forensic detective.

George Geder visiting John Stevenson's final resting place in Cazenovia, New York.

SEMPER FI

To bring the Grand Army of the Republic mystery full circle, Elyse brought George Geder to New York to meet Angelo Scarlato, and she presented Geder with a copy of the incredibly rare photograph. His ancestor, John Stevenson, served with the 29th Connecticut Colored Regiment Volunteer Infantry, which was active from 1863 to 1865 and was part of many battles, including the Battle of Chaffin's Farm (also called Chapin's Farm or New Market Heights) in 1864, which was instrumental in the Union Army's taking of Richmond, Virginia, a few months later.

Stevenson's final place of rest hadn't been seen by his great-great-grandson, so Elyse took Geder to pay his respects to a man whose bravery and courage in the face of adversity helped make the world a more open-minded place for his descendants. If the eyes are the window to the soul, then most certainly the faces of the men of the Grand Army of the Republic show that they have cast themselves into the warrior's abyss and managed to survive. Fortunately for us, a moment of their lives will continue to live on.

Technical Wonders of the Civil War

The Civil War produced staggering numbers of casualties, with more American losses than all other wars combined. Much of the reason for this was that army commanders used ages-old tactics of massing huge forces against one another while using recently developed weapons that were far more lethal and accurate than anything soldiers had ever encountered.

With the development of rifled muskets, breech-loading small arms, cartridges that permitted relatively rapid firing rates, and cannon batteries that literally mowed down rows of concentrated troops, the armies of both sides were ill prepared for the destruction that ensued. Not surprisingly, the Civil War era ushered a wide range of unique firsts into the battle arena during its four years, and a few of them eventually evolved into some of the deadliest instruments ever devised.

Invented by Richard Gatling and patented in 1862, the Gatling gun is one of the first "machine" guns ever devised. Despite the fact that the weapon was capable of firing at a high rate of speed utilizing a hand-operated crank, it was initially ignored by the government as being too radical and cumbersome. Union major general Benjamin Butler purchased twelve Gatling guns and used two of them in the battle for Petersburg, Virginia, in 1864, but it wasn't until after war's end that the gun gained a worldwide reputation as a killing machine. Several other rapid-fire weapons were developed during the Civil War, but because of operational difficulties, few were placed into service.

Babes in Arms

Frail, passive, and genteel may have been words used to describe women during the Civil War era, although for many entirely the opposite was true. As men by the hundreds of thousands enlisted or were drafted into the fight, untold numbers of women were left with the responsibilities of caring for families and farms, often single-handed.

On the battlefront, thousands more women rose to the unpaid task of nursing the wounded, and as casualties mounted the demand for nurses grew exponentially. Less well known are the estimated 200 to 400 women who actually changed their appearance and enlisted as soldiers. Although the practice was expressly forbidden by both the Union and the Confederacy, women fought side-by-side with soldiers in battle, were killed on the field, and were taken as prisoners of war.

In the case of a nineteen-year-old Irish immigrant who entered the Union Army in 1862 as Albert Cashier and fought in nearly forty battles over a four-year period, no one knew that "he" was a "she" until a year before she died at the age of seventy-one in 1914. Cashier lived most of the last years of her life in the Quincy, Illinois, Soldiers' Home. Although there's little doubt that female warriors during the Civil War didn't affect the outcome, the remarkable aspect of their involvement is that they purposely put themselves into the line of fire in such a bloody conflict.

time
TEASER What was the first metal-hulled U.S. Navy battleship?

Answer: The USS *Monitor*.

It may seem odd to note that the first military aircraft carrier sailed during the Civil War, considering that propeller-driven aircraft were yet to be invented, but the claim is technically valid. On August 3, 1861, John La Mountain tethered a hydrogen balloon to the stern of the Union transport ship *Fanny* to observe Confederate positions at Sewell's Point on Chesapeake Bay. Professor Thaddeus Lowe had already established the viability of balloon flight for military observation on June 17 of the same year when he ascended near the White House with President Abraham Lincoln looking on. Both La Mountain and Lowe recognized the inherent difficulties of inflating balloons and towing them to observation points, and reasoned that ships could be outfitted with the unwieldy gas pumps needed to produce hydrogen.

After Lowe convinced Secretary of the Navy Gideon Welles to place the coal barge USS *George Washington Parke Custis* at his disposal, the Navy outfitted the vessel with a hydrogen gas pump, storage for equipment, and a wide, flat deck. The morning of November 10, 1861, the steamer *Coeur de Lion* towed the barge down the Potomac River, and the following day, with the barge secured near Mattawomen Creek, Lowe lifted off to observe Confederate activities on the Virginia shore.

In 2005, History Detective Wes Cowan launched his own investigation into Professor Lowe's uplifting story when he was confronted with a swatch of fabric purported to have come from Lowe's 1862 balloon *Enterprise*. As one of the founders of American air power and commander of the Balloon Corps, Lowe was touted by historian Carl Sandburg as being "the single most shot-at man in the war," and while the swatch didn't actually come from *Enterprise*, Wes did uncover that it was collected by a regimental historian from one of the other Union Army balloons that were destroyed by Rebel gunfire.

DID YOU know

The submarine was not a Civil War invention, but the conflict brought the "infernal machine" into its first use as a warship. The Confederacy's *Hunley* is the first submarine credited with the sinking of an enemy vessel. Often referred to as the *H. L. Hunley* after its inventor, Horace L. Hunley, the submarine used explosives to sink the sloop USS *Housatonic* on February 17, 1863, in Charleston Harbor. The submarine's hull is thought to have been damaged by the force of the detonation and sank shortly after the attack, killing all eight crewmen. The *Hunley* was finally recovered on August 8, 2000, and the remains of the crew were interred with full military honors in Charleston, South Carolina.

Missing Links

D espite the passage of many decades, remnants of wars remain eternally woven into the fabric of our society, and while many of the names and faces are lost to time, the cause for which they fought and the inalienable liberties they hoped to achieve are continually resurrected in modern-day battles. A genuine war relic in good condition—especially one with a great story attached to it—is a truly exciting adventure for everyone involved. Sometimes these artifacts are items found at a garage sale or antiques fair, as was the case with a Revolutionary War speaking trumpet (see chapter 10). Others are purchased through dealers or online auctions or simply donated to an organization. Even more special are those family items that have been handed down from one generation to the next.

The History Detectives have become intimately familiar with the Civil War and the many, varied items they've been asked to investigate. The GAR photograph was but one of many reminders of the bloody conflict. So was a Civil War star flag, an abolitionist banner, a Stanhope spyglass, Robert E. Lee's General Order No. 9, a riding crop allegedly belonging to Preston Brooks, a pair of dueling pistols, and a whaling ship that became part of the Underground Railroad. All of those items and more gave us a glimpse of war and hell, and the endless spirit of the men and women of the era. A family heirloom and a yard-sale find provided two intriguing Civil War mysteries for the History Detectives to explore, and the investigative journeys were well worth the battle.

Richard Gatling with a redesigned version of his famous invention, the Gatling gun, circa 1893.

THE LUMINOUS LETTER OF 1858

The first of these fantastic Civil War finds is a letter that Tampa, Florida, firefighter Joe Skanks found amid a stack of photos he purchased at a yard sale. Signed "A. Lincoln," the letter is dated August 2, 1858, and written to a conservative Republican named Henry Clay Whitney. What are the odds of finding an original letter written by one of the United States' most famous presidents? If you bet that the letter couldn't possibly be authentic, you better start handing over your pennies.

In an investigation that took a few twists and turns, History Detective Elyse Luray was initially quite skeptical because the writing on the letter appeared to contain more than one color of ink. The content of the missive was also curious, its subtext suggesting that Lincoln was responding to a thinly veiled threat. At the time, he was running for Illinois senator against the popular pro-slavery Democrat Stephen Douglas, and clearly the letter was a response to a warning that Lincoln stay away from radical abolitionist and fellow Republican Owen Lovejoy.

With all due respect to Honest Abe, it's amusing and should be duly noted that historical politicking hasn't changed much. When Elyse consulted several historians regarding the letter, it turned out that its content was well known, as the original letter written to Lincoln by Whitney was documented. Both Lincoln and Whitney were lawyers and conservatives, and while Lovejoy was a Republican, he was walking a fine line that could well have ousted him from the party. Whitney's letter was a warning that Lincoln be aware of a Republican plot in which party members were willing to break ranks and vote for Douglas in the hope of thwarting Lovejoy's anti-slavery influence.

Elyse Luray with Joe Skanks and an 1858 letter written by Abraham Lincoln.

Considering the racism of the era, Lincoln was walking a razor's edge of political influence, but the intriguing aspect to the investigation was that two months before the letter was written, Lincoln spoke the immortal words: "A house divided against itself cannot stand. I believe this government cannot endure, permanently, half slave and half free." Known as the "House Divided" speech, it showcased Lincoln's exceptional and somewhat subversive abilities as a politician.

Scientific analysis of the letter authenticated Lincoln's signature, but the inks of different colors created skepticism. The underlying writing was done in iron gall ink (see DIY Detective). But under a microscope, it looked as if the letters had been traced over in black ink. Who might the tracer have been?

For years, historians have been bothered by a published copy of Lincoln's correspondence, as it appears that some of the letters don't quite match his handwriting. Evidently, the man who published the correspondence had traced over the letters to darken the writing. That man was Henry Clay Whitney. The letter that Joe Skanks found at a yard sale is an authentic missing piece of history, an extraordinary artifact that thrilled historians and Lincoln aficionados. Owen Lovejoy's opinions may not have been the zeitgeist of the Civil War era, but in forming a silent political partnership with Abraham Lincoln, both men executed maneuvers that ultimately contributed to the end of slavery.

Abraham Lincoln's signature at the bottom of the letter purchased by Joe Skanks at a yard sale.

THE TALE OF THE TACTICAL MAP

Fred Gumbart of Tucson, Arizona, is one of the lucky few who knows the provenance of his Civil War artifact—a map of the infamous Battle of Vicksburg, one of the most crucial battles of the conflict. The map belonged to Gumbart's great-grandfather, Captain George Conrad Gumbart, who as a Union soldier allegedly carried it during the Vicksburg battle, which began in the spring of 1863.

If proven authentic, it would not only be an astonishing piece of history, it would indeed be priceless, as no other original maps of the Vicksburg battlefield are known to exist. The map, which is in excellent condition, is dated June 20, 1863, and indicates various roads and gun positions that show it to be from the perspective of the Union Army. In addition, it says "Lauman's Division."

Taking on the challenging investigation was Tukufu Zuberi, who brought the map to the Library of Congress for authentication. The map itself was drawn on *drafting linen*, a type of woven cloth with a heavily

---

time TEASER

Confederate Stonewall Jackson's cousin William Lowther Jackson had an unusual nickname. What was it?

Answer: Mudwall Jackson.

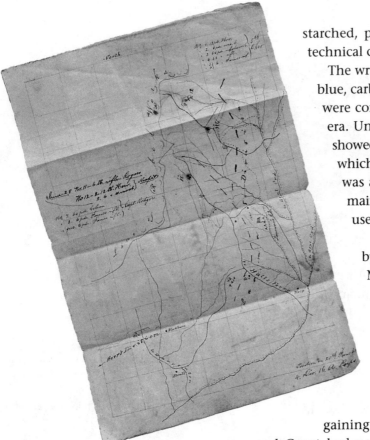

Fred Gumbart's rare and authentic map of the Battle of Vicksburg.

starched, polished surface typically used for technical drawings.

The writing was done in a combination of blue, carbon black, and iron gall inks, which were commonly used during the Civil War era. Under ultraviolet light, the linen also showed a lack of modern optical brightners, which helped confirm that the document was authentic. But the real question remained unanswered: what was the map used for?

By all accounts, the Battle of Vicksburg was a brutal assault. Located in Mississippi, Vicksburg became the target of Union general Ulysses S. Grant and his army of over 35,000 in their crucial attempt to maintain power over the Mississippi River, thereby cutting off Confederate supply lines. Prior to the battle, the Confederacy was gaining ground on the Union contingent, and Grant had no choice but to seize the powerful Vicksburg garrison, which he did—with a bloody and unforgiving siege of the city. From May through July, Grant's forces literally bombarded rebel forces to the ground, in part as revenge for the 3,200 Union soldiers who had perished in a mere two days at the beginning of the assault. A revision of his strategy worked, and on July 4, control of the Mississippi was surrendered to the Union after the rebels finally gave in to starvation and endless firepower.

Gumbart's map was analyzed by Vicksburg historian Terrence Winschel, who explained that the map was meant for Union troops under the leadership of Brigadier General Jacob G. Lauman to show the location of troop units and specific artillery batteries. This information would prove crucial in helping the Union destroy Confederate fortifications. A check of George Gumbart's military records proved that despite being wounded in 1862, he recovered and served as an artillery chief under Lauman during the Vicksburg siege, but that still didn't prove he carried the map.

At the Library of Congress, Tukufu met with Dr. John Hébert, chief of the Geography and Map Division, who was able to read between the lines of this cartographic conundrum. The map belonging to Fred Gumbart's great-grandfather was literally a missing piece of Civil War history. There was no doubt in Hébert's mind that the map was created at the time of the siege, a fact confirmed by Terrence Winschel, who later found a reference to a "skeleton map" belonging to a field report—a map that had never been found. George Gumbart ended his military career a mere ten days after the battle, and he took home with him one of the rarest and most extraordinary maps of the Civil War.

Hide and Go Seek

Civil War maps such as the Vicksburg map are astonishing finds, but there's more to map collecting than meets the eye. The journeys of early explorers during the fifteenth and sixteenth centuries are generally acknowledged, but we often tend to overlook the significance of one of their most important functional tools. Mapmaking, or *cartography*, was a vital skill and paved the way for future explorers to expand on limited knowledge of the structure of the world. All early maps were drawn by hand and depended on the skill, knowledge, and often preconceived biases of the men who drew them. Many of the first explorers were not cartographers per se; they drew crude charts and diagrams of their explorations, which were handed off to skilled artisans, some of whom developed cottage industries out of their mapmaking talents.

One of the most intriguing maps ever produced was created by German cartographer Martin Waldseemüller in 1507, just fifteen years after Columbus landed in the New World. Produced as a woodcut and reproduced in unknown quantities, the map consisted of twelve sections of a sphere that were meant to be pasted onto a ball. Based on letters describing explorations questionably attributed

Spanning the Globe

For navigational purposes, the most revolutionary idea in cartography was perfected by Dutch mapmaker Gerard Mercator in 1569. One of the primary obstacles to generating accurate maps was that the three-dimensional reality of earth was being translated onto flat, two-dimensional pages, with resulting distortions in lines of travel.

Mercator developed a process of incorporating that distortion into his maps and transferring the spherical shape of the world onto flat surfaces. The concept became known as Mercator's Projection and continues to be used in virtually all nautical maps. The breakthrough ushered in an age of Dutch superiority in cartography that lasted for nearly a century.

From exploration to waging war, and for such mundane purposes as simply driving from one city to the next, the visual aid and significance of maps has become so infused in the modern psyche that we tend to take them for granted. In reality, the science and surveying techniques of cartography are one of man's most enduring and important technologies.

to Italian explorer Amerigo Vespucci, Waldseemüller made an educated but incorrect guess at the size of the American continents and essentially "invented" the Pacific coast of North America many years before its actual exploration by European explorers. In the Vespucci letters, the explorer's name was Latinized to *Americus Vespucius*, and Waldseemüller named the newly minted continent for the feminized Latin first name, *America*.

Part of the significance of Waldseemüller's map is that it contains the first documentation of the name for the Americas that would eventually come into permanent use, and was very likely the first map to be printed as a globe.

DIY DETECTIVE

One of the most critical components to authenticating historical documents is analyzing the material they're made of and the ink that was used to write on them. Early documents were written on handmade cotton or linen paper, or on *parchment*. Made from the skins of young calves or sheep, parchment was far more durable than paper and was meant to stand the test of time. Most important documents were written on parchment, with still pristine examples dating back to A.D. 600. *Vellum* is a fine grade of parchment made from calfskin, although the two words are often used interchangeably. It's estimated that the manufacturing processes for making parchment and vellum required three weeks of stretching, drying, scraping, and polishing.

European papermakers in the mid-1400s developed a process for breaking down cloth fibers into a soupy pulp, which was then scooped into molds with hundreds of fine metal wires called *laid lines* woven closely together across a wooden frame. Thicker wires running at right angles every inch or so to provide support were called *chains*. After the paper was dried, the impressions left by the wire mold resulted in the so-called laid finish. Laid paper became the fastest and least expensive form of papermaking. Many historical documents and manuscripts are produced on laid paper, which is identifiable by marks left behind by the screening process, which usually include a faint watermark embedded into the paper fiber during the screening process.

Some of the standards for identifying vellum and laid papers can be misleading, so a word of caution is in order when attempting to identify paper age. Modern laid papers also invariably contain laid and chain lines and are normally watermarked, so the existence of these markings isn't necessarily proof of age.

Modern vellum-type papers, while commercially made with cotton fibers, have a translucence, feel, and durability similar to the real thing. One of the primary differences between early and modern

One of the four known existing copies of the Waldseemüller maps sold at auction in 2005 for $888,000. A wall map also produced by him in 1507 was purchased by the Library of Congress in 2003 for a whopping $10 million. With the same inscriptions as the globe map, the wall map is sometimes regarded as the "birth certificate" of America.

Another of the most significant influences on mapmaking was an atlas created by British cartographer Christopher Saxton and published between 1579 and 1590. Commissioned and financed by royal court official Thomas Seckford with the approval of Queen Elizabeth I, Saxton

papers is the industry-wide addition of optical brighteners that became common in the 1950s.

The purpose of these brighteners is to absorb light in the ultraviolet range and emit a "whiter" appearance, a trick that's commonly used in household detergents. Exposing optically brightened paper to a relatively inexpensive fluorescent ultraviolet source, commonly referred to as *black light*, produces fluorescence that is quite noticeable.

Still, the absence of fluorescence doesn't necessarily indicate the authenticity of a document, and the reason is as close as your public library. Forgers are well aware that libraries are sources for books produced long before the age of optical brighteners, and they're known to slice blank endpapers out of old publications for the purpose of drafting fraudulent historical documents.

The ink traditionally used for handwritten documents in the past is known as *iron gall* and was the ink of choice from the Middle Ages to the mid-1900s. The term

refers to the primary components of the ink, which are an iron solution and oak tree galls produced by the plant's chemical reactions to insect larvae. The resulting mutation, or gall, is often referred to as an oak apple and is quite common.

Iron gall has the unique quality of oxidizing and quite literally "rusting" and turning a sepia color with age. This effect can often be seen under magnification where the edges of written words tend to be more discolored.

While iron gall ink is commercially made only in very small quantities, it's still available in niche markets. Recipes for iron gall ink are also readily available and consist of relatively common items such as iron filings, vinegar, and vegetable tannins or hand-picked oak galls. Here again, forgers know the secrets of duplicating iron gall ink and speeding the aging process, which can be difficult for untrained eyes to identify. Expert authenticators are the last and best line of defense against forgeries, and can often spot even a well-done fake in minutes.

drew incredibly accurate and detailed maps of the counties of England and Wales that were reprinted for centuries and became a benchmark for future cartographers. A copy of Saxton's atlas, bound with five maps depicting Sir Francis Drake's exploration of the New World by Italian mapmaker Giovanni Battista Boazio, sold at auction in 2007 for $1.3 million.

Vestiges of War

U nique in all American conflicts, the Civil War was the culmination of the most divisive social discord in the nation's history and continues to generate keen public interest in the causes and aftermath of the only serious attempt to dissolve the Union. For collectors, the Civil War also generated a plethora of memorabilia that brings enthusiasts a small step closer to the reality of the conflict.

Although many high-profile auctions of Civil War–era relics produce staggering bids, there are many dealers who specialize in significant pieces of history for relatively reasonable prices. For example, the 2005 sale of one of the fifteen known copies of the Emancipation Proclamation signed by Abraham Lincoln reached $688,000 before the gavel fell, making headlines and adding to the aura of inaccessibility for truly rare relics. On the other end of the spectrum, less prestigious documents such as a stamp-signed officer's commission from President Andrew Johnson, who succeeded Lincoln after his assassination, can be found in the dealer's market for less than $500. The Civil War generated millions of documents on both sides of the battle lines, such as general orders, notices, resolutions, pay vouchers, and accounting forms, which regularly sell for prices well under $100.

Civil War–era newspapers provide some of the most interesting perspectives of the conflict and are filled with fascinating history. Confederate general John Hunt Morgan, attempting to divert Union troops from Vicksburg, led raids into Ohio and was captured and imprisoned on July 26, 1863. Morgan escaped on November 27 and returned to the South, where he published a call for his troops to reassemble. Many Southern newspapers, such as the Richmond, Virginia, *Sentinel*, printed his call to arms. Copies of that edition can be found through memorabilia dealers for prices between $100 and $200. There are also several Web sites that focus on reproducing Civil War–era newspaper editions and articles. A good starting point to investigate these offerings is the Historical New York Times Project at www.nyt.org.

Outside of Civil War documents and printed material, the list of collectibles from the era is endless. Badges, canteens, officers' spurs, ammunition boxes, sabers, holsters, caps, and uniforms are all available in various stages of cost and condition. Relics with established provenance that were actually used in battle are relatively rare and invariably bring much higher prices. Firearms in particular make up one of the most expensive niches in Civil War collecting. Even parts of firearms are considered highly collectible, with gun locks and hammer mechanisms selling for well over $1,000. Intact firearms from the period commonly sell for several thousand to tens of thousands of dollars, depending again on rarity and condition.

Although the Civil War was unquestionably one of the bleakest periods in American history, the causes and outcome helped to shape our daily lives and continue to play a part in our sense of solidarity and our differences. For many who acknowledge and appreciate the sacrifices, lives, and honor of the hundreds of thousands who participated in the Civil War, the opportunity to touch and hold relics that may have passed through their hands is enough to inspire awe and raise goosebumps.

time TEASER

What is the name of Robert E. Lee's favorite horse?

Answer: Traveller.

CHAPTER FIVE

IF WALLS COULD TALK

There are many approaches to history that can shed light on the culture, nature, and climate of a particular era and its peoples. The types of shelters that individuals and entire civilizations have constructed provide invaluable information on not only the technical advancement of particular cultures, but how they lived on a daily basis. As a historian and professor, Gwen Wright has taken on many *History Detectives* mysteries involving historically intriguing homes.

Several of these investigations proved that around every corner and behind every façade things aren't always as they appear to be. A perfect example is Gwen's research of an Ohio abode thought to be a do-it-yourself kit purchased from the Sears catalog. Equally compelling are her examinations of a stylish swinging sixties home in Florida and a New Jersey domicile believed to have been built by renowned inventor Thomas Edison. And in a heartfelt turn, we meet a humble family whose Japanese-style home bears extraordinary historical and emotional significance. From the early 1900s through the Cold War era and the Second World War, Gwen's investigations trace the legacy of hopes and fears, comforts and instabilities, historical allusions and modern technologies that underlies Americans' devotion to domestic architecture.

The Case of the Distinctive Domicile

For most of us, the decision to buy or build a house is one of the biggest choices we'll ever make. Today, we would probably retain the services of a broker or real estate agent when purchasing a house, but that wasn't always the case. During the first half of the twentieth century, many savvy individuals took a route that wasn't in keeping with prevailing home buying or building methods—they ordered a home from a catalog, much like the ones you see arriving in your mailbox from places like Sharper Image or Harry and David. Many purchased a home from the most famous of all mail-order companies—Sears, Roebuck and Company. The homes were sometimes called *kit homes*, and they arrived boxed up and ready for assembly, whether by the owner or a local builder. And though you might think it absurd to build your home from a kit with a set of instructions, these structures made home ownership more affordable in rural and suburban areas.

Raymond and Cherie Teuton of Akron, Ohio, believed that their vintage home might have been one of those Sears specials, a notion that came about as a result of a local bus tour they took. When the driver passed their home he singled it out, telling tourists that the home was a perfect example of a Sears abode. Curious about the assertion, the Teutons said they met with the son of the people who built the house. He insisted that it hadn't come from the Sears catalog. But the Teutons weren't convinced, and their need to know prompted their enlisting the help of Gwen Wright to investigate and determine their home's potentially historic origin.

Ray and Cherie Teuton in front of their historic home in Akron, Ohio.

A page from the 1928 Sears home catalog advertising their do-it-yourself homes.

Gwen paid a visit to the Teuton home, located in an idyllic neighborhood setting just outside the city of Akron, near the historic Firestone Park. It is a quaint area, and the streets are filled with foliage and trees that give it an air of quintessential Americana. To own a home in such a place is best described as having a "dream home," which is why the Teutons purchased it.

THE WHOLE KIT AND KABOODLE

After examining the house façade and floor plan, which she found quite well designed, Gwen's first task was to take a closer look at the mail-order-home phenomenon and see what the hubbub was all about. Not surprisingly, kit homes were the ultimate catalog offering. Imagine turning the pages of your newly delivered catalog and seeing the perfect dream house, knowing that it had only to be ordered and assembled. Over 75,000 kit homes were created in the early- to mid-1900s, but only 5,000 have ever been identified. In that regard, they are considered to be collector's items. The idea of pre-cut mail order houses had been around since the very early nineteenth century, and Sears Roebuck began selling the structures around 1908, featuring them in their catalog until the early 1940s.

To further her research, Gwen consulted with Sears house specialist Rosemary Thornton about the Sears home program. In total, Sears produced over 370 different home designs, from small cabins up to four-bedroom structures, ranging in price from $600 to $6,000. According to Thornton, the typical Sears kit home contained over 30,000 pieces, including 750 pounds of nails, twenty-seven gallons of paint and varnish, twenty-seven windows, and twenty-five doors, all shipped in a pair of railroad boxcars. Also included was a mere seventy-five-page instruction booklet. And you thought assembling a bookshelf was a chore?

After examining the outside of the Teuton home, Gwen and Thornton couldn't make a firm identification, since it didn't look like any of the known Sears models, so they headed indoors for further investigation. In the basement they searched for any identifying labels or three-digit stamped numbers that would indicate that pieces had been marked for assembly, but none were found. In the attic, they searched for the plasterboard sheets common to the typical Sears home, but again no physical evidence was found. Without some form of physical identification or documentation, there was no way to confirm or deny that the Teutons' beloved home was a piece of history. Or was there?

Curious to learn more, Gwen met with Cristine Braman, a local tour guide, who was able to paint a picture of the neighborhood history during the early 1900s. As it turned out, this history involved the rubber industry, which saw explosive growth between 1910 and 1920, fueled in part by munitions for World War I. At the forefront of the boom was Harvey Firestone, whose Akron factory helped make the city the fastest growing in America. This rapid growth compounded the problem of a significant lack of housing for factory workers. Braman's great-grandfather told her that during that time housing was so scarce that boardinghouses were renting out rooms in twelve-hour shifts.

Firestone's influence on the Akron area was majestic. He promised to build houses for his workers near the factory in a bucolic company town he called Firestone Park, including a huge park at the center of the neighborhood, conspicuously built in the shape of Firestone's company logo—a shield. In an effort to satisfy the urgent demand, Firestone set about building company housing. The question was, did he do so with the help of Sears Roebuck?

NEIGHBORHOOD WATCH

To give you some idea of just how much influence Sears, Roebuck and Company had on the American public, it's important to understand the company's impressive history. During the latter part of the nineteenth century there were almost sixty million individuals living throughout the thirty-eight states, over half of them in rural areas, and the entire U.S. national income was a mere $10 billion. It seems that Sears was started almost as a

time
TEASER

Henry Ford gathered wood scraps from his factory and developed what well-known product?

Answer: Kingsford Charcoal Briquettes.

fluke in 1886, when Minnesota train agent Richard Sears inadvertently received a shipment containing unwanted watches. The budding entrepreneur sold the timepieces and created the R.W. Sears Watch Company. Successful at his new endeavor, he moved his base of operations to Chicago, where in 1887 he advertised in the local newspaper for a watchmaker. Lo and behold, the man who applied was Alvah C. Roebuck. Six years later, in 1893, Sears, Roebuck and Company was created, and an American legend was born. But what really brought Sears to the forefront was their mail-order business and the needs they filled for rural American farm families. From watches to farm equipment, the Sears catalog expanded to include just about everything—including the kitchen sink and the house surrounding it.

Throughout the twentieth century, the company continued to flourish and open the eyes of every consumer. Second in literary popularity only to the Bible, the Sears catalog became a mainstay of American life. The company would eventually expand to include retail stores, the 1931 creation of the Allstate Insurance Company, the international landmark Sears Tower, acquisitions such as Dean Witter, Coldwell, Banker and Company, the Discover Card, and a 2005 merger with superstore Kmart. Quite an amazing history for a fellow starting out with a box full of cheap pocket watches.

THE CLUE IN THE CATALOG

Gwen's next step in her investigation was to follow the Firestone paper trail in an attempt to establish who actually built the Teuton home. A 1917 letter from Harvey Firestone's secretary mentioned that the firm's expert advisers believed that the company could build worker housing more cheaply on their own rather than buying from ready-made companies like Sears. Another letter from renowned New York architectural firm Trowbridge and Ackerman, who had designed Firestone's lavish estate, affirmed that they were interested in Firestone's housing project. Trowbridge and especially Ackerman had a great interest in high-quality housing for workers. Considering the sophistication of the building, it seemed likely that the Teuton home was designed by them and not by Sears.

Further digging revealed yet another source: Firestone's building contractor, Shannon Construction. In the Shannon files Gwen discovered correspon-

time
TEASER   What was the most requested reading material for wounded U.S. troops recovering in overseas hospitals during both World Wars?

Answer: The Sears Roebuck catalog.

Now You See It—Now You Don't

In the early 1900s, Hungarian immigrant Harry Houdini, arguably the best illusionist and escape artist the world has ever known, astounded audiences with mind-boggling illusions and his daring and inexplicable feats. Decades after his death, a roofer renovating a 1920s bungalow in Chicago made an intriguing discovery—dozens of Houdini posters that were used as roof insulation. Were they authentic? And what did they have to do with spiritualism?

Gwen Wright was sent to investigate, and as it turned out, the poster was from Houdini's final tour in 1926 at the Shubert Princess Theater in Chicago. Part of his performance was a segment to expose fraudulent mediums, whom he despised as a result of having been conned when trying to contact his dearly departed mother.

A poster of one of magician Harry Houdini's shows from his final tour in 1926. At right, Harry Houdini.

dence from 1920 that verified that at that time Firestone was awaiting a shipment of lumber supplies from Sears. Apparently, Firestone had changed his mind and decided to use Sears materials after all. A check of the Teutons' lot number confirmed that theirs was indeed one of the Firestone homes that used Sears materials. It was fantastic news, but the mystery still remained. Could it still be considered a true Sears home?

As is often the case when investigating a piece of history, crucial information sometimes surfaces when it's least expected. In this case, Gwen found her answer with Rosemary Thornton, who presented Gwen with a 1925 Sears catalog and took her to a second home in

Firestone Park, bringing a fitting end to this dubious domicile mystery. Meeting once again with Raymond and Cherie Teuton, Gwen was able to tell them that their dream home is indeed a historic Sears home—but not just any Sears model. The Teutons' house is a hybrid. It was financed by Harvey Firestone, but it was designed by Trowbridge and Ackerman and built using Sears materials. The second house Gwen was shown, along with a picture in the 1925 catalog, confirmed that while that particular house design was advertised in the catalog, it was never made available to the general public. The design of the home is exclusive to Firestone Park and very special, and the Teutons can take great pride in knowing that their Sears home holds a distinctive place in American history.

The Conundrum of the Cold War Kitchen

When it comes to politics there's no end to the rhetorical skills employed by most politicians, and while many of them may speak about the subject of housing in general terms, they rarely get involved in debating the architecture and interior design of a home. That wasn't the case, however, in 1959, when Soviet premier Nikita Khrushchev and U.S. vice president Richard Nixon engaged in a war of words over a quintessential American dwelling. Later developed as the Leisurama home, it contained state-of-the-art features geared toward pleasing the typical American housewife.

Over forty years later, Leisurama home designer Andrew Geller and his grandson Jake Gorst had a question. They had seen hundreds of Leisurama homes in Montauk, New York, but wanted to know if any of Geller's legendary designs were still standing in Lauderhill, Florida. It was an enticing question that combined Cold War intrigue and Swinging Sixties sensibilities—both of which were an irresistible challenge for History Detective Gwen Wright.

The mystery actually begins on October 4, 1957, with the mention of a single

Leisurama designer Andrew Geller and his grandson, Jake Gorst.

word: Sputnik. On that day, the Soviet Union reached new heights in the space race by launching the world's first artificial satellite from their Cosmodrome in Kazakhstan. Despite the fact that Sputnik was just over 180 pounds and was only slightly larger than the size of a basketball, it continued a wildly contested space race between the Soviets and the United States that stirred up a hornet's nest of political, scientific, and technological debate and discovery.

Vice President Richard Nixon showing off a Leisurama kitchen to Premier Nikita Khrushchev in Moscow in 1959.

Two years later, on July 24, 1959, Khrushchev and Nixon met in Moscow to attend the U.S. Trade and Cultural Fair in Sokolniki Park. What ensued was a dispute of epic proportions, as Nixon gave Khrushchev a tour of a typical American exhibit home, complete with color television and an all-electric kitchen designed especially for the modern housewife. Never had a home design been elevated to become a political, cultural, and ideological talking point between two of the world's most powerful leaders. Nixon's feeble attempts at pointing out the superiority of capitalist kitchen appliances were constantly countered by Khrushchev's insistence that the Russian people already had all of those things—and more. Who knew that the Cold War could so easily splatter onto America's shiny new Formica counters? The true winners of the debate were General Electric, housing developer Herbert Sadkin, and Leisurama designer Andrew Geller, whose visionary ideas captured the world's attention and took the model American home to new heights.

THE MYSTERIOUS AFFAIR AT LAUDERHILL

The 1960s marked a decade when the American housewife was coming into her own. Fueled by a carryover of the Donna Reed mentality of the 1950s, architectural innovators of the 1960s were undoubtedly motivated to market home efficiency and kitchen design. Andrew Geller's Leisurama

An advertisement for Leisurama homes sold by Macy's.

design was an example of suburban living, with its gal-friendly all-electric kitchen, Formica countertops, and ample closet space throughout the house, as well as the mandatory carport for the head of the household. The truly remarkable twist was that these homes were marketed as vacation homes or "second" family homes, *and* they were available from Macy's department store.

Amazing as it sounds, the Leisurama came completely furnished with appliances and every single item a modern 1960s home required, right down to the china, kitchen utensils, and toothbrushes. It's said that over 250 of these homes were built in Montauk, New York, around 1964, and a similar number in Lauderhill, Florida. But could any of those in Florida still be identified?

Upon her arrival in Florida, Gwen began researching newspaper articles in the hope of finding something about the history of 1960s home building in the area. What she found was a small map in an article about Herbert Sadkin, the developer of the Moscow exhibit. The article stated that Sadkin was building a $60 million project in Broward County in what would come to be known as Lauderhill. Further proof came in the form of an advertisement, which spectacularly touted the Leisurama home as "The greatest advance in housing since the invention of bricks." Finding a Leisurama home in Lauderhill, however, proved to be an exhausting task for Gwen, who scoured neighborhoods with colleagues hoping to catch a glimpse of the tell-tale pitched roof, ribbon windows, and carport integral to the Geller design.

The search proved fruitless, but after a meeting with Sadkin's son Marty, Gwen finally found the answer to her groovy 1960s mystery. With over

20,000 homes in Lauderhill, it may have seemed an impossible task to find even one Leisurama home. But find it Gwen did. As luck would have it, a real estate investor named Chester Gould had recently purchased an unusual home near the Sadkin Community Center and invited Gwen in for a tour.

What she initially saw was a home with ample closet space and cathedral ceilings, but it was the kitchen that ultimately told the tale—it was virtually identical to the Leisurama kitchen at the Moscow exhibition, right down to the cabinets and the Formica counters. Both Andrew Geller and his grandson were thrilled by the discovery, which afforded the octogenarian designer a brief glimpse into his youth and the remembrance of a home whose design and functionality had withstood the test of time and a long-ago debate between a capitalist and a communist.

Top, a rendering of a Leisurama home. Above, a Leisurama in Lauderhill, Florida.

Bottoms Up!

It may take some doing, but more often than not, old houses give up a few of their historical secrets. In Washington, Pennsylvania, Gwen met a woman named Allene Steinberg, who presented her with a curious bottle that her father found in the crawl space underneath their family cabin. He alleged that the bottle was part of the infamous 1794 Whiskey Rebellion. His wife, however, felt certain that it simply belonged to a poor old fellow hiding his indiscretions from his wife.

On the bottle were thirteen stars, a pair of clasped hands, a cannon, the word "Union," and "F.A. & Co." So which of Steinberg's parents had it right? It turns out neither of them won their bet. The bottle was made by Pittsburgh glassmaker Fahnestock, Albree & Company as a personal whiskey flask during the Civil War era.

The Curious Concrete Creation

In the early 1900s, it likely would never have occurred to anyone that they could reside in a house made entirely of concrete, but it did indeed happen. If you had to hazard a guess as to the concept's inventor, would you say that someone was Thomas Alva Edison? If you did, you'd be correct. Affectionately dubbed the "Wizard of Menlo Park," Edison produced a stellar list of scientific and technological advancements, including the phonograph, the electric lightbulb, the electric generator, loud-speaking telephones and transmitters, stock tickers, automatic telegraphy, and motion picture technology—an astonishing repertoire of inventions amid over a thousand patents (see chapter 15). Without a doubt, Edison is one of the most ingenious and prolific inventors in history. But did his ingenuity spread as far as constructing an all-concrete home?

That was the question Gwen Wright had to answer when she visited Antonio Cardozo at his home in Union, New Jersey, where his house and nine neighboring houses were rumored to have been built by Edison. After examining the Cardozos' basement and the neighboring home exteriors, it appeared to Gwen that all were virtually identical, constructed of concrete with a cubic shape, plain window frames, and little ornamentation. She surmised that the homes were built in the early twentieth century, a time when simplicity was appreciated and many dwellings were being mass produced. But would Edison have developed a home made of material that was so solid that it would have inherent logistical problems, such as accessing water pipes and electrical wiring for repair or upgrades?

Thomas Edison with the model for his perfect suburban home.

MINE YOUR OWN BUSINESS

Gwen began her search at the local library in Union, where she learned that in 1906, Edison had announced his plans to mass-produce low-cost worker housing. At that point, he declared that his "cement house" would be his greatest invention. Gwen then met with Dr. Raymond Frey, a New Jersey historian and an expert on inventors. Their meeting at a local mine shed a different light on Edison's master plan.

As it turned out, some years earlier, Edison had purchased an iron mine in the area—3,000 acres in total—and built an entire factory town for his 400 workers. But despite the fact that he invented new milling and crushing technology, he soon went bankrupt when the price of iron dropped, which resulted in his losing $3 million. But did that dissuade the savvy entrepreneur? Nope. He realized that the same techniques he'd invented for his iron mine could be used to crush limestone and make cement for concrete. As a result, he purchased a limestone quarry and began experimentation that eventually enabled him to make huge molds into which he would pour vast amounts of his own concrete. After it dried, he'd remove the mold and—*voilà*—he'd have a concrete house.

Antonio Cardozo in front of his curious concrete home in Union, New Jersey.

A particularly helpful resource when researching any historical subject is correspondence and personal records. In Edison's case, Rutgers University is currently at work cataloging the inventor's personal and professional records as part of their Edison Papers Project. Here, Gwen found numerous papers and queries from individuals who were interested in Edison's concrete work— including Franz Ferdinand, the Archduke of Austria and Hungary, whose infamous assassination on June 28, 1914, by a young Bosnian member of the Black Hand was said to have triggered the start of World War I. It appears that instead of producing his own concrete creations, Edison was banking on other interested individuals or companies to make use of his patents.

One of Edison's letters in particular proved highly significant to Gwen's investigation. Written in 1917, it was from watchmaker Charles Ingersoll, who made his fortune manufacturing

DID YOU know

Thomas Edison's concrete endeavor was not without serious flaws. At the end of the day, his concrete homes cost three times more than estimated, and his other cement-driven inventions—which included concrete furniture such as beds, phonograph consoles, and pianos—became a public gigglefest. Edison may have been a genius, but he was also stubborn, determined to find some way to make money off his mistakes. Unfortunately, not everyone was hip to the idea of plunking down on a concrete couch at the end of a hard day.

inexpensive brass "one dollar" watches, of which he sold a cool seventy-five million. Ingersoll asked Edison to inspect a concrete home he was pouring.

With a solution to her mystery in hand, Gwen was able to return to the home of Antonio Cardozo and his family and reveal her findings. The unusual abode was built in 1917 by Charles Ingersoll, whose well-intentioned goal was to construct affordable worker housing out of concrete. Instead of using the cumbersome cast-iron molds that Edison used, Ingersoll ingeniously used wooden forms produced from his own lumber planing mill. His method proved successful and enabled him to build close to a hundred concrete homes, but with likely very little profit. The homes built in Union, New Jersey, including the Cardozos', were the first concrete creations that Ingersoll built, and although the homes weren't built by Edison himself, they are still considered to be Edison homes. The icing on the cake? The Cardozos live on Ingersoll Terrace.

The Pavilion Palace

The quiet town of Gilroy, California, is a rural area known primarily for the crazy concoctions it features at its annual garlic festival. Located approximately eighty miles south of San Francisco, Gilroy is the last place you'd expect to find a masterpiece of Japanese architecture, but it does indeed exist—a traditional Japanese-style house that's unlike any of the local home designs. So how in the world did it get there?

The allure of the mystery drew Gwen Wright to visit the home belonging to Lawson and Mineko Sakai, a home that has been in Mineko's family, the Hirasakis, since 1941. The difference between the Sakais' home and that

Lawson and Mineko Sakai in front of their Gilroy, California, home in 2003.

of other traditional and modernized Japanese dwellings is that it has an air of sophistication and perfection that one typically finds in a museum. The home is enchanting, which becomes understandable when it's revealed that the central room was a big hit in the 1939 San Francisco World's Fair. It had been part of the Japanese Pavilion, the most expensive and, to many visitors, the most beautiful building ever seen at a world's fair. Mineko's father, Kiyoshi "Jimmy" Hirasaki, actually purchased the materials when the fair was being dismantled, and transported them to Gilroy.

In October of 1941, after nine months of construction and just two months shy of the bombing of Pearl Harbor, the home was finished, and while the sheer size of the project is impressive, it was the timing of the construction and the fair itself that became an intriguing mystery. With the Japanese walking a razor's edge of prewar hostility, why would they go to so much trouble to showcase their peaceful culture at the World's Fair?

FAIR PLAY

Long before folks were glued to the television watching *Gunsmoke* reruns, they were flocking to World's Fairs, where grand exhibitions and inventions showcased technological and futuristic wonders while at the same time introducing all types of international cultures. During her investigation, Gwen learned that the theme of the 1939 fair was "Pageant of the Pacific," a celebration of all of the countries whose shores rimmed the Pacific Ocean.

The Japanese Pavilion was one of the largest installations, its gorgeous rooms, gardens, and recreation of the Kyoto bridge delighting thousands of visitors. Somewhat optimistically, it was hoped that the fair would promote peaceful trade among the Pacific nations. The reality, however, couldn't have been further from that hope.

In 1931, Japan invaded Manchuria and created the puppet state of Manchukuo. Five years later, Japan signed an anti-Soviet pact called the Anti-Comintern Pact with Germany. By 1937, Japan invaded China and infamously captured

Worldly Goods

One of the easiest and least expensive collecting hobbies to pursue involves the memorabilia of World's Fairs or Expositions. World expositions are ranked close to the Olympic Games in terms of national exposure and cultural exchange, and have a profound economic impact on host cities worldwide. Thousands upon thousands of souvenir items are generated by participating nations at world expositions, ranging from silver spoon sets and glassware to banners, clocks, medallions, and pins.

The 1962 World's Fair in Seattle produced a plethora of collectibles that can be picked up at Internet auctions for little more than they cost over forty years ago. The most collectible American fair memorabilia is from events held in Chicago and New York in the early 1900s. Even those high-profile affairs spawned mementos that can be obtained for the cost of what you'd currently spend for a night out at the movies.

The "silk room," which was part of Japan's cultural display at the San Francisco World's Fair.

Nanking, a raid that resulted in over 350,000 Chinese deaths and the rape of over 100,000 women. That year also witnessed the Panay Incident, when the Japanese sank a U.S. ship sailing in Chinese waters, resulting in three American deaths. The true irony of the 1939 fair and the Japanese illusion of international amicability was that during that same year in Harbin, China, the Japanese created a research laboratory called Unit 731, which was geared toward biological warfare. On whom were they testing biological weapons? War prisoners—ten thousand of whom perished.

Given the political climate of the late 1930s, it seems obvious that Japan's glorious Pavilion was more than a bit of propaganda, a fact confirmed by one of Gwen's colleagues in Japan, who searched declassified government documents. Anti-Japanese sentiment in the United States was growing stronger at the time as Americans learned of the Asian atrocities, but by brilliantly showcasing their harmonious Zen-like culture, the Japanese hoped to rehabilitate their sagging public reputation. Gwen's San Francisco visit with historian Ken Brown at Golden Gate Park's Japanese Tea Garden further validated that assumption. According to Brown, the huge Japanese Pavilion at the Fair reflected a Buddhist-style, semi-samurai castle, showcasing a number of small rooms. The "silk room," a tranquil and very feminine room, highlighted the Japanese silk industry. Pictures of that room closely matched the Sakais' Gilroy living room.

time
TEASER

Lentil beans are a common household edible. What is a *lintel* in housing terms?

Answer: A decorative horizontal support over windows or doors.

BITTERSWEET HEROES

With the United States' declaration of war against Japan in 1941 came the unfortunate imprisonment of over 120,000 individuals in internment camps. These camps exemplify some of the darkest days of twentieth-century

DIY DETECTIVE

One of the great services of modern-home ownership comes from the tenacity of folks who purchase, renovate, and restore historic homes. As a result of their hard labor, many structures that could have been lost forever have been brought back to their former glory. Organizations like the National Trust for Historic Preservation, the National Historic Preservation Program, and hundreds of national and community groups have helped raise awareness of the importance of retaining America's architectural history.

Even more exciting for those individuals and families who take on a restoration project are the amazing time capsules of history they uncover when renovating their homes. For example, a Civil War cannonball was found buried in the cellar of a 1918 North Carolina plantation house, and in a South Carolina home, Civil War Union uniform buttons were discovered in the attic crawl space.

Bottles, wooden artifacts, letters, newspapers, clothing, artwork—all of these wonderful items give a voice to the families who once roamed the halls and staircases of their homes, and they give us a sense of what it was like to live in times of simplicity, turmoil, and the awakening of a nation whose past and present aren't always clear.

Getting your rookie badge as a history detective can start right inside your front door. What do you know about your own home? Do you know who built it, why it was built, or who lived there before you? To learn more about your humble abode, your first step should be to create a research plan. Your county recorder's office will have a record of every transaction that involved your property, and you can search through them to make a list of each owner and the purchase date. Records of deeds also include plat maps that show your property in relation to every other piece of property in the area.

Another good source of information is your local building permit department, which collects records of construction that will usually tell you the builder's name and even the original cost of construction. Also, talk to your neighbors and learn about the area's history. You may find that many of your neighbors have old photographs of the neighborhood with interesting stories that go along with them.

In addition, local historical societies are a valuable source for old photos and information about an area, as are *city directories*, which contain an alphabetical list of residents, often noting occupations and addresses. Your local library can put you on the right track for these directories, in which you can find out more information about the people who lived in your home in the past. For more details, visit *History Detectives* at www.pbs.org.

Lawson and Mineko Sakai's living room, which was originally part of the Japanese Pavilion at the 1939 World's Fair.

American history, a time when both Japanese immigrants and Japanese American citizens were deprived of their property and their liberty and herded into isolated camps (see chapter 12). For the Hirasakis and Lawson Sakai, there was no escaping the ordeal. Mineko's father, Jimmy Hirasaki, was shipped to a camp in Bismarck, North Dakota, while Mineko's mother and her eight children fled to Colorado, leaving their newly built home to an unknown fate. In 1943, after initially being rejected by the U.S. military, Lawson volunteered for service and eventually became a sergeant in the all–Japanese American 442nd regiment, the most decorated combat unit in the war.

By 1945, Jimmy Hirasaki was allowed to return to his home, which miraculously had been left undisturbed. Whether by fate or perhaps because of the spiritual peace the house evokes, it stands as a symbol of a nation whose tumultuous military aggression is in stark contrast to the harmonious nature of its ancient culture. As a final gesture, Gwen showed the Sakais a catalog of the Japanese Pavilion and the silk room, which became their family home for over six decades.

The *History Detectives* episode featuring the Sakais' beautiful home was shown in 2003 during the first season. During the writing of this book, we learned that sadly, in February of 2007, an electrical fire broke out in the middle of the night and totally destroyed the Sakais' beloved home. Both Mineko and Lawson Sakai fortunately escaped the flames unharmed, and for that we're very grateful. With the telling of their tale, we pay tribute to the Sakais, the Hirasakis, and their entire family, for the courage they faced in adversity and to all the memories they collected in their cherished abode.

CHAPTER SIX

American Icons

E ach generation, era, and civilization has its own revered icons, whether that icon is a Christian crucifix, an Egyptian obelisk, a legendary novel, a declaration of independence, or an extraordinary individual, and each can exude a certain power, be it spiritual, psychological, political, or historically significant. The History Detectives have encountered many such icons that on the surface appear to have absolutely no commonality, but whose subtle underlying effects indicate they are indeed linked.

War correspondent Ernie Pyle spoke for the common soldier, the common man, who when thrust into adversity overcame seemingly insurmountable pain, suffering, and odds in pursuit of liberty and survival. Equally profound in his writings was Mark Twain, whose outspoken and sardonic wit embodied social and political commentary. And then there's Superman, the ultimate defender of all humankind, a legend who keeps the spirit of true heroism alive to the present day. What do these paragons of power have in common? Each of them, in his own way, spoke out against evil empires and forces while at the same time encouraging and showcasing the best part of the human psyche, and each of them posed significant challenges for our stalwart History Detectives.

Voices of War

It's often said that war is hell. For those embroiled in war, from foot soldiers to sailors to pilots and every individual involved in their support, war is a grim and brutal experience. It's no secret that since the beginning of time wars have been, at best, sketchily reported primarily due to governmental restrictions handed down to media outlets limiting—or worse yet, dictating—what was allowed to be written or photographed about the true atrocities that were occurring. Journalists who choose to serve during times of conflict are heroes themselves, so-called war correspondents who risk life and limb to tell their stories in the sincere hope that readers and viewers the world over can make sense of an act that is inherently nonsensical.

Legendary war correspondent and anchorman Walter Cronkite, whose opinions on the Vietnam war played a part in swaying public sentiment.

War correspondents today are no less ambitious in their reporting than their historic counterparts, although they greatly benefit from modern conveniences such as satellite communications, body armor, computer systems, e-mail, and the Internet. Their job may appear glamorous to some, but *embedded journalism*, meaning the work of reporters who are attached and traveling with specific military units, comes with great risk.

This fact is all too often confirmed when war correspondents come to harm, as was the case with ABC anchorman Bob Woodruff, who on January 29, 2006, suffered traumatic brain injury while on assignment in Taji, Iraq, when a roadside bomb struck the Iraqi army transport vehicle he and his crew were traveling in. Even more heartwrenching is the loss of thirty-nine-year-old NBC journalist and co-anchor David Bloom, who was already a seasoned war correspondent when the strain of war took its toll. While embedded with the 3rd Infantry Division in Iraq on April 6, 2003, Bloom died from a pulmonary embolism.

Over the decades, many male and female war correspondents have literally brought our attention to the front lines. Irishman William Howard Russell, one of the first war correspondents, detailed the 1853 to 1856 Crimean War for the *Times* of London. In the late 1800s, a little-known British war correspondent named Winston Churchill provided frontline coverage for several London newspapers. Also working at that time was

Stephen Crane, author of *The Red Badge of Courage*. Gloria Emerson, a reporter for the *New York Times*, made her opinions clear about the Vietnam War. So did career war reporter and New Zealander Peter Arnett, who worked for both National Geographic and CNN, and won the 1966 International Reporting Pulitzer Prize for his Vietnam coverage. Arnett spent thirteen long years in Vietnam, from 1962 to 1975, and came to prominence again during the Iraqi Gulf War and at the end of 2002 during the American invasion of Afghanistan.

The late 1980s marked the arrival of renowned multiple Peabody Award winner Christiane Amanpour, who to this day remains one of the most successful and recognized international correspondents. All of these gutsy individuals left their mark on war reporting as a result of their actions and reactions, but there's one embedded journalist who towers above the rest, a man who won not only the respect of the world, but the hearts and utmost admiration and respect of every American soldier. That journalist was Ernie Pyle.

The Message in the Masterpiece

Owning any significant piece of history is a thrill, but owning an object you think might have been used by a legend is truly an honor. Eric Warlick of Portland, Oregon, called upon History Detective Wes Cowan to investigate an old Corona 3 typewriter he was told once belonged to Ernie Pyle. When meeting with Warlick, Wes was told a remarkable story about how Warlick's grandfather allegedly won the Corona in a poker game sometime during the 1950s or 1960s.

The fellow card player he procured it from was a man named George Pratt, who was said to have been part of the unit Pyle was traveling with during his tour in the Pacific during

A Corona typewriter allegedly used by renowned World War II correspondent Ernie Pyle.

Ernie Pyle hard at
work in the field.

the Second World War. More than anything, Warlick wanted to find out if the Corona did indeed belong to the legendary writer, and despite the daunting difficulty of the task, Wes was ready to find an answer to Warlick's mystery. To begin his quest, he set off to learn more about Pyle and the typewriter.

Ernest Taylor Pyle was born on August 3, 1900, to a farming family in Dana, Indiana. After serving as a reservist in the navy for the last few months of World War I, Pyle did a turn as a local reporter before relocating to Washington, D.C., distinguishing himself as the United States' first aviation columnist. In 1927, after several years of cross-country driving and on-the-road reporting, Pyle and his wife, Jerry, settled in Albuquerque, New Mexico. He became a war correspondent just after the United States entered World War II in 1941.

What makes Pyle's writings resonate is that he had the talent and intelligence to tell his tales from the common soldier's point of view, refusing to focus on upper echelon mucky-mucks or military strategy. He was also immune from the modern restrictions of traveling with certain units, instead moving freely wherever destiny led him. Being embedded with the foot soldiers was Pyle's forte, and he remained with his beloved troops for an astonishing three years, during which he no doubt used plenty of typewriters. The first question for Wes was, how old is Warlick's Corona 3, and did Ernie Pyle even use that particular brand?

Upon further inspection, Wes found a pair of patent dates on the typewriter—1904 and 1910—which meant that the Corona had to date after 1910. The fact that the machine was so old, however, immediately set off a red flag. By the time World War II was in full swing, the Corona was already over thirty

time
TEASER

What winner of both the Nobel Prize for Literature and the Pulitzer Prize for fiction was also a World War II war correspondent?

Answer: John Steinbeck, who reported for the *New York Herald Tribune*.

Ernie Pyle doing what he did best—communicating with the common soldier.

years old. Why would Pyle use such an antiquated piece of equipment? To learn more, Wes took the Corona to the Ace Typewriter & Equipment Company in Portland to meet with Matt and Dennis Mc-Cormack. Examining the typewriter's inner mechanisms, they were able to find a serial number and match it to a typewriter reference book that indicated that while that particular style of Corona was produced from 1912 to 1940, Warlick's was made between 1915 and 1916.

Wes then showed the McCormacks several pictures of Pyle with a typewriter, all of which turned out to be Underwood or Remington models. Without concrete identification, Wes needed to match the Corona's typeface with known pages Ernie Pyle had typed, so he had Matt repair the Corona to good working order. But later, while Wes was doing online research for Pyle's correspondence, the investigation took an unexpected twist when he learned that the Albuquerque Museum of

Art and History has in their collection a Corona 3 that was reputed to have belonged to Ernie Pyle.

At the Albuquerque Museum, Wes met with curator Deb Slaney, who showed him the Corona 3 in their collection of Ernie Pyle memorabilia. At first sight, their typewriter looked very much like Eric Warlick's, but with several noticeable differences. The museum's Corona was made in 1921, and the typewriter's case has "E. Pyle" written on it. The age of their Corona helped support the supposition that Pyle had no problem using older typewriters. Slaney also shared with Wes how the museum came to inherit the Corona. Army Sergeant Don Bell told the story of the time he and Pyle spent together in a foxhole just outside Saint-Lô, France, in the

The Nimble Newsmaker

Embedded journalism isn't just a man's game. Legendary maverick Martha Gellhorn was one of the first and most prolific female war correspondents, and during her sixty-year career she covered just about every major world conflict, beginning in 1936 with the Spanish civil war. In 1939, she covered Russia's war against Finland, known as the Winter War.

As a frontline journalist during World War II, Gellhorn reported the liberation of Dachau concentration camp and the D-Day invasion, for which she allegedly had no press credentials and pretended to be a stretcher bearer to get close to the action. She then covered Vietnam for *Atlantic Monthly* and continued with the Nicaraguan Contra war and the Middle East's Six-Day War in 1967, and amazingly even reported on America's invasion of Panama in 1989. Gellhorn, who was novelist and former war correspondent Ernest Hemingway's third wife, was eighty-one at the time. By the time the Bosnian war raged during the 1990s, the stalwart journalist finally gave up the fight, famously saying that for covering a war, "You need to be nimble." In 1998, she chose the same fate as Hemingway, committing suicide after an extended battle with cancer.

Legendary war correspondent Martha Gellhorn circa 1937 in Madrid covering a story.

summer of 1944. According to Bell, their hideout was bombarded by German artillery and caved in, burying the typewriter as both men scurried to safety. Later, when Bell inquired about the type-writer, Pyle told him that if he could actually find it he could keep it. As the story goes, Bell returned to the foxhole days later and found the machine, which he donated to the museum in 1990.

ERNIE PYLE'S WAR

Throughout his career as an embedded journalist, Ernie Pyle, just like the troops he was chronicling, was in constant danger. He'd been to North Africa, Italy, and France writing about ordinary GIs, their lives, and in too many instances, their deaths, but still he persevered. On May 2, 1943, he wrote a column titled "The God-Damned Infantry," which epitomized his devotion to the troops: "I love the infantry because they are the underdogs," he wrote. "They are the mud-rain-frost-and-wind boys. They have no comforts, and they even learn to live without the necessities. And in the end they are the guys that wars can't be won without."

Braving Japanese sniper fire, U.S. Marine Lt. Colonel R. P. Ross places an American flag during the Battle of Okinawa.

Pyle's columns appeared in hundreds of newspapers almost daily, with many people referring to the war simply as "Ernie Pyle's War."

In April of 1944, Pyle was awarded the Pulitzer Prize, but shortly after D-Day, June 6 of that year, the cumulative effects of combat bore heav-ily on him; too many men had lost their lives in battle and the psychological toll on Pyle was enormous. In his final column from Europe he wrote: "By the time you read this, the old man will be on his way back to America. After that will come a long, long rest. And after the rest, well, you can never tell. I do hate to leave right now, but I've given out. I've been immersed in it too long. My spirit is wobbly and my mind is confused. The hurt has finally become too great." And so Pyle left Europe after the liberation of Paris to return to Albuquerque, an action that he once likened to his wife as desertion. But fate was a cruel mistress to the weary writer, and it wasn't long before Pyle was back in the trenches. In 1945, he shipped out to the Pacific to document the inva-sion of Okinawa, the largest amphibious operation of the war.

Legendary Icons

Famous figures of every ilk leave a trail of iconic artifacts that in some way represents who they were and what they accomplished, and there are always those who gladly pay startlingly high prices to own a small piece of legendary history. Eric Clapton has played hundreds of guitars during his career, many of which were sold at auction in 1999 to fund his drug rehabilitation facility, the Crossroads Centre on Antigua. A 1956 Fender guitar he played during the 1970s sold for a jaw-dropping $450,000, with another ninety-nine instruments selling for a total of nearly $4 million. In 2004, Clapton's "Blackie," a Fender Stratocaster guitar, brought $959,500 at a Christie's auction.

In a 1999 sale, a baby grand piano owned by Marilyn Monroe was purchased for $662,000, while the dress she wore when she sang "Happy Birthday, Mr. President" to John F. Kennedy realized a record-breaking $1,267,500. Slightly less breathtaking, the dress Dustin Hoffman wore in the 1982 film *Tootsie* sold in 2006 for a relative steal: $25,200. In 2003, a Harley Davidson Fatboy motorcycle once owned by Cher went for $24,500, practically the retail price for an uncelebrated Harley. And for those who were looking for a real bargain in 2006, a set of drumsticks used by Led Zeppelin drummer John Bonham went for the bargain-basement price of $1,200.

THANKS, PAL

After leaving the museum in New Mexico, Wes traveled to the Lilly Library at Indiana University in Bloomington to research the Ernie Pyle Archives and meet with Pyle expert Professor Owen Johnson, who provided copies of documents Pyle typed while in the Pacific. Johnson also shared with Wes an original letter Pyle wrote to his wife. Perhaps in a portent of things to come, Pyle expressed his relief about completing the most recent invasion, stating: "For as you know, I had dreaded this one terribly. Now it is behind me and I will never make another landing. So I can't help but feel good about that." Wes submitted his copies to forensic examiner Jacqueline Joseph, who explained that typewriter keys often leave distinct, telltale marks on the documents they produce. When Joseph checked the authenticated Pyle documents against samples Wes typed on Eric Warlick's Corona, they were entirely different.

With all other avenues exhausted, the final step for Wes was to confirm if George Pratt—the man who allegedly lost the Corona in the poker game—even existed. A check of military records showed that Pratt did serve in the military and fought in the Pacific. Was it possible that he actually knew Ernie Pyle?

Already drained from his extended tour in Europe, Pyle was in no shape for a repeat performance, but he wasn't about to disappoint the troops or his avid readers. He'd managed to survive the initial landings in Okinawa, but a few days later his luck ran out. It was April 18, 1945, and Pyle decided to visit the small island of Ie Shima near Okinawa with Lieutenant Colonel Joseph Coolidge. Pyle, Coolidge, and several other soldiers were driving along in a jeep when they suddenly came under attack by Japanese machine-gun fire. The men quickly dove into a ditch, where shortly thereafter, Pyle went down, a single shot piercing his temple. In an instant he was gone.

When doing research into Ernie Pyle's final days, Wes uncovered information that at long last solved the mystery of Eric War-lick's curious Corona typewriter. When meeting with Warlick, Wes relayed that it was highly likely Pyle used multiple typewriters during his wartime endeavors, including Corona models, and that clearly Pyle was partial to vintage machines. He also told Warlick about his conversation with Owen Johnson, who men-tioned that Pyle was covering the Army's 77th Infantry—the same division that George Pratt was serving under. He even showed Warlick a photo taken of them in their jeep. But it didn't end there. What Wes revealed next was truly astonishing.

As Pyle and the other men hopped into the ditch that fateful day, Pyle was dodging sniper fire with a man named George Pratt. It was, in fact, Pratt who watched as Pyle and Coolidge raised their heads from the ditch to assess their precarious situation. Pyle then turned to Pratt and asked him if he was all right, and it was at that very second that the sniper fired. Though it couldn't be confirmed through forensic analysis that the Corona matched Pyle's document samples, the fact that Pratt was with Pyle when he was killed reinforces that Pratt could have come to own what may have been the last typewriter Pyle ever used.

Profound and humble, Ernie Pyle was a legend for all the right reasons, and the world loved him for it. In what could well have been his own epitaph, Pyle once wrote: "I guess it doesn't make any difference once a man has gone. Medals and speeches and victories are nothing to them anymore. They died and others lived and nobody knows why it is so. There's nothing we can do for the ones beneath the wooden crosses, except perhaps to pause and murmur, 'Thanks, pal.'"

Every soldier, from GI to general, was devastated by the loss of forty-five-year-old Ernie Pyle, whom they'd considered one of their own. A sign was placed at the ditch where he was killed, in honor of his service and the indisputable respect and admiration he showed to every soldier he ever met.

The Tip in the Timepiece

There's no denying that Samuel Langhorne Clemens, otherwise known as Mark Twain, is one of the most famous American writers to ever grace paper with a pen. His nineteenth-century works, including *Huckleberry Finn*, *The Prince and the Pauper*, *The Celebrated Jumping Frog of Calaveras County*, *Tom Sawyer*, and *A Connecticut Yankee in King Arthur's Court*, are considered classics, with their youthful exuberance and uniquely American viewpoints of the rags-to-riches myth. Perhaps the only thing rivaling the stature of his literature is Twain himself, his sardonic wit, political satire, and real-life adventures as a vagabond, prospector, Mississippi riverboat pilot, and reluctant elitist elevating him to larger-than-life status.

To own any part of Mark Twain's existence is a tantalizing dream, one that Oregonian Jack Mills hoped would prove true. To solve his timeless mystery, Mills enlisted the help of History Detective Wes Cowan, who upon meeting Mills was shown a beautiful pocket watch allegedly owned by none other than Mark Twain. According to family legend, the watch was given by Twain to Captain John Commingers Ainsworth, one of the founding fathers of Portland, Oregon, and great-grandfather to Jack Mills. Ainsworth was a transportation magnate of the late 1800s, having formed his Oregon Steam Navigation company in 1860 and later other institutions such as the Cascades Railroad Company. He also had business dealings that extended into Washington and California.

Captain John Commingers Ainsworth, one of the founding fathers of Portland, Oregon.

With that in mind, Wes couldn't help but wonder how Ainsworth and Twain may have come into contact, but as it turned out, Ainsworth once worked as a Mississippi steamboat captain, as did Twain. What Jack Mills wanted to know was if the watch could be authenticated to the early nineteenth century, if it was even possible that Twain could have given it to Ainsworth, and if so, where they met.

Before he could immerse himself in the backgrounds of Twain and Ainsworth, Wes needed to ascertain that the watch was from the correct time period. He traveled to San Francisco to meet with watch historian and appraiser Don Levison, who immediately noted the markings of the British "W. W. & Co." on the watch case. When he opened the dust cover, he found a serial number and the name of the watchmaker, Joseph Johnson. Checked against a

time
TEASER During Mark Twain's lifetime, what was his most popular book?

Answer: *The Innocents Abroad*.

reference text, Levison determined that John-son produced watches in Liverpool, Eng-land, between 1814 and 1851. Further database research showed that the watch was likely made between 1833 and 1835. Given that Twain was born in 1835, it was safe to assume he certainly hadn't purchased it new, although that didn't mean he couldn't have owned it.

As the mystery deepened, Wes delved into the backgrounds of both Twain and Ainsworth hoping to find common ground. In a delightful turn, he con-sulted Twain expert and renowned imperson-ator McAvoy Layne, who related that in 1857 Twain began an apprenticeship on a Mississippi riverboat, eventually earning his pilot's license. In 1862, with the Civil War at full throttle, Twain—despite being a Southerner—decided to "secede from the secession" and head west to Nevada with his brother Orion to explore the riches of silver mining. Two years later, he went to San Francisco.

To establish what Ainsworth was doing during that time frame, Wes consulted Norma Paulus at the Oregon Historical Society, where the cap-tain's watch is currently on display. Originally from Ohio, Ainsworth was orphaned at thirteen and decided to make his fortune on the Mississippi, eventually purchasing and captaining his own steamboat. In 1849, he sold his business and, like Twain, headed west to San Francisco and then to the Comstock silver mines in Nevada's Virginia City. Eventually ending up in Portland, Ainsworth began operating a steamboat along the Columbia River, one of the most unforgiving waterways in the nation. Ainsworth, however, was one of the few pilots who could successfully ne-gotiate the river, even forgoing the traditional side-wheel steamboat and introducing the first stern-wheeled steamer to the area.

The watch allegedly given to Ainsworth by Mark Twain. Below, a close-up of the watch showing its maker, Joseph Johnson.

Legendary writer
Mark Twain.

An excerpt from
the 1865 diary of
Captain Ainsworth,
showing his associa-
tion with magnate
W. C. Ralston.

In addition to his steamship and railroad operations, Ainsworth eventually added real estate, banking, and mining operations to his enterprises. When asked about a possible connection between Ainsworth and Twain, Paulus mentioned that the two men had mutual friends in San Francisco who were involved in the mining business. Could it be that the transportation magnate and the up-and-coming writer met somewhere in the Bay Area?

Determined to find an answer to his timepiece riddle, Wes hunkered down at the University of Oregon's Knight Library to find out more about Captain Ainsworth. The library boasts a collection of the captain's materials, including thirty-two volumes and over two dozen boxes full of information and personal correspondence. In reading Ainsworth's 1860s letters, Wes found correspondence from banker and financier William C. Ralston, who arrived in San Francisco around 1849 and eventually came to be recognized as "the man who built San Francisco." Ainsworth's 1865 diary mentions spending a month in San Francisco, in particular noting several times when he dined with the Ralstons and even stayed at their renowned estate in Belmont, just south of the city. So a connection was made between Ainsworth and Ralston, who underwrote at least one of the captain's Oregon business deals. But where did Mark Twain fit in?

To further establish a link between Twain and Ainsworth, Wes paid a visit to the Bancroft Library at the University of California, Berkeley, where general editor Robert Hirst showed him a letter Twain wrote to a friend in which he stated: "Do not let Ralston have the pamphlet unless he allows you to add it to the book." The letter suggested that at the very least Twain had a familiarity with Ralston. Wes also found a biography about Ralston that discussed his abilities as a host, saying that he "entertained everyone from a young, comparatively unknown lecturer named Mark Twain to the visiting Chinese embassy at Belmont." Given that Ralston regularly held literary salons at his estate, it was possible that Ainsworth and Twain had indeed met in Belmont.

Yet another possible connection is the Comstock Lode. After the gold rush of the 1850s, thousands of adventurers headed west to the silver mines of Nevada, which ultimately gave up over $300 million in ore. One of those hopeful individuals was Captain Ainsworth. Twain also went to Comstock in 1862, serving as a reporter for the *Territorial Enterprise* in Virginia City. And in a final ironic twist, the Union Mill and Mining Company acquired most of the Comstock Lode in June of 1867. Who was one of the owners of the Union Mill? None other than William Ralston. Twain once said: "As news, this is a little old, but better late than never." For Ainsworth's great-grandson Jack Mills, the fact that Twain could have given his great-grandfather a beautiful pocket watch was all the news he needed.

Inside the opulent estate of W. C. Ralston, a possible meeting place for Captain Ainsworth and Mark Twain.

The Man of Steel Mystery

Over the centuries there have always been mythic individuals whose legendary strength, power, and versatile skills brought them to iconic stardom. Thor, Hercules, Atlas, Zeus, Sampson, John Henry, and even the Incredible Hulk are rock stars of superhuman strength, tenacity, and vigilance. Of that elite group, however, there's one who flies circles around all others. He is, of course, known in this and other worlds as Superman. For over seven decades, the Man of Steel has been in the public eye, vanquishing abhorrent villains and malevolent nations through comic books, newspaper strips, radio shows, cartoons, toys, memorabilia, a television series, and a film franchise, becoming the premier superhero of the twentieth century.

One of the many battles Superman waged was a propaganda war against the Axis powers during World War II, and it was because of that fight that Diane VanSkiver Gagel contacted

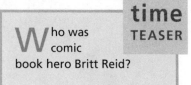

time TEASER

Who was comic book hero Britt Reid?

Answer: The Green Hornet.

Randall VanSkiver with his daughter, Diane.

The signed 1941 pencil sketch of the Man of Steel, acquired by Randall VanSkiver and investigated by *History Detectives*.

History Detectives. What VanSkiver Gagel found was a sketch belonging to her father, Randall VanSkiver, but it wasn't just any drawing. This one was signed to Randall from Superman creators Jerry Siegel and Joe Schuster and stored in an envelope marked: "Fort Dix, 1944." To get to the bottom of this super mystery, *History Detectives* summoned Wes Cowan, who went to Toledo, Ohio, to meet VanSkiver Gagel and examine the drawing, which she had found in her mother's attic rolled up in a tube. Sadly, Randall VanSkiver passed away in 1959, when Diane was a little girl. What she wanted to know was how her father came to meet Siegel and Schuster, and more importantly, could the drawing—a penciled profile of the Man of Steel—shed light on her father's military career?

Of the myriad superheroes the world has known, Superman is arguably the most popular, but his creation wasn't the result of an army of artists prodded on by rabid hordes of sales and marketing consultants. The Man of Steel was the brainchild of Cleveland, Ohio, high school buddies Jerry Siegel and Joel Schuster, who conceived the idea during the early 1930s.

Believe it or not, Superman began as an evil Nietzsche-based character, but when Hitler came to power the duo wisely swapped his alignment to portray good. With Siegel serving as writer and Schuster as illustrator, the two worked for several years to define their hero before coming up with their final character around 1934.

Four years later, in June 1938, Superman made his debut in the first edition of *Action Comics*. The public was fascinated by the larger-than-life action hero who

was shipped to Earth as a baby just as his home planet of Krypton exploded. When his craft landed in Smallville, Kansas, he was found and adopted by Jonathan and Martha Kent, who named him Clark. Of course the rest, as they say, is history. For decades, Superman and his alter ego worked tirelessly for the good of humanity, fighting foes like Lex Luthor and in later years even marrying vivacious reporter Lois Lane.

With Randall VanSkiver's drawing in hand, Wes flew to New York to visit comic illustrator Jerry Robinson, whose premier creation was one of Batman's most annoying foes—the Joker. Siegel and Schuster were among Robinson's close friends, and he was able to quickly identify VanSkiver's drawing as an original. For comparison, he showed Wes a drawing Schuster had done for him in the early 1940s. It was almost identical. To gain insight into Superman's inception, Robinson told Wes about a dream Siegel had one night in 1934. In it, he had a vision of a character who "was greater than Hercules and faster than a speeding bullet." Sound familiar?

From Robinson, Wes also learned about the birth of the comic book era, the so-called "Golden Age," which took place in the Big Apple during the Great Depression. Primarily a Jewish-dominated industry, comic books became hugely successful. One tip from Robinson that would prove particularly crucial to the investigation was the fact that many comic illustrators often made public appearances where they would pass out sketches to fans. This was substantiated by Comic Art Appraisal president Joseph Mannarino, who authenticated Schuster's drawing and Seigel's signature, but oddly enough, couldn't approve Schuster's signature. Compared against other signings, parts of his signature were atypical. The fact that VanSkiver's sketch appears to have been drawn in a hurry lent credence to his possibly having received it at an open event, but did that event take place at Fort Dix in 1944 as the envelope indicated, or was the investigation being impeded by kryptonite?

During World War II, the value of Superman's presence on the propaganda scene was immeasurable, a fact echoed by comic collector Ethan Roberts, who showed Wes examples of the Man of Steel fighting the Japanese and the Nazis.

time TEASER

Leonardo da Vinci's handwritten and sketched *Codex Leicester* is the world's most expensive notebook. Which wealthy businessman purchased it in 1994 for $30.8 million?

Answer: Bill Gates.

Jerry Robinson, renowned creator of one of Batman's archenemies, the Joker.

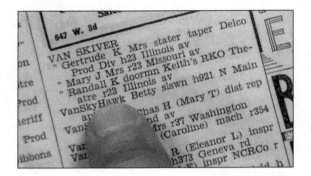

The 1942 *Dayton City Directory* showing Randall VanSkiver's employment.

Through comic books, Jewish illustrators were able to fight Nazi oppression in a very public way. American GIs loved comic books, especially one with a hero just like them (only with x-ray vision) who was helping them fight the good fight.

Superman as well as Batman and Robin were also used in the effort to sell war bonds with advertising slogans like: "Sink the Japanazis with bonds and stamps!" Roberts noted that both Siegel and Schuster attended bond drives and rallies, where they'd do signed sketches for fans. At that point, Wes had to consider that Randall VanSkiver may have met the two super men on a military base, so he ordered VanSkiver's service records. What Wes received would prove thrilling to Corporal VanSkiver's daughter—a 1944 picture of her father in Italy, and a memo noting his being awarded the good conduct medal. But there was nothing to indicate that VanSkiver, Siegel, and Schuster had ever crossed paths. Or was there?

Acting on a hunch, Wes did research closer to home. Randall VanSkiver enlisted in the army in 1943, but Wes needed to find out what VanSkiver was doing in Dayton, Ohio, *prior* to his enlistment. By checking the 1942 *Dayton City Directory*, Wes learned that VanSkiver worked at RKO Keith's Theater as a doorman. Theaters of the era were often used to sell war bonds, so this was a promising lead. Given that Siegel and Schuster were from Cleveland, Wes zeroed in on Cleveland newspapers, where he found the final clue to Diane VanSkiver Gagel's superhero mystery.

DID YOU know

In April of 2007, scientists at the British Natural History Museum and Canada's National Research Council identified a new mineral. What's so exciting about that, you ask? The discovery isn't a typical mineral; this one is a match for the unique chemical makeup of kryptonite—the singular substance that zaps the power out of Superman. In a bizarre twist, the "composition" of kryptonite was revealed in the 2006 film *Superman Returns*. In a case of fiction becoming reality, the powdery white non-radioactive substance was discovered by mineralogists and geologists working for the mining group Rio Tinto. The official name of the superhero-thwarting mineral is *Jadarite*, named after the Jadar Basin in Serbia, where it was found.

DIY DETECTIVE

When it comes to misplaced, lost, and tossed-out treasure troves, there are probably more than a few people over the age of forty who lament getting rid of their comic book collection. In today's market, a mint copy of the first *Action Comics* featuring Superman is worth a staggering $500,000, with many comic issues from the 1940s regularly selling for close to $10,000 apiece. These are astonishing figures for relatively youthful fantasy features that were produced monthly by the thousands and sold for a paltry ten cents.

Comic books featuring action heroes such as Superman, Batman, Spiderman, and Captain America are some of the most sought after, and issues featuring the first appearance of a popular action figure are invariably the most valuable. As with most collection hobbies, condition is an extremely important key to value, but even a slightly worn copy of a very rare issue can be worth thousands. With the publicity that extravagant prices can generate, it's easy to become enamored of the prospect of making a quick fortune, but be aware that virtually all comic dealers and most hobbyists know exactly what their collections are worth, and the investment outlook can be sketchy.

If you're bitten by the comic book bug, there are vast Internet resources that provide casual and serious enthusiasts a wealth of knowledge, including tips for collecting, how to preserve comics, and lists of reputable dealers and comic conventions. Protecting valued comic books is vital to their long-term survival and is of particular concern because of the inherently inexpensive wood pulp paper that comics are made with and their inevitable propensity for discoloration.

Your best bet for safeguarding comics is to store them in mylar bags made specifically for the purpose. Polyethylene and polypropylene bags that are also designed specifically for comics are a less expensive alternative to mylar but will eventually experience chemical breakdowns and should be replaced every two years or so. Acid-free archival backer boards are also a good idea to keep comics from curling and bending.

As with all valuable documents, avoiding exposure to sunlight and fluorescent lighting is important. Although aging is inevitable, proper storage in a cool, dark environment will extend the life of a comic for decades. And no matter how old you are, don't grow up too fast—and don't *ever* let your mom toss those comics!

Superman creators
Jerry Siegel and Joe
Schuster.

In 1941, Jerry Siegel and Joe Schuster made an appearance at a Cleveland movie theater to promote a Superman cartoon. At that gathering, they'd set up drawing boards in the theater's lobby and given fans autographs and signed sketches. When meeting with Diane VanSkiver Gagel, Wes surmised that her father likely acquired his sketch at a Superman promotion at an Ohio theater, possibly the theater he worked at prior to his enlistment in the military. Save for Schuster's odd signature on Randall VanSkiver's sketch, it was absolutely authentic, but more importantly, his military records at long last showed his daughter just how true a superhero *he* really was.

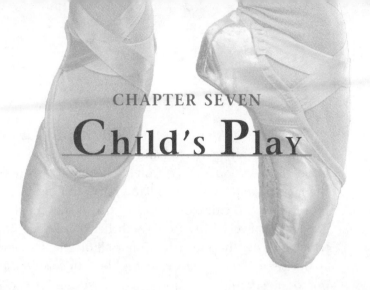

CHAPTER SEVEN

Child's Play

History is a legacy for all generations, one that the younger population will one day recall with the same vivid tenacity as their elders no matter the time, place, event, or object. *History Detectives* paid tribute to this commingling of young and old when detectives Gwen Wright and Elyse Luray took a trip down memory lane, and teamed up with two junior detectives for a pair of New York investigations that were uniquely personal and highly enlightning.

The first investigation brought us into the world of early twentieth-century ballet and a humble cobbler named Michele Savino whose dream was to create a shoe that would help a ballerina seem to float on air. It was Savino's great-great-granddaughter who enlisted the help of *History Detectives* in order to learn more about her ancestor. Another Gotham foray featured young film student, Sade Falebita, who researched the early history of one of the world's most renowned amusement parks—Coney Island—which as a landmark form of entertainment was unmatched in its technical innovations, creativity, and marketability and for the freedom it provided men, women, and children during the early 1900s. From center stage to a unique steeplechase, dance and merriment bring forth the inner child in all of us, no matter the place or decade, and we have scores of early innovators to thank for keeping us entertained.

The Ballet Slipper Mystery

There are few things in life as ethereal as a ballerina on stage, her methodically perfected and deliberate actions masked by her calm, graceful expression and movement. She has the swiftness of a gazelle and the magical appeal of a woodland fairy, and her pirouette gives the impression she's floating on air. This surreal action, while seeming to defy gravity, has everything to do with her dainty yet sturdy pointe shoes, which give her the ability to lift herself off the floor and spin effortlessly. To devise such footwear was no easy feat for cobblers, and most assuredly not for one of the most famous shoemakers in history, Salvatore Capezio. And while Capezio is one of the most renowned, there were other creative shoe gurus who played a big part in outfitting some of the most famous dancers of the twentieth century.

You've likely never heard of Michele Savino, who left his mark on the entertainment industry in a big way, but there were questions that three generations of women on Long Island, New York, had surrounding Savino, a relative who they believed could have served as mentor to Salvatore Capezio in the late 1800s. Young aspiring ballerina and amateur sleuth Mariel O'Connell, in particular, was driven to find out what part her great-great-grandfather played during the golden age of Broadway and his possible contributions to the art of ballet.

Amateur detective Mariel O'Connell and her great-great-grandfather Michele Savino. (Opposite page) A ballerina *en pointe*.

Elyse Luray was intrigued by the dancing dilemma and went to the Big Apple to visit with Mariel and her mother, Pamela, who explained that according to O'Connell family history, Michele Savino once owned a shoe store on 42nd Street in the heart of New York City's theater district. As evidence, the O'Connells have in their possession a patent that had been issued on April 3, 1934, to Savino for a ballet slipper, and a photograph of the cobbler taken at his daughter's wedding.

More than anything, the family wanted to know if Savino served as mentor to Capezio, and if he'd made shoes for renowned Broadway star Marilyn Miller. With Mariel as her detective dance

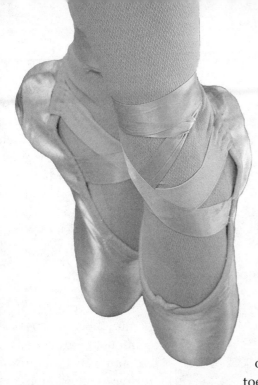

partner, Elyse began investigating the baffling ballet slipper mystery by researching the history of the dance and the dancer's footwear.

TAKING POINTE

The *pointe*, or *toe shoe*, has a fascinating evolution that runs parallel to the pointe technique of dancing, generally referred to as *en pointe*, or dancing on the tips of one's toes. The word "pointe" is the French word for "tip." Ballet is a dance steeped in history, its origins dating back to the thirteenth century during the Renaissance, when arts of many forms were coming into their own. In 1533, the Italian powerhouse Medici family married off Catherine de Medici to the son of King Francis I of France, and it was Catherine who introduced the French court to the Italian *balletto*.

Ballet became an officially recognized art form in the late sixteenth and early seventeenth centuries during the reign of King Louis XIV. Early productions in his courts and stages showcased dancers wearing enormous wigs, masks, and bulky costumes. By the Romantic era of the 1830s, however, women would adopt a bold new look. This in part occurred when Italian dancer Marie Taglioni peformed *La Sylphide* en pointe, wearing a risqué skirt that fell just below her knees and a top that left her arms and shoulders completely bare. Imagine the scandal! On their feet, Taglioni and those who followed in her footsteps usually wore leather-soled satin slippers with limited padding and virtually no support in the toe. To say these women had strong feet and ankles is a vast understatement.

Over the decades, pointe shoes, the pointe technique, and ballet in general evolved by leaps and bounds, with prestigious companies popping up all over the world.

DID YOU know

Ballet wasn't the only thing Catherine de Medici introduced to society. A staple of the fashionable woman's wardrobe for years, modern stiletto-heeled shoes were originally designed by Italian shoemakers in the 1950s. References to high-heeled shoes date back for centuries, but the first recorded use of fashionable heels was by de Medici, who had high heels made for her wedding to the French Duke of Orleans. The bold new look set off a trend in 1533 that swept through the royal courts of Europe.

The Ballets Russes rehearsing in New York in 1916.

One of most renowned ballet companies was the Russian Imperial Ballet (later known as the famed Kirov Ballet), which introduced the world to amazingly gifted dancers including Vaslav Nijinsky, Anna Pavlova, and later Rudolf Nureyev and Mikhail Baryshnikov.

Throughout that time, pointe shoe design was continuously enhanced to accommodate the growing needs of more technically proficient dancers and their wide range of feats, with shoes becoming sturdier at the toe through the use of padding and layers of fabric. Modern-day pointe shoes are now covered in canvas or satin with a rigid yet pliable shank, and front ends made of layered fabrics like canvas and burlap glued together. Shoe design is as important to dancers as the music to which they dance, and masterminds behind ballet shoe design, such as Salvatore Capezio, were artists in their own right.

Italian-born shoemaker Salvatore Capezio is said to have fallen into his fame by sheer luck. In 1887, the seventeen-year-old cobbler ambitiously opened his own business in a shop across from New York's Metropolitan Opera House, then on Broadway and 39th Street. Advertising himself as a "theatrical and historical shoemaker," Capezio rose to repute when dancer Jean De Reszke required an emergency pair of shoes—a repair that snowballed into many local dancers calling upon Capezio to make *their* shoes.

By 1910, he shot to the top of his game when Russian prima ballerina Anna Pavlova invested in his pointe shoes not only for herself but for her entire dance company during her first American tour. By the 1930s, the Capezio name was all over the footwear of famed Ziegfeld Follies dancers, and a true legend was born. But the real question surrounding that legacy was the notion that Capezio

time
TEASER

At age seventy-one, Charin Yuthasastrkosol holds an entertainment world record. What is it?

Answer: She's the world's oldest performing ballerina.

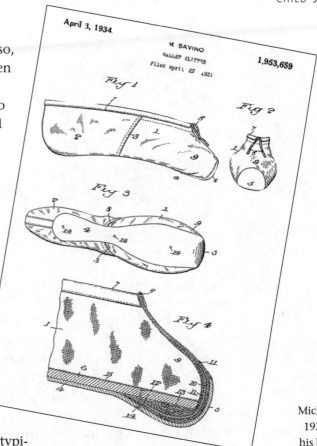

April 3, 1934

M. SAVINO
BALLET SLIPPER
Filed April 22 1931

1,953,659

Fig. 1

Fig. 2

Fig. 3

Fig. 4

indeed had a mentor, and if so, could that guiding light have been Michele Savino?

To learn more about Capezio and pointe shoe design, Elyse and Mariel took Savino's patent to Gotham's American Ballet Theater to consult Judith Weiss, a renowned Capezio expert with three decades' experience in the ballet industry who herself has designed a pointe shoe called Prelude. Weiss was able to quickly ascertain that Savino was attempting to create a pointe shoe with thick padding that would allow a dancer to be virtually silent. This was, and continues to be, an inherent problem of the pointe shoe, given that a hard front end typically makes noise when a dancer jumps. Compared to Capezio's shoes, Weiss concluded, Savino's were vastly different in design, which furthered her opinion that Savino wasn't Capezio's mentor.

In order to confirm that Savino even made ballet shoes, Elyse and Mariel went to Lincoln Center to the New York Public Library for the Performing Arts to research their world-renowned archives. What they found was a dance magazine containing an advertisement for toe dancing slippers made by M. Savino that also contained a patent number matching the patent left to his descendants. According to the United States Patent and Trademark Office, Savino's ballet slipper patent—number 1,953,659—was filed on April 22, 1931, and approved April 3, 1934. The address of his shop was 324 West 42nd Street, which was on the edge of the theater district. With that valuable information in hand, it was time to investigate whether or not the enterprising cobbler made shoes for Broadway superstar Marilyn Miller.

Michele Savino's 1934 patent for his ballet slipper design. Below, a magazine ad for Savino's shop on West 42nd Street in New York.

TWENTY-SEVEN

NEWEST DANCING SHOES

Prevents blisters on toes—no paste—soft, yet rigid. The greatest ease in dancing, longer wear and satisfaction. Guaranteed

Patent No. 1,953,659

NEW BALLET SLIPPER
—with full elk leather sole, no pleats— gives complete freedom of toes.

Patent Pending

Hand-turned. THEO TIE Tap Shoes, any color desired, made by SAVINO. We make all kinds of CHARACTER SHOES Send for Catalogue and Price List

M. SAVINO
TOE DANCING SLIPPERS
324 West 42nd St. New York City

Pictured above and below, Ziegfeld Follies star and Broadway sensation Marilyn Miller.

THE LEATHER TRUNK TRIUMPH

The quintessential blonde bombshell, Marilyn Miller had her first starring role in 1902 at the age of four as Sugar Plum in the Five Columbians, her family's vaudeville act. Over the years, she excelled at acting, singing, and tap dancing, which, after many gigs in America and Europe, brought her to the attention of Florenz Ziegfeld, whose Ziegfeld Girls were touted as "the most beautiful girls in the world."

Elaborate shows known as the Ziegfeld Follies, which ran from 1907 until 1931, were inspired by the Parisian Folies Bergères. The lavish Ziegfeld productions showcased a host of eventual A-listers, including Barbara Stanwyck, Paulette Goddard, Marion Davies, Josephine Baker, Fanny Brice, Ina Claire, Lana Turner, Gilda Gray, Ruby Keeler, Gypsy Rose Lee, and two of Ziegfeld's wives, Billie Burke and Anna Held.

In 1918, at age twenty, Miller took the Follies by storm, wowing audiences with her raw talent and charisma. With her peppy signature song, "Look for the Silver Lining," she spent the next decade performing to sell-out crowds at the Follies and on Broadway, and rose to superstardom, earning a whopping several thousand dollars a week. She married three times, and her bright career was sadly extinguished when she died in 1936 at the age of thirty-seven as a result of complications from sinus surgery.

Miller's amazing talent and tragic end were well documented, but what wasn't documented was her link to shoemaker Michele Savino. Luckily, Elyse had an ace up her sleeve. She called upon fellow History Detective Tukufu Zuberi, who traveled to New Orleans to meet with Miller's grandniece Sudee Campbell, and it was there that Mariel's family mystery began to rise to the surface.

During his visit with Campbell, Tukufu was shown a beautiful leather trunk with the embossed initials "MMP," which stood for Marilyn Miller Pickford, the star's married name from 1922 to 1927. According to Campbell, Miller was a woman of very particular taste and style, especially when it came to her costuming—and her shoes. Within her trunk, Tukufu found a time capsule of the star's life, including a fan, the boots she wore when playing Peter Pan on Broadway, and the linchpin of the ballet slipper mystery.

Back in Long Island, Elyse met with Mariel, her mother, Pam, and Mariel's grandma. Mariel shared with her family the advertisement that she and Elyse found for Michele Savino's New York shop, which confirmed that he was indeed a shoemaker working at the heart of the theater district. But it was what Elyse presented to the O'Connell family that gave true life to their enterprising ancestor. It was a pointe shoe belonging to Marilyn Miller—a shoe that Tukufu found in Miller's leather trunk. Generously given to the O'Connell family by Miller's grandniece, the shoe proved with absolute certainty that Michele Savino was a shoemaker to the stars, because on the bottom of the sole was inscribed: "Savino, New York."

In a stroke of pure irony, Miller's ancestors also had a family story, only theirs was about a shoemaker who stood backstage during Marilyn Miller's performances and tended to her shoes. In the end, two unrelated families with two mysterious family legends were linked together by a star and a cobbler who both left an indelible footprint on Broadway.

Michele Savino's imprint on the sole of Marilyn Miller's ballet slipper.

The Call of the Wild

In a world often filled with war and strife, there are few places on the planet that provoke a truly magical aura that gives us a break from the everyday realities of life. Amusement parks are such places, as they offer a wide range of activities, oddities, and mesmerizing attractions meant to encourage free-spirited attitudes and suspension of disbelief, if only for a few precious hours. In the modern era, Disneyland and all its fabled amusements fits the bill, but at the turn of the twentieth century, everyone was focused on the spectacular glitz, glamour, and wide-eyed wonder

Gwen and amateur detective Sade Falebita meeting with Jim Elkind to examine an unusual set of lion paws.

that was Coney Island. Unfortunately, few remnants have survived of the famed amusement capital that saw its heyday at the dawn of the twentieth century, but one New York collector called upon *History Detectives* to investigate a pair of lion paws that he believed came from the main entrance to Steeplechase Park, which provided stellar entertainment at Coney Island from 1897 to 1964.

Always game for a bit of investigative fun, Gwen Wright teamed up with student filmmaker and Brooklynite Sade Falebita to examine the lion paws and determine their potentially historic significance. Meeting Jim Elkind at his home in Pelham, New York, Gwen and Sade learned that he'd purchased the enormous paws, which presumably were once attached to a large ornamental lion, from the estate of amusement park archivist Frederick Fried, who helped dismantle Steeplechase Park in the 1960s. In order to determine if the paws were from the correct era, Gwen and Sade traveled to Columbia University's Graduate School of Architecture, Planning and Preservation for a consultation with Gwen's colleague Dr. Richard Pieper, who was surprised how lightweight the paws were, given their metal construction.

After his initial examination, Pieper showed Sade how to use an x-ray fluorescence gun, commonly used for elemental analysis, in an effort to identify what the paws were actually made of. Holding the gun against the surface of the paw, Sade pressed the trigger and checked out a screen attached to the mechanism, which indicated that the paw was primarily comprised of zinc. Pieper went on to explain that the type of stamped zinc the sculptor used required pieces being pressed together in dies to form specific shapes, which were then cut and soldered together. He estimated that zinc creations such as the lion would have been made between 1875 and 1925—the correct era for Steeplechase Park. With that information in their pocket, Gwen and Sade set out to learn more about the evolution of Coney Island.

time
TEASER Which famous amusement park performer has his own myspace.com Web page?

Answer: Sea World's famed killer whale, Shamu.

The panoramic grandeur that was Coney Island in 1910.

AMUSING DEVELOPMENTS

As with many innovations throughout history, the amusement park as we know it evolved from a relatively simple concept to one of multi-million dollar proportions. The idea was nurtured in the resort areas and gardens of Renaissance Europe and grew to become the traditional picnic grounds and beer gardens of America. While the practice of rest and relaxation with one's family was a popular pastime, it provided only a sparse glimpse of what would prove to be the true inspiration of the modern-day amusement park—World's Fairs and Expositions (see chapter 5).

Known for their exotic rides, cuisine, and other entertainments, fairs and expos opened a cultural and technological Pandora's box that emanates to the present day. In particular, the Chicago World's Columbian Exposition in 1893 served as a turning point, with its games, concession stands, and myriad rides, including the first Ferris wheel, all of which provided serious motivation for the creators of Coney Island's exceptional amusement parks.

Located on the southern edge of Brooklyn, Coney Island, a five-mile stretch of pristine sandy shoreline, was explored by Henry Hudson in the early 1600s, and named for its abundance of wild

Visitors racing around the tracks of the premier attraction at Steeplechase Park.

Blondes Have More Fun

American culture is loaded with entertainment icons, and one of the most enduring is unquestionably Barbie, the doll that made her debut in 1959 and took the toy world by storm. Barbie's creator, Ruth Handler, is credited with conceiving the idea of an adult-shaped doll after noticing her daughter, Barbara, playing with paper dolls and giving them grown-up roles. Handler's husband, Elliot, and his partner, Harold Matson, owned the eleven-year-old toy company Mattel, but they were initially uninterested in Ruth's idea.

During a 1956 European visit, Ruth became enamored of a sassy German doll called Lilli, which was based on a cartoon character for the German newspaper *Bild Zeitung*. Ruth purchased several Lilli dolls, and it was these samples that persuaded Mattel executives to give her novel idea a chance.

The Barbie doll, named after the Handlers' daughter, became an instant success, with over 350,000 sold during the first year of production for three dollars each. Barbie's companion, Ken, was named after the Handlers' son and introduced into the marketplace in 1961.

rabbits, called "coneys." By the mid-1800s Coney Island had a smattering of picnic grounds, local cuisine, a less-than-formal pier and pavilion, and scattered hotels. Some of the more unsavory happenings—mainly prostitution and various acts of thievery and gambling—gave it the nickname "Sodom by the Sea," a moniker that stuck with future amusement park critics.

By the 1870s, Irishman John Y. McKane took virtual political control of the area, and it began its first major evolution with a steam-powered elevator taking tourists up an observation tower previously showcased at the 1876 Philadelphia Exposition. Over the next decade, the area would also become home to the Switchback Railway, an 1884 invention by LaMarcus Thompson, followed by the highly precarious Loop-the-Loop and Flip-Flap roller coasters. And in true American style, visitors could also indulge in Charles Feltman's Coney Island Red Hots, otherwise known as hotdogs. But without question, the true innovator of Coney Island was a man named George C. Tilyou, whose dedication and inventiveness left a permanent mark on the entertainment industry.

A WILD RIDE

George Cornelius Tilyou was a born entrepreneur, having spent the majority of his formative years in Coney Island helping his parents build Surf House, a business offering tourists cuisine and bathing attire. In 1876, at the age of fourteen, Tilyou took advantage of the hordes of tourists who came to town after visiting the Philadelphia Expo, by selling authentic Coney Island beach sand and bottled salt water. From there he started his own transportation business and then went into real estate before helping his family open a theater.

During his 1893 honeymoon, Tilyou visited the Chicago World's Columbian Exposition, where he became enchanted with the entire atmosphere and technology and especially the Ferris wheel, created by

George Ferris. So taken was Tilyou with the ride that he attempted to buy the circular money maker, which had unfortunately already been sold. Undaunted, he had his own 125-foot wheel made and erected in Coney Island along with several other rides in the area.

Crammed in like sardines, tourists become part of the human roulette wheel at Steeplechase Park circa 1908.

By 1895, a new tourist attraction caught Tilyou's attention in a big way. It was Sea Lion Park, an enclosed area created by Captain Paul Boyton, who made use of the ingenious idea of charging a single admission fee. It was a concept that would ultimately strike gold for George Tilyou. In 1897, he unleashed his master plan for Coney Island by opening Steeplechase Park. Its signature attraction was a replica horse race featuring life-size saddled wooden horses that visitors could ride over a course of undulating steel tracks leading all around the park just like a real contest. It attracted tourists by the thousands. Another big hit was his Pavilion of Fun, including the Blowhole Theater and Insanitarium, which provided unusual but highly successful spectacles for the masses who watched as men received unexpected electrical shocks and women had their skirts raised by intentional gusts of compressed air.

Fortunately for Tilyou, instead of being shocked, people loved *being* the entertainment. It was a daring move for the era and something that set the tone of Steeplechase, which welcomed all measure of humanity from rich to poor and all ethnicities. It truly was a place where inhibition could run wild, free of Victorian repression.

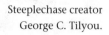

Steeplechase creator George C. Tilyou.

A photo taken by Charles Denson of one of the lions keeping watch at the entrance to Steeplechase Park.

Over the years, George Tilyou constantly added new rides and attractions, including a French Renaissance-style Palace of Pleasure, a Louis XIV ballroom, the popular "Chicken Carousel," a Human Roulette Wheel, the Barrel of Love, a Parachute Jump, "A Trip to the Moon" illusion ride, a sunken garden, roller coasters, spinning rides, and the world's largest swimming pool.

During the first few decades of the twentieth century there were several other parks in addition to Steeplechase that brought Coney Island to the worldwide stage. In 1903, Boyton sold Sea Lion Park to Elmer Dundy and Frederick Thompson, who transformed it into Luna Park, a spectacular attraction that rendered visitors speechless as it showcased over 25,000 electric lights strewn amid its glorious towers and replica Venice canals and Eskimo village. By 1904, politician William Reynolds built Dreamland Park, a biblically themed park with rides, attractions, and light displays meant to rival Luna. Dreamland only survived until 1911, while Luna managed to hold on until 1946, but ultimately, it was Tilyou's Steeplechase that stood the test of time and served as the true heart and soul of Coney Island. Despite several devastating fires and floods, Tilyou rebuilt and continued his innovations until his death in 1914. His family members maintained the park for decades, primarily with the help of general manager Jimmy Onorato, although their reluctance to modernize finally caused the park to close its historic doors in 1964. Ironically, it was Onorato who would provide Gwen and Sade with a wealth of information concerning their historic lion paw investigation.

A conversation with renowned Coney Island historian Richard Snow confirmed that Jimmy Onorato acted as gatekeeper and historian of

DID YOU know

George Ferris created one of the most enduring amusement rides in history as a crowd pleaser to rival the Eiffel Tower. Introduced as the Ferris Wheel at the 1893 World's Fair in Chicago, the incredible structure stood nearly 300 feet into the air and its thirty-six wooden cars could carry up to sixty people each, for an astonishing capacity of 2,160 delighted thrill seekers.

Steeplechase Park for forty years, and that he kept a daily diary of park activities. Snow also mentioned that the park was replete with ornamental animals. As luck would have it, the New York Public Library's Milstein Division houses a collection of Onorato's journals, including lists of all the rides and equipment that sold when the park closed. On May 14, 1965, Onorato noted that a lion was sold to Frederick Fried. But

The El Dorado Carousel, built for Kaiser Wilhelm II of Germany.

was it the same lion? In order to establish provenance, Gwen and Sade met with Charles Denson, author of *Coney Island: Lost and Found*, whose keen photography skills ultimately solved the mystery.

Meeting with Jim Elkind back in Pelham, Gwen and Sade showed him a picture that Charles Denson had taken of the entrance to Steeplechase when he was only twelve years old. Proudly displayed at the top of the façade was Elkind's lion. But that was only a small part of the story. In 1910, Dreamland Park acquired one of the most spectacular rides ever built—the El Dorado Carousel—which was constructed and carved by famed Leipzig sculptor Hugo Hasse for Germany's Kaiser Wilhelm II. The carousel was over four stories high, lit by thousands of lamps, elaborately decorated with Roman warriors, peacocks, and all types of animals, and was three-tiered, with each tier moving at differing speeds. Atop the fabulous creation was the pièce de résistance in the form of a golden chariot pulled by three enormous lions.

A Coney Island lion now decorating New York's Brooklyn Museum.

In 1911, the carousel was nearly destroyed in a fire, but George Tilyou purchased and restored the treasure to its former glory, using the lions at the entrance to his magical park. Jim Elkind's lion paws are a rare memento of a bygone era when men, women, and children of all ages and cultures had the time of their lives. But Gwen had an additional surprise for both Elkind and Sade. Adorning the Brooklyn Museum is another of Tilyou's lions. Donated by Frederick Fried, it proudly stands guard over the museum, just as it did over Steeplechase Park almost a century ago.

DIY DETECTIVE

Every generation has its popular teen mysteries and detectives, whether it's Nancy Drew, the Hardy Boys, Joe Sherlock, Encyclopedia Brown, Scooby Doo, or the Time Soldiers. Every kid loves a great mystery, and it's not only good for entertainment, it encourages creativity, logic, and reasoning. But how do you get your child interested in a history mystery? One way is to find an intriguing item at a flea market, antique fair, or even your own attic, something you can both research and learn about at your local library. Another is to select your child's favorite toy, perhaps a Barbie or a Hot Wheel and search the Web for its inventor.

One particularly helpful resource when researching a toy or almost any other object is running a patent search, but oftentimes there's confusion over the difference between the terms *trademark*, *copyright*, and *patent*. A word, phrase, or symbol that's unique to a product is trademarked to protect the rights of the creator, whereas a literary, artistic, or musical work is copyrighted. A patent establishes legal rights to a unique and useful invention.

Using those concepts, the name "Barbie" for America's favorite doll is trademarked, Harry Potter books are copyrighted, and the articulated joints that make action figures move so realistically are patented. Doing a patent search may sound intimidating, given the millions of patents that have been filed over the centuries, but fear not, because all it

takes is few clicks of your mouse to conduct a simple search.

The Department of Commerce's United States Patent and Trademark Office (USPTO) started in 1790 at the insistence of then Secretary of State Thomas Jefferson as a means of protecting the rights of inventors. The USPTO has an extensive research database that goes clear back to the first year. Their Web site at www.uspto.gov will get you started on a basic patent search. For instance, to take at look at the drawings for Michele Savino's ballet slipper patent, you can enter the patent number, the name "Savino," or even descriptive terms such as "sound deadening ballet shoe." That will lead you to a first-hand view of Savino's invention.

For in-depth patent searches, it's important to remember that there are millions of patents on file with the Patent Office, so you'll need to be tenacious. The Patent Office itself recommends the Web site of the Patent and Trademark Depository at the Richard W. McKinney Engineering Library of the University of Texas at Austin for a tutorial on conducting serious research. To begin that search, visit www.lib.utexas.edu/engin/patent-tutorial/index.htm, where you can get a comprehensive idea of the steps involved in launching a full-scale investigation. Above all, explore History Detectives Kids at www.pbskids.org/historydetectives for more tips on getting youngsters interested in history.

Fun and Games

For generations, anthropologists have had a field day studying human development and our propensity for tinkering with toys and playing games. We've been doing it since the beginning of civilization, and the array of toys we've created is absolutely astonishing. The first toys were created from the most mundane natural materials, like rocks, sticks, and pinecones, which kept kids happily occupied for hours, and continue to do so to this day. And while the purpose of toys is fairly obvious in regard to stimulating creativity and cognitive ability in children, the bottom line is that toys are just plain fun, and our enjoyment of childhood playthings stays with us for a lifetime. For a toys and games collector, this seemingly childish endeavor can quickly turn into a passionately gratifying hunt for the perfect memory.

Although the earliest commercially produced toys were handcrafted from wood, most collectors specialize in gathering examples of vintage toys made from materials of more recent eras. During the mid 1800s, mass-produced tin toys from Germany dominated the world market. As American manufacturing processes developed in the mid- to late-1800s, domestic toymakers jumped into the burgeoning market by producing tin, tinplated steel, and cast-iron toys, and in doing so provided German innovators serious competition. As early as 1860, American toymakers began incorporating clockworks into their inventions, thereby creating the first mechanical toys.

By 1880, European manufacturers responded by building toys with inexpensive spring-driven mechanisms, capturing a huge chunk of the toy market with cheaper products. Of course, American toymakers followed suit and eventually flooded the market with windup toys well into the 1900s. Examples of these early mechanical toys can be found at prices ranging from hundreds of dollars to many thousands. The current record price for a mechanical toy is held by a near mint condition nineteenth-century mechanical bank depicting Jonah and the whale. The iron bank realized $414,000 at auction in 2007. A number of toy manufacturers began working with plastic toy molds in the late 1950s, and although many hardcore toy collectors shun plastic creations, there's no question that some of the most enduring collectibles are plastic. As recently as 2006, a single pony-tailed Barbie doll sold at auction for $5,422.

time TEASER

What famous incarceration device did Joseph F. Glidden invent and receive a patent for in 1874?

Answer: Barbed wire. Glidden is known as the "Father of Barbed Wire."

THE LANDLORD GAME

One popular niche of the amusement industries is board games, which have given millions of people reason to sit around the kitchen table for long hours after the dinner dishes are cleared away. History Detective Elyse Luray probed into the fascinating legacy of one of the most popular board games ever created when she investigated the background of the obscure Landlord Game, which turned out to be the predecessor of Monopoly. The Landlord Game, patented by Elizabeth "Lizzie" Magie in 1904, was originally devised as a tool to demonstrate economic principles denouncing sole ownership of properties and the subsequent and inevitable enrichment of landlords and the impoverishment of those who rented from them. The game found limited popularity in intellectual and university circles and was considered a bit radical for the times. Of course these days, a fervent game of Monopoly can be just as radical—especially if you're stuck in the pokey without a "get out of jail free" card.

Lizzie Magie's 1904 patent for the Landlord Game.

Amazing as it may sound, the earliest recorded board game was found in Egyptian burial sites dating back to 3500 B.C. Known as Senet, the game was meant for two players and consisted of a thirty-square grid and at least five pawns for each side. A set of throwing sticks were used to control the number of moves a player could make, much the same as dice are typically used today. Although historians and scholars have made educated guesses as to the rules of gameplay, the technicalities are still debated, but the game was clearly a favorite pastime of the ancient Egyptians.

A MOUSE IN THE HOUSE

Toy collecting as a hobby is a fairly recent development that has been gathering a lot of steam over the last twenty years. As with all collection hobbies, the

The Greatest American Hero

When it comes to the ultimate male, one in peak physical condition who possesses amazing good looks and oozes utter masculinity, there is but one left on Planet Earth. GI Joe hasn't aged a day in over forty years, and his rugged military and adventurer visage continue to make him one of the most beloved action figures of all time.

Made by Hasbro, GI Joe has had many incarnations over the decades, from his kung fu grip to his flocked beard, all of which are highly collectible. Anyone interested in the immortal hunk can find plenty of books, Web sites, collecting clubs, and even conventions dedicated to one of the most enduring, heroic, and posable men in the world.

most important step is to learn as much as possible before leaping into the game with an open checkbook. The condition of a toy is of utmost importance for collectors, with the most desirable category being MIB (Mint condition In Box). Fashions and fads in toy collecting can also affect sales prices. For instance, Barbie's market value has declined from previous years, while the value of mechanical toys has soared.

Reproductions and outright frauds do exist in the market, and a few unscrupulous vendors sell fairly recent tinplated toys of the mid 1900s as "antiques," with inflated prices and implied histories of much earlier and more collectible eras. Many newcomers to the field rely on whimsy and impulse upon entering the market, but careful research along with visits to toy fairs and knowledgeable dealers will yield plenty of information and help protect your investments.

The world of fun and games is varied and complex, and the History Detectives have led us into fascinating new territory with a couple of intriguing investigations. Wes Cowan took us on an interesting journey into one of the biggest possible upsets in the toy industry when he scrutinized the suggestion that a toy figurine named "Micky" just might have been the original Mickey Mouse. Although the figure of Micky was patented in 1926, two years before Mickey Mouse debuted, it turned out that the two characters had little in common other than myth. The manufacturers of that Micky slipped quietly into obscurity during the Depression, while Mickey Mouse went on to become a major superstar.

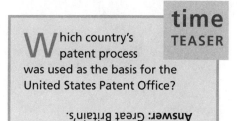

time TEASER

Which country's patent process was used as the basis for the United States Patent Office?

Answer: Great Britain's.

Mickey Mouse has been an American icon for eighty years, and is by far one of the most endearing and best recognized figures in entertainment merchandising and toy-making history. The brainchild of budding young animated film producer Walt Disney, the original Mickey was first drawn by Ub Iwerks, with Disney doing the voice work for the character. The first commercially successful animated film featuring Mickey Mouse was *Steamboat Willie*, a 1928 venture that made both Disney and Mickey household names. Since the character's inception, hundreds of Mickey Mouse merchandising products and toys have been produced, but among the most sought after collectibles are watches featuring Mickey's image on the face.

The first Mickey Mouse watches were manufactured by the Ingersoll Watch Company in 1933 and sold for $2.75. A near mint condition watch from that year, complete with original box and paperwork, was sold in 2004 for $3,650. In 1972, Swiss watchmaker Helbros manufactured a spin-off Goofy character watch with numbers placed in reverse order and hands that ran backward. Priced at $19.95, an original backward Goofy can bring over $1,000 in today's collector's market. In continuous production since 1933, Mickey Mouse and related Disney watches have been manufactured by a number of major manufacturers, including Ingersoll, Helbros, Timex, and Lorus. So next time you've got a mouse in the house, be sure and take a second look, because your Goofy old watch may be worth a bundle!

A 1926 "Micky" mouse figurine investigated by *History Detectives*.

CHAPTER EIGHT
Whispers in the Mist

The first inhabitants of North America were well established long before the arrival of European settlers and conquerors, although relatively little archaeological evidence remains of the most ancient cultures on the continent. The intriguing clues scientists are privy to often come from the remains of shelters, pottery shards, and stone tools that date back many thousands of years, and when those discoveries are made, they are absolutely mind-blowing.

In a very unusual turn for *History Detectives*, Elyse Luray investigated a startling artifact from a long-lost culture—a spearhead embedded in the skull of an extinct ancestor of modern-day bison. It was an amazing find, with results that startled even seasoned professionals and naysayers. To reinforce the concept of significant ancient discovery, we also delve into the equally remarkable tale of the oldest human remains ever found in North America, a find that triggered an epic battle for the legal rights to study them in laboratory conditions, and a group of unusual folks known as the bog people. These few whispers of man's ancient heritage in America are directly linked to later cultures that met their demise with the spread of European exploration of the New World. Also in this chapter we follow Gwen Wright and her investigation of a photograph of legendary Apache warrior Geronimo.

The Case of the Calf Creek Skull

The concept of Native Americans hunting buffalo on the plains of Oklahoma a few hundred years ago is nothing novel to students of Western history, but amateur fossil hunter Kim Holt's discovery of an ancient bison skull with a spear point stuck through its horn shocked even seasoned archaeologists. When it was found in the sandbars of the Arkansas River, some experts thought it was just a little too good to be true. When Holt contacted *History Detectives* for help, the challenge to discover the truth went to super sleuth Elyse Luray, who traveled to Tulsa to meet with Holt and see the skull firsthand.

When the skull was examined, it was clear that the point of a sharpened stone projectile had been driven deep into the base of one horn. It was also clear that expert opinions and testing were needed, so Elyse took the skull to forensic archaeologist Kent Buehler, who determined that it was from a predecessor to the modern bison, a species named *Bison occidentalis* believed to have lived at least 5,000 years ago before evolving into the buffalo we know today. With permission, Buehler removed a small sample for radiocarbon dating, the results of which would prove astonishing.

To dig deeper into the mystery, Elyse did some background research on ancient peoples who used similar stone hunting tools. It's known that the cultures of early Native American peoples experienced dozens of transitions over many millennia. Archaeologically, it's surmised that the vast glacial formations of the most recent Ice Age reduced sea levels by over 200 feet, providing a land bridge across the Bering Strait by which the first human inhabitants made their way to North America from Asia over 14,000 years ago.

Little evidence remains of the cultures that followed, with the exception of the tools early hunters and gatherers created and used—tools that have long provided a benchmark for dating eras of Native American development. So vital is the information that the identification of spear and arrowhead design has itself become

A spear point embedded in a bison skull found by Kim Holt in the sandbars of the Arkansas River.

an intriguing archae-ological specialty. In many cultures, pro-jectile points for tools were carefully fired in hot coals to improve shaping characteris-tics. Selected pieces of crystalline rock called *chert* were chipped into points and used for spears and arrow-heads, scrapers, drill

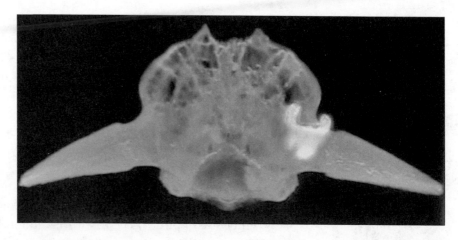

X-rays of the bison skull taken at the University of Texas at Austin show the embedded projectile point.

points, and knives and cutting tools. Among the most sophisticated spear and arrow projectile points are those of the Calf Creek people, named by archaeologist Don Dickson after he discovered and identified artifacts at the Calf Creek Cave in Searcy County, Arkansas, during the late 1960s.

The Calf Creek people crafted complex projectile points that are very difficult to reproduce even by modern-day practitioners of the ancient art. Of the dozens of projectile types Native Americans created over the millennia, the Calf Creek style is readily identifiable, but Elyse needed to clarify the origin of the projectile lodged in the bison skull, so she visited Calf Creek expert Dr. Don Wyckoff of the Sam Noble Oklahoma Museum of Natural History for an opinion. Wyckoff was unequivocal in his assess-ment—the projectile point embedded in the base of the horn of Kim Holt's bison skull was a Calf Creek prod-uct. Better yet, the Calf Creek are believed to have lived and hunted in what's known as the Middle Archaic period of North American culture—be-tween 5,000 and 7,500 years ago—during the same time frame as *Bison occidentalis*.

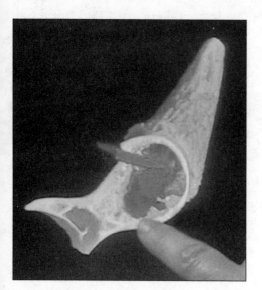

As a scientist, however, Wyckoff expressed reservations about the blade in the horn. For thirty years he'd strongly believed that similar Calf Creek projectile points were too large to have been used as spearheads, and were instead utilized as hand-held knives. With that information, Elyse wondered if it was possible that a hoaxster had purposely hammered an archaeological artifact into the bison skull to create the appearance of an event that never occurred. To answer this serious question, the archaeologists sent the skull to the High Resolution X-ray Computed Tomography Facility at the University of Texas at Austin for a photo shoot.

Research scientist Dr. Richard Ketcham at the University of Texas at Austin created cross-section scans of the skull and then refocused on the embedded point to create a three-dimensional image that replicated the position of the blade in the horn. Utilizing a new and amazing 3-D printer technology that deposits a layer-by-layer film of thermoplastic material, Ketcham was also able to create a precise replica of the projectile point. With the scans back in Oklahoma, archaeologist Dr. Leland Bement was able to determine that only the elastic bone and horn of a living animal could have responded with the limited fracturing defined by the x-ray images. There was no question that the projectile point had been thrown or thrust into the skull of a live bison. The final piece of evidence fell into place when Kent Buehler's radiocarbon dating of the skull proved its age to be over 5,000 years.

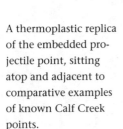

A thermoplastic replica of the embedded projectile point, sitting atop and adjacent to comparative examples of known Calf Creek points.

Through the resources of two universities, several top-level scientists and archaeologists, and Elyse Luray, the authenticity of Kim Holt's Calf Creek skull was indisputably determined. Wishing to share his remarkable and extremely rare find, Holt donated the skull to the Sam Noble Oklahoma Museum of Natural History in Norman, Oklahoma, where it's currently on display.

Place and Time

The twentieth century set into motion an astonishing acceleration of scientific discovery, the results of which are clearly evident with the Calf Creek bison skull. One of the most important of those revelations is *carbon*, or *radiocarbon*, *dating*, a process whereby the age of organic objects can be determined with relative accuracy. For the first time scientists could actually assign a relevant chronological order to history in regard to geological happenings, and to many of the significant objects the world's population holds dear, such as the controversial Shroud of Turin, the Dead Sea Scrolls, Egyptian artifacts, and all measure of items in antiquity as far back as the Pleistocene and Holocene eras.

Considered to be one of the best absolute dating methods, radiocarbon dating was discovered in 1949 by Dr. Willard F. Libby and his team of University of Chicago scientists, including Dr. James Arnold and Dr. Ernest Anderson, working under a grant of only a few thousand dollars. In developing his method, Libby and his team established that any organic object could be dated by analyzing the ratio of carbon-12 (C-12) to its naturally occurring radioactive isotope carbon-14 (C-14).

With a half-life of 5,730 years, C-14 decreases very slowly at a predictable rate, making it an ideal marker for measuring archaeological samples. The team's first tests were conducted on acacia wood collected from the tomb of Djoser, the second pharaoh of Egypt's Third Dynasty. Estimates were then matched with a date established by using *dendrochronology*, a testing procedure employed by Gwen Wright during her *History Detectives* investigation of a hanged witch (see chapter 19).

Though the timing was slightly off, the test taught Libby to adjust for the cosmic intensity of the ancient era. Other Egyptian samples followed, the process was honed, and a new testing methodology was born. Ultimately, Libby's discovery resulted in his earning the Nobel Prize for chemistry in 1960. By the late 1970s, the process advanced, primarily due to Accelerator Mass Spectrometry (AMS), which offered even more precise dating. As with most scientific methods, certain protocols must be enforced in order for the process to be effective.

In the case of radiocarbon dating, results are better achieved with organic matter that is not older than approximately 50,000 years. Precautions must be taken to assure that samples are carefully collected and

time TEASER

What artificial and permanent addition to Earth's atmosphere in the 1950s aided the accuracy of radiocarbon dating?

Answer: Nuclear weapons testing.

DID YOU know

Using radiocarbon dating, a wide range of samples can be tested, including textiles, fabrics, soil, wood, pollen, hair, bloodstains, paper, animal remains, resins, and even ice core samples. A truly amazing innovation, this technique breathed new life into the disciplines of archaeology, anthropology, and geology, and many other cultural and climatological sciences.

stored to avoid any cross-contamination, and additional samples should also be procured from the immediate area for comparison. It's also important to have a large rather than a small sampling, because during the process some matter is removed due to distilling and purification. Another crucial aspect to the process is the fact that over the millennia changes have occurred in our atmosphere and in the radioactive cosmic bombardment of the planet, meaning that the C-12 to C-14 ratio is inconsistent. All of these factors and the complex scientific methodology applied to radiocarbon dating truly make it one of the most fascinating and occasionally controversial discoveries of our time.

The Kennewick Controversy

The discovery and analysis of ancient human remains in the United States is typically a highly debatable undertaking, primarily as a result of the Native American Graves Protection and Repatriation Act (NAGPRA), which was enacted in 1990. The act decrees that remains and associated artifacts discovered on Federal lands can be claimed and returned to descendants and Indian tribes who have a cultural affiliation to a deceased individual.

As one can imagine, NAGPRA continues to be a hotly contested subject between scientists and Native American groups, both of whom pose compelling arguments when it comes to archaeological discovery. This has never been more evident than with the fascinating case of *Kennewick Man*, whose remains were the center of controversy for nine years as various parties, including Native American tribes, the Federal government, and a group of scientists publicly argued their moral positions while also fighting their legal case in the judicial system.

On July 28, 1996, an annual hydroplane race was being held on the Columbia River near Kennewick, Washington, when two spectators discovered a skull along the riverbank. Further searching produced a male skeleton, nearly intact save for his sternum and several bones in his hands and feet. Radiocarbon dating showed the skeleton to be over 9,000 years old, which makes Kennewick Man the oldest and most complete ancient skeleton ever found in the United States.

The skeleton's age sparked immediate debate, with scholars revisiting several theories of early human settlement, wondering where Kennewick Man originated and if he'd migrated over the Bering land bridge stretching from Alaska to Siberia, or if he'd arrived via a Pacific coastal route, or even over the Atlantic. But that was only the beginning of the controversy. The evening of Kennewick Man's discovery, archaeologist, anthropologist, and paleoecologist Dr. James Chatters was called in to consult with local coroner Dr. Floyd Johnson. In the days that followed, Chatters estimated that Kennewick Man was a slender male, likely between forty and fifty-five years of age, who stood approximately 170 to 176 cm (five foot five to five foot six), and who showed evidence of multiple injuries. Chatters also surmised that the ancient man didn't appear to be Native American, his characteristics being more typical of a Caucasoid, or Caucasian, with other traits suggesting Polynesian, Aboriginal, or Asian descent. The assumptions made by Chatters, however, didn't stop the Colville, Nez Perce, Umatilla, Wanapum, and Yakima tribes from uniting to claim Kennewick Man under the repatriation act.

The remains of Kennewick Man, estimated to be over 9,000 years old.

Just over a month after the remarkable skeleton was discovered and after the initial round of radiocarbon results were released, all examinations of Kennewick Man ceased and he became a ward of the U.S. Army Corps of Engineers, thus beginning a decade-long battle between the tribes and a group of renowned scientists led by the Smithsonian Institute's Dr. Doug Owsley, who filed suit for the rights to examine the remains under laboratory conditions. An innovator in his field, Owsley was featured in one of Gwen Wright's 2004 *History Detectives* investigations (see chapter 16).

In 1998, the skeleton was ordered to be moved to the University of Washington's Burke Museum of Natural History and Culture. Two years later, Native American tribes rejoiced when the Interior Department awarded them custody, only to have that rescinded in 2002 by an Oregon federal court, which ruled Kennewick Man be given to a team of scientists for study. An appeal followed and was denied in 2004. For the scientists, the decision was a victory for the study of America's ancient heritage and history. Extensive examinations produced a vast array of information concerning Kennewick Man, including age estimates, skull measurements, tooth casts, and facial reconstruction. Although the studies are ongoing and will probably take several years to complete, Kennewick Man is thought to have been buried after death alongside the Columbia River, where he remained undisturbed for over 9,000 years.

The Bog People

Few individuals can properly prepare themselves for viewing a deceased human body, much less one that has been resting in peat moss for centuries. Indeed the very term "bog people" sounds like a race of aliens that only a science fiction genius such as Ray Bradbury or Arthur C. Clarke could conjure up. Yet these miraculously preserved souls have pushed scientists to their limits while at the same time providing a wealth of information about how our ancestors lived and, in most cases, died by violent means.

As their name suggests, bog people are individuals whose bodies have been preserved in peat moss bogs in areas of Northern Europe and the United Kingdom and even in America. The characteristic dark tan coloring of the bodies occurs as a result of cold temperatures combined with a stagnant and acidic anaerobic (oxygen-free) environment that decalcifies bone matter yet prohibits tissue decay and preserves the body's organs, skin, and even facial hair and tattoos. So well preserved were some of these individuals that one of the two Weerdinge Men, who were determined to have lived between 100 B.C. and A.D. 50, was found with his intestines outside of his abdomen as a result of a chest wound.

Over the past few decades, hundreds of bog people

The amazing slumbering face of Tollund Man, found in a Danish bog in 1950.

The Sky Is Falling

In 1942, a forest ranger in India made a startling discovery at India's Roopkund Lake, a body of water located 16,000 feet high in the Himalayas. What the ranger found was a mass grave around the lake containing hundreds of skeletons. Were they pilgrims, soldiers, traders, or victims of disease or other violence, as indicated by the evidence of sharp blows to their heads?

Radiocarbon dating on the bones in the 1960s dated the remains to between the twelfth and fifteenth centuries, but a later test at Oxford University's Radiocarbon Accelerator Unit put the time of death around A.D. 850. In 2004, National Geographic launched an expedition and scientific investigation into the baffling mystery. DNA tests were conducted on the frozen bodies, which were found intact and complete with clothing and adornments.

While the origin of the unfortunate victims and what they were doing at Roopkund is still pending, their cause of death was surmised to have been a fierce hailstorm—one that bombarded them with ice the size of cricket balls.

have been found, dating from the Iron Age, the Roman era, and clear up until the Medieval Age. Koelbjerg Woman, who is said to be the matriarch of the bog folk, was proved after the testing of her skull to have lived around 8000 B.C. Another famous bogwoman named Haraldskaer Woman was found in 1835 at Gunhild's Bog in Demark. A wild controversy ensued when her remains were identified as those of Queen Gunhild of Norway, who reigned in the late A.D. 900s and who was allegedly killed and tossed into a bog. By 1977, the decades-old mystery was solved when radiocarbon testing dated her remains to around 500 B.C.

Tollund Man, whose remains were dated between 300 and 400 B.C., was found in Denmark in 1950. He is perhaps the most famous of the bog people, and his peaceful and highly detailed angelic face, beautifully preserved sheepskin cap, and calm body positioning stand in sharp contrast to the braided leather noose still hanging around his neck. Two years later in 1952, one of the most amazingly well preserved bogmen was found a few feet below the surface of a peat bog not far from Tollund Man. Dubbed Grauballe Man, the remarkable body had a healthy coif of hair, fingernails, fingerprints that could actually be printed, and a rather nasty gash extending from one ear to the other.

time TEASER

What characteristic did the slain bog peoples discovered worldwide have in common?

Answer: They are generally considered to be members of the affluent class.

Radiocarbon testing indicated that Grauballe Man lived sometime between 100 B.C. and A.D. 100, and quite astonishingly, his last meal was identified as a soup or gruel containing various seeds and possibly hallucinogenic fungus. The bog people, including Lindow Man, Oldcroghan Man, Gallagh Man, Clonycavan Man, Meenybraddan Woman, and Windeby Girl, are a fascinating study, made all the more real by facial reconstructions like the one performed on sixteen-year-old Yde Girl, who was found in 1897 but had been stabbed to death sometime between 100 B.C. and A.D. 50.

The Ghost in the Glass

As a direct result of NAGPRA, the discovery of Native American remains are hotly contested, primarily because of the efforts of tribes to protect the legacy and sanctity of their ancestors. Much of what we know of the oldest Native American cultures is derived from experience with the tribes who existed during America's growth into the West. During the 1800s, America's relentless expansion into the Western frontier brought white settlers into direct conflict with dozens of native cultures with ancient roots.

In the southwestern territories, one of the most fiercely independent of the native American cultures were the Apache tribes who inhabited the lands of modern-day New Mexico, Arizona, and northern Mexico. For the Apaches, the concept of borders and boundaries was unimaginable, and they responded with stubborn contempt and deadly retribution to all attempts by U.S. and Mexican authorities to control their lives. Frustrated military commanders dedicated over 5,000 soldiers—nearly a quarter of the U.S. Army—to the capture and imprisonment of a single warrior whose leadership embodied the spirit and determination of the Apache people. His Chiricahua name was Goyaaté, which translates into English as the relatively sleepy "One Who Yawns." For inexplicable reasons, his enemies gave him a name that would haunt their own dreams: Geronimo.

The alleged photo of Geronimo investigated by *History Detectives*.

Robin Isele of Walton, Kentucky, contacted *History Detectives* with a tale about a photograph of the legendary Apache war chief that she believed was taken on her great-great-grandfather's ranch in New Mexico. Intrigued, History Detective Gwen Wright visited Isele to investigate the possibility of a historic moment captured on film. During their meeting, Gwen saw that the subject of the photograph was a man wearing a feathered headdress amid a group of what appeared to be soldiers, all astride horses. The caption on the back of the photo read: "Geronimo saluting a crowd of 100,000 people and surrounded by U.S. soldiers at Ranch 101, June 12, 1905." Isele explained that her ancestor,

Geronimo (far right) with his fellow warriors circa 1886, the year he was captured.

William Ritch, was the lieutenant governor and acting governor of the New Mexico Territory during the late 1800s, and owned a large ranch in the southeast region of the territory. For Gwen, Robin Isele had a simple request. Was this a genuine photograph of Geronimo, and was it taken on William Ritch's ranch?

HOME ON THE RANGE

With limited information and the photograph in hand, Gwen began her search in Santa Fe, New Mexico, where she met with photography historian and teacher Dr. Eugenia Parry. Parry confirmed that the photo could easily date to the early 1900s, but poor facial detail couldn't provide positive proof that the figure was actually Geronimo. Moving on, Gwen uncovered information on William Ritch and his New Mexico ranch that presented yet another obstacle—there seemed to be no connection between Ritch's ranch and the 101 Ranch cited on the photo.

Acting on a hunch, Gwen contacted fellow History Detective Wes Cowan, who'd recently sold at auction an authentic photograph of Geronimo that was taken at the 101 Ranch. Wes e-mailed Gwen a scan of the photo, and much to her delight, the image was a close match to Robin Isele's photo. Clearly, the second image was taken at the same location and highlighted the same subject: Geronimo and a company of soldiers. Adding to the good news, Wes had located the elusive 101 Ranch, providing Gwen with a name and address that turned out to be in Oklahoma.

Oklahoma's 101 Ranch, famous for its Wild West shows during the early 1900s.

At the Woolaroc Ranch and Museum in Bartlesville, Oklahoma, the mystery of Geronimo's photograph was solved with the help of noted Western author and historian Michael Wallis. Wallis explained that the 101 Ranch had been a working Oklahoma cattle ranch for many years until the enterprising owners added to the mix by organizing a Wild West show and recruiting some of the most famous names in Western history. Featured attractions at their well publicized "Gala Day" in 1905 were Buffalo Bill Cody, African American cowboy phenomenon Bill Pickett, and a young Tom Mix, who would later become the first Western cinematic superstar. All of these renowned cowboys, however, were trumped by the event's main draw—famed Apache warrior Geronimo, who at age seventy-six was approaching the end of a long and legendary life. Despite his advanced years, Geronimo participated in what was touted as his "last buffalo hunt" by firing arrows at a bison from a moving car inside the show arena. Reportedly, several armed cowboys eventually entered the ring and finished off the hapless beast.

Because bison are generally associated with the American Great Plains and Geronimo's Chiricahua Apache people lived in the Southwest, some controversy exists over whether Geronimo's "last buffalo hunt" was actually his first. Historically, buffalo ranged throughout the plains of America, including those of Texas and eastern New Mexico, and were a common source of food and hides for the Apache people. Evidence of Apache reverence for and reliance on buffalo exists in the work of famed artist and sculptor Allan Houser, whose Chiricahua parents, Sam and Blossom Haozous, related stories of buffalo hunts that inspired many of Houser's artworks. In fact, Sam Haozous was

Geronimo's grand-nephew and translator during much of their coinciding time at Fort Sill. Perhaps the best evidence comes from Geronimo himself, who relayed to biographer S. M. Barret, writer and editor of *Geronimo's Story of His Life*, the following words: "Out on the prairies, which ran up to our mountain homes, wandered herds of deer, antelope, elk, and buffalo, to be slaughtered when we needed them. Usually we hunted buffalo on horseback, killing them with arrows and spears. Their skins were used to make teepees and bedding; their flesh, to eat."

LUMINARY LEGEND

Much of Geronimo's life was spent in conflict with encroaching Mexican and U.S. settlers and soldiers in the ancestral homelands of the Apache tribes. When he was in his early twenties in 1851, Geronimo's tribe encampment was attacked by 400 Mexican soldiers commanded by Colonel Jose Maria Carrasco while the Apache men were away trading for supplies. The troops slaughtered Geronimo's wife, his mother, and his three young children. Enraged, the young Apache helped organize a band of vengeful warriors from separate tribal groups to hunt down Carrasco's troops.

Outnumbered and outgunned, the Apache war party lured a company of soldiers from the town of Arizpe in Sonora and attacked them in a bloody two-hour assault. Geronimo led the Apaches in hand-to-hand combat that wreaked havoc on the soldiers, killing or wounding over seventy. His successful retaliation cemented his position among the Apache people as a skilled war chieftain and began his legacy as a fierce opponent to the intrusions of Mexicans and Americans alike.

For the next thirty-five years, Geronimo raided settlers throughout the hills and mountains of Arizona and New Mexico and ran the armies of two nations ragged. But decades of running and hiding eventually took an enormous toll on the great warrior and his people. When Army agents promised him peace for his people and a new home in Florida, he laid down his weapons and surrendered to General Nelson Miles on

---

DID YOU know

Geronimo's "last" buffalo was butchered, barbecued, and mixed with previously prepared beef to make sandwiches for the hungry crowd at the 101 Ranch Gala Day. The sandwiches fetched a pricey fifty cents apiece. The enterprising show operators also sold cups for ten cents each, and cold water to fill them up for another dime.

Geronimo himself was quite the entrepreneur. During his many Wild West shows and fair excursions he was known to cut the buttons from his coat and sell them for a quarter each. He also had the foresight to bring replacements to be sewn back on later. Originally sold for ten cents in the early 1900s, penciled Geronimo autographs can sell for as much as $6,000 in today's antiquities market.

Geronimo skinning his "last" buffalo at the 101 Ranch Gala Day in 1905. Below, the great warrior photographed earlier the same year.

September 4, 1886, and was immediately imprisoned. After a brief period of confinement at Fort Pickens, Florida, and four years in Alabama, Geronimo was eventually brought to the army prison at Fort Sill, Oklahoma, in 1894. He would spend the rest of his life there.

Although technically a prisoner of war, Geronimo became a major celebrity at Wild West shows and fairs like the 1904 St. Louis World's Fair. On March 4, 1905, he was even summoned as a novelty to ride in Theodore Roosevelt's inaugural parade. That same year he was invited to the 101 Ranch Wild West show, which took place just four years before the old warrior succumbed to pneumonia, on February 17, 1909. From the historical background that Gwen gathered, she was able to tell Robin Isele that her rare photograph was unrelated to her ancestor William Ritch's ranch, but there was little question that the picture depicted Geronimo and his soldier guard preparing to return to Fort Sill after his last buffalo hunt at the 101 Ranch Gala Day extravaganza.

Jurassic Fever

The end of the American Civil War in 1865 triggered an explosion of social and economic change, as a nation still in its infancy redirected its efforts toward expansion into the frontier territories that had been the domain of native cultures for centuries. At the same time, an explosion of another sort was brewing in the scientific communities, and the fuse was lit by two natural historians whose intense rivalry would alter the course of our understanding of the ancient world. Before Othniel Marsh and Edward Drinker Cope immersed themselves in the field of paleontology, only eighteen species of dinosaurs were known to have existed, and most of those were determined from incomplete bits and pieces discovered in the eastern United States. That would

Peace Offering

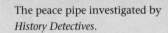

One of the few successful war campaigns waged by Native American tribes against the U.S. government ended in 1868 when Chief Red Cloud of the Oglala Sioux agreed to a treaty after forcing the Army to evacuate his remaining ancestral lands in the Black Hills of western South Dakota, Wyoming, and Montana.

The peace pipe investigated by *History Detectives*.

An uneasy truce lasted until the discovery of gold in the Black Hills in 1868, prompting the government to renege on the treaty by forcing the Sioux to relocate to small reservations. Red Cloud realized the overwhelming futility of combating the flood of white settlers, though he still insisted that the government should honor the Treaty of 1868.

Red Cloud dedicated the rest of his life to negotiating with government authorities on behalf of his people, and the Sioux continue to do so to the present day. One of the few white men he could trust was Indian agent James Irwin, who came to Red Cloud's Pine Ridge Reservation in 1877. Irwin's great-grandaughter, Pat Smith, and her daughter Susan possess a treasured Oglala Sioux peace pipe allegedly presented to Irwin by Red Cloud. History Detective Wes Cowan's investigation of the peace pipe found it to be a rare and meaningful ceremonial gift likely given to Irwin by the legendary Native American war chief.

Evidence of Red Cloud's tendency to present trusted white men with a peace pipe as a token of respect was corroborated by an 1883 photograph in the Smithsonian Institute's National Portrait Gallery. The photo depicts Red Cloud offering a pipe to famed paleontologist Othniel Marsh, who had first met Red Cloud in 1874 on a fossil expedition and appealed to him for rights to explore Sioux land. Marsh later argued vehemently for the improvement of living conditions for the Sioux, and won Red Cloud's admiration by taking their grievances all the way to the White House.

Red Cloud, chief of the Oglala Sioux.

Professor Edward Cope's infamous study circa 1897. And you thought your desk was piled with paperwork?

change dramatically as surveyors preparing the way for the transcontinental railroad began reporting incredible fossil finds in the West.

The Indian tribes who were in the midst of a losing battle to maintain their homelands were well aware of the existence of the fossilized remains of long-extinct creatures and had incorporated them into myths and legends. The Oglala Sioux had a name for them: "Thunderhorses." For Othniel Marsh and Edward Drinker Cope, the opportunity to scour the untamed land for unknown species was a godsend, and throughout the decades following the 1870s the combative duo frantically strove to outdo each other. Between the two men, 136 new dinosaur species were identified and named, and their work crews collected tons of fossil specimens in the western territories by the boxcar load. Major fossil sites excavated through the efforts of Marsh and Cope, particularly in Colorado and Wyoming, continue to attract the attention of paleontologists, with new finds being uncovered on a regular basis.

COLOSSAL FOSSILS AND FOLLIES

The field of archaeology is sometimes confused with *paleontology*. The simplified definition of archaeology is the study of ancient cultures, while paleontology focuses on the study of ancient life forms. The first major players in the budding science of paleontology couldn't have been more different than Othniel Marsh and Edward Cope. Born on March 29, 1831, as the nephew of millionaire George Peabody, Marsh developed an early interest in collecting bones and fossils, and went on to study natural history at Yale University with continued studies in Europe. After graduating, Marsh convinced his wealthy uncle to donate heavily to Yale in

1866, founding Yale's Peabody Museum of Natural History (now called the Peabody Museum of Archaeology and Ethnology). Peabody's endowments ensured Marsh a chair with Yale's faculty as the first American professor of paleontology, along with a curatorship of the new museum.

Still in his early thirties, Othniel Marsh was in the unique position of turning the as-yet-untapped field of paleontology into a self-indulgent personal playground, although he led only four expeditions of Yale students into the field. Sustained by his uncle's fortune, Marsh was content spending most of his career being a masterful delegator and political player, taking much of the credit for the efforts of his university staff and paying work crews to do his digging.

Nine years younger than Marsh, Edward Cope was born in Philadelphia on July 28, 1840, to a prosperous Quaker family. Like Marsh, Cope developed a youthful interest in natural science and history, going on to study for a year at the University of Pennsylvania and spending three years investigating the herpetology collection at Washington's Smithsonian Institute. Cope also spent a year visiting museums and archaeological sites in Europe, reportedly to avoid involvement in the Civil War. In 1864, at the relatively tender age of twenty-four and with a limited

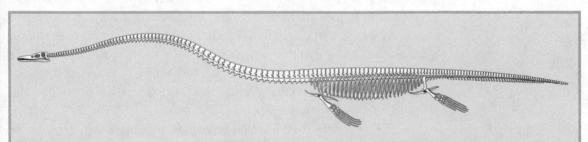

A Fossil Faux Pas

Edward Cope's infamous *Elasmosaurus* (above) was a *plesiosaur*, the same species of creature that has long been speculated to be stealthily swimming around in a Scottish loch. Perhaps the most famous of all elusive and mythical creatures, the Loch Ness Monster has been the subject of public and scientific debate for centuries. Despite truckloads of disputed evidence in the form of photographs and videos and myriad proven hoaxes, the sea monster's legendary existence has yet to be substantiated. With any luck, both the believers and the naysayers will one day be rendered speechless by definitive evidence of the legendary beast affectionately known as "Nessie."

formal education, Cope's natural brilliance, background, and knowledge gained him a seat as a professor of natural science at Haverford College in Pennsylvania. A year later, he was named curator of the Academy of Natural Sciences.

Unlike Othniel Marsh, Edward Cope was arrogant and brash, relentlessly conducting dozens of field expeditions into the wilds of the Western frontier. Cope and Marsh reportedly came into personal contact while the two men were studying in Europe, but the first meeting of note occurred in 1868 when Cope invited Marsh for a professional visit. Cope had an ongoing agreement with local quarries to provide him with fossils and bones and proudly gave his colleague a tour of the sites, but shortly after the meeting and much to Cope's horror, his stream of local artifacts from the quarries mysteriously dried up. Upon investigating the matter, Cope could only surmise that Marsh had made separate financial arrangements with the quarry operators, who were now redirecting their finds to the Yale museum. Although Cope couldn't prove his suspicions, he would never forgive Marsh for his interference, and a recurring fossil feud of epic proportion was born.

The enmity that would become known as the "Great Bone Wars" between Cope and Marsh was elevated to new heights in 1870 after Cope published a legendary blunder about a newly reconstructed skeleton excavated in Kansas that was dubbed *Elasmosaurus*, an aquatic reptile of the dinosaur age that reached over forty-feet in length. In his description, Cope noted that the vertebral structure of the beast ran in the opposite direction of other known species. Upon inspecting the specimen, Marsh suggested that the backbone was not backward, but rather that Cope had reversed the head with the tail.

The resulting heated exchange was resolved by Cope's former professor at the University of Pennsylvania, Joseph Leidy, who'd described the first complete dinosaur ever discovered in America, *Hadrosaurus*, in 1858. To Cope's dismay and Marsh's utter glee, Leidy agreed that the head and tail were indeed swapped. To make matters worse, Cope had already published descriptions and drawings of the backward *Elasmosaurus*. Although he frantically attempted to purchase and destroy every copy of the printed error, he failed to get them all out of circulation. Marsh happily capitalized on the mistake by casting suspicion on Cope's credibility and professionalism at every opportunity.

time
TEASER   The dinosaur *velociraptor* was made famous in the 1993 film *Jurassic Park*. What does "velociraptor" mean?

Answer: Fast thief.

DIY DETECTIVE

Do you fancy yourself to be the next Indiana Jones, tomb raider Lara Croft, or *Jurassic Park* entrepreneur? If so, you'll no doubt be on the hunt for everything from fossils and rare gems to Noah's Ark and the Holy Grail. You may not have much luck with the latter two, but you could hit pay dirt when searching for ancient bones and stones—assuming you know what to look for. In both cases, research will help get you one step closer to being a genuine rock star or dino hunter.

Field guides and identification books are a great place to start. When it comes to geology, the most important thing you need to know is that a rock isn't just a rock—it's actually composed of various minerals like quartz, copper, turquoise, malachite, iron, and pyrite (fool's gold), to name a few. These minerals are primarily evaluated for their luster, density, hardness, transparency, and even crystal formations.

Rocks typically fall into three categories: sedimentary, which have distinct layers such as sandstone and shale; metamorphic, which are formed by extreme underground conditions like heat or water; and igneous, which come from lava or magma. If you happen upon a rock you believe could be valuable, don't conduct any home chemistry tests. Instead, hit the library and see if you can find similar pictures or visit your local museum or university geology department to compare your sample. The same logic applies to fossil finds, some of which can be very fragile and difficult to identify. If you make an exciting discovery, the best thing you can do is leave the artifact in place and take extensive photos of it and the surrounding area. In this way, you have more information to share with experts who'll benefit from knowing exactly where your item was located.

More often than not, you may find an artifact and not even realize it's an ancient relic. That was the case in June 2007, when two ten-year-old boys from McMinnville, Oregon, stumbled upon what they thought was a hiker's boot stuck in the mud of a streambed near their home. After much debate, the boys finally gave the "boot" a tug and pulled out a nearly pristine ten-pound mastodon tooth. Experts identified the fossil as a molar from a nine-year-old mastodon calf that died in the area a remarkable 12,000 to 15,000 years ago.

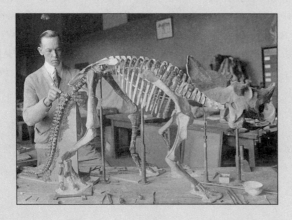

In this 1921 photo, Norman Ross, of the division of Paleontology at the National Museum of Natural History, examines the skeleton of a baby dinosaur said to be seven or eight million years old.

THE LEGENDARY BITTER END

When we think of a paleontologist, it's easy to picture an individual hunched over a dig, meticulously excavating a rare specimen. It's a seemingly laborious yet peaceful image. But that wasn't the case for Cope and Marsh, who took their feud into the field by dragging their work crews into the mess. Both men's collectors spied on one another, destroyed and sabotaged competing fossil sites, and even stole from one another. Scientific scrutiny and prudence went out the window as the bitter opponents cranked out volumes of articles that were increasingly used as forums for professional attacks, criticism, and thinly veiled slander. The quarrel spilled over from scientific circles into the public domain in 1890 when a Cope ally and reporter from the *New York Herald* published a long list of accusations and criticisms directed at Marsh.

A week later, Marsh lashed back with counteraccusations and allegations of professional chicanery and theft, along with a rehash of the still stinging *Elasmosaurus* debacle. Cope and Marsh's public conflict permanently damaged the reputations of both men, although Marsh's tenure at Yale and the Peabody Museum afforded him a measure of protection. The feud technically ended with Edward Cope's death from renal failure on April 12, 1897, although his last, sadly comical wish was to have the volume of his brain measured and compared to that of Othniel Marsh after Marsh's passing, in a ridiculous effort to prove that Cope was the more intelligent of the two. Marsh may not have had Cope's raw intelligence, but he was certainly wise enough to decline the challenge. Othniel Marsh passed away two years later, on March 18, 1899. It remains unclear whose brain outweighed the other's.

time
TEASER   Which of the first three Indiana Jones films (*Raiders of the Lost Ark*, *Indiana Jones and the Last Crusade*, and *Indiana Jones and the Temple of Doom*) makes reference to Indiana's fear of snakes?

Answer: All of them.

CHAPTER NINE

Dollars and Sense

Numismatism is the study and collection of coins and currency, and remains one of the more popular hobbies for both amateurs and high-end dealers. When it comes to the latter, rare and historic currency can generate hefty sales prices, but for many amateur collectors the thrill of the chase is finding a piece of currency that has a tale to tell. On several occasions the History Detectives have had the opportunity to investigate some unique currencies and their profound impact on the societies who created them.

If you happened to find a six-dollar bill, would you know its significance? What about a Mexican peso from the late 1800s? These were the questions posed to detectives Gwen Wright and Elyse Luray, each of whom delved into tricky currency conundrums. The two investigations appeared to be entirely different, but at their core they were inquiries into whether the currency in question was of historical significance to two families and whether it had present-day value—or was worth no more than a penny on the dollar. In this chapter, we also delve into the production of counterfeit currency and the technically advanced processes employed by the U.S. Treasury and the Secret Service to help protect one of the most basic foundations of our economy.

Money Matters

The elaborately crafted paper bills we trade back and forth in this country for goods and services have real value for two very basic reasons. First, the U.S. government says they have value, and second, we believe it. Although national economies often guaranteed the worth of paper currency with precious metals such as gold and silver, for the last several decades the value of paper currency has been accepted on nothing more than faith—and it works. The technical term for this economic system is *fiat* currency and it's used throughout the world today. The use of paper currency in the Western Hemisphere was first developed in colonial America and is one of the world's oldest.

Beginning in 1690, various American colonies began producing their own paper money, called *bills of credit*, to use for paying internal government expenses and as mortgage loans to citizens who used their own property as collateral. Because the bills technically had value to the government and to landowners for paying taxes, they also came into general use within the issuing colony for private trade and were usually accepted as readily as gold or silver coins.

After writing and producing a pamphlet titled *A Modest Enquiry into the Nature and Necessity of a Paper Currency* in 1729, an enterprising young Philadelphia printer named Benjamin Franklin was awarded a contract for production of Pennsylvania's paper currency. The experience would serve him and the colonies well in later years as he helped engineer the development of a struggling young nation. Of course, as with most objects of value, a host of talented counterfeiters over the centuries have pulled the wool over the eyes of unsuspecting individuals and entire governments.

Gwen Wright with Paulette Hammerstrom and Paulette's daughter, Brooke.

The Curse of the Deceptive Dollar

P eople can make extraordinary discoveries in the most unlikely places, and this was certainly the case when Omaha, Nebraska, residents Paulette Hammerstrom and her daughter Brooke were going through one of Paulette's husband's old books. Tucked between the pages they found an intricately designed six-dollar bill dated February 17, 1776, a bill that was apparently produced by the "United Colonies." Intrigued and baffled, they called upon Gwen Wright to help them learn the origins of the curious note.

Examining the faded bill, Brooke and Gwen could see elements of its intricate design strewn with imagery, including a beaver gnawing a palmetto tree, with pyramids in the background. Gwen realized that the beginning of the Revolutionary War in 1775 had posed a significant challenge for the fledgling, cash-poor colonial Continental Congress. The only way to finance an all-out battle with Great Britain was to create and authorize the printing of paper currency that would be accepted throughout the colonies. In order to determine if the six-dollar bill was genuine, Gwen enlisted the help of professional currency authenticator Glen Jorde in New York.

According to Jorde, the paper stock the bill was printed on was true to the paper produced in the 1700s, and the ink and printing processes also appeared to be correct for the period. But Jorde had one unforeseen concern. Soon after the revolt broke out, the British made a serious

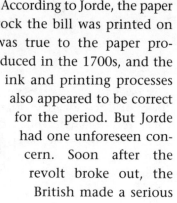

Paulette Hammerstrom's American six-dollar bill, circa 1776, issued by the Continental Congress.

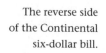

The reverse side of the Continental six-dollar bill.

An illustration of renowned American inventor and statesman Benjamin Franklin, circa 1847.

effort to negate the value of Continental Currency by producing counterfeit bills in enormous quantities. He pointed Gwen to a newspaper account from the 1770s in which the British offered travelers to the colonies as much fake currency as they wanted, for the express purpose of undermining the value of colonial bills.

Fortunately for the colonial government, they had an invaluable ally in Benjamin Franklin and his unique experience in the design and production of currency. Franklin developed several methods to assure merchants of the legitimacy of the fledgling government's currency. He captured the impressions of tiny leaves onto metal stamps that were imprinted onto every bill, using a different leaf type for each denomination. Since the pattern of the veins is slightly different on every leaf, other people could not duplicate them. On the six-dollar bill one of the signature images was a buttercup leaf. Franklin also added crushed mica to the paper. This shiny silicate mineral not only added substance and resiliency to the notes, it also produced a noticeable sparkle. Fortunately, these crucial elements were all intact on the Hammerstrom's bill and Glen Jorde was certain that it was the genuine article.

One intriguing detail on the six-dollar bill that was of particular interest to Gwen was the inscription which read: "This Bill entitles the Bearer to receive Six Spanish Milled Dollars, or the Value thereof in Gold or Silver, according to a resolution of Congress passed at Philadelphia February 17th, 1776." So how much gold and silver did the new government have in its reserve? The answer came as a shock. Researching the bill

DID YOU know

Symbolism was an important factor in the creation of Benjamin Franklin's Continental Currency, and he often incorporated imagery to convey the triumph of the meek over the mighty. The six-dollar bill's depiction of an industrious beaver gnawing down a venerable palmetto struck a responsive nerve in the patriots' resolve. As a result, the image was painted onto the battle flag of the Second Regiment of the Continental Light Dragoons, which was captured by the British and sold at auction in 2006 (see chapter 10).

at the New York Public Library, she discovered that the Continental Congress passed a resolution in June of 1775 to issue currency backed by two million Spanish dollars to finance the American Revolution. By the end of the war with Britain, Congress had gone back to the table several times and issued a total of $245 million worth of currency—all of it supposedly backed by Spanish silver dollars that simply didn't exist.

Given this economic instability, it's not surprising that the value of the currency continually eroded over the course of the war. With a tale of fiscal intrigue, Gwen once again visited Paulette and Brooke to reveal her findings. When the Hammerstroms' genuine six-dollar bill was printed in 1776, that six dollars would have been a soldier's wages for a month. By the end of the war just a few years later, it wasn't enough to purchase a pound of butter.

This phenomenon was actually anticipated by Congress and Benjamin Franklin to be to the nation's ultimate advantage. As the bills depreciated in value, the government would owe less on the debts. Many years later, Franklin described the process as the equivalent of an involuntary tax on the population. The longer people held on to a given note, the less it would be worth to them. The real beneficiary was the new government of the United States. Franklin's intricate bill design and its underlying significance was a powerful message to the rest of the world that the new nation was sticking to its principles and permanently declaring its independence. One of the words printed on the bill was the Latin word *Perseverando*, which means "by perseverance," and by all accounts that motto served America well.

A close-up of the iconic symbol of the beaver gnawing down the palmetto tree on the six-dollar bill.

Not Fit to Print

In the worldwide marketplace, items of value such as watches, purses, jewelry, musical recordings, and electronic software are often counterfeited by underground crime syndicates and terrorist groups who pass forgeries off to an unsuspecting public for huge profits. The counterfeit article that most concerns national security and the safety of the economy is counterfeit currency. The U.S. Treasury has played a cat-and-mouse game with counterfeiters by producing bills that are extraordinarily difficult to duplicate. For every addition to the technology of manufacturing nonreproducible notes, there are dedicated criminal attempts

time TEASER

In what year did George Washington's image first appear on the one-dollar bill?

Answer: 1869.

to sidestep the technical difficulties by printing an undetectable fake. Fortunately for the vast majority of us who work hard for our genuine dollars, the federal government is prepared to go to every extreme to stop counterfeiters in their tracks, but they've got their hands full with the challenge.

One of the primary problems in combating counterfeit currency is the ubiquitous little timesaver sitting right on our desktops—the personal computer. Digitally produced counterfeit bills have overtaken every other technically demanding form of production, such as offset printing, which requires a great deal of expertise and expensive equipment. According to the Secret Service, an estimated amount of counterfeit bills in excess of $60 million entered circulation by the end of September 2006, and approximately 50 percent of that was produced digitally.

Because digital technology is readily available to anyone with a scanner, desktop computer, printer, and a few hundred dollars' worth of software, high-tech counterfeiting has experienced a huge shift from being a highly specialized art form to becoming the dedicated focus of small-time crooks. To put the counterfeit statistics into context, the Secret Service estimates that only about 0.03 percent of the total bills in circulation are fakes. Regardless, the amount is growing as a result of home computers, with the number of bogus bills more than doubling in the past ten years.

DID YOU know

The counterfeit U.S. currency that's the most worrisome to the Secret Service are so-called *Supernotes*, which are near-perfect duplicates of genuine currency. They're produced on specially manufactured paper with the same printing process used by the U.S. Treasury, and only high-tech equipment can consistently detect them as fakes. Foreign governments are suspected to be involved, with much attention focusing on North Korea. Don't worry about what's currently in your wallet, though. Most Supernotes are thought to be in circulation overseas.

THE NOT-SO-SECRET SERVICE

Many people are familiar with the most visible role of the Secret Service. After all, who hasn't seen those menacing guys sporting dark suits and sunglasses who have little wires and communication devices plugged into their ears and who keep watch whenever the president is out and about? Although the protection of major political figures is taken very seriously, the primary function of the Secret Service is the prevention and investigation of the counterfeiting of U.S. currency.

Established in 1865, the Secret Service is the oldest of the national investigative law enforcement agencies. In March 2003, it was shifted from the Treasury Department and is now under the wing of the Department

Making a Buck

Continental Currency notes are some of the most well crafted bills in existence, and they're one of the few Revolutionary War era collectibles that remain within the means of the novice hobbyist. In today's market it's still possible to purchase very fine bills for $200 to $300. Although many counterfeits exist, period fakes also maintain collectible value.

The bills were initially issued in 1776 in denominations ranging from one-sixth of a dollar to eight dollars. Inflation eventually took its toll on the value of Continental Currency, and bills were produced in ever-increasing denominations. The final Continental Congress issue of the eighty-dollar bill in 1779 signaled the demise of confidence in

An eighty-dollar bill issued in 1779. At left, the reverse side of the bill.

paper currency, and by the early 1780s, it took well over $100 in Continental Currency to obtain one dollar in specie, or metal coinage. In the end, Congress did eventually make good on the value of Continental Currency—to a degree. The bills were redeemed at a hundredth of their value in bonds that didn't mature until 1811, giving the new United States a pretty good bang for its buck. The U.S. government would not return to the use of official paper currency until 1862, a decision triggered by the financial burdens of the Civil War.

For an in-depth review of Continental Currency, including superbly detailed images of various issues, visit the Coin and Currency Collections Web site of the Department of Special Collections, University of Notre Dame Libraries at http://www.coins.nd.edu/.

Two Secret Service agents on duty, circa 1908, in Oyster Bay, New York, at the home of President Theodore Roosevelt. Roosevelt was the first president to be guarded by the Secret Service.

of Homeland Security. Because counterfeiting now falls under the category of terrorist activity, the shift has given the Secret Service unprecedented authority and latitude for investigating counterfeiting operations at any level. As for the specifics of that authority, the Secret Service is decidedly tight-lipped.

Much of the Secret Service's activity in putting a dent in counterfeiting involves educating the general public and training professional money handlers to detect fraudulent currency. Digitally produced fakes are generally much easier to identify than bills produced by highly skilled counterfeiting rings, given that the majority of computer-generated currency is of mediocre quality. Genuine notes are invariably highly detailed in manners that home printers can't duplicate, and the paper stock is specialized and unavailable to the public. Ultimately, it's the easy availability of cheap computer equipment that's contributing to the sheer volume of bad bills that are usually passed off to unwary recipients who are unfamiliar with the real thing.

The threat of computer-generated counterfeits in the early 1980s triggered a manufacturing change in 1993 that introduced an embedded polyester security thread in currency paper. Running vertically and printed with the denomination of the note, the security thread is visible only by holding the bill up to a light source. Another tactic is the technique of microprinting "THE UNITED STATES OF AMERICA" around the edge of currency portraits. The wording can be seen clearly only with magnification and is virtually impossible to reproduce on office copiers or printers.

In 1996, another copier and printer reproduction impossibility was added to the mix in the form of a watermark of each bill's portrait, along with optically variable ink used in the number on the lower right-hand corner that changes color from green to black when viewed at different angles. Yet another counterfeit trap was set by desktop printer manufacturers who incorporated a

time
TEASER What was the highest denomination of bank note produced by the U.S. government?

Answer: The discontinued $10,000 bill featuring an image of Chief Justice Salmon Chase.

unique code that allows any copies made on their machines to be traced back to a specific piece of equipment. Many new high-end digital printers also contain built-in software that will disable the machine if certain design elements are detected during copying. Who says Big Brother isn't watching?

THE ART OF FAKERY

Criminally minded craftspeople have haunted the production of genuine currency since the very inception of money as a valuable commodity. Before the computer age, men were traditionally trained in the dirty and tedious printing industry, so it's no mystery that males are historically linked to counterfeiting. In the digital era, however, computerized fakery is unquestionably gender neutral, and a sampling of state records shows that roughly one-third of counterfeiting and forgery arrests are female.

Although men are usually the culprits in most things criminal, the art of counterfeiting in the distant past lured a handful of talented but unscrupulous ladies toward the economic dark side, and while some paid for their offenses with their lives, others got off without a hitch.

It's difficult to imagine that a conviction for counterfeiting could result in one of the most hideous executions imaginable, but in the 1700s, Great Britain treated counterfeiting, or *coining*, as high treason against the Crown, and dealt with lawbreakers in the harshest possible manner. Ironically, as Gwen revealed in her investigation of the six-dollar bill, the British had no problem counterfeiting currency to be passed around in the American colonies, but that obviously didn't extend to their own citizenry. British men were given the comparatively "civil" death sentence of being dragged to the gallows behind a horse and hanged by the neck, but women were executed by a combination of strangulation and burning.

A counterfeit fifty-dollar note printed circa 1778. One of the indicators that the bill is a fake is the missing comma after the word "Philadelphia." Several penned "X's" were added over the emblem to cancel this detected fake.

Between 1702 and 1734, eight women were convicted of coining and suffered the ghastly consequences. Toward the end of the century, three more women committed the crime of coining, but by this time public horror and the disgust of the executioners themselves were shifting Parliamentary sentiments. The last woman strangled and burned in England was Catherine Murphy, who was put to death on March 18, 1789. The spectacle provoked an editorial by the *Times* of London that read: "The execution of a woman for coining on Wednesday morning, reflects a scandal upon the law and was not only inhuman, but shamefully indelicate and shocking." The practice was abolished the following year, and female coiners were subsequently executed in the same manner as their male counterparts.

One of the many styles of Confederate currency from the Civil War.

The Confederacy's Sour Note

On the eve of the Civil War in April, 1861, the Confederate States of America made a bold attempt to follow in their forefathers' financial footsteps by issuing their own paper currency. Notes were created in denominations from ten cents to $1,000 and initially brought high value for private trade in the South.

The Confederacy didn't pretend to back the notes with silver or gold, instead relying completely on the faith of the populace. Over the course of the war, they produced almost $2 billion worth of notes, and by the end of the conflict, Confederate currency was virtually worthless the moment it was printed.

After the war, the value of the South's monetary bills was declared invalid and reduced to zero. In today's collectible marketplace, rare denominations can fetch up to $30,000, while more common printings sell in the neighborhood of fifty dollars.

There's Something about Mary . . .

Paper currency in the colonies was still a relatively novel commodity in 1716 when Puritan wife and mother Mary Butterworth decided to make her own handmade copies. She was born into a prosperous Massachusetts family and married to a successful home builder, and the origin of her criminal counterfeiting tendencies remains a mystery, but by all accounts she was very good at it and turned the process into a family cottage industry. Utilizing an ingenious method of transferring ink from genuine currency onto a starched sheet of muslin cloth, Butterworth developed a technique for ironing the image onto a blank piece of paper. With fine quill pens, she added detail to the image and created notes that were virtually indistinguishable from the original.

After seven years of producing and passing fake notes, the family counterfeiting ring had increased to at least a dozen co-conspirators when suspicions became too obvious for colonial authorities to ignore. Butterworth's innovative cloth transfer system, however, permitted easy disposal of evidence into the kitchen fireplace, leaving no trace evidence save for quills and ink containers. It wasn't until fellow ring member Nicholas Campe caved under intense questioning that the fiscal femme fatale was finally arrested for suspicion of counterfeiting on August 15, 1723, and charges against the group were presented to a grand jury. Tightlipped to the end, the family confessed nothing, and with no credible evidence of wrongdoing all charges were summarily dropped. Apparently impervious to karma, Mary Butterworth returned to the quiet life of a Puritan housewife and died peacefully at the age of eighty-nine.

time TEASER

During the Civil War the public hoarded coins, which created a shortage. What was the government's response?

Answer: It printed paper currency in denominations of three, five, ten, twenty-five, and fifty cents.

An Inconvenient Adversary

For most American citizens of Mexican ancestry, the term "revolution" conjures imagery that has nothing to do with the colonial war with Great Britain in the 1700s. Mexico has in fact been involved in two major revolutions, the first of which gained the country's independence from Spain in 1821. The second revolution, the Revolución Mexicana, began on November 20, 1910, when Francisco Madero issued a call to arms and the country became engulfed in an internal revolution that ended the dictatorship of

Despotic Mexican president Porfirio Diaz. At right, his political adversary, Francisco Madero.

Porfirio Diaz and pitted bitterly opposing political and armed factions against one another for seven years, until the enactment of the Constitution of Mexico finally brought major hostilities to an end. The bloody conflict cost the lives of nearly two million Mexicans, but it brought about major reforms that ended rampant exploitation of peasant farmers and mandated the reallocation of land back to the populace.

Leading up to the revolution in Mexico, Porfirio Diaz had ruled as Mexico's president since 1876 and was noted for bringing industrialization and encouraging the construction of dams, roads, and factories in the country in a process that increased the wealth of the relatively few members of the affluent classes, while alienating the vast majority of poor working farmers. Diaz also instituted land-holding policies that took land away from farmers who didn't own clear title to their property. In a country where peasant farmers lived and farmed the same land for many generations without the benefit of papered ownership, the co-opting of their ancestral land created enormous resentment among the hundreds of thousands who suffered as a result. During his first term in office, Diaz established a constitutional policy of no re-election, which was designed to keep presidents from serving consecutive terms in order to prevent corruption in the government or create a dictatorship rule.

After his first term, Diaz indeed stepped down and essentially turned the presidency over to Manuel Gonzalez, a handpicked puppet and political crony, who wasted no time filling high political offices with his own cohorts. His presidential tenure was a mess of corruption and self-interest that included draining the national treasury. Diaz ran for election the following year and easily won. From that point on, Diaz ignored the constitutional policy and ran for consecutive terms until the revolution in 1910, and his use of the Mexican Army and hordes of thugs ensured easy victories by bullying and threatening voters at the polls. Diaz also consistently rigged the polling process, further

time
TEASER What is the average lifespan of a $100 bill?

Answer: Eighty-nine months.

establishing himself as a president who would never be voted out of office.

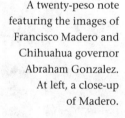

What saved the population from greater tyranny under Diaz was an inconvenient adversary named Francisco Madero, who was one of the few affluent politicians who actively opposed Porfirio Diaz's stranglehold on power and had enough public support to represent a real threat to his reelection in 1910. Up to that point, Diaz's political adversaries had been weak and were easily swept aside with fixed elections, but Madero's growing popularity with the poor majority made the appearance of an uncontested election unlikely. Madero capitalized on the unconstitutional nature of Diaz's many reelections and became known as the "Apostle of Democracy" among the poorer classes. Diaz responded to the threat by arresting Madero and 5,000 supporters, who were jailed on trumped-up charges.

A twenty-peso note featuring the images of Francisco Madero and Chihuahua governor Abraham Gonzalez. At left, a close-up of Madero.

Madero was placed under limited house arrest and permitted daily horseback rides, but on October 4, 1910, he managed to evade his guards and rode across the border to Texas. Once in San Antonio, he made quick plans to instigate a revolution against the despotic Diaz and called for an armed revolt on November 10 that quickly spread throughout Mexico.

Tens of thousands of determined Mexicans responded to Francisco Madero's call for revolution.

Diaz's regime ended on May 25, 1911, with his pressured resignation, after which Madero was elected into the presidency. Continued political upheavals, however, ended Madero's political career in February of 1913 when he was forced to resign his presidency. He was assassinated four days after leaving office, and the Revolution raged on for another chaotic four years.

The Case of the Peculiar Pesos

I f there's a single theme of revolutions of any nature, it's the willing-ness to bring about change at any cost, and if there's one common requirement for every successful revolt, it's financing. Millions of pesos were printed during the Mexican Revolution, and many of those were printed in the politically neutral United States. Russell Hill is the third-generation owner of Clarke Printing Company in San Antonio, and according to his family legend, Clarke Printing, which started doing business in 1874 as Maverick-Clarke Litho Company, had something to do with the printing of Mexican currency during the Revolution. Hill contacted *History Detectives* to help him solve the mystery of Maverick-Clarke's rela-tionship with the revolutionaries, and Elyse Luray jumped at the chance to resolve the peso pandemonium.

The Maverick-Clarke Litho Company in San Antonio, Texas, during the 1940s.

Meeting with Russell Hill in San Antonio, Elyse discovered that all records and printing samples of Maverick-Clarke's early days had long been lost, but Hill was able to direct her to the local Witte Museum, which had peso notes in their collection. At the museum, Elyse inspected a collection of three early Mexican notes in ten-, twenty-, and fifty-peso denominations printed for the State of Chihuahua, but with no known origin. The notes were printed with images of famous revolutionary figures Francisco Madero and the governor of pro-revolu-tionary Chihuahua, Abraham Gonzalez.

From historian Dr. Gilberto Hinojosa, Elyse discovered that San Antonio was a hotbed of revolutionary activity and served as a central point for agents from several separate revolutionary factions, including Madero and legendary revolution-ary hero Pancho Villa. Arms and supplies were gathered in the city, deals were made with opposing forces, and strategies were developed. Researching the archives of the *San Antonio Express*, Elyse found an article detailing another of the city's contributions to the Revolution—specific references citing the production of Mexican pesos in San Antonio.

Taking the investigation another step, Elyse visited the University of Texas at Austin to inspect their Latin American collection, and it was there she hit pay dirt. In miscellaneous correspondence in the archives she discovered a Western Union telegram dated October 31, 1914, specifically citing Maverick-Clarke Litho Company and a shipment of currency paper. While the message presented strong evidence

Renowned Mexican revolutionary leader Pancho Villa (third from left) with his compatriots.

that Maverick-Clarke was in the banknote business, it still didn't prove the company had direct ties to the Revolution. On a hunch, she refocused her efforts on the three banknotes owned by the Witte Museum and obtained permission to have them analyzed.

With the trio of Mexican peso notes in hand, Elyse traveled to Massachusetts to meet with renowned currency expert Gene Reid, whose extensive numismatic records proved conclusively that all three notes were printed for revolutionary leader Pancho Villa, and better yet, that the fifty-centavo note was produced by the Maverick-Clarke Litho Company in San Antonio. Armed to the teeth with historical resolution, Elyse shared with Russell Hill all the information she'd learned about the revolutionaries and his family business. She'd also acquired a small collection of peso notes produced by Maverick-Clarke, which she presented to the grateful proprietor of the Texas printing company that had played a fiscal role in the greatest cultural and social revolution Mexico ever experienced.

A fifty-centavo note investigated by *History Detectives.*

DIY DETECTIVE

When pondering the activities of your local Boy Scout troop, you tend to envision hiking, camping, and performing good deeds, but what you probably can't picture is one surprising Scout merit badge that is awarded for learning the basics of coin study and collecting, or *numismatism*.

One of the world's most popular leisure hobbies, the so-called hobby of kings developed popularity in fifteenth-century Europe when nobility began active collections by hiring agents to seek out desired examples of rare coins.

Although the collection of coins as a pastime was a bizarre concept to the poor majority of the population, who cherished coins for the simple purpose of paying day-to-day expenses, the idea eventually drifted down the economic chain as the collectors market grew and some coins gained worth beyond their face value.

Today, coin collecting is wide open to anyone with a little change to spare. Even panhandlers have been known to carefully inspect every handout, searching for rarities that can be peddled to pawnshops and dealers for a little extra cash. Coin collectors usually begin the hobby with coinage they receive in their daily business transactions, sometimes running across the occasional odd

The U.S. Mint 1990 Prestige collection.

specimen. If the collecting bug bites, the next step often becomes the general pursuit of looking for examples of everything available on the market.

Most serious collectors specialize in particular aspects of interest, such as subject collections featuring specific images, period collections, which focus on defined time frames, or composition collections, which center on coins made of particular metals, such as gold, platinum, or silver.

Thematic collections might feature relatively common coins along with particularly rare and elusive objects like the 1933 Double Eagle gold coin, which sold at Sotheby's for $7.59 million in 2002. Close to 500,000 of the twenty-dollar double eagles were made by the Mint in 1933, but only a few survived as a result of Executive Order 6102, which assured they'd all be melted down.

The best way to become a numismatist is to visit a local coin shop or coin show to get a feel for what you'd like to collect. Shows in particular are a terrific source of hands-on information. American coin collectors have adopted a coin grading system called the Sheldon scale, which allows for judgment of coin quality on an exhaustive scale of one to seventy, with seventy being an example of a perfect uncirculated specimen and one representing the worst-case scenario of a barely identifiable coin. A modern addition to the Sheldon scale is a descriptive initial ranging from "P" for poor condition to "MS" for Mint State, meaning that the coin has never been circulated

The value of collectible coins is directly tied to the condition and grading of each sample. Generally, a coin graded at MS 70 on the Sheldon scale is worth many times more than one with a very low rating. While many numismatists gather collections for investment purposes, fluctuations in coin prices and the potential risks of tying up cash in a static collection usually make the practice a questionable investment strategy.

Most numismatists get hooked on the hobby for the challenge of searching out a rarity at bargain prices and for the artistic and aesthetic qualities of creating a highly personal collection. The best part about getting started in coin collecting is that it's as easy as taking a closer look at what's hiding in your piggy bank. For more helpful hints, visit *History Detectives* at www.pbs.org.

CHAPTER TEN
LET FREEDOM RING

Unlike artifacts from the Civil War, artifacts from the American Revolution are relatively rare, so a discovery of a relic from that era generates a lot of excitement and curiosity. As far as brutal conflagrations go, the Revolution was no different than any other war, but it remains a permanent milestone, as it established the most powerful nation on earth. In this chapter, you'll be swept back in time over 200 years to the American Revolution with a trio of mysteries whose outcomes no one could have guessed.

History Detectives Elyse Luray and Tukufu Zuberi had their work cut out for them as they negotiated their way through a conflict rife with bloody battles, propaganda, and an unusual dose of old-fashioned espionage. Is it possible that a Scottish Highlander could have lost a small piece of metallic identification on a scouting expedition during Britain's "Southern Campaign"? How did the British Army lose entire cannons to colonialists pulling off a heist in broad daylight? And what part did a trumpetlike instrument play in the first stages of America's pesky uprising? In typical *History Detectives* style, these seemingly un-related artifacts and historic episodes form pieces of the puzzle that united a fiercely independent population and gave birth to a nation.

The War of Independence

Beginning with the "shot heard round the world," on April 19, 1775, and ending on September 3, 1783, the "little" colonies of America took on the mighty British with all the force they could muster, and until the bitter end, no one could have predicted the outcome—especially an American win. The end of the war is particularly fascinating: the English news media has a historically unabashed obsession with chronicling the unvarnished truth, and the British public got an eyeful of it when they read the details of one of the worst military defeats in Great Britain's history. The event kept British journalists hopping, as recriminations, investigations, and resolutions flew through Parliament and the entire United Kingdom. Through it all, one thing was obvious to England's hardcore newshounds and their readers: Britain's celebrated military had surrendered to an upstart army and world history had just taken an irreversible twist.

The event that sent those shockwaves through Great Britain occurred during the Revolution in October of 1781, when General Charles Cornwallis, the British governor and military commander in the colonies, was forced to surrender to the combined forces of the French and Colonial armies after a severe trouncing in Yorktown. After a dozen years in office, British prime minister Lord Frederick North was on the ropes. Parliament gathered in February of 1782, four months after the Yorktown debacle, to debate the merits of a resolution that would discontinue the war effort against the rebellious American colonies, with disastrous results for Lord North's administration. After North lost his composure during a heated exchange and then made a feeble apology, his fate was virtually sealed, and in March of 1782 the prime minister resigned his office after the first Parliamentary vote of no confidence in British history. The following year, the final peace treaty was

John Turnbull's renowned 1797 painting depicting the surrender of British general Charles Cornwallis at Yorktown, Virginia, an event marking the end of the American Revolution.

signed in Paris between Parliamentary representatives of King George III and America's John Jay, John Adams, and Benjamin Franklin. The fledgling United States of America had stretched its wings and survived its harrowing fight for freedom, and in doing so, participants of the conflict left a few historic gems in their wake, several of which were prime targets for *History Detectives*.

The Mystery in the Muck

A Revolutionary War badge found by Darryl Boyd and investigated by *History Detectives*. At right, a detailed rendering of the badge.

Over the centuries, countless artifacts of this crucial era have been lost to the ravages of time, and for most of us, the viewing of pristine Revolutionary War artifacts is usually confined to museum outings and exhibitions. For a very few, the occasional tidbit of history can turn up in the most unlikely locations. The Revolutionary War campaigns waged by British troops are most often identified with the northern colonies, but the English military and political strategists of the late 1770s became convinced that the southern colonies held the key to victory.

A medallion-like relic from that strategic move was discovered by amateur scuba diver Darryl Boyd on the muddy bottom of the South Carolina side of the Savannah River, which forms most of the border between Georgia and South Carolina. Boyd found his object in 1993 and was convinced that the silver dollar–sized medallion was somehow associated with British troop activity in the area during the Revolutionary War. He was baffled that a British relic would be lost in fifteen feet of water so close to the riverbank of patriot-controlled South Carolina, so History

Detective Elyse Luray was invited into the case to find the answers to this metallurgic mystery.

Upon meeting Boyd, Elyse observed that the relic appeared to be made of copper with a hook on the back and evidence of two more missing hooks, which convinced her that the object was most likely a type of badge. On the face were the raised images of a crown and thistle, with two Latin inscriptions around the bor-

Elyse Luray meeting with Darryl Boyd on the banks of the Savannah River where Boyd discovered the badge.

ders, and a clear image of the number 71. Initially, she was puzzled. How could a nearly pristine concave copper British relic be sitting in plain view at the bottom of a major river for over 200 years?

To fully grasp the strategic maneuvering of the American Revolution, one must understand the military mind-set of the mid- to late eighteenth century. For starters, the armed insurrection in the American colonies was nothing unusual for England. With a vast empire that had a presence on nearly every continent, the British were accustomed to occasional irritating rebellions, and to quashing them with virtually invincible military power. From 1775 to 1778, the Brits concentrated on crushing rebel forces in the major cities and ports of New York, Philadelphia, and Boston. So confident were English generals that they were known to have placed bets with each other as to who would be the first to crush the rebellion and how quickly they'd do it.

At the outset of the conflict, even the Revolution's Continental Congress recognized that a good two-thirds of America's inhabitants were skeptical of the revolt and supportive of Great Britain's dominion. Although English troops and naval fleets effectively put a stranglehold on major colonial trade centers when hostilities began, those centers were economically reliant on the products of the vast majority of colonists who lived and worked in the wide outlying regions. As British war efforts moved into the backwoods of the colonies, the war became infinitely more complicated. Military blunders and much-publicized atrocities by English forces continually swayed public sentiment toward the goals of the revolutionists.

A major victory at Saratoga in the New York colony by the Continental Army in 1777 convinced a growing number of colonists that the struggle for independence was becoming a feasible reality. The subsequent alliance of France with the American revolutionists in February of 1778 added considerable fuel to the fire of the effort for colonial freedom, and as a result, the British were forced to re-examine their approaches and options for putting out a rebellious brushfire that was quickly growing into an unmanageable conflagration.

The theory that it was possible to "win the hearts and minds" of local inhabitants by sending in occupying forces is hardly exclusive to the modern political and military mind-set. The British government in the 1770s was crystal clear that the power of the empire depended on the blessings and support of American colonists. Seemingly convinced by the exaggerations of loyalist colonial exiles in London that the southern colonies held the key to loyalist support, King George and his Parliamentary ministers initiated a campaign to disrupt the south. On December 29, 1778, 3,500 British troops sailed into Savannah under the command of Lieutenant Colonel Archibald Campbell and captured the city in a single day with the battle-hardened 71st Highlanders at the forefront of the attack.

From all accounts, Campbell's assault on Savannah was a military masterstroke. The British suffered the loss of one officer and two privates, while the patriot casualties numbered over 450. The attack and the subsequent British garrisoning of Savannah put a chokehold on the Atlantic coastline, and within two weeks the English had routed most of the patriot army from Georgia, chasing them across the Savannah River into South Carolina and placing virtually all of the Georgia colony under British control. The only exception was the patriot-held city of Augusta on the Savannah River. So where does Darryl Boyd's extraordinary underwater treasure hunt fit into this bold military campaign?

time
TEASER What hill was the Battle of Bunker Hill fought on?

Answer: Breed's Hill.

ELEMENTARY, MY DEAR WATSON

The 71st Highlanders were Scotsmen who wore the red bonnets and green tartans of the Highland clans. The Highlanders had a long history of fighting for the Crown and were a vital part of the British forces in the colonies. Many of the lower-ranked officers in the Highland Regiment were in fact Highland clan chieftains. Notorious for their ferocious fighting skills and dedication to the Crown, this group of warriors had garnered a deadly reputation with the patriots, who simultaneously respected and feared them.

Their commander in the southern colonies, Archibald Campbell, was himself a Scotsman whose family ties and military career were firmly entrenched in the Scottish Highlands.

During her examination of Darryl Boyd's relic, Elyse quickly spotted the possible connection between the "71" image on Boyd's badge and the fact that the 71st Highland Regiment was directly involved in the British war effort in Georgia.

In a meeting with Carl Borick, assistant director of the Charleston Museum in

Viscount Kirkwall, captain of the 71st Highland Regiment, circa 1855.

Charleston, South Carolina, Elyse discovered that the museum had a nearly identical badge in its extensive Revolutionary War collection. According to Borick, the piece was an identification badge that was attached to cartridge boxes containing ammunition carried by each soldier in the 71st Highland Regiment. Borick was also able to shed light on the other images embossed on the badge. The thistle is the national flower of Scotland, and the crown is representative of the British monarchy. The first Latin phrase translates to: "Whatever is to be performed or endured;" the other, the intimidating statement "No one assails me with impunity," which is the national motto of Scotland.

There was no question that Boyd's badge was the real deal, but despite determining its authenticity, Elyse was still stymied by its unbelievably good condition. A visit with Jon Leader at the South Carolina Institute of Archaeology and Anthropology solved that part of the mystery. After studying the badge through a stereoscopic microscope, Leader noticed a single spot of sulfide corrosion. In his opinion, the badge fell into the Savannah River and quickly sank into the mud, in an *anaerobic*, or oxygen-starved, environment, keeping it in a state of remarkable preservation over the centuries. But how far did the badge travel in the flowing current before it sank?

Elyse Luray reviewing documents concerning Archibald Campbell with Dr. Edward Cashin of Augusta State University. Below, one of Campbell's journal entries.

RIVER RATS

At the South Carolina Institute, underwater archaeologist Chris Amer explained that the shape and weight of the badge would have quickly taken it to the bottom of the river. Much as the concave shape of an airplane wing forces the wing upward in flight, the concave shape of the badge worked to force the object downward through the river current and into the mud.

With that revelation, Elyse had solved three mysteries surrounding one surprising war relic. The knowledge that the badge sank almost exactly where it went into the water over 200 years ago makes the final mystery much more interesting. How did the badge end up on the side of the river controlled by patriot forces?

Soon after securing Savannah and routing the patriot forces scattered throughout Georgia, Archibald Campbell and his 71st Highlanders marched on the last holdouts in Augusta. In another decisive victory, Campbell seized the patriot-held city and chased the last of the rebel army across the Savannah River. It had been only a month since the 71st Highlanders first set foot on Georgia soil, and Campbell was the first and last British officer to "rend a star and stripe from the rebel flag of Congress." For the British, it appeared that gaining complete military control over one of the thirteen rebellious colonies would be a first important step in turning the tide of the revolution. Campbell issued proclamations to Georgia colonists, requesting oaths to the Crown and offering rewards for the capture of patriots and invitations to join his loyalist regiments. It was presumed that Augusta would become a mecca for loyalists in the colony and that they would soon arrive in droves.

After learning the details of Campbell's amazing feat in the southern colonies from Dr. Edward Cashin of Augusta State University, Elyse gave Darryl Boyd the answer to how the cartridge-case badge found its way so close to the South Carolina shore. Just after Archibald Campbell captured Augusta, he sent scouts across the river to reconnoiter patriot positions in South Carolina. Who better to send on a dangerous mission in enemy-held territory than members of his trusted 71st Highlanders? It's probable that the badge was lost during one of those intelligence missions and sat quietly in the river muck for more than two centuries. There's no way of telling what natural forces stirred the badge from its muddy resting place, but whatever it was, Darryl Boyd just happened to be in the right place at the right time to find it.

The British capture of Augusta triggered a massive movement of southern colonial warriors into the area, but much to Archibald Campbell's dismay, they weren't loyalists flocking to Augusta—they were patriots in South Carolina bent on retaking the city, and their numbers were increasing daily. It's doubtful that Darryl Boyd's 71st Highlander badge was in the water for more than a few days before the British realized that without sufficient reinforcements, Augusta would soon face a numerically superior contingent of patriot troops.

> **DID YOU know**
>
> Fluorescence spectroscopy is an analysis technique that utilizes a beam of light, usually ultraviolet, that excites the electrons in compounds and causes them to emit light of a lower energy. This generated light is compared to readings for known compounds and provides an accurate analysis of the makeup of the test subject within seconds. Any metal composition can be determined through fluorescence spectroscopy.
>
> To analyze paint, a spectrophotometer is used to measure a color sample and obtain reference values. These are compared to known values to arrive at the composition of the sample. A stereomicroscope can then be used to analyze the pigment composition of paint. Metals and metal finishes such as gold leaf can also be identified.

Campbell staged a tactical retreat from Augusta on February 13, just two weeks after taking the city, and soon returned to Savannah. Despite the setback, the British effectively retained military control over the Georgia Colony until the end of the war in 1783. Lieutenant Colonel Archibald Campbell fell ill and relinquished his command just three and a half months after beginning the campaign in the southern colonies. He set sail to recover in London on March 12, 1779, and the British army lost one of its most talented Revolutionary War commanders.

The Southern Strategy provided the British with many of their most profound successes of the Revolutionary War. By the middle of 1780, Charleston, South Carolina, fell to the English, and subsequent British victories throughout the colony virtually destroyed organized patriot military activity in the lower southern colonies. Still, the cost in lives and supplies, as well as the increasing threat of French military intervention, would soon undermine Britain's war strategy. They were winning battles, but they were losing the war. As British forces worked their way into North Carolina and eventually Virginia, they faced increasingly reorganized and resolute patriot forces. By 1781, the British suffered a humiliating and irreparable defeat in an attempt to hold Yorktown, Virginia, and conceded independence to the colonies the following year. The last action between the patriots and the British was a minor skirmish in South Carolina in August of 1782.

The Adventure of the Absconded Artillery

The minor skirmish that concluded revolutionary hostilities was preceded seven years earlier by the far more celebrated first engagement at Concord, in Massachusetts. On April 19, 1775, the British governor and military commander in Boston ordered 800 regular British troops to disarm and arrest suspected rebels in the notoriously anti-British town of Concord. At the North Bridge near Concord, colonial militiamen faced off with the British soldiers, shots were fired, and the Revolutionary War began. By the end of the British retreat back to Boston, 94 colonists and 273 Redcoats were dead, wounded, or missing in action. For Bostonian Kate Barrett, the incident at Concord had a close family connection. Her ancestor Colonel James Barrett was the commander of the militia regiment based in Concord, and according to Barrett's family legend, the reason the British marched on Concord was to retrieve cannons stolen from a Boston armory.

In 2005, the National Park Service unveiled a cannon dating back to the Revolutionary War, and Barrett thought it might be one of the cannons the British were after. History Detective Elyse Luray heard about the controversial cannon and went to Boston to meet with Barrett and ascertain if there really was a connection. Elyse's first step was to take Barrett to

Bell of the Ball

A little-known but important event in post–Civil War Georgia was brought to light by Sandy Fisher of Charlotte, North Carolina, when she approached *History Detectives* with a beautifully crafted pin depicting the Liberty Bell, and her family's story that the piece was allegedly created with metal from the bell itself.

Elyse Luray's investigation revealed that Fisher's great-grandfather, John M. Stratton, was instrumental in bringing the bell, one of the nation's most prized possessions, to Atlanta, Georgia, in 1895, just thirty years after the end of the Civil War. The event was the Cotton States and International Exposition, which was designed to showcase the city of Atlanta as a good location for Northern investments.

The Civil War had created lingering social and economic rifts between the North and the South, and the exposition's developers were intent on establishing that Atlanta had reconciled those differences and was actively seeking to participate in the economic growth of a united country. Placing the Liberty Bell on display was a brilliant public relations strategy, and an estimated 800,000 people visited the exposition. It's uncertain, but possible, that Stratton's pin could have been made from the leftover metal saved when the bell cracked and was repaired, thus keeping intact Fisher's family legend.

Clockwise from top left, Sandy Fisher wearing a pin that once belonged to her great-grandfather, John M. Stratton; the front and back of the pin; a detailed rendering.

see the cannon, which was being stored at the Charlestown Navy Yard, part of the Boston National Historical Park. As Elyse examined the cannon, she noticed an inscription on the barrel which read in part: "possessed by the British Colonies of North American at the commencement of the war on the 19th of April, 1775." On the breech, she noticed what appeared to be a worn seal or emblem. The cannon itself was made of brass, which was much lighter and more maneuverable and durable than the older style iron cannons. The inscription gave Elyse a time frame and starting point for the investigation, but with the worn seal, there wasn't much more to go on.

In a meeting with National Park Ranger Jim Hollister, Elyse discovered some intriguing background information about the motivations that triggered the British march to Concord. It seemed that growing tensions between British authorities and the colonists in Massachusetts in 1774 were pushing colonists toward stockpiling an arsenal of military supplies. Rebels raided armories and forts throughout Massachusetts for weapons and ammunition and funneled much of it to the anti-British militia in Concord. Cannons were exceedingly expensive and difficult to acquire, and most of the militia's cannons were old and unreliable, made of iron, and too heavy to be of real value for a moving army in the field.

In Boston a colonial militia group, the Boston Artillery Company, commanded by Major Adino Paddock, kept four brass cannons in a gun house on Boston Commons. Paddock, a loyalist to the Crown, intended to turn the cannons over to British authorities and kept them under the guard of Redcoat troops. On September 16, 1774, in broad daylight, rebel members of the artillery company slipped into the gun house during a changing of the guard, lifted the cannons from their carriages, and spirited them away to a nearby schoolhouse, where they stashed them in a wood bin. Upon

Above and below, the cannon investigated by *History Detectives* that was allegedly stolen by rebels in 1775.

discovering the theft, a British sergeant reportedly exclaimed: "I'll be damned if these people won't steal the teeth out of your head while you're on guard." Later, the cannons were smuggled to Concord and added to the growing cache of hidden supplies. As it turned out, the cannons were taken to the farm of Colonel James Barrett, Kate Barrett's ancestor and leader of the Concord militia. But did the cannon thefts actually trigger the British march on Concord?

IMPERIAL INDISCRETIONS

During the years leading up to the thefts, the British committed a vast number of intrusions on colonists' rights, and tensions grew from angry grumblings into furious preparations for bloodshed. Would a relatively petty theft bring the most powerful nation in the world to the brink of warfare? The British Army had remained a major part of colonial life since the French and Indian War with France, beginning in 1756 and ending in 1763 with a treaty that ceded Canada and all of North America east of the Mississippi River to Great Britain. Much of the reason British troops remained in the colonies was to protect Britain's newly acquired interests. After the war, the English moved a large part of their scattered army into major port cities, particularly New York and Boston, implementing the Quartering Act in 1765 to give British troops free access to vacant private dwellings and public buildings for use as barracks.

Beginning that same year, a series of unpopular tax acts were also initiated in the colonies to help defray the cost of maintaining an already unwanted military presence. After colonialists strongly, and sometimes violently, protested against arbitrary taxes and vociferously denounced the army's intrusions, the punitive "Coercion Acts" added dry tinder to a growing fire of resentment by allowing British troops to move into any private dwelling in the province of Massachusetts Bay and requiring inhabitants to provide them with food, day-to-day living supplies, and even alcohol.

The Acts also abolished colonial administration of the courts and permitted British authorities to replace locally elected officials with loyalists of their choosing. The "Intolerable Acts," as they were called by colonists, self-destructively served to unite

The inscription on the cannon, which notes that it was "possessed by the British Colonies of North America at the commencement of the war on the 19th of April, 1775."

The Boston Tea Party in 1773 was a Colonial response to British taxation.

the sympathies and hostility of all thirteen colonies against British authority. Massachusetts and particularly Boston, having suffered as the focal point of Britain's heavy-handed pressure, also became the nucleus of rebel activity and preparation.

Dissident colonists, who became known collectively as the Sons of Liberty after a comment by one of the few colonial supporters in Parliament, began forming into an organized and closely knit brotherhood. In the outlying communities of Boston, one of which was the small town of Concord, the revolutionaries stored the arms of full-blown rebellion. Because General Thomas Gage was instrumental in implementing British penalties in the colonies, the British administration felt he was best suited to quell the growing crisis. London named him Royal Governor of the province of Massachusetts Bay in May of 1774, replacing the colonial governor and essentially making Gage the commander in chief of British forces. Although his own officers thought he treated the colonists too leniently, Gage became one of the most hated British figures in Boston.

CANNONBALL RUN

After General Gage seized stockpiled colonial gunpowder in Somerville, Massachusetts, in September of his first year as Governor, his orders and troop movements fell under the constant scrutiny of the Sons of Liberty. Even before Gage decided to make his move on the colonial stockpiles in Concord, the intelligence network of the Sons of Liberty spread the word that the British were coming—weeks in advance of the actual march. As a result, members of the revolutionary militia redistributed the stockpiled arsenal long before the British regiment left Boston for Concord.

In order to determine Gage's motives for moving on Concord, Elyse visited the Massachusetts Historical Society, a treasure trove of Revolutionary War documents, where she found correspondence between Gage and his staff. Secret intelligence written in French from a spy in Worcester, Massachusetts—another known colonial arms arsenal—revealed that "the brass cannons which were once in Mr. Paddock's hands never got here and are probably presently in Concord."

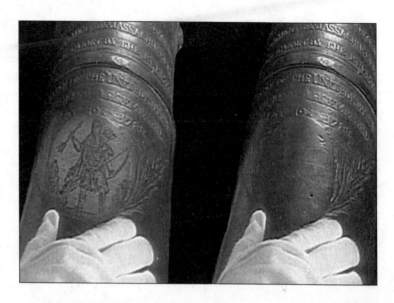

Two images of the cannon at the Charlestown Navy Yard. At left, a juxtaposed image of the Massachusetts coat of arms shows how the seal would have appeared.

In the same archive, Elyse found a draft of Gage's orders to his troop commanders describing the stockpiled supplies for which they would be searching. At the top of the list were four brass cannons, but those orders were just a draft. The final marching orders moved the cannons down the list, beneath ammunition and supplies. Regardless, there's no question that Gage knew the stolen cannons were at Concord—and he wanted them back. Elyse found another clue in an archived copy of the *Boston Gazette* from 1768, which described the arrival of "two beautiful brass field pieces" from London on the merchant ship *Brigantine Abigail*. The newspaper also described the cannons as having the seal of the Massachusetts coat of arms on the breech and being destined for the Boston militia—Major Paddock's artillery unit.

Although the seal on the cannon at the Navy Yard was almost completely worn away, Elyse soon discovered that the matching fieldpiece was on display at the Bunker Hill Monument in Boston. After taking measurements and making comparisons of the two cannons, there was no question that these were the cannons stolen from the Boston Artillery Company. Kate Barrett's ancestor, Colonel James Barrett, was in possession of the stolen cannons at his farm in Concord before hiding them away prior to the arrival of Gage's troops. Colonel Barrett was in command of the rebel militia when the first shots of the Revolutionary War were fired, and those cannons were part and parcel of one of the most famous days in U.S. history.

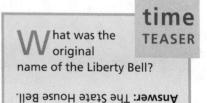

time TEASER

What was the original name of the Liberty Bell?

Answer: The State House Bell.

The Legend of the Row Galley Trumpet

Over the years, *History Detectives* has investigated a number of artifacts that people have found at garage sales and fairs, and some of them, like a women's suffrage painting (see chapter 1) and a letter written by Abraham Lincoln (see chapter 4), turned out to be unbelievable discoveries. Howard Szmolko is one of those individuals: he approached *History Detectives* with an interesting metal object that he thought might have played—quite literally—a part in the Revolutionary War.

He first saw the unusual piece under a table at an antiques fair, and it intrigued him enough that he purchased it. But in order to establish its potential historic significance he needed help, so Elyse Luray and Tukufu Zuberi traveled to Bucks County, Pennsylvania, to examine the artifact firsthand. What the detectives saw was a trumpet-shaped instrument bearing a partial inscription that read: "This trumpet was used in the Revolutionary War in a Row Galley between West Point and Fort Washington." Also inscribed was a name: "Captain Lewis."

Although the widest end, or *bell*, and the general shape of the trumpet were quite similar to a modern trumpet, the tube ran straight from the bell to a telescoping mouthpiece that extended the length of the instrument, close to three feet. Was it really an instrument? And who was Captain Lewis? With a potentially rare object on their hands, Elyse and Tukufu embarked on a high-tech investigation that would produce several startling conclusions. While Tukufu checked on the meaning of the inscriptions, Elyse took the trumpet to musicologist Professor Daniel Abraham at American University in Washington, D.C. According to Abraham, the trumpet didn't match the construction of a musical instrument, as there was no valve assembly, and the width of the mouthpiece and tube didn't permit the backpressure of air needed to produce a musical tone.

The telescoping speaking trumpet investigated by *History Detectives* in its short and extended configurations.

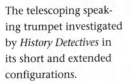

Read All About It!

One of the most important tools for polarizing colonial sentiment during the Revolutionary War years was the newspaper. Although the British were highly adept at spreading propaganda, they came nowhere near the inspirational brilliance of America's revolutionary forefathers for getting their views into print.

On the eve of the Revolutionary War, there were just over twenty newspapers being published in the thirteen colonies, most of them in Massachusetts and New York. By war's end, there were forty-three papers in print. America's first multi-page newspaper appeared in print on September 25, 1690, in Boston, ninety years prior to the bid for independence. Titled *Publick Occurrences, both Forreign and Domestick*, the three-page newspaper lasted for a single edition. Miffed by the printed insinuations of incest among the French royal family—and especially by the fact that the paper was published without legal authority—the Governor promptly shut it down, and all available copies were gathered and destroyed. The Governor and Council of the Massachusetts Bay colony issued a proclamation four days after the first edition was published, denouncing *Publick Occurrences* by name and forbidding the production of "anything without License first obtained from those that are or shall be appointed by the Government to grant the same."

It would be another fourteen years before a continuously published newspaper would see print in the colonies. The *Boston News-Letter*, published by politically well-connected Boston postmaster John Campbell, produced its first edition on April 24, 1704. Ownership of the paper stayed in the Campbell family for seventy-two years; the paper finally closed its staunchly pro-British editorial doors in the face of overwhelming public scorn when British troops evacuated Boston in 1776.

For Abraham, there were only two possible purposes for the instrument—it was either an ear trumpet for listening or a speaking trumpet for projecting the human voice. Based on his knowledge, the obvious conclusion was that the trumpet was used as a speaking aid, or type of megaphone. To check that out, Elyse met with Navy Museum curator Ed Furgol, and while he'd only seen a dozen examples of a speaking trumpet, he knew exactly what this one was—a custom-built speaking trumpet for directing crew activity on board a sailing vessel.

The next stop for Tukufu was the Library of Congress in Washington. While researching row galleys, he learned that the vessels were triple-masted sailing ships with openings cut into the sides to accommodate

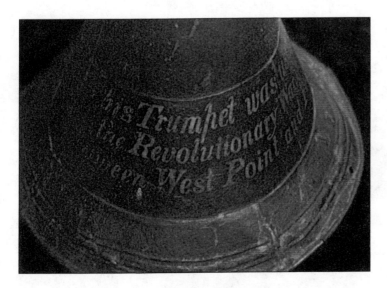

The inscription on the speaking trumpet.

oars, making the craft highly maneuverable with or without cooperative breezes. The vessels were over seventy feet in length with a twenty-foot beam, and were very heavily armed with two eighteen-pound cannons, two twelve-pounders, and two four-pound pieces. Without a doubt, the row galley was a formidable opponent against virtually any enemy warship. Tukufu also found a letter from Continental Army generals to General George Washington stating that the purpose of the row galleys was to provide firepower and protection as part of a huge blockade on the Hudson River.

Additional documents proved that three galleys were built and commissioned to protect iron cables and chain that stretched across the banks of the Hudson to form a barrier against British warships. Further research turned up a muster roll for the row galley *Lady Washington*, and first on the list of her crew was Captain Abraham Lewis. As it turned out, Lewis was assigned to *Lady Washington* on June 27, 1777, ten days after the British began a campaign southward from Canada that would bring them into the Hudson River. What Tukufu found was concrete evidence that connected Captain Lewis to a Continental Navy row galley.

At the Smithsonian Institute, Elyse anxiously awaited results of a battery of specialized forensic tests performed on the trumpet. Analyst Carol Grissom took minute scrapings from the trumpet's metal and the paint from the inscription for elemental analysis in a scanning electron microscope. The high-tech instrumentation performed an analysis of the molecular structures of the trumpet materials, proving the trumpet to be constructed of iron and the paint composed of red lead. Both were indicative of Revolutionary

A popular and evocative image during the American Revolution, this appeal for colonists to unite is thought to have been designed by Benjamin Franklin during the French and Indian War, which ended in 1763.

JOIN, or DIE.

DIY DETECTIVE

One of the primary resources for serious historical research, *archives* provide access to records created for an individual, families, or organizations. In the United States, the National Archives is the leading institution for acquiring that source material. With the mission of preserving and making accessible a vast collection of information, the National Archives is essentially the nation's record keeper, with thirty-three locations throughout the country.

The primary difference between archives and libraries is that archives contain original records, while libraries contain published books and periodicals. Because of the original and therefore irreplaceable nature of archive material, direct access is closely monitored and controlled, but for those with specific interests, archives are an indispensable source of information.

Fortunately, the National Archives has embraced the computer age and opened the door to much of their research on the Internet. The best and easiest way to explore the holdings of the National Archives and how to access them is by visiting their Web site at www.archives.gov. Another online innovation for the National Archives is a pilot program launched in 2006 in cooperation with the Internet search giant Google that has made hundreds of digitized videos available to the public. That site can be accessed at http://video.google.com/nara.html.

Many other organizations, such as museums and historical societies, contain archival material specific to a region or time period, and provide glimpses of their holdings via the Internet. The Massachusetts Historical Society, for instance, has a fascinating online catalog describing an enormous amount of material covering much of the Revolutionary War era. Just as the History Detectives do, you'll find that the Internet can provide an immense amount of information for those with the tenacity and presence of mind to sift the wheat from the chaff. Bear in mind that anyone with a little technical savvy can create pages on the Internet, and information should be viewed with more caution than published material.

Here are a few questions to ask yourself about Internet information: Does the information present a balanced point of view or is it emotionally slanted? Is the content updated? Is the Web site part of a permanent organization? Does the appearance of the site reflect professional production, and has the content been edited for typos and grammatical errors? Can you verify the information through other sources?

If your answers to these questions are positive, you can feel somewhat secure that the information is reasonably accurate. Still, it's important to verify all of your data by researching similar Web sites to compare and weigh the information you're seeing. Sound Internet research requires a lot of practice and patience, but with a solid dose of skepticism and common sense, you'll be amazed at just how much information is available right at your fingertips.

Tukufu Zuberi testing out Howard Szmolko's speaking trumpet.

War–era construction. To complete the scientific scrutiny of the trumpet, the Smithsonian also took x-rays, which indicated the irregularities of hand-hammered construction and even evidence of a minor modern repair. The results of the Smithsonian tests revealed that the speaking trumpet was authentic to the mid-1700s.

Tukufu's subsequent research filled in the final chapter in the known history of Captain Lewis, his fighting ship the *Lady Washington*, and the speaking trumpet he used to command her. In October 1777, as the British sailed up the Hudson with overwhelming firepower, Captain Lewis and his crew rescued retreating American forces under withering barrages and took them to safety. Lewis continued to defend the Hudson until 1778 and then disappeared from record. For Howard Szmolko, the speaking trumpet belonging to Captain Lewis is a truly historical and extremely rare prize that continues to carry the echoes of a young nation in conflict.

DID YOU **know**

When Sotheby's announced the impending auction of Tarleton's Revolutionary War battle flags, a number of historical groups in the United States attempted to raise the funds needed to bring the flags home. The final selling price was millions more than even Sotheby's anticipated, and the historically priceless relics went to a telephone bidder who remains anonymous to this day.

Flying High

While most of the physical remnants of the Revolutionary War have been lost to history and the ravages of time, amazing antiquities still come onto the open market on occasion. The most notable of those relics usually sell for tens of thousands of dollars, although obscure examples, such as a battered land-grant document signed by Revolutionary-era notable John Hancock can sometimes be found for less than $1,000. On June 6, 2006, Sotheby's auction house in New York sold four battle flags flown by the Continental Army during the Revolutionary War for an astonishing total of over $17 million. Just one of those flags, flown by the Second Regiment of the

Continental Light Dragoons, accounted for $12 million of the total sale price. Among the very few remaining Revolutionary War–era flags still in existence, the four flags were captured by the cavalry unit of Lieutenant Colonel Banastre Tarleton, who was celebrated in Great Britain after the Revolution as a national war hero.

In America, Tarleton was one of the most notorious and despised field officers to ever face the Continental Army. Three of the auctioned flags were captured after a bitter and controversial loss by American forces at the Battle of Waxhaws in South Carolina. Tarleton's Seventeenth Light Dragoons had pursued the Third Virginia Detachment commanded by Colonel Abraham Buford for over a hundred miles when they caught up with them on May 29, 1780. Tarleton's force of 270 was outnumbered by the Third Virginia unit, but the mounted British held a distinct advantage over the foot soldiers of the Third Virginia. It's known that Tarleton offered Buford the opportunity to surrender before the battle took place—an offer that was promptly dismissed. Tarleton responded by leading a headlong cavalry charge that resulted in the massacre of over a hundred of Buford's men, with 150 more seriously wounded. The British reported just nineteen casualties.

English accounts indicate that patriot forces attempted to surrender and many were in the process of laying down their arms when Tarleton's horse was shot from under him. Believing the surrender to be a ruse and that Tarleton was murdered, the British fell on the patriots and cut them to pieces. American survivors of the battle concurrently insisted that the "shot horse" story was bogus and that Tarleton, infuriated by Buford's initial refusal to surrender, had no intention of offering quarter again.

The incident at Waxhaws, coupled with a variety of other anecdotal horrors committed by Tarleton during his years in

The flag of the Second Regiment of the Continental Light Dragoons captured by Colonel Banastre Tarleton in 1779.

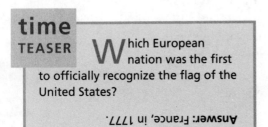

time
TEASER

Which European nation was the first to officially recognize the flag of the United States?

Answer: France, in 1777.

America, served in many ways to reinforce colonial hatred of Britain's authority, and it very likely became a deciding factor in swaying the opinions of colonists who were ambivalent in their loyalties. The year after Waxhaws, General Cornwallis surrendered at Yorktown, and the Revolutionary War was over. Banastre Tarleton returned to England with his four captive battle flags and passed them down through succeeding generations until they were finally sold at Sotheby's in 2006.

CHAPTER ELEVEN

Family Ties

In our lifetime there's but one thing that takes precedence over everything else in our busy existence—family. They keep us grounded, whole, and uniquely individual amid a world filled with personal and professional motivations, affected by unforeseen events, tragedies, and joyous occasions. Many of the mysteries that *History Detectives* has explored offer very personal sagas of men, women, and children who want nothing more than to understand and feel a closer connection to their ancestors, no matter how many generations separate them. Their joy in learning new information about a family member—regardless of the outcome of their investigation—is what makes every foray a rewarding experience.

Three investigations that particularly tugged at the heartstrings took us back to post-Revolutionary Canada, a notorious detention center in the San Francisco Bay, and Kansas City during the 1960s. For everyone involved, the investigations proved deeply emotional, as their outcomes were unique and entirely unforeseen. No words can pay homage to the emotions investigators and participants endured, but perhaps in the telling, their stories bring life and hope to families the world over.

The Mystery of the Unwed Mother

Throughout the course of our lives, each of us has experienced defining moments. For Dodie Jacobi of Kansas City, Missouri, two such moments proved to be life-changing occurrences. *History Detectives* has explored dozens of fascinating investigations involving genealogy, but in the history of the series, Jacobi's mystery stands alone in regard to the nature of the answers she was seeking. In a dramatic turn for the show, Jacobi wanted to know where she was born and hoped to find her birth family. This emotional investigation took Gwen Wright back to her own youth in the 1950s and 1960s, an era when the ignominy of being pregnant and unmarried forced many women to give their babies up for adoption. Dodie Jacobi was one of those children.

Born in 1961 in the vicinity of Kansas City, Jacobi was never told the names of her birth parents or where she was adopted from, and it was a mystery whose time had come due. Like something out of a classic film, the linchpin of the investigation was a tiny medal that was pinned to Jacobi's diaper when her adoptive parents came to collect her. It's the Medal of the Immaculate Conception, and Jacobi cherishes it as the only clue to her first days on earth and even wore it for over a decade until its gold plating began showing wear.

The search for her birth family was not a decision Jacobi took lightly. Chosen by loving parents who also adopted three other children, she didn't develop an interest in finding her birth parents until she was in her late twenties. As a testament to her strength of character and unwillingness to cause any pain to the loving adoptive parents she adored, Jacobi didn't pursue a search until they had passed on. Of particular interest to Gwen was what Jacobi's mother told her about the day she was adopted in 1961. Her mother described a ceremony in a beautiful chapel with a huge, colorful stained-glass window. With the morning sun streaming through the window, a trio of nuns—one of whom was holding the infant girl—were clad in blue velvet robes and standing before the altar. The tiny medal was pinned to her diaper.

Kansas City native Dodie Jacobi enlisted the help of *History Detectives* to find her birth mother. At right, Jacobi when she was approximately six months old.

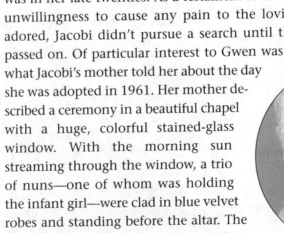

Dodie Jacobi with her adoptive parents, Bob and June, and brother Bobby shortly after her adoption in 1961.

Jacobi's parents were brought before the nuns at the altar, after which one of the nuns said: "Here is your gift from God" and introduced the proud parents to their new daughter.

FOOTLOOSE AND FANCY-FREE

With Jacobi's baby medal in hand, and the intriguing prospect of helping a woman learn the circumstances of her birth, Gwen began her investigation by taking a closer look at the medal itself and the pamphlet that had accompanied it. On the face of the tiny medal is a haloed woman and the phrase: "Mary conceived without sin. Pray for us who have recourse to thee." According to the pamphlet, the original concept of the Medal of the Immaculate Conception was revealed to a novice nun named Sister Catherine Labouré on an evening in July 1830, after she was awakened by a small child thought to be her guardian angel, who

Dodie Jacobi (far right) with her three adopted siblings, Bobby, Wick, and Mindy, during the late 1960s.

The tiny miraculous medal pinned to Dodie Jacobi's diaper when she was adopted in 1961.

summoned her to the chapel at the community of the Daughters of Charity in Paris. There she was greeted by a vision of the Virgin Mary, who told her that she had been chosen for a mission.

Over the course of several months and visitations, Sister Catherine's vision instructed her to create a medal, with the aid of her priest confessor, that would grant holy blessings to anyone who wore it with trust and faith. After initial hesitation, the priest ordered the medals to be made and distributed to the faithful, and the graces they received were deemed miraculous. For over forty years Sister Catherine quietly went about her duties and remained silent about her involvement with the creation of the Medal of the Immaculate Conception, finally revealing the truth after receiving another vision to do so shortly before her death in 1876. In 1933, Catherine Labouré was exhumed, and reinterred in a glass coffin. She remains on display in a Paris church where she allegedly experienced one of her visions of the Virgin Mary. Sister Catherine was canonized in 1947 by Pope Pius XII, who called her the "saint of silence."

To find out more about adoptions in Missouri in the 1960s, Gwen met with historian Dr. E. Wayne Carp at the former Union Station in Kansas City, Missouri, where he explained that thousands of childless couples arrived from across the country to adopt children after the baby-boom years following World War II. Since abortion was illegal and single mothers faced the stigma of bearing children out of wedlock, thousands of pregnant young women went to Missouri to give birth and give their babies up for adoption. Missouri was one a handful of states where adoption was unregulated, and Kansas City became a national destination for unwed

The pamphlet accompanying Dodie Jacobi's baby medallion, describing the story of St. Catherine Labouré.

mothers and hopeful couples who could adopt newborns with relative ease. Dozens of commercial homes known as "baby mills" offered secrecy in the process of birthing and quick adoptions, but several Catholic charities began offering similar services with more selfless hopes of redeeming and spiritually supporting young mothers while providing new babies with good homes.

A close-up of the pamphlet accompanying Dodie Jacobi's medal.

Dr. Carp also explained that Jacobi's search for her birth parents could prove difficult because birth records were legally sealed, and in many states birth certificates are even now altered to substitute the names of adoptive parents. Undaunted, Gwen researched the task and learned that a court-appointed researcher could be hired to look into Jacobi's records. Gwen contacted researcher Sandy Sperazzo, who herself had given up a child for adoption years earlier and felt a calling to the work of connecting children with their birth parents. Sperazzo explained that once Jacobi filed a formal request to contact her parents, Sperazzo could personally contact them and ask if they were interested in meeting. If they agreed, a court order would permit Jacobi to make first contact. When asked if she would like to proceed, Jacobi replied enthusiastically and emphatically, "Yes!"

IMMACULATE CONCEPTION

Dodie Jacobi had no guarantees that the search would provide her with a direct link to her birth parents, so Gwen continued the investigation by searching the library for information on the Daughters of Charity, discovering that the religious order was dedicated to working among the poor and sick, and had long been involved in hospitals, prisons, and caring for abandoned children. Could they be the same nuns who pinned the Medal of the Immaculate Conception to Jacobi's diaper?

time TEASER

In 2006, a woman in Barcelona became the world's oldest mother by giving birth to twins. How old was she?

Answer: Sixty-seven. The previous record holder was sixty-six.

Top, St. Anthony's Home for Infants, circa 1950. Above, Gwen Wright and Dodie Jacobi standing in front of the same building in 2005.

Taking a break from her investigation, Gwen met with an excited Jacobi, who shared with her the tantalizing information she had received from the court about her birth mother. Although identifying details were omitted in the report, Jacobi learned that her mother was just fifteen years of age when she gave birth. Other tidbits included a brief description of her mother as being 5' 6" tall and weighing 120 pounds, with blond hair and a "cheerful disposition," traits obviously handed down to her daughter. Even more intriguing was the fact that Jacobi's mother had a passion for horseback riding—an avid interest Jacobi also possesses.

Before Gwen's investigation, Jacobi believed that her mother stayed at a maternity home prior to giving birth, but the court report indicated she'd only been seen twice by doctors before delivering. Since all maternity homes required weekly medical examinations for residents, she had probably not stayed in such a home. Moreover, the girl's mother was with her at the birth, and her parents had given her the final choice, supportive of any decision she made. Given cultural attitudes during the early 1960s, it became clear that Jacobi's birth family was willing to stand up against the norm. Despite the new information, however, the intriguing report failed to solve the mystery of exactly which home Jacobi was born in and who her mother was.

Gwen continued the investigation by searching the local library for maternity homes run by the Daughters of Charity in Kansas City during 1961, the year of Jacobi's birth, and discovered St. Anthony's Home for

Finding Your Roots

Few people have done for genealogy what Pulitzer Prize–winning author Alex Haley did with his investigation into his family history, which began in 1767, when his ancestor Kunte Kinte was captured in Gambia, Africa, as a teenager and enslaved in Annapolis, Maryland. Kinte's life as well as his successive generations is, of course, the basis of the award-winning *Roots: The Saga of an American Family*.

Haley's 1976 book made history in January of 1977 when it was adapted into an incredible twelve-hour television miniseries seen by over a hundred million viewers. *Roots* reinvented television with its innovative format and remains one of the highest-rated programs of all time. Haley's passionate storytelling coupled with the tenacity of his genealogical research triggered worldwide interest in not only African American genealogy, but the origins of all races and cultures. Many became instantly motivated to trace their familial roots. The willingness of Haley, the father of this genealogical renaissance, to share his family history resulted in a wide range of resources being made available to a public inspired by names like Kunte Kinte, Binta, Kizzy, and Chicken George.

A young Alex Haley when serving in the U.S. Coast Guard.

Infants run by the Sisters of Charity, which suggested a possible link to the Daughters of Charity. After talking with archivist and researcher Laura Long, Gwen was able to put the final piece of the puzzle together. She then met with Jacobi at St. Anthony's to share the good news. Now a drug rehabilitation center, St. Anthony's Home for Infants was indeed where the Sisters of Charity pinned the Medal of the Immaculate Conception onto the diaper of newborn Dodie Jacobi. Gwen also revealed that when Jacobi was born, her grandmother was at her mother's side.

In the end, the tiny medal was the key to learning about the conditions of Jacobi's birth, but it wasn't just Gwen who provided a revelation during the emotional meeting. Dodie Jacobi had exciting news of her own. While Gwen was immersed in her investigation, court researcher Sandy Sperazzo contacted Jacobi to give her the amazing news that her birth mother happily agreed to reunite with the child she had given to a wonderful family so many years ago.

The *History Detectives* episode featuring Dodie Jacobi first aired in 2005. Shortly after the program was filmed, Jacobi did indeed meet with her birth mother and family. From Jacobi's perspective, it's difficult to describe that first meeting, given the complexity and sheer emotion of the situation. In what can best be characterized as a case of "like mother, like daughter," both Jacobi and her birth mother brought to their first meeting a homemade family photo album as a surprise gift. The albums proved to be the perfect icebreaker, initiating conversation and setting the stage for what has become true friendship between Jacobi and her birth family, sharing laughter, holidays, and a mutual love of horses. Most importantly, the experience has given Jacobi a new and valuable perspective on life. In her own words: "The mirror remains the best metaphor for this experience. In looking at my birth family and my adoptive family, I am finding the most important acquaintance I sought—a greater understanding of myself."

Kindred Spirits

By our very nature, we humans are intensely curious, especially when it comes to our individual history. Those of us who are fortunate enough to know our grandparents and even great-grandparents are given the priceless gift of personal history—one that cannot be understated. What we can learn from our close relatives is a vast amount of information about our ancestors, including their names and professions, where they came from, how they lived, and what kind of people they were. During the course of the show, each of our dedicated History Detectives has faced a wide range of genealogical conundrums that posed significant challenges. For Dodie Jacobi, the outcome of her mystery is extreme in the sense that it physically reunited an adoptive mother and child. For Hanno Shippen Smith, the resolution to his mystery was different but no less endearing. Gwen Wright and Elyse Luray's investigation of a golf club owned by Smith shed light on the amazing career and personal life of his grandfather John Shippen, who in 1896 became the first African American to play golf in the U.S. Open.

One of Tukufu Zuberi's mysteries proved to be a poignant experience for brothers George and Joe Rutledge, who wanted to know if their uncle, Tom

time
TEASER Who played the role of Kunte Kinte's grandmother Nya Boto in the 1977 miniseries *Roots*, for which she received an Emmy nomination for Best Supporting Actress?

Answer: Poet and scholar Maya Angelou.

Rutledge, built the engine for Charles Lindbergh's historic *Spirit of St. Louis*, in which "Lucky Lindy" made the first transatlantic flight in May 1927. The fact that Tom Rutledge, who was twenty-four at the time, was indeed the builder of the plane's engine was an emotional revelation to his nephews, one that gave them enormous pride and a strong sense of legacy. Such was the case with another unique pair of *History Detectives* investigations that transported us to two very different eras, when war and prejudice permeated U.S. society, leaving a permanent scar on several nations and future generations.

The exterior of the Angel Island detainment building.

On Angels' Wings

Like many individuals whose ancestors are immigrants, Oakland, California, resident Kathleen Wong was searching for answers about her family and how they came to the United States. But this was no ordinary tale of immigration and ultimate liberty, for Wong's ancestors, like many other Chinese immigrants of the early twentieth century, were detained on an island in the San Francisco Bay, in an immigration station seemingly lost

The bleak interior where detainees were confined.

Unsigned poems written on the walls by immigrants detained on Angel Island. Below and opposite at top right, close-ups of the lettering.

to the winds of time. What remains of their experiences are several outbuildings and scores of heart-wrenching poems carved into the walls of what were once the barracks of Angel Island. Kathleen Wong wanted to know if her grandfather, Wong "Doong" Kay, and great-grandfather, whose name she didn't know, had been confined on the island, and if any of the poems could be attributed to them.

For History Detectives Wes Cowan and Gwen Wright the investigation would prove both challenging and highly emotional, given the plight of the immigrants and the inherent difficulty in the ongoing deciphering of hundreds of unsigned poems. The name Angel Island itself is somewhat of a misnomer, as from 1910 to 1940 during its stint as a detainment and processing station for an estimated 175,000 to 200,000 individuals, it was anything but heavenly.

Unlike the immigrants at New York's Ellis Island, who were typically processed within several hours, Angel Island detainees, including individuals from China, Russia, Australia, New Zealand, Canada, Japan, Korea, the Philippines, Mexico, and India, endured horrible travails while awaiting word as to whether they were approved for admission into the United States or would be immediately deported to their home country. Incarceration would last for days, weeks, months, and even years if they chose to appeal their rejection. Conditions on the island were deplorable, with detainees suffering overcrowding, harsh interrogations, degrading medical exams, and facilities segregated by race and gender. One deciphered poem paints a grim picture of the incarceration: "The insects chirp outside the four walls. The inmates often sigh. Thinking of affairs back home, unconscious tears wet my lapel." And so it was on the island, as detainees endured the misery of the government's heavy-handed treatment.

Angel Island was originally named Isla de Los Angeles, meaning Island of the Angels, by Spanish naval lieutenant

Juan Manuel de Ayala, who on August 5, 1775, sailed his ship the *San Carlos* into San Francisco Bay. It's said that he and his crew were the first Europeans to sail into the bay. The island's sordid past remained secret largely because most detainees refused to speak about their time spent at the station or denied it altogether for fear of future reprisals at the hands of the U.S. government. It was only because of renewed interest in ethnic awareness and cultural heritage during the late 1960s and early 1970s that the story of Angel Island began to unfold.

Much like the internment of the Japanese in the 1940s, incarceration on the island was the result of prejudice and fear, only this time it wasn't due to war. In the 1850s, Chinese immigrants flooded to the States hoping in vain to make their fortunes in California's Gold Rush, but instead they became a strong, inexpensive work force, building the Transcontinental Railroad, clearing land, building levees, and working as farm laborers. An economic depression during the 1870s, brought on by business overexpansion, resulted in widespread antagonism against Chinese American laborers, a malevolence that reached its crescendo with the Chinese Exclusion Act. With the approval of the 47th Congress, President Chester Arthur signed the act in 1882, effectively barring almost all immigration from China and setting further restrictions on Chinese immigrants already in the United States.

Though it was to expire after a decade, the act was extended in 1892 as the Geary Act, which for the most part would remain in place until President Franklin D. Roosevelt's administration, when all exclusion acts were repealed and quotas were established, primarily because China joined the Allied forces during World War II. While foreign-born Chinese were allowed to become naturalized citizens, only 105 Chinese immigrants were allowed entrance each year. It wasn't until 1965 that the influence of the civil rights movement resulted in Congress passing the Immigration and Nationality Act, which again allowed Chinese immigration. For individuals incarcerated at Angel Island, however, progressive thought and actions would come much too late.

The search for information about Kathleen Wong's patrilineal heritage sent Gwen and Wes in two different directions. At Angel Island, Wes

Chinese immigrants arriving at the immigration station at Angel Island circa 1931.

A typical interview conducted at the Angel Island detainment center.

joined up with a group of Chinese language scholars who were working on deciphering the poems inscribed on the barrack walls. At that time over 175 had been transcribed, the words baring the haunting and emotional turmoil and frustration felt by the detainees. "America has power, but not justice," says one poem. "In prison, we were victimized as if we were guilty. Given no opportunity to explain, it was really brutal. I bow my head in reflection but there is nothing I can do." For Wes, the powerful sentiment was a sad reminder of a dark stain on U.S. history, which stands in sharp contrast to the divine hope of Chinese immigrants brave enough to depart their homeland in search of a better life in the so-called land of liberty. Sadly, most of the poems are unsigned, which made it impossible to verify that Kathleen's ancestors wrote any of the verses as yet translated.

To begin her part of the investigation, Gwen visited Kathleen's aunts and uncles to see if anyone had additional information about her grandfather or great-grandfather. As it turned out, their parents hadn't shared much regarding their past, but Kathleen's aunt, Phyllis Wong, mentioned to Gwen that on her brother's birth certificate Kathleen's grandfather was listed as Wong Song Kay, an alternative of the Chinese version of Wong "Doong" Kay which Kathleen provided. Phyllis also mentioned that in

DID YOU know

If you're looking for one of your ancestors who may have passed through Angel Island, your first stop should be the Web site for the National Archives and Records Administration (NARA) for the Pacific region, which you can access at www.archives.gov/pacific/san-francisco/index.html. You can also visit the San Bruno archives, but be sure to call 650-238-3501 to make an appointment to do research. What will greatly assist you in your search is any information you have on a particular individual, including his or her full name and approximate date of arrival at the station. Further early immigration records can be accessed and downloaded at http://casefiles.berkeley.edu. In 1997, the Angel Island Immigration Station was declared a National Historic Landmark; it is open for tours during its preservation process.

Wong Song Kay
(left) and his father,
Wong Tsue. Below,
their descendant,
Kathleen Wong.

the spring of 1924, Wong and his wife sailed to the United States on what she vaguely remembered was the *Abraham Lincoln*.

With that lead, Gwen embarked on a search at the National Archives in San Bruno, just south of San Francisco, where immigration records can be accessed by researchers and family members. A passenger list for the SS *President Lincoln* from July of 1924 not only confirmed that Wong Song Kay was on board, but it gave his identification number, which Gwen used to access his file. That particular trip wasn't his first, as he most likely was already a citizen and had returned to China to bring his wife back to the States.

In looking back through his records, Gwen learned that at age eighteen, Wong, who was born on October 29, 1902, first sailed on the SS *Nanking*, and arrived on Angel Island on September 18, 1920. As a matter of luck, he spent a mere twelve days as a detainee and was approved for entrance to the United States on September 29. To determine the name and status of Kathleen's grandfather, Gwen dug deeper and finally came up with a name and picture of Wong Tsue, who arrived on the island June 21, 1915. Sadly, he was not as fortunate as his son, for on July 27, his bid for entrance was denied. For the next few months, Wong Tsue awaited the outcome of his appeal, but that was never to occur. On October 12, he passed away as a result of heart disease, and his body was shipped back to China.

Much of what is now known about Angel Island is gathered from governmental documents, archives, oral histories of detainees and their descendants, and, of course, the hauntingly beautiful poems. During the Second World

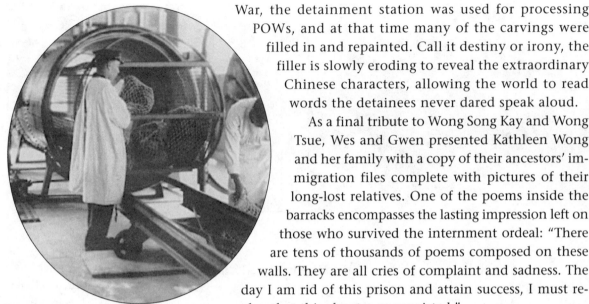

Immigrants work to disinfect clothing in the Angel Island laundry facility circa 1931.

War, the detainment station was used for processing POWs, and at that time many of the carvings were filled in and repainted. Call it destiny or irony, the filler is slowly eroding to reveal the extraordinary Chinese characters, allowing the world to read words the detainees never dared speak aloud.

As a final tribute to Wong Song Kay and Wong Tsue, Wes and Gwen presented Kathleen Wong and her family with a copy of their ancestors' immigration files complete with pictures of their long-lost relatives. One of the poems inside the barracks encompasses the lasting impression left on those who survived the internment ordeal: "There are tens of thousands of poems composed on these walls. They are all cries of complaint and sadness. The day I am rid of this prison and attain success, I must remember that this chapter once existed."

THE STRANGE CASE OF DUNHAM BAY

For many of us, the process of generating a family tree requires years of patience and research that doesn't always yield complete results. College dean Dr. Kristin Bruno of Northridge, California, is one of the lucky few who has a family member who generated a familial lineage. Left to her by her great-aunt is a family tree that Bruno found very intriguing, particularly the label under the names of several of her ancestors that indicated they were United Empire Loyalists. As most of us learned early in our education, the American Revolution was a war of independence fought to gain liberty from the British Crown. A fact that isn't as widely known is that many Americans actually took up arms for the British. They were called *loyalists*, and though they had a variety of reasons for defending Britain, most supported the traditional dominance of the British Crown and feared the instability that a new and unproven government would bring to their own prosperity.

Taking up arms for Kristin Bruno's cause was Tukufu Zuberi, who embarked on an investigation of Bruno's ancestor Daniel Dunham. To first

time
TEASER
Who shot William McKinley, and what disorder did McKinley's wife suffer from?

Answer: Anarchist Leon Czolgosz shot the president, whose wife, Ida McKinley, suffered from epilepsy.

The Ghostly Guard

On September 14, 1901, the United States lost its twenty-fifth president, William McKinley, to an assassin's bullet. McKinley's body was permanently moved to the McKinley National Memorial in Canton, Ohio, in 1907, but for the first six years it remained in a receiving vault guarded by the Army.

Over a century later, Shawn Kennedy asked History Detective Wes Cowan to investigate a forty-five-star flag that according to his family history was once draped over McKinley's casket. Even more mysterious was the additional story that Charles Kennedy, Shawn's great-grandfather, was one of McKinley's body-guards. The family knew very little about Charles, having only a few medals to remember him by; one indicating he was part of Company C of the 14th Infantry and another that he was a sharpshooter.

The flag was proven authentic to the period, but Wes could not say with certainty that it actually draped McKinley's coffin. What he did find was far more important to Shawn Kennedy: his great-grandfather's obituary, which indicated that Company C was the honor guard that stood watch over McKinley's temporary resting place. For over a year, Sergeant Charles Kennedy watched over McKinley as a sexton, and Wes found a photo showing just that. Even more poignant, Wes took Shawn to the McKinley Monument, and, with a view overlooking the monument, he showed

Shawn his great-grandfather's resting place, where he continues to keep watch in death of a fallen president, just as he did in life.

Clockwise from top left, Wes Cowan analyzing Charles Kennedy's flag; Kennedy's 14th Infantry medal; Charles Kennedy; his sharpshooter medal; and, with the McKinley Monument in the background, Shawn Kennedy pays his respects to his great-grandfather.

United Empire
loyalist descendant
Kristin Bruno.

gather background on the loyalists, Tukufu met with loyalist researcher and Revolutionary War reenactor Todd Braisted, who noted that during the war, Britain offered compensation to loyalists in the form of free land. However, because the Americans proved victorious, the British had to look to Canada to make good on their promise. As a result, thousands of so-called United Empire Loyalists were welcomed in Canada, which was still under Crown rule. To this day, descendants of loyalists are allowed to use the initials "U.E." after their names as an honorific.

Tukufu's next endeavor was to research Kristin Bruno's family tree, starting with family patriarch Daniel Dunham, who Tukufu surmised

DIY DETECTIVE

Adding leaves to your family tree can be a long and tedious process. Fortunately, there are a plethora of resources to help you get started and they're not intimidating. By definition, the term *genealogy* is the study of tracing the lineage of one's ancestors. The best place to start is with yourself and your immediate family by making a list of everyone's birthdays, marriages, divorces, children and their birthdays, schools, graduation dates, professions, dates and type of military service, death records, news clippings, photographs, diaries, immigration records—literally anything you can find that will help you in your documentation process.

Once you feel confident that you've gathered enough info, make a list of questions you can ask your parents, grandparents, great-grandparents, and all aunts, uncles, cousins, and close family friends. Oral histories and interviews are an excellent source of information, especially if you hone your interviewing skills by

asking specific questions and carefully writing down, tape recording, or even videotaping your meetings (see chapter 20). No doubt you'll be astounded by what you learn, whether it be a relative's surprising thoughts and perceptions, family folklore, rumors, or even a few black sheep or hidden skeletons. Once you've collected the most information you can from your immediate relatives, the research floodgates will open and you will find an abundance of genealogical options in addition to archives and libraries.

On the Internet, a terrific place to start is www.cyndislist.com, which offers over 260,000 genealogical links to help you track your ancestors, from obituaries to ships and passenger lists. It's an astonishing free reference library that has been in existence for over a decade. Also free of charge is the genealogy site for the Church of Jesus Christ of Latter-day Saints (www.familysearch.org), which in addition to its vast online information offers microfilm and documents at over 3,400 of its Family History Centers worldwide.

was a loyalist, as his progeny had the "U.E." designation on the lineage chart. A crucial clue to Dunham's history is the fact that he was born in New York near Saratoga—the site of one of the Revolution's most critical battles, which raged from September to October of 1777 and was led on the British side by General John Burgoyne. The Brits ultimately took a beating against an overwhelming force of close to 20,000 patriots, registering over a thousand casualties, with the Americans suffering only half that number.

To dig deeper into Dunham's history, Tukufu visited the David Library of the American Revolution in Washington Crossing, Pennsylvania, where

If you're looking for access to business directories, newspapers, historical biographies and a wide range of government records, such as World War I draft registration cards (which give vital information such as age, physical description, citizenship, and next of kin), you might consider joining www.ancestry.com, one of the more popular commercial sites. Both of the latter sites offer searchable census records, as do a host of governmental sites such as www.collectionscanada.ca/genealogy and http://ssdi.genealogy.rootsweb.com, where among other things you can search the Social Security death index for death records.

Joining a genealogical community is yet another option that can help in your research. Sites such as www.rootsweb.com offer a wide range of research tools and focus on connecting their members to one another in the hopes of sharing interests and research techniques and even finding long-lost relatives. Almost everyone involved in the genealogy community is very generous about sharing information and especially helping out newbies. Other online possibilities are special-interest groups.

For example, at www.theshipslist.com you can research ships' passenger lists, or visit www.ellisIsland.org for information about over twenty million European immigrants. Also of interest is www.afrigeneas.com, which walks beginners and pros through slave data, state and international resources, and surname data; www.dar.org, hosted by the Daughters of the American Revolution; and www.jewishgen.org, which features guides, databases, and discussion groups.

In addition, many groups with specific surnames also have sites you can explore, while other sites offer free calendars, charts, and forms to assist you in various stages of research. Exploring your genealogy is a terrific individual or family project, so don't be afraid to dig in, because the fruits of your labor will be rewarded tenfold once your family tree starts to grow and grow.

Otto Knirsch's painting of the surrender of British general John Burgoyne at Saratoga, New York, on October 17, 1777.

he found an archived testimonial from 1786 that confirmed that Dunham served under General Burgoyne at the Battle of Saratoga. Additional information on a compensation claim to the British Crown proved interesting. Dunham, like many other loyalists, lost everything as a result of the war. His loss was deeply personal, as his wife was sent away, his mill and farm were seized, and his animals were stolen by a rebel major. A loyalist to the bitter end, however, Dunham continued fighting and in 1780 provided aid to Canadian scouts.

An 1864 publication revealed that in 1783, Dunham was granted land in St. John, New Brunswick, and like over 50,000 other loyalists, departed the land he fought so hard to maintain. Kristin Bruno's family tree presented a strong showing of Canadians, with Dunham's grandson and great-grandson born in Brockville, Ontario, so at that point it was time for Tukufu to head for the border, where he rowed along the St. Lawrence River with Fred Hayward. As a member of the United Empire Loyalists' Association of Canada, Hayward relayed the hardships loyalists faced when relocating across the St. Lawrence River to their land, which lay in colonial Quebec in uninhabited terrain. These families lived in tents during harsh winters until their new homes could be built.

To determine exactly where the Dunhams relocated, Tukufu met with Brockville historian Myrtle Johnston, an expert in loyalist genealogy, whose records showed that in 1784, Dunham and his family were aboard the first brigade of boats arriving in Canada. She

General John Burgoyne.

further noted that a mill was eventually con-structed by Daniel Dunham's son James, who was also noted on the family tree as being a loyalist. What finally broke the case for Tukufu was yet another family tree shown to him by Myrtle John-ston—one that would prove astonishing to

Tukufu Zuberi and U.E. member Fred Hayward rowing along the St. Lawrence River.

Kristin Bruno, whom he invited to Brockville.

Upon her arrival, Tukufu took her to a stretch of land of over a hundred acres, rimmed by a gorgeous bay. What makes *this* stretch of land so interesting? The scenic body of water is called Dunham Bay, named for the family who literally helped build the area from the ground up. But was that the bottom of the family tree? Not a chance. No Dunhams remain in the area, but one of Kristin Bruno's relatives does—William Hamblen, Bruno's fifth cousin once removed. That Bruno and Hamblen should meet epitomizes the earnest goals of genealogical undertakings and the importance of family ties.

Kristin Bruno meeting her fifth cousin, William Hamblen, at Dunham Bay.

CHAPTER TWELVE
THE QUEST FOR EQUALITY

I n this life, there are many roads to equality and none of them is direct. There have always been and will always continue to be struggles and conflicts to affirm the belief that all men and women are created equal. In truth, global awareness and global equality are a direct reflection of cultural, societal, and, most importantly, individual liberties that in a perfect world would be granted to all human beings. Sadly, that has never been the case, and while strides have been made to effect change, it often comes with a steep price. Methods of resisting unjust actions have varied tremendously over the decades, yet every such attempt has a single thing in common—belief.

In their search for truth behind each investigation, the History Detectives have come across a host of remarkable men and women. For Tukufu Zuberi, three of these individuals displayed an intense courage and belief in themselves that elevated each of them to extraordinary heights of action and awareness during explosive eras. Famed abolitionist John Brown fought for the rights of African Americans, and in doing so passed down to his descendants the ability to continue fighting for their beliefs. You won't recognize the names George Tamura or Groote Manuel, who lived centuries apart and who both endured harsh incarceration, but they, like John Brown, brought about change—whether they knew it or not—as a result of their bravery and belief that the world could and should be a better place.

The Secret of John Brown's Letters

On October 16, 1859, twenty-one determined men in Harper's Ferry, Virginia, raided a federal arsenal in a valiant effort meant to incite a slavery rebellion, and while the fervent raiders were unsuccessful in their attempts, with most being killed or captured, their actions contributed to the start of the Civil War and ultimately, the abolition of slavery. The leader of the attack was renowned abolitionist John Brown, and what set him apart was not just his views about each individual's right to civil liberty and his abhorrence of slavery, but the fact that John Brown was white.

To tell the tale of such a man is to recount a courageous fervor and belief system that resulted in some calling him a hero and others a murderer, since his actions caused the loss of innocent lives. Brown took up a fight he could never win in his lifetime, but his attempts at abolition spoke volumes long after he was hanged for treason for his involvement in Harper's Ferry. At his core, Brown was a deeply religious family man who lived among people of color, and whose twenty children learned that despite life's injustices and hardships, a seamless harmony might one day be achieved if one believes strongly enough in a cause and can find a peaceable means to achieve success.

Over 150 years after Harper's Ferry, Lori Deal was informed by her grandmother that her family may be related to John Brown, a revelation fueled by a cache of personal letters and photographs found in her grandmother's garage. A mystery involving John Brown would prove to be an emotional journey for History Detective Tukufu Zuberi, who counts Brown among his personal

Abolitionist John Brown.

A rendering of the raid on Harper's Ferry in 1859.

heroes. If the letters were proven authentic, they'd be a rare find, offering insight into a family whose progressive and staunch beliefs were far ahead of their time. If there was a link between Deal's family and John Brown, Tukufu was determined to find it.

One of the remarkable letters Tukufu examined was written in 1854 by Brown to his wife, Mary Ann. A very personal missive written from Norfolk, Connecticut, it included a reminder and instructions for their sons on how to care for the family's livestock. Five years after the letter was written, two of those boys would perish while fighting by their father's side at Harper's Ferry. Another letter, dated June 15, 1872, proved even more curious, as it was written to the now-widowed Mary Ann by one of the nation's most renowned abolitionist leaders, Wendell Phillips. In his letter, Phillips included a check for $1,350, with instructions that she was to cash it in the same manner as a previous check. Clearly, members of the abolitionist movement were helping support Brown's family after his death.

Fortunately for Tukufu, on the back of the letter was an important lead—a note that the letter had been given to a woman named Lucy Higgins by Brown's daughter Sarah. What makes the inscription so astonishing is that Lori Deal's great-great-grandmother was Lucy Higgins, an identification that immediately linked Deal's family with John Brown. But Tukufu was puzzled as to why Sarah Brown would have relinquished her father's correspondence, a potentially priceless family heirloom and an important part of history, to Lucy Higgins. Why didn't the letters remain with the Brown descendants?

A Tale of Two Women

Wondering if Lori Deal might indeed be related to John Brown, Tukufu set about establishing a family lineage by making note of all the family surnames he could find. Searching through Deal's genealogy, he came up with six names: Bates, Crabb, Harlow, Slate, Smith, and Higgins, which he then needed to compare to the names in Brown's family tree. Of course, given the fertility of the Brown family, this would prove interesting—between Brown's grandfather, father, and John himself they had a total of sixty offspring. Around 1820, John Brown married Dianthe Lusk, who bore him seven children before succumbing to a fever in 1832. The next year, he married Mary Ann Day and set about adding another thirteen children to his brood. Only half of his children would survive to adulthood, but nonetheless, his descendants total over 1,500.

A compilation of the letters and photographs Lori Deal found in her grandmother's garage.

To research those names, Tukufu paid a visit to Gwendolyn Mayer in Hudson, Ohio, who oversees the John Brown genealogy index. Unfortunately, none of the surnames in Lori Deal's family tree crossed branches with the Brown family. Lucy Higgins and Sarah Brown weren't related to each other, which deepened the mystery significantly. But as it turned out, not all the leaves fell far from the tree.

Sarah Brown (left) and Lori Deal's ancestor Lucy Higgins.

After Brown's death, life became difficult for the Brown family, as they were ostracized by pro-slavers and fell on hard financial times. Mary Ann Brown moved from the East Coast to the northern California town of Red Bluff in 1861, and then three years later to Rohnerville with her son Salmon and daughters Ellen, Annie, and Sarah. In 1881, they relocated

A picture of the woman who is thought to be John Brown's wife, Mary Ann, and two of their daughters.

At left, the Saratoga property Mary Ann Brown transferred to her daughter Sarah in 1882. At right, a census search conducted by Tukufu Zuberi yielded records of Lucy Smith and her marriage to Rufus Higgins.

south to Saratoga, a sleepy town several hours west of Sacramento.

Tukufu's census search at the National Archives San Bruno division showed that a woman by the name of Louise Smith, who was born in Maine in 1818, gave birth to a daughter, Lucy, in Missouri in 1846. Lucy eventually married a real estate agent named Rufus L. Higgins. This was important information, as it showed a possible intersection between the Brown and Higgins families, both of whom moved from the East Coast via the Midwest before arriving in the Saratoga area. Taking his research a step further, Tukufu paid a visit to the Santa Clara County Office of the Clerk-Recorder, where he did a search of properties and land deeds related to both families. An 1882 land deed showed that Mary Ann Brown, who died of cancer in 1884, transferred her Saratoga property to her daughter Sarah, and the deed was recorded at the request of R. L. Higgins. Without a doubt, the two families knew each other, but was that the first time they'd met, and were Sarah and Lucy friends or mere acquaintances?

SINCERELY YOURS

When searching for information about a historical home, a great place to visit is a local historical society or museum. At the Saratoga Historical Foundation, Tukufu learned more about Sarah Brown from April Halbersta, who

characterized Sarah as a very "principled" person who was much like her legendary father. An active Congregationalist who taught Sunday school, Sarah was a natural leader who exhibited her familial propensity toward helping people of other cultures. When a group of Japanese farm workers approached her with an interest in learning about the Bible, she actually taught herself to speak Japanese so she could teach them. By all appearances, Sarah Brown was a well known and revered nineteenth-century woman who practiced what her father preached. But what of Lucy Higgins and her mother, Louise Smith?

At left, Sarah Brown in her later years. Below, a newspaper article amid the box of John Brown's letters shows Sarah Brown and Lucy Higgins together. The article mentions their likely conversation on abolition.

Research at the California State Library in Sacramento yielded a newspaper called the *Grizzly Bear* in which an obituary was listed for Louise Harlow Smith, who was a pioneer of the women's suffrage movement in California. Tukufu surmised that the families were likely to have been brought together by a common belief system that held dear the rights of all races and sexes. That fact was confirmed by an old newspaper article located among John Brown's letters that showed an elderly Sarah Brown and Lucy Higgins having an afternoon chat on a porch. The article noted their likely discussion of the abolitionist movement.

Lucy Higgins ended up with Brown's letters because his daughter Sarah never married and wished to keep his legacy intact after her death in 1916. Lori Deal's letters and photos, passed down from her great-great-grandmother Lucy Higgins, are in fact, the real deal. They are a rare and priceless find, and she can take great pride in knowing that her ancestor did all she could to give American women the right to vote.

Miss Sarah Brown, daughter of John Brown of Harper's Ferry, chats on the porch with her first acquaintance in Santa Clara County, Mrs. Lucy Higgins (on right) of Santa Clara. Their talk undoubtedly included a few comments on "abolition days," a favorite topic of Miss Brown's visitors as late as 1911, when ___ture was taken.

Miss Brown is ___ lived in Saratoga longer ___ other

An illustration of the final moments of John Brown's life just prior to his execution.

DEADLY CONVICTIONS

John Brown was a man of action, who despite his religious ardor came to the conclusion that the only way to abolish slavery was to resort to violence. It was a principle that in many ways resulted in the Civil War. At his trial on November 2, 1959, Brown addressed the court. As part of his final statement, he said: "Now if it is deemed necessary that I should forfeit my life for the furtherance of the ends of justice, and mingle my blood further with the blood of my children and with the blood of millions in this slave country whose rights are disregarded by wicked, cruel, and unjust enactments. I submit; so let it be done!"

Brown was willing to die for what he believed in—the abolition of slavery—and it was a difficult battle to wage. But he held true to his beliefs, meeting with renowned African American abolitionist Frederick Douglass, aiding in the Underground Railroad, giving land to slaves who were on the run, and even raising an African American child as part of his own family. John Brown practiced what he preached and his actions spoke louder than his words, although the bloody result of his fight didn't necessarily justify his violent methods. Writer Henry David Thoreau once said of Brown: "No man in America has ever stood up so persistently and effectively for the dignity of human nature. . . . He could not have been tried by a jury of his peers, because his peers didn't exist."

The Haunting Paintings of the Calamitous Camp

Pretend for a moment that you're standing outside. It's a warm, sunny day and the ground upon which you stand is surrounded by mountains. If you close your eyes and soak in the sun it feels like heaven, but when you open your eyes what you see is a horizon marred by watchtowers, armed guards, and high, barbed-wire fences enclosing wood-and-tar-paper barracks. You're a prisoner, and not because you've committed any crime. You're incarcerated simply because of your race.

Sculpting a Statement

Although the name Wedgwood has been synonymous with fine china since the English company's inception in 1759, few are aware that its founder, Josiah Wedgwood, was an active humanitarian who devoted the last years of his life to the abolition of slavery. In a forthright display of his beliefs in 1787, Wedgwood issued a stone and ceramic medallion that featured the image of a kneeling slave in irons with the inscription: "Am I not a man and a brother?"

Modeled after the seal of the Committee for the Abolition of the Slave Trade, the figure was created in England the same year that a social and political effort began to cease British involvement in the slave trade, and was inspired by outspoken abolitionists in the American colonies.

Wedgwood produced the medallion at his own expense and sent a number of them to Benjamin Franklin in the colonies, who distributed them among his many friends and allies. The medallions quickly became a popular social accessory in England and the colonies and were worn as brooches, hatpins, hairpins, and bracelets. Although the abolitionist movement in Britain was a sensitive issue, political activism and social pressure eventually forced Parliament to end the slave trade in 1838. Josiah Wedgwood's unconventional fashion statement helped pave the way.

Sadly, over 120,000 Japanese and Japanese Americans suffered this fate during World War II, as a paranoid U.S. populace and heavy-handed military herded them into internment camps. It was a travesty born of anti-Japanese sentiment after the attack on Pearl Harbor on December 7, 1941, and as is the case with all human injustices, it seems there's never enough that can be done to make restitution for actions against a targeted sex, race, religion, or genetic disposition.

Over six decades later, Kenji Liu found ten hauntingly poignant watercolor paintings he felt shed light on a very dark period in U.S. history. Liu made the discovery inside an unmarked box when he was working at San Francisco's National Japanese Historical Society. All of the paintings depicted a daunting scenario of obvious imprisonment, a fact that was confirmed when Liu turned the paintings over to look at the back sides. When positioned together, it became clear that the paper used was part of a public internment notice instructing Japanese Americans where to assemble for transportation to an

time
TEASER

Which song is most closely related to Word War II, with lyrics responding to the attack on Pearl Harbor?

Answer: "Praise the Lord and Pass the Ammunition."

internment camp. Realizing the potential historical value of his find, Liu called upon the expertise of History Detective Tukufu Zuberi, who was determined to uncover the secrets behind the paintings and their artist, who signed his name as "Geo Tamura."

A painting by George Tamura of an infamous photo representing anti-Japanese sentiment during World War II.

West Coast Quarantine

On February 19, 1942, with Congressional approval, President Franklin D. Roosevelt signed Executive Order 9066, which gave Secretary of War Henry L. Stimson the broad power to "prescribe military areas in such places and of such extent as he or the appropriate Military Commander may determine, from which any or all persons may be excluded, and with respect to which, the right of any person to enter, remain in, or leave shall be subject to whatever restrictions the Secretary of War or the appropriate Military Commander may impose in his discretion." What resulted were military "zones," primarily in Washington, Oregon, California, and southern Arizona, where individuals from certain ethnic groups were rounded up by the War Relocation Authority and incarcerated. It's estimated that over two-thirds of those Japanese American prisoners were born in the United States, which illustrates that the paranoia of the government was such that it was willing to imprison its own citizens.

The ten major internment camps—located from California to Arkansas— typically included over a dozen cramped barracks, crude latrines, a mess hall, a laundry area, and a recreation building, although nothing about the Japanese incarceration gave rise to recreation. Deemed to be a threat to national security, with the underlying subtext of prejudice and fear, families and individuals who were interned faced physical and financial ruin, most having to relinquish their hard-earned businesses, homes, and

A view of the general quarters of the Japanese internment camp in Arcadia, California, circa 1942.

personal property to the government. Emotionally, the toll was even more dire. Accounts from inside the relocation camps paint a bleak picture of despair, humiliation, cold, hunger, coercion, extreme sorrow, and ultimate betrayal by the U.S. government (see chapter 5).

To begin this haunting journey into the nation's past, Tukufu went to San Francisco's Presidio, which served as the military's predominant western post during World War II. The oldest operational base in the United States, the Presidio was used by the military until 1994 and is now a historic landmark and part of the Golden Gate National Recreational Area.

An internment camp notice instructing Japanese civilians where and when they must report for relocation.

There, Tukufu met with Presidio historian Randy Delehanty to compare the internment camp notice on the back of Tamura's paintings with original notices in the hope of determining which camp the artist had been sent to. Examination of the original public notices showed them to be instructions for Japanese Americans, informing them of the meeting place for their transport to a camp and listing what they were allowed to carry with them.

While Tamura's recycled paper was indeed a public notice, the crucial center section citing where the notice was posted was missing. To learn more, Tukufu made tracks for the University of California–Berkeley's Bancroft Library, which boasts a collection of over 7,000 internment camp photos. Taken during the 1940s by the War Relocation Authority, the images are somewhat deceptive in their attempts to show calm and content among inmates. Comparing Tamura's watercolor paintings to landscapes shown in the archive photos, Tukufu found similarities to the Northern California

A close-up of one of the notices.

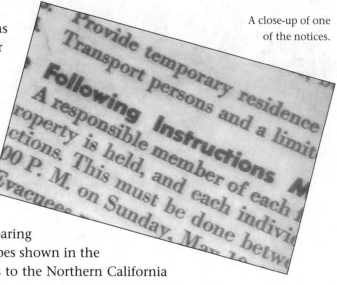

A trio of haunting original images of the Tule Lake internment camp painted by George Tamura.

camp known as Tule Lake, the largest of the internment camps and the one with the highest security. Opened in 1942, the camp was rife with protests and labor issues as a result of overcrowding, shoddy medical care, and horrible sanitation and housing. If "Geo Tamura" was indeed at Tule Lake, his incarceration would have been sheer misery.

WHY THE CAGED BIRD SINGS

To confirm his suspicions that Tamura's paintings had been done at Tule Lake, Tukufu met with anthropologist and internment camp expert Dr. Akemi Kikumura-Yano in Los Angeles at the Japanese American National Museum. What he learned was that Tule Lake initially housed families like any of the other camps, but in 1943 it shifted focus to become a segregation center meant to house dissidents, individuals who wished to be repatriated or expatriated to Japan, or those unfortunate individuals who simply gave the wrong response on a very confusing loyalty questionnaire.

According to Kikumura-Yano, Tule Lake was the most difficult of all the camps, as it was heavily guarded and enforced a strict curfew. She also asserted that it was common for internees to paint pictures during their incarceration as a method of escapism. For Tukufu, there was no escaping the fact that finding "Geo Tamura" in the museum's War Relocation Authority records might be an impossibility. After a lengthy search, he was able to narrow his list down to four possible individuals named George Tamura, one of whom had penned his autobiography. When searching through Tamura's book, entitled *Reflections*, Tukufu encountered a telling passage where Tamura revealed his artistic ability. After a number of phone calls, Tukufu actually found the elusive artist, living peacefully in Sequim, Washington.

In 1942, George Tamura was a mere fifteen years old when he was incarcerated at Tule Lake, just prior to its conversion to a maximum security camp. Upon meeting Tamura in Washington, Tukufu laid out for him the watercolor paintings, which he was able to identify as his own. When asked why he chose not to include people in his paintings, Tamura replied: "I felt that there was simply no place for people to be living there at that time"–an assertion that is, no doubt, a massive understatement. For student Kenji Liu, discovering the internment camp paintings proved to be more than he could ever have dreamed in terms of personal and historical significance.

As a final surprise, Liu traveled to Washington to meet Tamura and was shown several larger paintings that the artist created of Tule Lake, which was closed six months after the end of World War II. For George Tamura, however, the door has never fully closed on his tragic internment, sharing that despite his best efforts, he has never been able to forget his internment number: 27449. In his memoir, Tamura wrote of his first impressions of the prison that would be his home, and his words say it all: "The alien walls of wood and tar paper would then cover the emotions, sorrows, and happiness of the people who lived in them; would conceal the feelings hidden deep inside all of us."

Internment camp survivor George Tamura as a young man, and now.

DID YOU know

Japanese Americans weren't the only victims of Franklin D. Roosevelt's Executive Order 9066. Individuals of German and Italian descent were also singled out. Estimates show that over 5,000 Germans living in the United States at the time—some of whom held naturalized citizenship—were incarcerated and about 11,000 arrested. Those of Italian heritage were also targeted, with more than 3,000 arrests and 300 individuals imprisoned. Over 150,000 Japanese Americans, who made up more than one-third of Hawaii's population, managed to escape the debacle, most likely because of the logistics of relocating them to the mainland. They were, however, still under martial law. Unbelievably, Order 9066 wasn't rescinded until 1976, under Gerald Ford's presidency.

Setting Sail

One of the most remarkable periods in U.S. history encompassed the efforts of Marcus Garvey, who fought for the rights of African Americans in the early 1900s, decades before the emergence of Martin Luther King and Malcolm X. Rachael Clifford of Williamston, North Carolina, discovered a pair of stock certificates signed by Garvey that belonged to her great-grandfather Cornelius Martis. Her story brought History Detectives Tukufu Zuberi and Elyse Luray into a search for the origin of the certificates and their remarkable significance. The certificates, dated 1919, were stock shares in the company Black Star Line, Inc., and showed an investment of $400, a sum that would equal about $5,000 in modern currency.

Garvey moved from Jamaica to New York's Harlem district in 1916, and responded to the prevailing racism and persecution of his people by developing the Universal Negro Improvement Association (UNIA). His message was clear and reverberated throughout the world, demanding equality and encouraging racial pride and self-reliance. The UNIA helped open black-operated businesses throughout Harlem and triggered the largest mass movement in African American history up to that time. One of Garvey's goals was the repatriation of African Americans to an African nation with the aid of the Black Star Line shipping company. Thousands of passionate people responded to Garvey's powerful message and made an investment in his dream.

Sadly, the shipping company ultimately failed through poor business advice and the actions of the U.S. Justice Department, which arrested and convicted Garvey for soliciting funds through the mail in 1922 in what many consider a politically motivated witch hunt. Although Garvey's plans dissolved, his message and determination left an indelible mark on the social fabric of the United States. Garvey died of natural causes in 1940, but his legacy lives on. You can explore much of Marcus Garvey's extraordinary vision at www.marcusgarvey.com.

Clockwise from top left, trailblazer Marcus Garvey; Cornelius Martis; the authentic Black Star Line stock certificate belonging to Martis and now his descendants.

The Peculiar Deed of Groote Manuel

Although most U.S. citizens are familiar with the British colonization of America, we often overlook the significant part the Dutch played and how they viewed the New World in a much different light. Although trade routes to the Indies were well established by the 1600s, the Dutch East Indies Company hired English sea captain Henry Hudson to discover a northern Pacific route in 1609. The journey failed to discover an Indies route, but instead it established a Dutch foothold in what are now the states of New York, New Jersey, Connecticut, and Delaware, in a venture that was based not on colonization and territorial expansion but on monopolizing an emerging and highly lucrative fur trade.

Tukufu Zuberi examining the 1667 land grant now owned by Mark Mitchell. Below, the aged and delicate land grant.

Several Dutch businesses began taking advantage of the new business enterprise, and by 1624 the Dutch had established a settlement of thirty families on Noten Eylant (modern-day Governor's Island, off the southern tip of Manhattan) fulfilling a final obligation of European law that required discovery, charting, and settling before a formal claim could be made. The establishment of the new colony also gave the recently incorporated Dutch West Indies Company an exclusive monopoly on the new territory, which officially became the Province of New Netherland. From the beginning, New Netherland was a company-owned and operated business run for profit, and in 1625 the town of New Amsterdam was established on what is now Manhattan Island as the administrative center of the Dutch West Indies Company.

A year later, the Dutch West Indies Company introduced a disturbing aspect to New Netherland by bringing eleven black slaves into the colony, and as the general population slowly grew, the number of slaves grew with it.

time
TEASER

Which song is most closely related to the U.S. civil rights movement?

Answer: "We Shall Overcome."

It was during this period of company-run colonization and slavery for profit that a surprising land grant deeded to the wife of a deceased former slave would be written, a document that eventually came into the hands of historian and collector Mark Mitchell from Fairfax, Virginia. In the hope of verifying his astonishing find, Mitchell contacted *History Detectives* for help in a quest that would send Tukufu Zuberi on a remarkable journey through uncharted New World territory.

Inspecting the land deed with Mitchell, Tukufu quickly saw the historical significance of the document. Written in 1667, four years after the British had taken control of New Netherland with a show of force that left the Dutch militarily helpless in the New World, the deed recognized the ownership of a significant piece of property on the outskirts of New

DIY DETECTIVE

Although genealogical research has become one of the favorite hobbies of do-it-yourself historians, those with African American heritage face daunting obstacles linked directly to slavery. Before the 1870 U.S. census, slaves were considered property, and few personal records of those held in bondage exist in government archives. Another major problem is the state-enforced illiteracy of slaves, who were denied basic reading and writing skills by law.

Although the 1870 census included African Americans, the literacy issue prevented most freed slaves from spelling their own names, and census takers were free to apply any spelling they chose to the pronunciations they heard. Because of this, variations in spellings from one census to the next don't necessarily negate a family link. It's important to remember that census records are only as good as the data the census taker entered and only as accurate as the person who provided the information.

One of the most important tools for genealogists is oral history. Family and relatives are an invaluable source of information and can provide you with links to other relatives you never knew you had. Building a trusting relationship is vital to speaking with distant relatives who may not entirely understand your motives or who fear that the information you're gathering might be used to hurt them or someone else. Face-to-face meetings are generally much more productive than relying on telephone interviews or written

Amsterdam by a deceased freed slave named Groote Manuel in 1644 and legally passed all rights to his wife, Christina. With Mitchell's permission, Tukufu took the deed to African Americana appraiser Wyatt Day of Nyack, New York, for authentication. After determining that the document was written with seventeenth-century iron gall ink on period handmade, watermarked paper, Day confirmed that the land deed was genuine. At the New York State Library in Albany, Tukufu traced the exact location of Groote Manuel's property, discovering that at one time it was farmland. Today, the property is in the heart of Greenwich Village. So, how did a slave in 1644 New Amsterdam come to win his freedom and actually own a piece of property?

Meeting Dr. Charles Gehring, director of the New Netherland Project, which was begun in 1974 by the New York State Library and the Holland Society of New York to research, translate, and publish documents of

correspondence and help establish your credibility and desire to perpetuate your family's oral legacy. Oral histories can often lead you to searches for church records and cemeteries.

Before the Civil War, most slaves were buried in unrecorded graves, but after the war, African Americans were free to create their own churches and cemeteries. Many churches keep records of memberships and burials from their earliest days that can usually be investigated after contacting administrators or church elders. Church records can also provide leads to other relatives who may have been involved in the congregation.

The National Archives holds millions of documents related to African Americans after 1870, including census data and records of the Commissioners of Claims, the Freedman's Savings and Trust, and the Bureau of Refugees, Freedmen, and Abandoned Lands (also known as the Freedmen's Bureau).

The Freedmen's Bureau was established in 1865 as a relief agency for Civil War refugees and freed slaves, and their Web site, www.freedmensbureau.com, contains a searchable database. Although the search for African American lineages can be intimidating, there are plenty of methods for researching the past (see chapter 11). The Center for African American Genealogical Research, Inc., maintains a Web site (www.caagri.org) with excellent information and tips for developing a research plan and getting started.

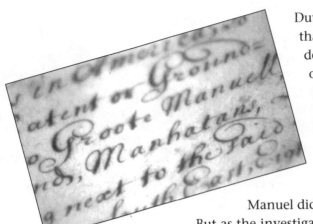

A close-up of the 1667 land grant with the Dutch spelling of "Groote Manuell."

Tukufu Zuberi meeting with historian and Groote Manuel descendant Chris Moore.

Dutch colonization in America, Tukufu discovered that the first historical record of Groote Manuel described a dark past. In 1641, Manuel and eight other slaves were accused of murdering another slave. In a show of solidarity, none of the nine men accused of the murder volunteered any information as to the identity of the true killer. Frustrated Dutch authorities forced the group to draw lots to determine who would go to the gallows for the crime, and luckily Manuel didn't draw the decisive verdict.

But as the investigation into the murder unfolded, a little-known piece of Dutch slavery history came to light when it became clear that ultimately no one was punished for the crime. Under Dutch commercial colonization, New Netherland was sparsely populated by settlers bent on making a profit, and slaves were a vital source of labor. Unlike the English settlers, who had a plantation crop orientation, the Dutch actually held relatively few slaves, with most slaveholders owning no more than two or three. Economically, it made no sense to execute an able-bodied man, and the fact that the slaves had murdered one of their own undoubtedly played a large part in the final decision to ignore the entire sordid affair.

The value of manpower in the new Dutch colony became even more apparent when Tukufu met with historian Chris Moore at the New York Public Library's Schomburg Center for Research in Black Culture. According to Moore, the Dutch declared war on the indigenous inhabitants in February of 1643, killing eighty of them in New Jersey and another twenty or thirty in New Amsterdam.

In retaliation, the tribes attacked and burned every farm north of the town, turning the outlying region into a potential deathtrap. In this direst of circumstances, eleven longtime

slaves cited their enduring service to the Dutch East Indies Company and petitioned for freedom and property. With frightened settlers moving nearer the fortifications of New Amsterdam, the wily Dutch agreed to the bargain, imposing heavy annual taxes on the freed slaves in the process. The newly freed slaves survived and prospered on their new land holdings and developed the earliest free African American community in the New World.

With his investigation complete, Tukufu returned to Virginia to meet with Mark Mitchell and relate his incredible findings. The land grant was unquestionably authentic and Groote Manuel was one of the first free black landowners in America. Tragically, although the English initially recognized the ownership of the property by Manuel's heirs, they abolished the rights of people of color to inherit land in 1712, thereby ending an era of freedom to possess property. But that wasn't the end of the story. In an unexpected turn of events, Tukufu discovered that Chris Moore was directly related to Groote Manuel and considered Manuel's son, Nicholas, born in 1649, to be the first freeborn African American in his family.

CHAPTER THIRTEEN
ARMED AND DANGEROUS

One of the most colorful periods in U.S. history is often referred to as the "public enemy era" of the early 1930s, a time when social pressures of the Great Depression and the ill-conceived Prohibition Act of 1919 triggered a wave of criminal activity, along with public opinions that often romanticized dangerous thugs. Political and law enforcement corruption in urban areas was out of control, and it was often difficult to separate the obviously criminal behavior of politicians and cops from the activities of outlaws. Desperadoes who rebelled against authority were often viewed as heroes and modern-day Robin Hoods who despite their outrageous actions were fighting the "good" fight.

Over the seasons, a variety of *History Detectives* mysteries have involved personal weaponry, including Napoleon's sword, Custer's bayonet, and even a shotgun said to have been owned by Nazi warmonger Hermann Göering. But for Wes Cowan and Tukufu Zuberi, there were two inquiries in particular that highlighted a bunch of unsavory characters whose actions left a trail of destruction in their wake. Both of these investigations proved that for some individuals, there are no limits to what they will do and how many people they take down in the process.

The Deadly Downfall of Bonnie and Clyde

Young love and life on the road and on the run epitomize the escapades of Bonnie Parker and Clyde Barrow, who mixed romance and crime sprees during the first years of the 1930s. The truth about the duo was much harsher than the glamorous fantasy that surrounded them, a fact that was especially evident when Bonnie and Clyde were finally killed in a hail of bullets during a carefully laid out Louisiana roadside trap by a law enforcement task force in 1934. *History Detectives* received a call for help from Cassandra Goss of Brodhead, Wisconsin, regarding the infamous ambush. Cassandra owns five spent bullets that she believed might have killed the fugitive duo, and with intrepid haste, Wes Cowan and Tukufu Zuberi responded to the call.

Upon meeting with Cassandra, they learned that her grandfather-in-law, J. D. Goss, had worked for the Dallas Police Department at the time of the infamous shootings. She showed Wes and Tukufu authenticated forensic photographs that seemed to back up J. D.'s claim that the bullets had been removed from the bodies of Bonnie and Clyde, but the slugs raised some serious questions for the detectives. Why would a police officer retain evidence from such an important criminal investigation? And could these be the actual bullets that were fired during the ambush? While Tukufu arranged for forensic testing of the bullets, Wes decided to do some background research on the events leading up to that fateful day.

SPREE OF LOVE

The fifth of eight children, Clyde Barrow was born into a poor sharecropping family in Texas in 1909. When Clyde turned twelve, his father gave up the struggle of farming and went to work at a filling station in West Dallas, where Clyde and his older brother Buck developed a local reputation as young toughs and troublemakers. A string of petty thefts and burglaries gave the Barrow brothers their first brushes with the law and put Buck into Huntsville State Prison in 1929. Undeterred, Clyde assembled a crew of hoodlums and continued committing relatively minor crimes on the western side of Dallas.

Five bullets allegedly pulled from the bodies of Bonnie Parker and Clyde Barrow.

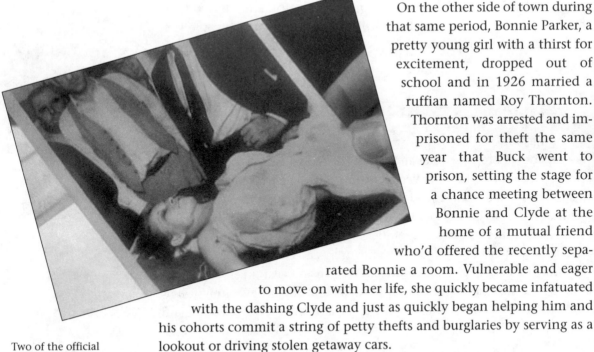

On the other side of town during that same period, Bonnie Parker, a pretty young girl with a thirst for excitement, dropped out of school and in 1926 married a ruffian named Roy Thornton. Thornton was arrested and imprisoned for theft the same year that Buck went to prison, setting the stage for a chance meeting between Bonnie and Clyde at the home of a mutual friend who'd offered the recently separated Bonnie a room. Vulnerable and eager to move on with her life, she quickly became infatuated with the dashing Clyde and just as quickly began helping him and his cohorts commit a string of petty thefts and burglaries by serving as a lookout or driving stolen getaway cars.

Two of the official forensic images owned by Cassandra Goss of Bonnie Parker (above) and Clyde Barrow (below) after the ambush.

Bonnie's devotion to Clyde was soon solidified after he was arrested and jailed in Waco, Texas, after a botched burglary. The lovelorn Bonnie stayed in regular contact with her paramour and happily agreed to an escape plan by slipping a firearm to her beloved right under the noses of jail attendants. Clyde, with the help of fellow inmate Frank Turner, put the weapon to a guard's head, and he rationally unlocked their cell and let them go free. With lawmen quickly on their trail, the escape proved to be short-lived, and the pair were picked up in a stolen vehicle and returned to Waco, where Barrow was sentenced to fourteen years in prison.

Yearning for her lover, Bonnie kept vigil and visited Clyde often during the two years he would ultimately serve in the pen. Desperate and always clever, Clyde made a play for sympathy from the courts by convincing a fellow prisoner to cut off two of Clyde's toes during work duties, pretending he'd suffered a horrible accident. The painful but clever scheme worked perfectly, and Clyde was granted parole in February of 1932. Hobbling on crutches, he made his way straight to Dallas to be with Bonnie, and there the pair launched a murderous crime spree that rocked the nation and catapulted them to headline celebrity.

On April 30, 1932, during a bungled robbery in Dallas, Clyde and his sidekick Ray Hamilton shot and killed a grocery store owner in front of the owner's horrified wife. The fiasco forced Clyde to accept his new fate as a known killer, and Bonnie willingly agreed to stick with him until what they both knew would be their inevitable bitter end. On the run and contemptuous of the law, Bonnie, Clyde, and a varied gang of stray hoodlums, including recently paroled brother Buck and his new wife, Blanche, went on a rampage throughout the Southwest, committing a series of car thefts and armed robberies that left a trail of murdered police officers and in- nocent civilians in their wake.

After holing up at the Red Crown Tourist Camp near Platte City, Missouri, the gang was seen by an alert citizen and trapped into a har- rowing gunfight with city policemen. Buck Barrow was seriously wounded, but the gang managed to pile into their stolen car amid a rain of lead and make their escape. It would be one of the few shootouts for the Barrow Gang that didn't result in the death of a police officer. Days later, the shell-shocked gang was licking their wounds in a state park when they were once again spotted. The sheriff deputized a group of locals, and over a hundred armed men descended on the camp- site. Another gunfight broke out, and this time Buck was killed. Blanche Barrow was captured in the melee, but the natural-born killers Bonnie and Clyde made yet another narrow escape.

A lighter moment in 1933 that belies the trail of destruction left by outlaws Bonnie Parker and Clyde Barrow.

Saddened but undeterred by Buck's death, Clyde masterminded a Texas prison breakout several months later, presumably to add to his gang's thinning ranks. Ironically, one of the freed inmates, Henry Methvin, would eventually become a rat in the pack, aiding in the demise of the notorious duo by conspiring to save his own neck. The prison raid left a

time
TEASER

Which notorious mobster plotted assassinations of Benito Mussolini, Hermann Göering, and Joseph Goebbels and later provided funds to Holocaust victims settling in Israel?

Answer: Bugsy Siegel.

guard shot to death. Lee Simmons, the frustrated and angry head of the Texas Department of Corrections, hired retired Texas Ranger Frank Hamer to hunt down the Barrow Gang and put them away for good.

Hamer had a solid reputation as a relentless man-hunter and would prove to be the perfect choice for the job. He went to work in February of 1934 and quickly realized that Clyde, Bonnie, and the gang had developed a habit of skirting the borders of Texas, Louisiana, Arkansas, Oklahoma, Missouri, and Kansas, committing crimes and running in a circle throughout the states while periodically hiding out with families and sympathetic friends. Clyde was well aware that state and local police were bound by jurisdictional rules that prevented them from pursuing fugitives across state lines, and he took every advantage of the one law that actually helped protect him. By bouncing back and forth across borders, the gang was always on the run—but also a step ahead of the law.

SHOOT TO KILL

After a series of bungled car thefts, robberies, and police chases that resulted in a mounting death toll, Henry Methvin realized that he'd gone from frying pan to flame by joining the Barrow Gang. Edgy and trigger-happy, Henry himself instigated the cold-blooded murders of a naive motorcycle cop and his partner on a desolate Texas highway on Easter Sunday in 1934. For Bonnie and Clyde, a deadly end to the path they'd chosen seemed inevitable and close at hand, and Methvin had no intention of going down in a blaze of gunfire or dangling from the end of a hangman's noose. He wanted out. Holed up in his home territory in Louisiana with Bonnie and Clyde, Henry related his fears to his father, Iverson Methvin.

DID YOU know

Law enforcement officers during the public-enemy era often found themselves outgunned by desperadoes with superior firepower. Modern police forces often find themselves engaged with similarly well-armed outlaws. Several incidents, such as a 1997 North Hollywood bank robbery that left seventeen officers and civilians wounded at the hands of a pair of crooks wielding illegally modified high-powered assault rifles, led to increased police access to equally powerful military-style weaponry.

For the elder Methvin the alternative was obvious—cut a deal with the law and help bring Bonnie and Clyde down.

Acting on his own suggestion, Iverson Methvin contacted Shreveport sheriff Tom Bryan and offered his son's treacherous proposition, which Bryan immediately relayed to Frank Hamer. In a meeting with Iverson, Hamer learned that Bonnie and Clyde were staying at the Methvin cabin near Sailes, Louisiana, and had fallen into the daily habit of driving into town for supplies. By this time, Hamer had assembled a small posse, including fellow Texas Ranger Manny Gault and two Dallas deputy sheriffs who knew both Bonnie and Clyde by sight—Bob Alcorn and Ted Hinton.

Knowing that the Barrow Gang were armed to the teeth with stolen military weapons and had a history of shooting their way out of tough

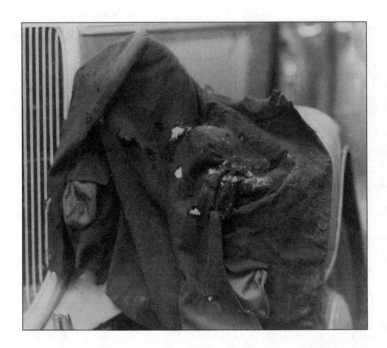

Clyde Barrow's bullet-riddled jacket after the final showdown in 1934.

situations, Hamer decided that a roadside ambush would be more sensible than an assault on the cabin itself. Hamer planted Iverson Methvin's beat-up Model A pickup on the side of Sailes Road, anticipating that Clyde would recognize the truck and assume the old man was stranded and in need of help. Hamer and the posse, which now included Bienville Parish Sheriff Henderson Jordan and Deputy Prentiss Oakley, set up in the trees and brush opposite the parked Model A and waited. Hamer was aware that Bonnie and Clyde prevailed in many of their infamous gun battles because they used a number of powerful Browning automatic rifles stolen from armories. To even the odds, Hamer equipped several members of the posse with exactly the same weapons. The six men were also armed with shotguns, semi-automatic rifles, and sidearms—enough firepower to stop a small army or start a full-scale war.

At 9:15 A.M. on May 23, 1934, Bonnie and Clyde rolled into view in a stolen V8 Ford sedan and slowed to a crawl after noticing Iverson Methvin's parked pickup truck. Disinclined to offer a warning, Hamer gave the order to fire, and all six officers opened up with every weapon at hand. Seconds later, the pincushioned Ford rolled slowly to the side of the highway and came to a feeble halt. The car was hit by 167 bullets, and no one could determine how many rounds may have missed their target entirely. Bonnie and Clyde were struck by an estimated fifty rounds and likely died within a few struggling heartbeats of the first shot.

The two .45 caliber bullets belonging to Cassandra Goss.

Inside the destroyed Ford, Hamer found a weapons arsenal of three .30 caliber Browning automatic rifles, two sawed-off shotguns, half a dozen Colt semi-automatic pistols, and thousands of rounds of ammunition. Bonnie and Clyde met the bloody end they'd expected, and probably never knew what hit them.

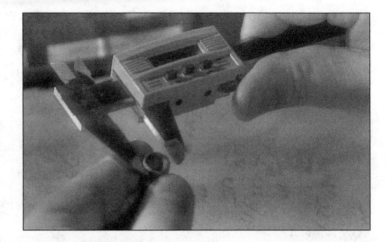

THE CLUE IN THE CALIBER

With a sobering yet confounding investigation on their hands, both Wes and Tukufu were stymied as to whether or not Cassandra's five bullets were part of the fusillade that ended the lives of Bonnie and Clyde, so they decided that the projectiles themselves required expert testing. Tukufu took the bullets to Chris Lucky, a leading ballistics expert, who determined that two of the five were .45 caliber and the other three came from .38 caliber rounds.

A ballistics expert taking precise measurements to verify the caliber of the bullets under investigation.

While records indicate that no .38s were used in the ambush, there is evidence that Hamer carried a Colt Model 1911 in .45 caliber. After testing impressions on the bullets left by the barrel *rifling*, or grooves that impart spin to bullets, Lucky was able to determine that at least one of the collection had indeed been shot from a Model 1911. Out of the five bullets, one may have been fired on that fateful day.

To follow that line of speculation, Wes set out to determine just who J. D. Goss was and how he may have been involved in the aftermath of the infamous ambush. In the Dallas public library, Wes discovered that Goss was a ballistics expert for the Dallas police. Further searching in the library newspaper archives revealed that Goss was instrumental, not in the deaths of Bonnie and Clyde, but in the investigation of the death of the two motorcycle officers whom Clyde and Henry Methvin brutally gunned down in Texas on Easter Sunday in 1934. What Wes found next would no doubt surprise Cassandra Goss.

Microscopic analysis of the stria of the bullets.

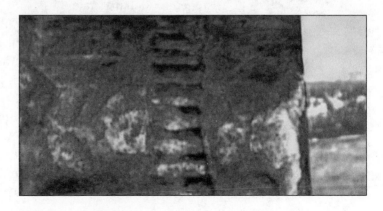

At the Dallas Public
Library, Wes Cowan
discovered a city
directory that listed
J. D. Goss as a
ballistician.

When meeting with Cassandra, Tukufu and Wes shared with her reports of ballistics testing done by J. D. Goss concerning the Easter Sunday murders, which proved that the bullets that killed the officers were fired from guns found in the Ford in which Bonnie and Clyde perished. In a bizarre twist, Bonnie Parker's sister Billie Parker and her husband, Floyd Hamilton, were charged with killing the two Texas motorcycle officers. Expert forensics testing and testimony by J. D. Goss actually helped free Billie and instead pinned the crime squarely on Bonnie and Clyde. In the end, all five of Cassandra's bullets were part of the investigation of the Easter Sunday murders.

The Case of the Contentious Colt

The public-enemy era produced another romanticized outlaw during the 1930s by the name of Charles Arthur Floyd, better known as Pretty Boy Floyd. As an outlaw he was highly admired, but as a criminal, like Bonnie and Clyde, he was just another natural-born killer. Richard Kee of LaVerne, California, is the owner of a .32 caliber pistol that was thought to have been a gift from Floyd to Kee's Uncle Ted when Ted was just seventeen. In an effort to determine the authenticity of the gun and ascertain if the family legend was true, Richard Kee called upon Wes Cowan, who was more than intrigued by this Colt conundrum as he listened to Richard's tale.

According to Kee's family story, Pretty Boy Floyd's car broke down in the small town of Bolivar, Missouri, and was taken for repairs to the local service station. A wanted fugitive, Floyd allegedly asked young Ted Kee to keep lookout while the car was being serviced and repaid the boy for his vigilance by giving him the pistol. The year was 1934, and by that time Pretty Boy Floyd had spent years building his own reputation as a bank robber and outlaw.

Born in Georgia on February 3, 1904, Floyd was the fourth of eight children, who grew up helping their family pick cotton as tenant farmers. After moving the brood to Oklahoma in 1911, his father, Walter Floyd, continued

Richard Kee's
uncle, Ted Kee.

Locked and Loaded

In 1783, the American Revolution was winding down after Great Britain had called it quits with the colonies and was close to ratifying a peace treaty. But in Bucks County, Pennsylvania, a gang of loyalist sympathizers continued robbing and harassing patriotic colonists.

The so-called Doan Gang (also spelled Doane) had no intention of accepting Britain's defeat, so they began robbing colonial tax collectors and treasuries. Branded as outlaws and with a price of $300 on their heads, the Doans were tracked down to an isolated cabin in the woods, where a final shootout occurred and the Doans were disbanded.

Elyse Luray and Wes Cowan investigated a flintlock rifle at the request of Doan Gang descendant Donna Doan, to determine if it was used in the shootout. As it turned out, many of the gun parts had been replaced, but the barrel was original. The real irony in the Doan Gang story is that there's little question that had the British prevailed in the Revolutionary War, the Doans would have been hailed as heroes and handsomely rewarded for their efforts.

working as a tenant farmer and succeeded in making a respectable living. By all accounts, the younger Floyd was a good kid, well liked and trouble free, until his late teens, when he and a buddy broke into the local post office and made off with $3.50 in change. The boys were caught immediately after the theft but managed to get off with only a stern warning.

For several years after the post office incident, Charles Arthur Floyd stayed clear of trouble and went on to marry a local girl named Ruby, who soon gave birth to son Dempsey, named after renowned boxer "Manassa Mauler" Jack Dempsey. Floyd continued working in the cotton fields, but after turning twenty-one in 1925 he'd had enough of the farming life and took off with new-found buddy John Hilderbrand, who enticed Floyd with tall tales of thievery, easy pickings, and, above all, wild living. Together, the pair began a spree of grocery store and gas station stickups that netted only a few dollars here and there, but enough to hook Floyd on the lifestyle of an audacious outlaw. The pair eventually hit the jackpot when they teamed up with Joe Hlavatry,

The .32 caliber Colt allegedly given to Ted Kee by Pretty Boy Floyd.

time
TEASER

What little-known African American mobster ran drug-trafficking operations for the Lucchese crime family in New York?

Answer: Leroy "Nicky" Barnes.

another small-time hoodlum, and held up a payroll transfer at a major food store in Missouri that netted them over $11,000.

Excited and celebrating their first big heist, the trio purchased a brand-new Studebaker to cruise the streets, a naive decision that attracted the attention of local police, who wanted to know what three punk kids were doing with a flashy, expensive car. Arrested and frightened, the three criminals could not keep their stories straight and implicated themselves in the robbery. They were tried and convicted, and to add insult to injury, newspaper articles described Floyd as "a pretty boy with apple cheeks." Much to his annoyance, the name stuck, and Charles Arthur Floyd became Pretty Boy Floyd overnight. Along with earning a new nickname, he also earned himself a five-year sentence at the Missouri State Penitentiary in Jefferson City. While in prison Floyd kept to himself for the most part, but he did become good friends with an experienced outlaw and bank robber named Red Lovett. Shortly before Floyd's release from prison, he received word that his wife had filed for divorce, so with his former life in shambles, Pretty Boy walked out of prison in 1929 and headed for Kansas City, Missouri, to reconnect with his criminal mentor Red Lovett, who was also finally out of the slammer.

Under Lovett's tutelage, Floyd learned the ropes of criminal life in Kansas City, which was teeming with crooks, crooked lawmen, and crooked politicians. Floyd blended in like a chameleon and eventually hooked up with the Jim Bradley Gang to begin a series of bank heists in Ohio. After several successful jobs and the killing of an investigating policeman, Floyd was arrested, tried, and sentenced to prison once again. But his detention would be short-lived. He managed to escape from guards on a prison-bound train and made his way back to the relative security of criminal acquaintances in Kansas City.

Teaming up with another desperado, named William Miller, the pair resumed the bank robbing business until they had a close encounter with Ohio law enforcement. During a wild gunfight with police officers, Miller was shot dead, and Floyd made a daring escape amid a hail of gunfire.

Charles Arthur Floyd, aka Pretty Boy Floyd.

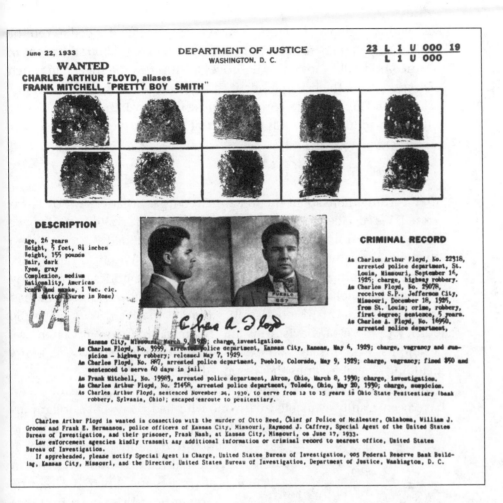

June 22, 1933

WANTED

CHARLES ARTHUR FLOYD, aliases
FRANK MITCHELL, "PRETTY BOY SMITH"

DEPARTMENT OF JUSTICE
WASHINGTON, D. C.

23 L 1 U 000 19
L 1 U 000

DESCRIPTION

Age, 26 years
Height, 5 feet, 8½ inches
Weight, 155 pounds
Hair, dark
Eyes, gray
Complexion, medium
Nationality, American
Scars and marks, 1 Vac. cic.
(Tattoo: Nurse in Rose)

CRIMINAL RECORD

As Charles Arthur Floyd, No. 22318, arrested police department, St. Louis, Missouri, September 16, 1925; charge, highway robbery.
As Charles Floyd, No. 29078, received S.P., Jefferson City, Missouri, December 18, 1925, from St. Louis; crime, robbery, first degree; sentence, 5 years.
As Charles A. Floyd, No. 16950, arrested police department,

Kansas City, Missouri, March 9, 1929; charge, investigation.
As Charles Floyd, No. 5999, arrested police department, Kansas City, Kansas, May 6, 1929; charge, vagrancy and suspicion - highway robbery; released May 7, 1929.
As Charles Floyd, No. 887, arrested police department, Pueblo, Colorado, May 9, 1929; charge, vagrancy; fined $50 and sentenced to serve 60 days in jail.
As Frank Mitchell, No. 19985, arrested police department, Akron, Ohio, March 8, 1930; charge, investigation.
As Charles Arthur Floyd, No. 21458, arrested police department, Toledo, Ohio, May 20, 1930; charge, suspicion.
As Charles Arthur Floyd, sentenced November 24, 1930, to serve from 12 to 15 years in Ohio State Penitentiary (bank robbery, Sylvania, Ohio); escaped enroute to penitentiary.

Charles Arthur Floyd is wanted in connection with the murder of Otto Reed, Chief of Police of McAlester, Oklahoma, William J. Grooms and Frank E. Hermanson, police officers of Kansas City, Missouri, Raymond J. Caffrey, Special Agent of the United States Bureau of Investigation, and their prisoner, Frank Nash, at Kansas City, Missouri, on June 17, 1933.

Law enforcement agencies kindly transmit any additional information or criminal record to nearest office, United States Bureau of Investigation.

If apprehended, please notify Special Agent in Charge, United States Bureau of Investigation, 905 Federal Reserve Bank Building, Kansas City, Missouri, and the Director, United States Bureau of Investigation, Department of Justice, Washington, D. C.

Mugshots and fingerprints of Charles "Pretty Boy" Floyd from a 1933 FBI wanted poster.

Figuring he'd overstayed his welcome, Pretty Boy sought the safety of friends and family in Oklahoma. Back in his home territory, he quickly turned up the heat on banking institutions. At the time, the Depression was in full swing and the lives of the poorer classes were being destroyed by poverty and unemployment. Banks were viewed as the enemy as mortgage foreclosures took the homes of people who'd lived on their land for generations. Through Oklahoma, Arkansas, and Missouri, Floyd robbed banks, tore up mortgage papers, and handed stolen money back to dozens of the grateful poor. Pretty Boy Floyd was becoming a legend in his own time—and the public loved him for it.

In 1931, he paired up with a boyhood friend named George Birdwell, a former preacher who was well liked and respected by his neighbors and friends. Working as a team, Floyd and Birdwell held up scores of banks and lending institutions. Legend has it that when the duo decided to rob the bank in Floyd's hometown, he let the neighbors know about the event in advance, and folks showed up in droves to sit across the street and watch the action. Even the bank president thought the whole spectacle was just a show that Floyd was presenting to amuse the crowd; that is, until Pretty Boy informed him that it was the real deal and took every penny.

ANATOMY OF A COLT

After learning more about the romanticized legacy that Pretty Boy Floyd created, Wes decided to research Ted Kee and how he could possibly have received the pistol as a reward. Wes learned that Ted had a sister, Mildred Ward, who was living in Southern California, so Wes paid her a visit. During their conversation Ward recalled vague memories of Pretty Boy Floyd being in Bolivar, but she hadn't a clue about how the handgun had come into her brother's possession. After leaving Ward, Wes made the journey to the J. M. Davis Arms and Historical Museum in Claremore, Oklahoma, which houses an extensive collection of outlaw weaponry, including several firearms that belonged to Pretty Boy Floyd.

According to Executive Director Duane Kyler, a .32 Colt pistol would have been readily available to anyone who had the twenty-dollar purchase price, but it seemed an unlikely amount of money for seventeen-year-old Ted Kee, who was living in a small rural town during the Depression. Kyler did affirm that Pretty Boy was partial to Colt pistols, and felt it was likely he could have carried a pistol like the .32. Kyler also verified that the manufacture date of Kee's gun was between 1904 and 1905, which would have placed the piece in circulation during Floyd's era.

The next stop for Wes was to show the pistol to firearms expert John Cayton. Hoping to find Floyd's fingerprints on metal parts of the gun not normally exposed to handling, Cayton removed the grips

Wes Cowan and firearms expert John Cayton looking for fingerprint evidence.

and put the weapon into a forensic fume box. (For fans of the hit *CSI* television series, this process should sound familiar.) When heated, a few drops of superglue in the box cause the glue fumes to stick to latent fingerprints, which could then be compared to known fingerprints of Pretty Boy Floyd. Unfortunately, the test yielded negative results, so Cayton's next step was to dismantle the firearm and check for signs of heavy wear.

time TEASER

I n what year did the FBI recognize the Mafia as a national crime syndicate?

Answer: 1957.

During Floyd's era, most civilians didn't have enough spare cash to waste expensive ammunition, whereas outlaws made their living with weapons and practiced shooting them extensively. The .32 Colt that once belonged to Ted Kee proved to be nearly worn out from a great deal of regular firing. This wasn't definitive evidence that the gun belonged to Pretty Boy Floyd, but there was evidence that the gun had seen use similar to that in the guns of outlaws.

With these tantalizing new pieces of information, Wes sought the advice of Floyd historian and biographer Michael Wallis, who confirmed that Pretty Boy was the kind of guy who might have given a kid a gun as a reward. He also mentioned that it was just as likely that a teenager in Missouri during the 1930s would have fallen all over himself in an effort to help a popular, bigger-than-life outlaw like Pretty Boy Floyd. But Wallis also had some bad news. During much of 1934, the year the pistol was supposedly presented to Ted Kee, Pretty Boy Floyd was holed up in Buffalo, New York, and was nowhere near Bolivar, Missouri.

THE BOLIVAR BOONDOGGLE

Wes ultimately took his investigation as close to the geographic source as he could get—to the Polk County Genealogical Society Library in Bolivar. Searching the archives of the local newspaper, Wes hit paydirt when he first found a *New York Times* article with the headline: "Floyd Takes Sheriff For Buggy Ride." The date was mid-June 1933, a year before the date Richard Kee thought the Colt was given to his Uncle Ted. The newspaper research

Expert John Cayton's comparison of the Colt's firing pin striker plate (left) to a Colt with normal use showed it had been fired extensively.

then produced even better results when Wes discovered an article in the *Bolivar Herald*.

The story stated that Pretty Boy Floyd had lined up bystanders at the point of a revolver while his car was being repaired at a local garage. Apparently the local sheriff walked in on the incident and was taken for a little ride, only to be released later as the outlaw made his way out of town. In the end, Wes was able to tell Richard Kee that although the evidence

Wes Cowan's search of the *Bolivar Herald* archives proved to be the linchpin of his Pretty Boy Floyd investigation.

proving the authenticity of his family story was circumstantial, it was still strong enough to make a good case. Allowing for the one-year discrepancy, Uncle Ted's amazing tale about Pretty Boy Floyd's brief visit to Bolivar courtesy of a broken-down car, and a priceless souvenir for a starstruck kid, had all the earmarks of a family legend come true.

The Robin Hood Syndrome

Considered one of the most difficult eras for the United States, the Great Depression, which began with the infamous stock market crash of 1929, ruined livelihoods and families across the nation. Although the causes of the Depression have filled volumes, it was ultimately the panic of Wall Street that resulted in an enormous economic downturn that affected every U.S. citizen. Manufacturing and construction plunged to new lows, and massive layoffs raised the unemployment rate to a record-

DID YOU know

Though it was rare for the most famous gangsters to pull a job together, it did happen. Pretty Boy Floyd reportedly once teamed up with the equally infamous John Dillinger to rob a bank in South Bend, Indiana. On June 30, 1934, tellers and customers at the Merchants National Bank were greeted by two of the most frightening holdup men in U.S. history, a scant few months before both were finally killed by police.

high 25 percent. The hundreds of thousands of consumers who had bought homes, farms, and vehicles on credit began losing everything they owned to foreclosures, and, not surprisingly, banks and bankers were directly blamed for the profound suffering that ensued.

A father and his sons enduring a dust storm in Cimarron County, Oklahoma, in 1936.

Class distinctions between the rich and the overwhelming number of poor, not to mention those hanging on by an economic thread, were glaringly obvious, and resentment was reaching a boiling point. In light of this edgy social atmosphere, the moral compass spun in a disturbing direction, as outlaws were increasingly viewed as rebels fighting an unjust system.

Part of the sympathy for the behavior of outlaws stemmed from the increasingly despised National Prohibition Act, commonly known as the Volstead Act, passed by Congress in 1919. The act made the manufacture, possession, and sale of alcohol a criminal act, and because of it, crime syndicates jumped at the chance to cash in on an enormous black market in alcohol trafficking. Their efforts proved successful, and despite law enforcement's diligence, alcohol was readily available to nearly anyone who wanted it.

The cost in public respect for the common sense of the government and law enforcement was incalculable, and the overall effect was to heighten the notoriety and wealth of criminals, while highlighting the perceived stupidity of politicians. In large urban settings, such as Chicago and New York, Prohibition gave major crime organizations a clear path to riches by bootlegging illegal liquor. Chicago's Al Capone, a notoriously cold-blooded killer, was idolized by the poor for his flagrant disrespect of the law. For years,

A mug shot of Al Capone while still a teenager.

time
time
TEASER

A t what location was the last attempt on Al Capone's life made?

Answer: At Alcatraz prison in the San Francisco Bay. The failed attempt in the mid-1930s was made by a fellow inmate.

Capone actually was the law in Chicago, having hundreds of police officials and even Chicago mayor William Thompson on his payroll. In New York, a number of competing Mafia families similarly controlled the bootlegging business, and, just as in Capone's Chicago, they controlled both law enforcement and politicians.

In rural areas, outlaws such as Bonnie and Clyde, Pretty Boy Floyd, John Dillinger, Alvin "Old Creepy" Karpis, and Ma Barker and the Barker Gang were viewed in a slightly different light. Many of the crimes they committed were against the much-despised lending institutions and banks. The lives these outlaws led and the media attention

DIY DETECTIVE

Collecting valuable firearms is one of the most highly specialized hobbies you can engage in, but beware—it involves many potential pitfalls. The ownership of even a single relatively inexpensive firearm requires experience and training to ensure safe handling, and most states set specific age limits. In many jurisdictions the ownership of firearms—even antique weapons that aren't intended for firing—is strictly limited. One of the niche specialties of firearms collecting is acquiring weapons that were actually used by notorious outlaws and famous lawmen. The Remington Model 8 rifle used by Deputy Prentiss Oakley in the ambush of Bonnie and Clyde sold at auction in 2006 for $69,000. An ordinary Model 8 manufactured in the same era can be purchased for about $600. The difference between the two guns is the historical significance of Oakley's rifle and verifiable documentation, or provenance, that the gun was the real deal.

When it comes to so-called "notorious" firearms, accurate provenance is far more valuable than the actual weapon. Another fascinating niche of the gun hobby is the collection of miniature firearms. Handcrafted by a handful of highly skilled artisans, exact tiny replicas of famous handguns, shotguns, and rifles only a few inches long can fetch several hundred to several thousand dollars. These pint-sized reproductions are anything but toys, and serious collectors take great pride in their unique artistic qualities. Another upside to the specialty? No one makes really tiny bullets, so they'll never go off accidentally!

they received played out many of the fantasies and frustrations of the rural poor, who often went out of their way to shield criminals from the law. In truth, many of those highway-burning desperadoes handed out stolen cash and goods to those in need, and their handful of kindnesses helped soften the images of desperate men and women who would not hesitate to murder anyone who stood in their way. Folk songs and glorified legends of the day also enhanced the romantic view of outlaw behavior and notoriety.

In 1929, agents pour liquor down the drain under the supervision of New York City Deputy Police Commissioner John A. Leach.

To shed a harsher light on the reality of outlaws and the company they kept, it's worth mentioning that Alvin Karpis, one of the romanticized characters of the public-enemy era, wrote in his memoirs about a kid and fellow inmate he'd met at the McNeal Federal Penitentiary during the mid-1960s. He wrote: "This kid approaches me to request music lessons. He wants to learn guitar and become a music star. I decide it's time someone did something for him. He never has a harsh word to say and is never involved in even an argument." The kid Karpis took under his wing actually became a fairly capable guitar player, but his longed-for musical career never came to pass. After being released from that first experience in prison, the youngster applied a different set of lessons to achieve fame. That kid's name was Charles Manson.

Alvin "Old Creepy" Karpis.

CHAPTER FOURTEEN

THE TREASURE TROVE

There aren't many humans on the planet who wouldn't love to find buried treasure, and for a lucky few, unbelievable treasures have been discovered, from prehistoric remains to Roman coins to millions in gold and silver. The concept of treasure depends entirely on what one considers valuable. To an archaeologist, it may be finding a tomb or remnants of a lost civilization. To the maritime historian, it may be finding a centuries-old shipwreck.

In this chapter you'll become immersed in several amazing expeditions and investigations that marine archaeologists live for and some treasure hunters died for. You may recognize the name *Nuestra Señora de Atocha*, but History Detective Tukufu Zuberi's unique investigation into this famed ship's legend and riches will astound you. The same goes for Elyse Luray's research into the valiant steamer SS *Portland*, although the steamship's story is rich in an entirely different way. We'll also explore advances in maritime archaeology, and the story of one of history's most famous pirates, who, it is said, literally lost his head. Those who hunt successfully for treasure, from scientist to explorer to the average Joe, all have one thing in common—tenacity. And it was that tenacity that sent the History Detectives on a pair of surprising and unforgettable voyages.

The Quest for the Sunken Silver

The search for hidden treasure is a very individual pursuit, whether it be finding the perfect piece of art at a Sotheby's auction, a beloved baseball card at a sports memorabilia shop, or an antique jewelry box at a local flea market. For an elite group of treasure hunters like legends Mel Fisher, Bob Marx, Kip Wagner, and Burt Webber, the discovery of astonishing maritime treasure was the icing on the cake. Ultimately, what drove these men and their teams toward spectacular treasure was the thrill of the chase—uncovering bits of elusive history that for hundreds of years were unseen by human eyes.

To acquire a piece of history from a sunken vessel is a pipe dream for most of us, but for scuba diver Chuck Sotzin of Cedartown, Georgia, that dream is a reality—one that comes with a tantalizing tale of intrigue. Sotzin owns a silver bar, known as an *ingot*, that in 1622 was being transported by the Spanish galleon *Nuestra Señora de Atocha*. How did Sotzin happen to come into possession of such a valuable piece of maritime

Tukufu Zuberi with Chuck Sotzin and his silver ingot from the Spanish galleon *Nuestra Señora de Atocha*.

history? He spent five years helping his uncle, Mel Fisher, in his search for the *Atocha*, and as payment he received the silver ingot.

By all accounts, there should be nothing mysterious about the silver bar; after all, it was common for Spanish galleons of the era to be carrying such booty. But this sixty-eight-pound ingot is special, a fact that's immediately evident from a strange deeply-cut slash accompanying the standard Spanish identification markings imprinted on the face of the bar. Who did it belong to? Where did it come from? And what do the markings indicate? Those were the questions posed to History Detective Tukufu Zuberi, whose first step was to learn more about the *Atocha*.

To understand the sheer magnitude of Mel Fisher's success, and ultimately solve the mystery behind Chuck Sotzin's silver ingot, one must

A close-up of Chuck Sotzin's sixty-eight-pound silver ingot from the *Nuestra Señora de Atocha*.

travel back to a time when intrepid explorers sought to claim New World riches for their countries—riches that were highly prized by infamous pirates. By the late fifteenth century Spain set about conquering and colonizing the New World and establishing the Spanish Main, which included a host of Caribbean islands and parts of Central and South America. The natural resources of the lands and the wealth of civilizations, including the Aztecs and the Incas, were manifest in the mind-boggling caches of gold, silver, and gems that made Spain one of the richest nations on earth.

In gaining their wealth, the Spaniards massacred thousands of the indigenous people and enslaved thousands more in their zeal for New World domination. Spain transported its riches aboard massive cargo-bearing vessels called *galleons*. Spectacular in their construction, the galleons were built by shipwrights who combined the design of huge triple-masted caravels with that of fast, lightweight carracks. The result was an impressive 400-ton vessel that could carry tons of treasure, yet use its twenty to forty cannons to defend itself from the inevitable scourge of pirates.

To protect themselves from ruthless rogues, the Spanish began traveling in convoys, or *flotillas*, and it was just such a flotilla that embarked from Cuba's Havana Harbor in 1622 in the hope of avoiding Dutch warships that were rumored to be in the area. On September 4, 1622, the twenty-eight ships of the Tierra Firma flotilla set sail, taking the serious risk of traveling during hurricane season. Bringing up the rear of the convoy was the over-500-ton galleon *Nuestra*

time
TEASER

In June 2004, an artifact from the RMS *Titanic* was sold at Guernsey's auction house for $88,500. What was it?

Answer: The only known surviving first-class menu from the final dinner served aboard the *Titanic* before it sank.

Señora de Atocha. The vessel was heavily armed and carrying a crew of 265 men; its holds were overloaded with Mexican and South American treasure that was anxiously anticipated in Spain.

By the standards of any era, the *Atocha's* cargo was astonishing: 100 gold bars, tons of silverware, silver and copper ingots, contraband gemstones and jewels, and silver bullion amounting to over twenty-four tons. Two days after leaving port and just off the coast of Florida, a raging hurricane quickly engulfed the flotilla, sending eight of the fleet to a watery grave. Among them was the *Santa Margarita* and her sister ship, the *Atocha*. Of the 265 men aboard the *Atocha*, 260 perished, but despite the human loss, Spain wasn't about to give up its riches. For the next fifty years they attempted to haul up the *Atocha's* precious cargo, an arduous feat made worse by a second hurricane a month after the sinking that unleashed its wrath on the wreckage and scattered it more than ten miles across the ocean floor. Over the centuries, many tried and died while attempting to recover the *Atocha's* elusive treasure, but the perseverance of one man finally unlocked her secrets and recovered her amazing riches.

A DATE WITH DESTINY

Treasure hunter Mel Fisher is that rare breed of individual whose optimism and tenacity in the face of pure adversity led him to the pot of gold at the end of the rainbow. A chicken farmer turned treasure hunter, Fisher began seriously searching for the *Atocha* in 1969, but he was by no means the only treasure hunter determined to salvage her. In doing his research, Tukufu traveled to Key West to meet with Fisher's grandson, Sean Fisher, who showed him charts indicating that the *Atocha's* position was in the Lower Matecumbe Islands, an assumption made from seventeenth-century references to its sinking. The area encompassed an eighty-mile stretch of Florida's mid-Keys. Of course, navigation in the 1600s didn't include GPS coordinates, and the *Atocha's* exact position was a mystery to all of the various treasure hunting teams who were competing to find her.

DID YOU know

In 1994, a team led by French archaeologist and Egyptologist Jean-Yves Empereur was conducting a salvage inspection in Egypt's Alexandria Harbor when they made an astonishing discovery. They were only a few hundred meters offshore when they found an over-twenty-ton statue of Ptolemy II made of rose-colored granite—a stunning work of art that was said to have stood at the base of the Lighthouse of Alexandria. Called the Pharos, the lighthouse was one of the Seven Wonders of the Ancient World.

Since then, thousands of fragments, artifacts, obelisks, columns, and sphinxes have been uncovered—a virtual underwater museum of Egyptian dynastic history. The Pharos, once the tallest building on Earth (about forty stories), was built by Ptolemy II around 280 B.C. and is thought to have collapsed in the early 1300s as a result of seismic activity.

Mel Fisher's grandson, Sean Fisher, showing the type of treasure that divers pulled from the *Atocha*.

A chart showing the Lower Matecumbe Key, where Mel Fisher and his team focused their salvage efforts off the coast of Florida.

In an effort to nail down a location, Fisher called upon his academic friend Eugene Lyon to help make sense of the complex, almost entirely indecipherable translational discrepancies in Spanish documents, charts, and accounts. Lyon soon discovered that the Spanish included *all* of the Florida Keys under the heading of "Matecumbe Keys," so he dug deeper and finally hit the jackpot in a Seville, Spain, archive. In a disintegrating document he made out the words "Cayos del Marques," which translates to "Keys of the Marquis." Further research brought him to the conclusion that the *Atocha* sank approximately forty miles west of Key West, Florida, near what is now known as the Marquesas Keys.

Every day that Mel Fisher set sail for another arduous search for the *Atocha* he repeated his now famous mantra: "Today's the Day!" In June of 1971, Fisher and his Treasure Salvors team found their first inkling of success in the form of a galleon anchor, fragments of olive jars, and a gold chain over eight feet long. Two years later, more artifacts were recovered, including several thousand pieces of eight, weapons, an unmarked gold bar, and a rare pilot's *astrolabe*, which was used for making astronomical calculations. Not long after, a silver bar was found with markings matching the *Atocha's* manifest, but still the mother lode refused to show itself.

After years of discouragement, cutthroat competition, and legal battles, Fisher learned firsthand just how high a price one has to pay to be a treasure hunter. In July 1973, a week after he'd discovered five bronze cannons, Dirk Fisher, Mel's son, died when a boat occupied by him, his wife, Angel, and diver Rick Gage tragically capsized. Grief stricken but determined, Fisher and his team continued their operations, and by 1980, they discovered the *Santa Margarita* and her treasure. But that was only a portent of things to come.

On July 20, 1985, Kane Fisher delivered the news to his father that the *Atocha* had finally given up her secrets and revealed a huge reef of silver bars. The mother lode, with an estimated worth of over $450 million, included 1,000 silver ingots, emeralds from Colombia, gold coins, hundreds of gold and silver artifacts, jewels, and over 100,000 pieces of eight. In total, Fisher's treasure amounted to a staggering cache of gold and silver weighing in at over forty tons, making it one of the largest treasure finds in U.S. history and arguably one of the greatest finds since Howard Carter's discovery of King Tutankhamen's tomb in 1922. So, just how lucky *is* Chuck Sotzin to own a small piece of maritime history?

Mel Fisher's crew with an astonishing cache of silver ingots recovered from the *Atocha*. At the far left is Chuck Sotzin.

A SILVER LINING

According to Chuck Sotzin, in the first year alone—from 1985 to 1986—Fisher and his faithful team brought up 986 silver ingots from the ocean floor. During Tukufu's library research he learned that many of the markings on the *Atocha's* ingots had been deciphered, with a variety of them being private ownership marks of wealthy, well-connected merchants. A portion of the ingots bore a mysterious slash mark similar to the marking on Sotzin's silver bar.

In order to learn more about the markings, Tukufu met with staff archaeologist Cory Malcolm at Fisher's nonprofit Maritime Heritage Museum in Key West. Right away, Malcolm knew by the inscriptions that Sotzin's ingot was mined in the former Peruvian town of Potosi

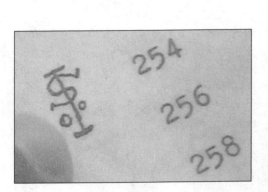

A documented seal that matches the seal on Chuck Sotzin's ingot.

(now part of Bolivia), from silver mines that to this day are among the word's richest. He was also able to determine that the ingot was indeed pure silver produced by a mercury amalgam process that was introduced by Spanish colonial mining operations. The process involved silver ore being crushed into powder and mixed with liquid mercury for several days before refining. Out of a possible 2400 points that indicate purity, Sotzin's ingot registered 2380. Further examination showed a unique serial number of "254," which Malcolm checked against the *Atocha's* manifest. The ingot originally belonged to Spanish merchant Juan Delgado and was registered at a weight of seventy-eight troy pounds (a weight system for gems and precious metals).

Unfortunately, the unusual slash mark on the ingot proved elusive to Malcolm, so he suggested Tukufu meet with Jon Van Harpen, a researcher on the *Atocha* team. Interestingly, it was Van Harpen who first noticed that most of the ingots with the slash mark belonged to Delgado. During recovery operations of the ingots, Van Harpen kept track of the manifest weights and the recovered and cleaned weight of each ingot. When he converted the weights from pounds to troy pounds, his calculations didn't match. All of the bars with the slash mark weighed more than was listed on the manifest. Van Harpen's theory regarding the unusual ingots was the final piece of Tukufu's high-seas whodunit.

His investigation complete, Tukufu once again met with Chuck Sotzin to share his startling revelations. Tukufu first relayed to Sotzin Cory Malcolm's findings that the ingot was indeed pure silver and very unique. He then explained where the bar was mined, and noted the unusual weight discrepancy. According to the *Atocha's* official manifest, each of Juan Delgado's ingots was listed as weighing sixty-three pounds, but in reality, they weighed

A close-up of the seal, indicating that the ingot had once belonged to Juan Delgado.

sixty-eight pounds each. Jon Van Harpen surmised that the slash was meant for inspectors in Spain, and that it was possible that Delgado was not only a businessman but a smuggler. Smuggling was a common practice, given that tax laws of the day were so stiff that passengers often turned their gold and silver into jewelry because anything they were wearing on their person was tax exempt.

One possibility is that the slash mark meant that an additional tax was to be charged, in which case more ingots if not all of them would bear the mark. More than likely, the slash was a signal to bribed inspectors that they should clear the ingots without weighing them, which allowed Delgado to bring in five extra pounds of untaxed silver per bar. Unfortunately for Delgado, karma can be a vindictive guardian. The alleged smuggler happened to be on board the *Atocha* during her fateful journey and didn't survive its tragic demise. Sotzin's ingot, kept safely stowed in a safe deposit box, is worth between $20,000 and $50,000 in today's market, a price that would no doubt cause Delgado to spin in his watery grave.

> ## time
> ### TEASER
>
> Powder monkeys were typically part of a pirate crew. Who were they and what did they do?
>
> **Answer:** A powder monkey was usually a boy who prepared cartridges, filled canisters with gun powder, and loaded them into muskets and cannons.

Maritime Archaeology

In the mid-1600s, the Spaniards desperately tried to recover the riches they'd lost from their 1622 flotilla, going so far as to offer slaves their freedom if they could dive deep enough to recover any treasure. If they had the advantage of modern-day underwater breathing gear, they might have succeeded. For centuries, divers had no choice but to hold their breath and take the plunge. Diving bells didn't make their first appearance until the 1600s, with various inventors attempting to engineer open-bottomed chambers that would supply their user with a sufficient amount of air. This process evolved into diving with compressed air filtered to a diver from a vessel, and eventually advanced with the invention of SCUBA, or Self-Contained Underwater Breathing Apparatus.

In the 1940s, a French Canadian engineer named Emile Gagnon partnered with an ambitious French naval lieutenant named Jacques-Yves Cousteau. Using a car regulator as their base mechanism, they reengineered it to deliver compressed air to divers as they naturally breathed in and out. Their patented Aqua-Lung, which became commercially available to the international market between 1946 and

Legendary underwater explorer and innovator Jacques-Yves Cousteau.

Sin City

Since the inception of piracy, there have always been safe havens that raging rogues could use to make repairs, replenish supplies, or come ashore to spend their hard-won riches on drinking, gambling, and whoring. The most infamous of these hideouts was an area off the southern coast of Jamaica. Dubbed Port Royal, the ten-mile Palisadoes sand spit and the commercially successful town sitting atop it were so infested with pirates, privateers, buccaneers, and prostitutes that it was dubbed "the richest and wickedest city in the world." But all of that debauchery and self-indulgence changed in an instant.

On June 7, 1692, at 11:53 A.M., Port Royal, a town often compared to Sodom for its illicit reputation, fell victim to a huge earthquake followed by an enormous tidal wave that literally swept the town and somewhere between 2,000 and 5,000 residents into the sea. Since that time, Port Royal has been preserved, its underwater archaeological importance secured in large part by the efforts of Bob Marx, who first excavated the area in 1964 and later worked with the Jamaican government to secure the site. To this day, nautical archaeologists continue to uncover priceless historical artifacts that tell the tale of Port Royal's lurid past.

Above, an illustration of Jamaica's Kingston Harbor and the notorious pirate hideaway Port Royal.

1952, revolutionized the science and practicality of diving, and opened up a vast world of underwater exploration. Following on the heels of that technology were wetsuits, which were first developed by the U.S. Navy in 1951, and made available to the public in 1956. Arguably one of the greatest beneficiaries of diving technology is the discipline of maritime archaeology, which enables individuals to salvage a wealth of historical data, especially in the search and study of sunken vessels such as the *Atocha* and, in some cases, entire towns such as Port Royal.

As with all precarious modes of transportation, ships of all shapes and sizes have fallen to Poseidon's lair as a result of accidents, enemy fire, or technical failure, or simply at the hand of Mother Nature. Like the *Atocha*, the *Nuestra Señora de la Concepcion* also fell victim to a hurricane as it was guarding the rear of a flotilla that set sail on September 20, 1641. The *Concepcion* managed to stay afloat and sailed for more than three weeks before finally running aground and sinking. In 1687, American William Phipps managed to find her and salvage a small portion of her cargo, including over 450 silver ingots, over 300 pounds of silver plate, and over 450,000 pieces of eight. In modern currency, the treasure is worth more than $30 million. For over 300 years, the *Concepcion* slumbered until being resurrected by legendary treasure hunter Burt Webber in 1978. His tenacious seventeen-year search resulted in the salvage of additional artifacts and coins worth over $14 million.

Of equal repute is modern-day Indiana Jones Bob Marx, whose treasure hunting extends to both land and sea. For over forty years, Marx has been credited with a wide variety of historical discoveries, including Mayan temples, Phoenician shipwrecks, Civil War vessels, and, in 1972, perhaps his most famous discovery, the Spanish galleon *Nuestra Señora de las Maravillas*. Carrying a weight of 900 tons, the *Maravillas* sank off the Bahamian coastline in 1656. What remained quietly hiding in the Atlantic was a mother lode of silver, gold, and emeralds that would remain undisturbed until 1972 when Marx and his team recovered her after years of searching.

Two deep-sea divers of the late 1800s wearing early diving suits that were attached to compressed air apparatus.

The Devil and the Deep Blue Sea

Magnificent Spanish galleons loaded down with tons of riches, like the *Atocha*, the *Concepcion*, and the *Maravillas*, were an irresistible lure to high-seas villains. When you mention the word "pirate" these days, most people immediately think of Johnny Depp and his alter ego Jack Sparrow, the charismatic pirate captain of the amazingly successful *Pirates of the Caribbean* franchise. But when push comes to shove, Captain Jack could not hold a cutlass to the pirates of antiquity, the majority of whom were incredibly brutal sea robbers. Since around 2500 B.C., pirates have plagued individuals, nations, and continents, and in the case of the ancient Egyptians and Greeks, have brought entire civilizations to their knees. High-seas piracy evolved over the centuries, as better weaponry, faster ships, and New World riches became available. From the ruthless Sea Peoples to the Vikings to infamous Golden Age pirates, raging rogues were the scourge of the sea, one that unfortunately continues to present day.

But when we think of piracy we usually think of the so-called Golden Age, which really only lasted between thirty and fifty years, from around 1680 to 1730. The majority of piracy was focused in the Caribbean, where ruthless scallywags such as Bartholomew "Black Bart" Roberts, Charles Vane, Edward Low, Black Sam Bellamy, Calico Jack Rackham, Anne Bonny, and Mary Read terrorized anyone who had the misfortune of crossing their bow. Throughout the Golden Age, however, there was but one pirate who literally stood head and shoulders above the rest; a man so feared that the mere sight of his flag elicited surrender. That man was Edward Teach, and his rule-by-fear tactics and zest for power were legendary even among pirates themselves. In 1717, Teach was famously described as being "a tall spare man with a very black beard which he wore very long." He was a fiercely tenacious man, a

An illustration circa 1896 of pirates using a typical ruse to lure unsuspecting merchantmen into their trap.

strategic fighter, and an enigmatic captain who could alternately be ruthless or ardent about protecting his crew. He was and shall always be known as Blackbeard.

THE QUEEN ANNE'S REVENGE

The curious thing about Blackbeard was that he was by no means the most successful pirate when it came to securing priceless booty, but during his short four-year reign of terror, from 1714 to 1718, he struck absolute horror into the hearts of everyone he encountered, from merchant crews to the entire city and port of Charleston, South Carolina, where he lay siege in 1718. As is common with pirate history, much is known only through scattered written and oral accounts handed down through generations and has been hotly debated by historians for centuries.

What makes Blackbeard unique is that a part of his history is now surfacing in the form of his prized flagship *Queen Anne's Revenge*, a 200- to 300-ton French slaver, formerly named *La Concorde*, which Blackbeard modified as his personal fighting machine. With forty cannons on board, the *Revenge* was a formidable warship captained by a rogue who was equally intimidating. Just prior to battle, to give himself the appearance of the devil himself, Blackbeard was known to place slow-burning cannon matches under his hat and set them alight, sending wispy smoke around his menacing face.

In 1718, Blackbeard made the mistake of sailing the *Revenge* into North Carolina's Beaufort Inlet, where she became trapped in the shallows. Surprisingly, he abandoned her as well as the majority of his crew, in a move that's still debated by historians as to whether

Eye Spy

Moore Memorial Public Library in Texas City, Texas, asked *History Detectives* to investigate the provenance of a spyglass in their possession that they believed was owned by famed privateer, pirate, and war hero Jean Lafitte. A known smuggler operating near New Orleans in the early 1800s, Lafitte made a fortune bringing contraband English products into the United States despite an embargo that was designed to strangle Great Britain's economic interests in the States. In the ensuing War of 1812, Lafitte switched sides and helped U.S. forces win a decisive victory over the British in the Battle of New Orleans.

History Detective Tukufu Zuberi investigated the history of the battered spyglass and, after establishing its date of manufacture, determined that it couldn't have been in Lafitte's hands before his death in 1821. Fortunately, Tukufu determined that the spyglass did belong to James Campbell, one of Lafitte's trusted captains and a notorious pirate in his own right.

The inscription on the spyglass allegedly belonging to infamous pirate Jean Lafitte.

or not it was intentional. Blackbeard was never again to lay eyes upon the *Queen Anne's Revenge*, as he died in an infamous battle on the deck of the British man-of-war *Jane*, on November 22, 1718.

Over two centuries later, in November 1996, research divers swimming in the area of Beaufort Inlet happened upon a huge cache of ballast stones, anchors, and more importantly—cannons. An official search was instituted in 1997 by the nonprofit Maritime Research Institute (MRI) and the North Carolina Department of Cultural Resources for the wreckage of what many believed was the *Revenge*. For the past decade, painstaking research and conservation efforts have been rewarded, as the *Revenge* relinquished her secrets. Cannons, anchors, the ship's bell, pewter chargers, tobacco pipe paraphernalia, a finial, guns, lead shot, wine bottles, and grains of gold are but a few of the items recovered. In 2007, almost 2,000 artifacts were sent to the North Carolina Maritime Museum.

HEADS UP

When Blackbeard finally met the Grim Reaper on November 22, 1718, during a battle against Royal Navy lieutenant Robert Maynard aboard the *Jane*, it was a scene unbelievable to most. So incredibly resilient was the rogue that he reportedly sustained over twenty cuts to his body and over a half dozen gunshots—and still continued hand-to-hand combat. What he didn't see coming was the final blow of a sword at the hands of one of Maynard's Scottish crewmen.

The skull alleged to be Blackbeard's.

In keeping with the true spirit of piracy, any rogue worth his or her salt would sooner dwell in Davy Jones's Locker for eternity than not have a legend about them. It is said that after Blackbeard perished, Maynard lopped off his head and tossed his body overboard, after which the body swam three laps around the boat before finally sinking to glory, fathoms below. The infamous scallywag's head wasn't so lucky. Maynard ordered it tied to the *Jane's* bow as a trophy, where it remained for the entire trip home.

You might surmise that the decapitation of the world's most famous pirate clearly signified the end of his mortal presence. That assumption would be incorrect. After being retrieved from the *Jane's* bow, Blackbeard's head was allegedly on display in the town of Bath, after which it began yet another legendary journey. In his 1958 book *Dig for Pirate Treasure*, Robert I. Nesmith shared an encounter with author and pirate-lore expert Edward Rowe Snow. On a stormy night, Nesmith met with Snow, who revealed to him a silver-coated skull he believed was Blackbeard's. He went on to tell Nesmith that the skull, after being covered in silver, had been owned by a college fraternity and later by a tavern owner and his subsequent descendants. It had even been used intermittently as a drinking cup.

Nesmith's telling of the tale notes Snow's sanity and sobriety, despite the fact that he was absolutely convinced that the skull was indeed Black-beard's. How was he so certain? Because it spoke to him. Today, the skull remains on display in Salem, Massachusetts, at the Peabody Essex Museum, donated after Snow passed on. Experts and pirate fanatics alike continue to hope that the skull can be officially identified or at the very least have a facial reconstruction performed to show just what the world's most infamous pirate might have looked like.

> **time TEASER**
>
> How many times did Blackbeard marry?
>
> **Answer:** No one knows for certain, but it is said he had about thirteen wives.

The Golden Steamer Mystery

For thirteen years, the legendary steamer SS *Portland* plied the treacherous waters of the Pacific Northwest until she struck uncharted rocks off the Alaskan coast during a brutal winter storm. On November 12, 1910, the captain steered the sinking ship onto a sandbar at the mouth of Alaska's Katalla River and abandoned her to the forces of nature. She would lie undisturbed and nearly forgotten until Gabriel Scott, an Alaskan ecologist with the Cascadia Wildlands Project, noticed the remains of a ship in 2002, and sent photographs to shipwreck specialist Michael Burwell, who passed the information on to state archaeologist Dave McMahan.

Alaskan ecologist Gabriel Scott, whose discovery prompted a *History Detectives* investigation.

Although McMahan lacked the resources or expertise to explore the possibility that this might in fact be the long-lost SS *Portland*, he knew the discovery could be a significant addition to Alaska's cultural heritage. Overwhelmed by the tantalizing maritime mystery, he contacted *History*

The SS *Portland* in her heyday during the early 1900s.

Detectives, hoping they could expose an important piece of Gold Rush history. Unable to refuse such a challenge, and armed with her laptop and long johns, detective Elyse Luray made tracks for the Alaskan wilderness.

Finding the SS *Portland* would indeed be an archaeological coup, as the role she played in saving the U.S. economy was staggering. To start the investigation, Elyse had to research the social and economic history of the era, which showed that during the late 1800s, vast overexpansion of nationally subsidized railroads throughout the United States sent a signal of booming economic growth and triggered wildly speculative business decisions. Unfortunately, it was the wrong signal, as uneasy foreign investors began bailing out of the U.S. market and cashing in bonds, nearly draining the U.S. Treasury of gold supplies. The stock crash that followed in 1893 ruined thousands of businesses and threw millions of U.S. citizens out of work and into desperate times. In the midst of a hopeless situation, the country needed an economic wakeup call, and it came from a most unexpected source—Alaska.

The headline in an 1897 issue of the *Seattle Post-Intelligencer*.

Since gold first became a precious commodity, tough and independent gold miners have clawed stubborn livings from the ground. Throughout the 1880s, an estimated 250 hard-bitten miners toiled in the relative seclusion of Canada's Yukon Territory, barely scraping by until a veteran California prospector named George Carmack and two Yukon Indian comrades hit the mother lode in the spring of 1896, literally hand-picking chunks of gold from the bed of a tiny Yukon River tributary. Word spread quickly, and local miners descended on the area like moths to flame, staking out claims of their own. For nearly a year, miners panned small fortunes out of the area before the rest of the world heard a word of the discovery.

The United States had formally purchased Alaska from Russia in 1867, and by 1890, a fleet of about two dozen ships regularly supplied U.S. forces and settlements in the sparsely populated new territory, subsidizing their freight business with a small but steady tourism sideline. In July of 1897, the steamship *Excelsior* set sail from Alaska to San Francisco, and the SS *Portland* soon followed, destined for Seattle. The *Excelsior* arrived in San Francisco on July 15, 1897, with a party of prospectors laden with gold. Although the miners were generally treated as a curiosity in California, news of the imminent arrival of the *Portland* was quickly telegraphed to Seattle, and the local news-paper, the *Seattle Post-Intelligencer*, hired a tugboat and sent reporter Beriah Brown to investigate.

The wreckage found by Gabriel Scott in Alaska's Katalla River.

After interviewing passengers, Brown raced back with the story that more than a ton of gold was on board. The *Post-Intelligencer* put out a special edition of the paper, and when the *Portland* arrived, thousands of spectators lined the docks to see for themselves. Sixty-eight miners left the ship, staggering under the weight of their fortunes, and the population of Seattle went wild. Within ten days, nearly 1,500 locals booked passage for Alaska, including Seattle Mayor William Wood, who resigned his position by telegram. The rush was on, and the economic wake-up call for the United States was ringing off the hook.

The SS *Portland* was a steamer with a sketchy past. Originally christened the *Haytian Republic*, the ship was launched in Bath, Maine, in 1885, and saw service hauling freight in the West Indies, where the captain was arrested for smuggling arms. After nearly sinking on a rocky coast, the *Haytian Republic* was repaired and sailed around Cape Horn in order to service Alaskan fisheries. But instead, the steamer was allegedly used to smuggle opium and Chinese laborers into Canada. In 1893, she caught fire and sank near Portland, Oregon, after which new owners resurrected her into a respectable vessel, hauling freight and passengers from Oregon and Washington to Alaska. They renamed her SS *Portland* after the city of

The Chilcoot Option

Eager Klondike Gold Rush prospectors flowed into Alaska through the port of Skagway. Of the two overland routes to the gold fields, the Chilcoot Pass provided the quickest but unquestionably the most arduous choice. Only thirty-three miles long, the Chilcoot Trail, a steep and treacherous path over which the "stampeders" carried enormously unwieldy bundles of supplies, was then followed by a hair-raising boat trip down the Yukon River.

Dealing with ill-prepared prospectors during the first years of the rush forced the Royal Canadian Mounted Police to establish the strictly enforced requirement that a year's worth of supplies weighing a ton be packed in. Of the estimated 100,000 gold-hungry pioneers who attempted the journey, only a third reached their goals, with most of them ditching heavy, bulky items along the way—and eventually giving up. To this day, relics of cast iron stoves, frying pans, and collapsible boats still litter the "world's longest museum."

Hundreds of hopeful prospectors make their way up Alaska's Chilcoot Pass circa 1898.

her rebirth. After delivering her wealthy party of miners to Seattle in 1897, the *Portland* was busier than ever supplying booming gold-rush enterprises—that is, until her tragic sinking in 1910.

Working with Dave McMahan, Elyse organized an expedition of experts that included Michael Burwell, nautical archaeologist John Jenson, and historical archaeologist Karl Gurcke. Careful timing with chartered planes put the team into a base camp near the site during the low seasonal tides in May 2004. Elyse and her team choreographed their movements with the ebb and flow of the tide, and in the scant few hours of lowest water waded to the impressive remains. Careful measurements of the exposed hull proved to closely match the known thirty-six-foot width of the *Portland*, but absolute proof would come by measuring the boilers.

A group of prospectors in Sheep Camp, Alaska, making their way to the Klondike circa 1898.

After a precarious climb to the top of the old steam engine, Jenson calculated the sizes of the boilers and established that they matched the *Portland's* refitted 1893 steam boilers perfectly. To the delight of Gabriel Scott, Elyse confirmed that he had indeed found the wreckage of the SS *Portland*, and that her resting place would be nominated for the National Registry of Historic Places, making the old steamer a permanent reminder of a gold rush that turned the tide of the country's economic plight.

Elyse Luray in front of the *Portland* wreckage with expedition members (from left) John Jenson, Karl Gurcke, Elyse, Gabriel Scott, Dave McMahan, and Michael Burwell.

DIY DETECTIVE

So you want to be a full-fledged treasure hunter? What would you like to search for? How much time and money are required? Where do you start?

The first thing to bear in mind is that seekers like Mel Fisher, Bob Marx, and Burt Webber spent the majority of their adult lives, not to mention hundreds of thousands of dollars, securing their legacies. Maritime treasure hunting is not for the faint of heart. Of course, you never know when you'll get lucky, and that's part of the addiction of treasure hunting.

In 1948, a fellow by the name of Kip Wagner was walking along Florida's Sebastian Beach when he found a few Spanish coins, and that was all it took for the treasure bug to bite. By the 1960s, Wagner's Real Eight Corporation (which Fisher worked with) had located a number of wrecks that yielded millions of dollars. But sometimes, the best treasures have far more historical significance.

In the very first episode of *History Detectives* in 2003, Elyse Luray investigated a curious stone found in Mantoloking, New Jersey, by avid beachcomber Betsy Colie. Carved into the stone was a human face. Was it simply a ceramic object someone had dropped, or was it a Native American

Elyse Luray with beachcomber Betsy Colie in Mantoloking, New Jersey. Opposite, the amazing stone face Colie discovered on the beach.

artifact, or was there more to it? As it turned out, a cargo ship named *Vizcaya* went down off the Jersey shore in 1890. Betsy's stone likely came from that shipwreck, and it wasn't just a trinket—the stone was from the Mexican region of Teotihuacán and dated from around A.D. 250.

If you're going to embark on a treasure hunt, there are a few things you should know, whether you're doing research or are out in the field. For starters, always keep detailed records of any investigation you take on, including dates, locations, and photographic evidence. If you're researching in archives, libraries, courthouses, or any other local, state, or national resource, always follow their rules and guidelines.

If you happen upon an artifact, first take pictures, and if you suspect it's Native American in origin, *leave it alone* and contact authorities. When doing field work, take special care to plan excursions and be aware of unfamiliar surroundings. If you're diving, snorkeling, or hiking in a remote area, for example, always travel with a buddy and notify others of your expedition itinerary.

Above all, don't hesitate to contact a professional or expert if you find something you think has historical or financial value, or even if you're simply uncertain what an artifact might be or how to examine it. You may not find a treasure chest brimming with gold on your first hunt, so prepare to be patient and tenacious.

For example, since 1795 hundreds of individuals have atempted the recovery of an alleged treasure buried at the bottom of the legendary money pit of Oak Island, located just off the Nova Scotia coast. Despite a few alluring bits and pieces, no one has actually found significant treasure as yet, but legend has it that everything from the Holy Grail to the French Crown jewels and from pirate treasure to the original works of William Shakespeare are rumored to have been buried in the pit. For more happy hunting tips, visit *History Detectives* at www.pbs.org.

CHAPTER FIFTEEN
That's Entertainment!

From the earliest days of herky-jerky hand-cranked silent movies to today's computer-enhanced mega-million-dollar blockbusters, the film industry has affected the lives, imaginations, and entertainment decisions of virtually everyone on the planet. Many black and white classics from the first half of the 1900s are still considered some of the finest films ever made, and stand up against more recent efforts despite the advantages of increasingly sophisticated digital film techniques.

The simple truth is that a first-class director with a great screenplay and a cast of gifted actors can tell a timeless, powerful, and captivating story that captures the hearts of an audience, and many film producers did exactly that decades ago. To this day, everything about the film industry, movies, and the individuals who make them remains a public fascination.

In addition to providing years of historic entertainment, the History Detectives have gone Hollywood on several investigations, including the mystery of Grace Kelly's Sunbeam Alpine, a Lincoln Heights movie studio, a lighter belonging to studio chief Harry Warner, and even Disney's iconic character, Mickey Mouse (see chapter 7). During one of these film forays, Wes Cowan and Elyse Luray took us on a larger-than-life, behind-the-scenes look into the production of one of the most famous and influential early blockbusters—*King Kong*. And while the film made headline news and changed the face of science fiction film production forever, it was one of the thousands of films that sadly drifted quietly into obscurity. Or did it?

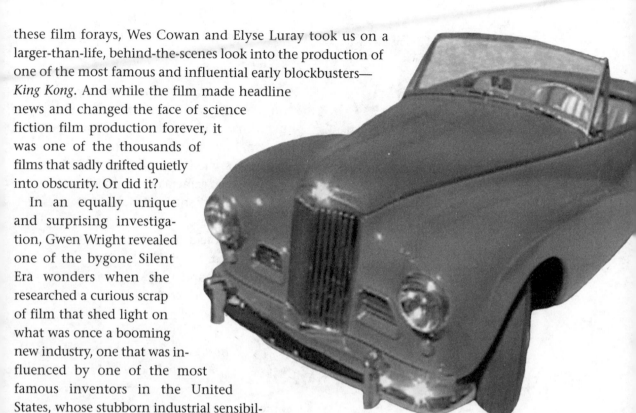

In an equally unique and surprising investigation, Gwen Wright revealed one of the bygone Silent Era wonders when she researched a curious scrap of film that shed light on what was once a booming new industry, one that was influenced by one of the most famous inventors in the United States, whose stubborn industrial sensibilities inadvertently helped create Hollywood.

The Clue in the Camera

In 1933 the United States was still languishing in the spirit-crushing mire of the Great Depression, which began after the stock market crash of 1929. Although the financial depression was international in scope, most of the U.S. population endured the situation on a deeply personal basis, with millions of individuals out of work and banks repossessing property that had been passed down through generations. For many families the Depression was an unmitigated, life-altering disaster.

On March 2, 1933, a small shred of distraction entered movie theaters when the innovative monster movie *King Kong* presented a far more palpable—if fleeting—horror. Audiences were shocked to see a hundred-foot-tall gorilla rampaging through the streets of New York City, blithely scrambling up skyscrapers and reaching into homes at will in a beguiling performance that by film's end left many in sympathetic tears. The makers of *King Kong* at RKO Studios developed

A vintage Swedish movie poster for *King Kong* demonstrates the universal appeal of the giant ape.

ingenious filming techniques by utilizing the talents of the most innovative cinematographers in Hollywood.

Unbelievably, a man in Lake Bay, Washington, thought he had a crucial piece of equipment that helped create the movie: one of the original film cameras used on the set. A dedicated movie buff, Sam Dodge came across the classic camera at an auction in England and quickly snapped it up. After investigating the history of his prize, Dodge believed the camera might have originally been owned by Eddie Linden, chief cinematographer of *King Kong*, so he contacted *History Detectives* to help confirm his suspicions.

Dodge's story caught the attention of Wes Cowan and Elyse Luray, who met with Dodge to investigate the story and gather background on his camera, a first-rate example of quintessential Hollywood machinery with a recognizable round "Mickey Mouse" ear style magazine that held a huge roll of film. The camera, a Mitchell Standard, appeared to have been most recently used for cartoon animation and had come with a 1970s celluloid transparency, known as a *cel*, from a version of *Alice in Wonderland*. The cel was important because it gave evidence of the camera's past life in major studios.

To investigate the inside story about the making of the *King Kong* simian, Wes met with legendary cinematographer Ray Harryhausen, the most renowned stop-action film animator in movie history. Harryhausen

DID YOU know

When enormous monsters made their first appearance on the silver screen, they scared people to death, and discussion about them focused mainly on their shock value. In truth, however, the subtle and in some cases deliberate messages they sent were warnings and direct reflections of events occurring at the time. King Kong was portraying public rage and frustration. Godzilla was born as a result of the atom bomb. The Cold War–era film *Them!* was crawling with giant ants created by nuclear testing, and in 1957, scorpions the size of skyscrapers were unleashed by volcanic eruptions in *The Black Scorpion*.

was just thirteen when he first saw *King Kong*, and he remembers the event as the inspiration for his career aspirations. The man responsible for bringing the great ape to life was animation pioneer Willis O'Brien, who began his career as a marble sculptor before turning to film. His first animation endeavor was with Thomas Edison's film company, where he produced the 1917 short film *The Dinosaur and the Missing Link* using a unique *stop-action*, or stop-motion, filming technique with handcrafted clay models that were photographed and repositioned one frame at a time.

Sam Dodge with the Mitchell Standard camera allegedly used by Eddie Linden to film *King Kong*. Below, a close-up of the camera.

Stop-action filmmaking was agonizingly tedious work, but when the film was projected onscreen the sequence of single shots created the amazing illusion of seamless movement. Hired by RKO producer David O. Selznick, who would later produce the timeless *Gone with the Wind* in 1939, O'Brien perfected his stop-motion technique using an eighteen-inch-tall model of Kong built on a metal ball-and-joint skeleton covered with foam rubber and rabbit fur. A life-sized gorilla head was also created for close-up shots, but the smaller model proved to be so emotionally convincing that it was used almost exclusively throughout the production.

In its time, RKO Studio's *King Kong* was a risky production for a struggling five-year-old film company on the brink of bankruptcy. The Great Depression had taken a toll on the once booming movie industry, and most films weren't even making as much money at the box office as they cost to produce. On top of that, *King*

Stop-motion legend
Ray Harryhausen
during his 2004
interview with
Wes Cowan.

Kong's production cost of $672,000 was an enormous investment in the face of an unstable economy, but Selznick's faith in the project proved to be well founded. Willis O'Brien was the perfect choice to create the character of King Kong, and he went to great lengths to tug at the heart strings of his audience by humanizing the creature's movements and facial expressions.

Willis O'Brien brought cinematographer Eddie Linden into the production knowing full well that he completely understood the art of stop-action cinema, a process that required long and tedious hours of painstaking precision. The Mitchell Standard camera was the tool of choice for nearly all major cinematographers and studios of the period and was an industry mainstay since its development in the early 1920s. Although O'Brien and Linden went on to make films for decades after *King Kong*, neither of them received the same financial support or achieved the same overwhelming superstar status and industy acceptance that their collaboration on the beguiling great ape afforded them.

With Wes gathering background on the production of *King Kong*, Elyse concentrated on the history of Sam Dodge's Mitchell Standard camera. Sales records from the Mitchell Camera Company proved that the serial number on Dodge's find matched the camera sold to Eddie Linden in

A King Kong model.

Mighty Ray Harryhausen

Since his first teenage exposure to *King Kong* in 1933, Ray Harryhausen has achieved a cultlike status as the premier stop-motion animator in the film industry. Long before the advent of computer-generated animation, stop-motion was the only method of realistically integrating fantastic creatures into real-world situations, and Harryhausen was a master artist of the technique.

His first major film was *Mighty Joe Young* in 1949, when King Kong's creator Willis O'Brien hired him as an assistant animator. The film won an Oscar for special effects, with Harryhausen generally credited with creating most of the animation himself. *The Beast From 20,000 Fathoms* in 1953 was his first solo effort and was a major box-office draw, further securing his reputation as a studio moneymaker.

Ray Harryhausen working on the infamous Kraken from the 1981 film *Clash of the Titans*.

In 1957, the cinematographer continued to perfect his craft with the creation of the startling emotional characteristics of the Venusian beast Ymir featured in *20 Million Miles to Earth*. In 1963, the technical wizardry of *Jason and the Argonauts* resulted in what many consider to be Harryhausen's masterwork, one that's still carefully studied by filmmakers. Released in 1981, *Clash of the Titans* was the last film made by the brilliant artist, earning over $41 million in U.S. box-office receipts. For fans of science fiction and cinematic special effects, and with his enduring influence on generations of movie producers, Ray Harryhausen is as close as a filmmaker can get to being a national treasure.

The serial number on the tag on Sam Dodge's Mitchell Standard camera matched the number of the camera recorded as having been sold to Eddie Linden in 1926.

early 1926. While researching records at the American Film Institute, Elyse learned that RKO Studios originally had an inventory of twelve Mitchell Standards. With thirty-five films in production during the year *King Kong* was made, there's little doubt that Eddie Linden would have rented his personal camera to the busy studio for filming.

Wes provided further circumstantial evidence after discovering the obituary marking Linden's death in November 1956. Appropriately for a die-hard filmmaker, Linden suffered a heart attack while working on what would be his last film. Elyse and Wes shared their findings with Sam Dodge, including Linden's obituary, which read in part: "It was his camera which filmed the spectacular *King Kong*." Perhaps a respectful turn of the phrase, but all of the evidence gathered by Elyse and Wes indicated that Sam Dodge now owned Eddie Linden's camera—a genuine piece of stellar cinematic history.

The Pivotal Tale of the Black Maria

If you want to stump your friends during your next dinner party, ask them if they know who built the first commercial film studio. Odds are they'll never come up with one of the greatest inventors of all time. In 1893, the world's first film studio was built by none other than Thomas Edison (see chapter 5). Dubbed "the Black Maria" (pronounced *muh-rye-uh*) after the dark, cramped, and forbidding police wagons of the era, the studio, built in West Orange, New Jersey, produced an enormous number of short films that changed the face of entertainment forever. Ironically, Edison's 1879 invention of the first practical lightbulb didn't solve the lighting requirements of film production, so the Black Maria was built on a swivel axis so that the entire structure could be rotated to capture the daily passage of the sun's light.

The films from the studio were designed to play on a single-user film projector called a *Kinetoscope*, which Edison's company built and distributed to hundreds of arcades across the nation. A shrewd invention that made its public debut in 1891, the Kinetoscope was a

time
TEASER   Which famous television detective starred in the 1956 film *Godzilla, King of the Monsters!?*

Answer: *Perry Mason* star Raymond Burr.

cabinet measuring approximately twenty by twenty-four inches wide and four feet tall with a peephole for viewing. When a patron inserted a coin, the machine played a fifty-foot reel of film in a continuous loop backlit by one of Edison's own lightbulbs. The production values and content of those first films was incredibly mundane by today's standards, featuring simple performances by acrobats and dancers, short skits, and a famously amusing clip of one of Edison's own employees, aptly titled *Fred Ott's Sneeze*. But in its time, the Kinetoscope proved to be a fascinating draw, and eager audiences loved the innovation of watching lifelike moving images for the first time in history.

The Black Maria was also built around Edison's creation of the first practical and commercially viable motion picture camera. Called the *Kineto-graph*, the camera was an unwieldy contraption that utilized a fixed lens and expanded on Eastman Kodak's creation of perforated film, developed

Renowned inventor Thomas Alva Edison in his lab circa 1904.

to be hand-wound in single-shot hand-held cameras. Edison's research team reasoned that the concept could be applied to a hand-cranked camera movement that would take a steady series of still shots in sequence that would replay to convey the illusion of continuous movement. The idea worked, and has been used by filmmakers ever since. Edison's camera also ushered in the first commercial use of thirty-five-millimeter film in a format that remains an industry standard to this day.

By 1895, however, Edison was forced to rethink his position on the single-user Kinetoscope concept. Although his system was still profitable, cinematic competitors were busy exploring an idea with much more potential by building projectors that would play the same images to a wider audience on a large screen. The economic benefit became obvious for the savvy businessman, and by 1896, Edison's company created the *Projecting Kinetoscope*. With the aid of a newly developed mobile camera that could be taken outside the studio, the

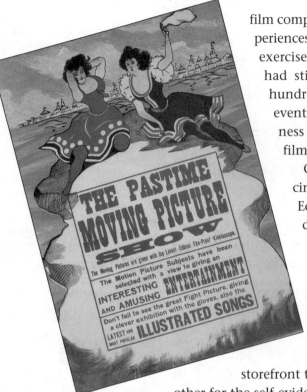

A poster for the Kinetoscope, the film projector developed by Thomas Edison and his crew during the late 1800s.

film company focused on *actuality* films of everyday experiences such as parades, vaudeville acts, and military exercises. At this point, the concept of storytelling had still not been explored, and after watching hundreds of monotonous social events, audiences eventually became bored with the tiresome sameness of motion pictures. By the early 1900s the film industry was in trouble.

Gradually, a slow but significant shift in Edison's cinematic priorities occurred with the hiring of Edwin Porter near the end of 1900. After producing several narrative films, Porter made *The Great Train Robbery* in 1903, and it turned out to be one of Edison's most famous and profitable films, its success triggering a shift toward fictional cinematic storytelling with an emphasis on highly popular comedies.

By 1905, the historically significant *nickelodeon* first appeared in the form of small storefront theaters that played film shorts one after the other for the self-evident admission price of a nickel. The gimmick paid off: three years later, in 1908, there were an estimated 8,000 nickelodeons in operation in the United States. That same year, Edison attempted to counter growing competition in the industry by forming the Association of Edison Licensees, followed by the creation of the Motion Picture Patent Company, commonly known as the Edison Trust. These moves were generally considered to be an effort to monopolize the film industry, and drove many independent filmmakers to the balmy, cinema-friendly climate of Southern California. In the end, it was just these rebels who formed the essential structure of Hollywood and eventually turned the tables on Edison's East Coast conglomerate.

It's nearly impossible to overstate the impact of Thomas Edison's cinematic endeavors on the nature of entertainment in the United States, and arguably the entire world. Entertainment seekers quickly grew accustomed to popping into a movie theater, where they could escape the realities of everyday life for the affordable price of five cents. To this day, the film industry continues to

time
TEASER   How did technicians create Godzilla's famous roar for the 1956 film *Godzilla, King of the Monsters!*?

Answer: They used a leather glove coated in resin, and dragged it across the strings of a low-pitched contrabass.

affect the lives of individuals the world over, whether they eagerly flock to every weekend blockbuster or idly switch on their televisions. Although the industry would no doubt have been created with or without the influence of Edison, the inventor's incessant drive to push the boundaries of nearly every technical innovation within his grasp left an indelible mark on modern life. But in the face of growing competition from Hollywood studios, and primarily because cinema was never the sole focus of his vast business interests, Edison sold the Black Maria and permanently ended his involvement with the film industry in 1918.

Thrilled moviegoers gather in front of the Leader Theater in Washington, D.C. during the early 1920s.

The *Devil Dog Dawson* Mystery

Of the thousands of films made during the silent-film era of the early 1900s, very few remain intact, but John Eytchison of Elsmere, Kentucky, came across a fragment of one of them while cleaning out his deceased grandfather's house. Thinking he'd discovered a piece of cinematic history, Eytchison asked *History Detectives* to help determine the provenance and significance of his find, and investigative historian Gwen Wright was happy to lend her expertise in solving this silent-screen mystery. Meeting with Eytchison, Gwen learned that his grandfather had no connections to the film industry, but for some reason he had held on

The film clip investigated by *History Detectives*, allegedly from the silent film *Dangerous Hour* starring Eddie Polo.

Prolific silent-screen star and action hero Eddie Polo.

to a thirty-five-millimeter film canister with the intriguing label "Dangerous Hour with Eddie Polo." Eytchison was able to determine that a film with that title was made, but no copies were known to exist and the film in the can was only a fifty-foot fragment of a full-length feature. With so little information, such a small piece of film, and so many silent films lost to time, Gwen had her work cut out for her. The first question was: Who was Eddie Polo?

Hundreds of film stars came and went during the Silent Era, and Eddie Polo was one of the many who shot to fame for a few brief years before fading into obscurity. A circus performer turned cinema stuntman, the 5'9" Polo was a man of almost superhuman physical strength. Universal Studios was one of the Hollywood studios formed by independent film producers who escaped Thomas Edison's attempted cinematic stranglehold, and, hungry for talent, they hired the thirty-nine-year-old Polo in 1914 as the perfect action star for their early efforts. A popular box-office draw, Polo was perhaps an even bigger star in Europe; he was reputed to be the favorite film actor of England's Dowager Queen Alexandra. But after hundreds of successful films, Polo's star appeal slowly waned and finally plummeted with the introduction of sound to the movies in the late 1920s. His motion picture appearances dwindled to uncredited bit parts throughout the 1930s and 1940s, and he had all but disappeared by the time he died from heart failure while playing poker with old cinema friends in Hollywood in 1961.

The Library of Congress Motion Picture Conservation Center in Dayton, Ohio, has the mission of restoring, preserving, and protecting the nation's cinematic heritage, and holds more than a hundred million feet of film in their climatically monitored and controlled facilities. In an effort to glean more information from John Eytchison's alleged Eddie Polo film clip, Gwen traveled to Dayton to meet with Ken Weissman, who heads the Conservation Center. Included in their vast high-tech library is the only film negative of Thomas Edison's seminal film *The Great Train Robbery*, which is considered a priceless national treasure. According to Weissman, early film stock was made with silver nitrate, a chemical with highly combustible and degradable properties that contributed to the permanent loss of an

time
TEASER

In 1987, Christie's sold two of Charlie Chaplin's trademark items. What were they and how much did they sell for?

Answer: His trademark bowler hat and cane, which sold for over $150,000.

estimated 80 to 90 percent of all silent films ever produced. His assessment of the Polo clip indicated that it was made with nitrate and was far too fragile to risk feeding through a projector. In fact, the library's practice is to never take the chance of running their precious archival film through any projection devices.

The impressive climate-controlled facility at the Library of Congress Motion Picture Conservation Center in Ohio.

Closely inspecting the clip, Weissman determined that film date stamps indicated that the manufacture date was 1921. Since Eddie Polo's *Dangerous Hour* was produced in 1923, there was a slim possibility that this film might have been used for part of the filming, but most movie producers of the day preferred to use fresh film because it became unstable very quickly. Weissman took photos of a few frames and blew them up to reveal what appeared to be the film's star playing a drunken lawman in a Wild West setting. Comparing the images to known photos of Eddie Polo proved that the actor in the film clip wasn't Polo at all. Facing a dead end on identifying the hero in the film, Weissman offered to put Gwen in contact with one of his many outside film experts for help.

A still that expert Ken Weissman was able to pull from the film, which showed that the movie's star didn't resemble Eddie Polo.

While Ken Weissman searched for historical help, Gwen made a side trip to visit with nitrate film expert Larry Smith at Dayton's Victoria Theatre, a film house with its own Silent Era history. According to Smith, Western films were a mainstay of independent Hollywood studios, and literally hundreds of actors starred in many hundreds of cowboy

Got a Light?

The controversial 1930s German Ufatone lighter owned by Warner Bros. studio chief Harry Warner.

Frequently, a historical object isn't what it appears to be, as History Detective Elyse Luray learned when investigating the intriguing story of a solid brass Kaschie lighter purchased by Robert Gallant at a flea market. Engraved on the lighter is the name "Harry Warner" on one side, and "Ufatone" on the other. The ironic coincidence was that Warner, studio chief of Warner Bros. film studio, was Jewish and an avowed and active anti-Nazi, while Ufa was Germany's largest film studio and one of Hitler's major purveyors of Nazi propaganda.

Elyse's research showed that the lighter probably fell into Warner's hands before Hitler came into power in Germany during the late 1930s, and most likely was a gift from the German film studio in an effort to woo collaborative business ventures with Warner Bros. before the advent of Nazi aggression. When Hitler's early regime began showing signs of warfare and anti-Semitism, Warner volunteered his studio's services to the U.S. government and lit a personal fire by producing a number of his own anti-Fascist propaganda films.

action movies. Studios shipped films to theaters throughout the country by the crate loads and when interest in the new productions waned, theater owners simply tossed the films out.

A few entrepreneurs took advantage of the vast oversupply of old films by cutting them into segments and peddling them through magazine advertisements. For a dollar or so the average movie buff could purchase a few moments of film history to play on a cheap home projector—a device that was the predecessor of the modern DVD player. Smith also theorized that the clip of a drunken cowboy might have been edited out of a full-length film under pressure from Prohibition-era movie censors. Either way, it appeared that discovering a small section of a feature film tucked away in an attic, while unusual, wasn't farfetched. It was at that point in her investigation that Gwen was contacted by Ken Weissman, who had found a film historian who might be able to shed some light on the mysterious film clip.

As it turned out, independent film collector Richard Roberts had the clue Gwen needed to solve her cinematic conundrum. Having spent hundreds of hours watching silent movies, he recognized the lead actor and identified him as another Silent Era Western star: Jack Hoxie. Unlike Eddie Polo,

Hoxie was the real deal, an Idaho cowboy who found fame in Hollywood beginning in 1910. By 1919, he was a major Western star, particularly in small towns where Westerns were the primary theatrical attraction. During his career, Hoxie was known to have made at least 130 Westerns, often starring in as many as a dozen a year.

Perusing the captured still shots from the clip, Roberts also recognized the leading lady as Helen Rosson, another silent-screen star. This was the defining moment for Gwen's investigation because Helen Rosson and Jack Hoxie appeared in film together only once. Thrilled by the revelation, Gwen was able to tell John Eytchison that his

A frame from what is, according to the Library of Congress, thought to be the obscure 1926 film *The Highwaymen*, starring Jack Hoxie and Helen Holmes.

grandfather's elusive clip was a piece of the 1921 Hollywood Western *Devil Dog Dawson*. To top off the discovery, the Library of Congress reconstructed the film clip by painstakingly photographing and digitally sequencing every frame. The result? Thirty-eight seconds of priceless Hollywood history, which you can view by visiting the *History Detectives* Web site at www.pbs.org.

A restored frame from John Etychison's clip of *Devil Dog Dawson*, starring Jack Hoxie and Helen Rosson.

DIY DETECTIVE

Movies have had such a profound impact on popular culture that film memorabilia has unquestionably become one of the hottest collection hobbies, generating millions of dollars in annual transactions and trades and occasionally even making headline news when sales of significant cinematic treasures are made.

Famous films involving popular actors often generate the most impressive auction prices, as was the case in 1999 when Sotheby's sold a Best Picture Oscar for the film *Gone with the Wind*. It was purchased by Michael Jackson for $1.5 million. Seven years later, in 2006, Audrey Hepburn's little black dress from *Breakfast at Tiffany's* was sold by Christie's for $807,000.

Even the sale of collectible one-of-a-kind pieces from the television industry produces some amazing prices from hardcore fans and investors. That was certainly the case when more than a thousand props, costumes, miniatures, and models used in the enormously successful *Star Trek* television and film franchises hit the auction block at Christie's in October 2006 during a three-day event that triggered over $7 million in sales. The bidding action was almost surreal when a model of the legendary starship USS *Enterprise*—which was estimated to go for between $15,000 and $25,000—sold to a determined collector for a whopping $576,000. By the end of the sale, nine miniatures and models of *Star Trek's* legendary space-conquering warships had sold for well over $100,000 each.

Aside from the *Star Trek* frenzy, which dealt strictly with studio artifacts, even such relatively mundane items as studio giveaways can reach collector status, such as a mint-condition limited edition promotional wristwatch for Tim Burton's 1993 feature-length animated film *The Nightmare Before Christmas*. The watch is currently valued at over $250.

The term *mint condition* is the key when evaluating consumer-oriented film collectibles. A slightly used wristwatch with less than perfect packaging from the same film promotion can drop the value to less than $25. Bear in mind that collecting limited editions as investments is tricky and requires careful research. Most are produced in such large quantities that their resale value actually drops from the original purchase price.

Whether collecting for fun or profit, the necessity of keeping memorabilia in pristine condition cannot be overemphasized. As with all collections hobbies, the seemingly easiest way to find movie memorabilia is through online auctions. Auction sites that cater specifically to transactions between private sellers and buyers have a number of pitfalls for the unwary, and it's important to do your homework before placing any online bids. These online auctions are fully aware that forgers and scam artists take advantage of the relative anonymity of their Web sites and take steps to prevent crooks from using their services, but the simple truth is that fraudulent dealers rip off unsuspecting customers every day. Reputable online auctions guarantee their lots, and you can find a number of honest dealers and sellers through careful research.

The simplest method of protecting yourself is to research the sites and learn exactly how they operate before committing yourself. Nearly all of them sponsor forums where members can voice their concerns, relate past experiences, and offer advice. You can also find buying guides written by members that will help you spot and avoid unscrupulous dealers. As a rule, you should explore forums and

guides thoroughly, understand how auctions operate, and take advantage of the payment accounts that most sites use. Those accounts may cost a few pennies for every dollar you spend, but they offer recourse to recover your money if you've been misled. Careful research is the key to finding the perfect addition to your collection.

Also keep in mind that original film memorabilia is often priced far out of the reach of the average collector. Perhaps the most recognizable pieces of costuming collectibles in cinematic history are Dorothy's legendary ruby slippers from *The Wizard of Oz*. At least five pairs are known to have been used in the film, either by Judy Garland or her stand-in, Bobbie Koshay, who wore a different shoe size. The last pair known to have been sold went through Christie's in 2000 for a staggering $690,000. The auctioneer for that transaction was none other than History Detective Elyse Luray. What was the final selling price for the first pair to be auctioned in 1970? A paltry $15,000. The wizard is reaching for his wallet as we speak.

CHAPTER SIXTEEN

Skeletons in the Closet

I n exploring the mysteries of history, it's easy to be overwhelmed by the sheer number of events that shape our understanding of the past. But one of the joys of exploring seemingly unrelated historical incidents is the surprising number of links those episodes have to one another. People have explored uncharted territory, made significant technological discoveries, cured diseases, learned to feed themselves and their families, developed protections against enemies, and destroyed one another in seemingly senseless hostilities in a never-ending journey of trial and error with one common goal—survival. The irony is that survival is fleeting and mortality is inevitable. Or is it?

In a highly unusual investigation History Detective Gwen Wright explored the shocking death of a single individual that highlights the struggle of a new world. An equally daunting task fell to Tukufu Zuberi when he examined a fascinating experiment of limited colonization that resulted in the near extermination of an entire culture in North America. In the telling of these tales, one fact becomes increasingly clear: whether we examine seemingly insignificant individuals or the most powerful individuals of their day, the stories are equally compelling.

The Secret in the Cellar

Archaeologists excavating a 1660s Maryland home site weren't surprised to find ceramic fragments, broken bottles, tobacco pipes, and even spare change entombed at various levels in a trash pit of the home's cellar, but they certainly didn't expect to find human remains crammed in with the refuse. The discovery puzzled archaeologist Dr. Al Luckenbach, head of the Lost Towns Project, a community-based group that for fifteen years has located and excavated colonial sites in Maryland's Anne Arundel County. It also confounded project team member Cory Seznec, whose parents own the site where the skeletal remains were found. Knowing it was an unusual discovery and hoping to better understand the historical significance of the unexpected find, Seznec called upon History Detective Gwen Wright, who went to work uncovering the secret in the cellar.

Upon meeting with Luckenbach at the dig site, Gwen learned that dozens of excavations in the former British colonies revealed similar cellar trash pits that contained invaluable artifacts that helped document early life in the colonies, but none contained a human skeleton. Without a doubt, this find was a bizarre anomaly, and it also attracted the attention of a team from the Smithsonian Institute, headed by renowned forensic anthropologist Dr. Douglas Owsley. His initial appraisal of the exposed part of the skull was that the individual was a male who was likely of European descent.

Al Luckenbach,
Doug Owsley, and
Gwen Wright examine
skeletal remains at a
dig site in Maryland.

A view of the skeleton's position in the cellar pit during its excavation.

A few of the glazed earthenware fragments found with the skeletal remains.

Owsley also noticed an ominous fracture in the side of the skull, which could indicate that the individual had suffered a violent end.

As with all skeletal remains, there was much more to be learned through careful laboratory examinations, so piece by piece the team meticulously documented and disinterred the skeleton for further analysis at the Smithsonian's high-tech facility in Washington. Gwen's conversations with Luckenbach revealed that the excavation site had been part of an early settlement named Providence, established in 1649 by the English. The refuse piled above and below the skeleton provided clues for dating the burial of the body, with glazed earthenware fragments and a 1664 brass farthing indicating that the death occurred between 1655 and 1665.

To better understand the circumstances that might have led to the individual's death, it's important to examine the political and religious climate of the era. The English Civil Wars between Puritan Parliamentarians and Catholic Royalists that brought an end to the reign of King Charles I had spilled over into the religiously divided colonies in a long-running dispute that would be decided by the battle of Severn, fought in 1655 near the excavation site. Virginia Puritans asserted their ties to Oliver Cromwell's new English regime by ousting the Royalist governor, Richard Stone, who quickly retaliated by leading a company of 250 in an attack on Providence, where the Puritans had taken power.

Commanded by landowner Captain William Fuller, the outnumbered Puritans overwhelmingly prevailed in the battle, killing or wounding nearly fifty Royalists and executing four more after the attack. Could the unceremoniously tossed-out body be one of those unfortunate soldiers killed in the conflict?

A complete analysis of the skeleton after its excavation.

At the Smithsonian laboratories in Washington, Gwen once again met with Doug Owsley, who had been patiently piecing together the life and death of the mysterious skeleton by investigating the evidence in the bones. After examining the tooth development, Owsley concluded that the age of the victim was no more than sixteen years. Wear on the spinal column and advanced muscle attachment growth indicated that the young man had experienced a great deal of physical exertion and likely carried heavy loads. All of Owsley's findings implied that the man had been a laborer in the colony and probably an indentured servant, one of the least likely to be afforded a decent burial.

A close-up of the skull clearly shows a fracture that Doug Owsley believed occurred post-mortem.

A close-up of the skull prior to its removal. The remains were ultimately revealed to be that of a teenager who died between 1655 and 1665.

The practice of indentured servitude in the New World provided economic benefits to the labor-hungry colonies of the 1600s, but it came with significant risks for the impoverished young men and women who signed up. They were guaranteed passage to the colonies by selling themselves into virtual slavery for a period of three to seven years, after which they were sometimes given a few acres of land and the chance at a new life. Many adolescents and young adults jumped at the chance, despite the fact that fair treatment was never guaranteed and laws could be excessively brutal. Indentured servants were often treated even worse than slaves, who by contrast were seen as a long-term investment.

In Maryland in the late 1630s, the penalty for an indentured servant running away was typically lashing and even death, although in later years punishments were less harsh—depending on your point of view— and resulted in a longer period of servitude as ordered by the court system. Under the best of circumstances, life in the New World was ruthless and unforgiving, and indentured servants were near the bottom of the social scale.

Doug Owsley's analysis of the skeleton also indicated that the young man had suffered from a severe dental infection that was exacerbated by the onset of spinal tuberculosis. The cause of his death was attributed to a blood infection brought about by the ravages of disease and tooth decay that overwhelmed his weakened immune system. It's possible that the boy's master simply buried his body in the cellar for the sake of convenience. But why the cellar?

time
TEASER   One of the most famous founding fathers of the United States was once an indentured servant. Who was it?

Answer: Benjamin Franklin.

Gwen discovered the answer to that crucial question in the Maryland State Archives, after which she was finally ready to share her research with Cory Seznec. What Gwen showed Seznec was a proposed 1663 Maryland law outlawing the private burial of indentured servants, a law designed to prevent the practice of treating deceased servants with such barbaric disregard. Although the economic life of the early colonies depended on the sacrifices of indentured servants, there's strong evidence that part of that sacrifice in this tragic case encompassed a wretched end in the family trash.

Bone Detectives

Every episode of *History Detectives* provides valuable information from a wide range of experts, scholars, and historians who graciously participate in solving a a mystery. Dr. Doug Owsley's interest in the indentured servant in the Lost Towns Project investigation is compelling testimony to the importance of understanding our cultural heritage through the remains of our ancestors. As a pre-med student at the University of Wyoming in the early 1970s, Owsley was so intrigued by his participation in an archaeological dig in Mexico that he immediately altered his career choice. He is currently the division head for physical anthropology at the Smithsonian's National Museum of Natural History and is one of the most renowned forensic anthropologists in the world.

Renowned forensic anthropologist Doug Owsley with Gwen Wright during his examination of the Maryland skeleton for *History Detectives*.

Over the course of his career, he has been called on to identify the remains of Croatian war casualties, Confederate soldiers, U.S. servicemen from the Persian Gulf War, and victims of the 9/11 terrorist attack in New York. He also examined 286 pieces of broken bone and teeth, leading to the conviction of notorious serial killer Jeffrey Dahmer. In addition, Owsley was instrumental in the lawsuit that allowed

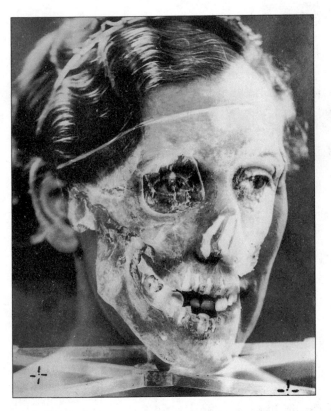

In a fascinating 1935 investigation of murder victim Isabella Ruxton, investigators confirmed her identity by superimposing a photograph of her over a previously unidentified skull.

scientific investigation of Kennewick Man, and leads the forensics team in an ongoing study of this most remarkable and significant link to North American history (see chapter 8).

In the past few years, forensic anthropologists have enjoyed more celebrity than their historical kin, primarily due to television exposure of their work on a wide variety of educational programming and also on serial dramas and high-profile crime shows such as *Bones*, *Skeleton Stories*, the *CSI* franchise, and a host of Discovery and TruTV documentaries. Popular programming has increasingly drawn on the talents and experiences of real-life forensics professionals for authenticity. For example, Dr. Kathy Reichs, consultant on the *Bones* television series, which is based on her bestselling books and real-life cases, is a highly renowned forensic anthropologist working in South Carolina and Quebec, while also serving as professor of anthropology at the University of North Carolina at Charlotte. While there may be some glaring exaggerations and oversimplifications about the field of forensic anthropology when the science is crammed into a one-hour time slot, these programs do offer a glimpse into a fascinating discipline.

A forensic anthropologist is a rare individual, one who is scientifically disciplined and can piece together an event with Spock-like logic and arrive at conclusions with Sherlock Holmes–like tenacity. Without these experts, thousands of unfortunate victims might never have been given names or a proper burial, or received justice for a brutal crime inflicted upon them. By definition, the forensic anthropologist is a highly trained specialist who combines *osteology*, the study of the function and structure of the human skeleton, with the anthropological subfield of *physical anthropology* (also known as biological anthropology), which focuses on evolution, genetics, fossils, blood groupings, and primate morphology, among other aspects. A relatively

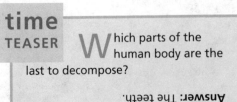

time
TEASER   Which parts of the human body are the last to decompose?

Answer: The teeth.

Power and Patronage

A rare statue of Egypt's most powerful female pharaoh, Queen Hatshepsut.

Excavations of human remains by archaeologists and forensic anthropologists like Doug Owsley and Kathy Reichs occur every day all over the world, but in the summer of 2007, results of an investigation of four mummies yielded a fairly positive identification of Egypt's most powerful female pharaoh, Queen Hatshepsut, whose legacy was virtually obliterated after her reign as "king" during the prosperous eighteenth dynasty. Three millennia later, a team of scientists and archaeologists embarked on a historic examination of the mummies, two from a remote clifftop cave known as DB320 and two in the tomb KV60, originally discovered in 1903 by Howard Carter of King Tut fame.

One of the KV60 mummies, surmised to be Sitre, Hatshepsut's wet nurse, was found in a lidless coffin. The second mummy was found lying on the tomb's floor. Intense scientific procedures were applied, including 3-D x-rays and tomography, yielding 1,700 images of each mummy, a study of facial features and body positioning, and scans of Hatshepsut's direct relatives, Thutmose I, II, and III. After that round of testing, both mummies from DB320 were ruled out. DNA testing was then done on the pair from KV60—miraculously, the genetic material had survived after 3,500 years. It was subsequently compared to mitochondrial DNA extracted from Hatshepsut's grandmother Ahmose Nefertari.

What proved to be the key to the entire discovery was a funerary box bearing Hatshepsut's royal seal, found in DB320. The forensics team took the unorthodox measure of putting the box in the CT scanner, which showed that it contained a liver, intestines, and a single tooth. The two KV60 mummies were each missing a tooth, one an upper incisor and the other a molar. An oral surgeon analyzed the scan and determined that the tooth was a molar with a single intact root. Measured against the two mummies, only one was a match. The mummy found lying on the floor of KV60 is very likely that of Queen Hatshepsut, a woman whose impressive reign was nearly erased from history, most likely in an effort to preserve Egypt's patrilineal traditions.

"new" science of the past seventy years, this specialty comes into play in a variety of legal, historical, and medical circumstances, from finding ancient skeletal remains to helping solve criminal cases where remains require identification or determination of the cause and method of death, or further still, assisting in the identification of victims of wars or disasters.

The majority of forensic anthropologists work in the academic field and serve as consultants when needed for a case, such as Gwen's indentured servant mystery. When they're called upon, they first determine if remains are human or animal, and then study the bones and teeth and any plants or pollens associated with the skeleton. Osteology techniques help determine a victim's size, age, sex, and stature, and any possible illnesses or wounds he or she may have suffered.

Taking measurements is crucial to the process, and it's usually extremely helpful if a skull is found, because a database of craniosacral information gives the examiner a firm idea of an individual's ethnicity, among other aspects. Teeth are also helpful in determining age, sex, and an individual's diet. Likewise, pollens, plant material, and insects indicate diet, and more importantly, time of death and a possible location where an individual may have died. All of these factors combined contributed to the analysis Doug Owsley provided for *History Detectives*— an invaluable assessment that played a huge part in answering crucial questions. Without Owsley's scientific expertise, the mystery of the body in the cellar would no doubt have remained unsolved.

time
TEASER Who were the first people to practice ritual mummification?

Answer: The Andean Chinchorros, who began the practice an estimated 7,000 years ago.

The Quartz Cross Controversy

If you happen to be traveling to Mission San Luis near Tallahassee, Florida, you'll discover one of the oldest "living" museums and the earliest fully reconstructed Franciscan mission in the nation. The mission was established nearly a century after Spanish explorer Hernando De Soto made landfall in the New World in 1539, and the site has provided invaluable insight into the lives and culture of the Apalachee Indians, the indigenous people of the area for thousands of years.

During archaeological excavations in 1991, an intriguing faceted cross made of crystal or glass was unearthed beneath the floor of the mid-1600s Spanish church that had been built over an ancient burial site where hundreds of Apalachee had been interred. The mysterious origins of the cross-shaped artifact was enough to lure History Detective Tukufu Zuberi to meet with Apalachee leader Gilmer Bennett, who was convinced that the relic was created by his ancestors in the early days of Spain's New World colonization. Ultimately, Tukufu's research and investigation would shine an illuminating light on a unique period of Native American history.

A circa 1893 illustration of Spanish explorer Hernando De Soto and his forces entering an Indian village on the Mississippi.

When you think of mortal conquest, wars are often the first thing that come to mind. After all, traditionally it's weaponry that inflicts death. But that's not always the case, and odd as it may sound, some killing devices bring together the most bitter of enemies. Although Florida's native population resisted Spain's first efforts toward conquering the New World during the 1500s, the invaders brought with them unseen weapons far more lethal than muskets or swords—they brought deadly pathogens to which the native people had no immunity. With their people decimated by disease and growing weary of their inability to protect themselves, native Apalachee chiefs entered into alliances with the Spaniards in the early 1600s, reasoning that the only way to control growing tribal dissension was with outside help.

By acquiescing to the Spanish Crown and relinquishing limited power, the chiefs were guaranteed substantial rights under Spanish law, thereby recovering their leadership status and bringing the native population under the control of a coalition of traditional tribal hierarchy and

DID YOU know

The predominantly peaceful relations between the Spanish and the Apalachee natives were repeated in the relatively congenial coexistence their Cherokee brethren just a few hundred miles to the north in Georgia had with settlers during the late 1700s. The Cherokee people's way of life, however, was finally and irrevocably destroyed in the late 1830s after the horrific Trail of Tears (see page 277).

The historic church Mission San Luis located outside Tallahassee, Florida.

Spanish authority. This highly developed social structure lasted for more than a century; it is one of the New World's most unusual cases of limited colonization and subjugation, with the most pervasive Spanish influence being the indoctrination of the native population into Catholicism.

THE MANY FACETS OF FAITH

The Spanish approach to colonization in Florida was a significant counterpoint to the havoc they wreaked in South America in the 1500s, and also to the control the British exerted in their settlements to the north. The English viewed native peoples primarily as trading sources and military allies, virtually excluding them as a permanent economic or social factor. History would prove that as far as the English and their American descendants were concerned, the native population was essentially dispensable. While the Spaniards in Florida indisputably capitalized on the original inhabitants as a labor force, they also saw them as an inherent element in the success of Spain's colonial efforts and established missions to convert them to the Catholic faith.

A little-known facet of Spanish colonialism in Florida was the active encouragement of intermarriage with the indigenous people, a practice designed to "civilize" the natives. Records indicate that the Apalachee readily accepted the social and religious transitions, integrating many of their own beliefs into the process under the generally acquiescent eye of the Franciscan friars who oversaw numerous missions throughout Florida. The 1991 discovery of the crystal cross in a burial site was evidence that the artifact had been interred with an individual and implied a significant acceptance of Christian symbolism

time
TEASER How far north did the Spanish establish missions on the eastern coast of North America?

Answer: They reached as far as present-day South Carolina.

Lost in Translation

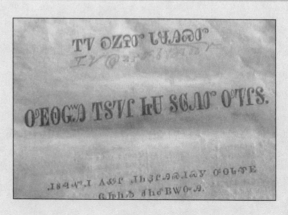

The title page of the Cherokee Bible written in 1860.

An 1860 Bible written in the Cherokee language led History Detectives Gwen Wright and Elyse Luray down one of the saddest paths in Native American history. The Trail of Tears was the name given to the uprooting and forced march of 16,000 Cherokee from their native lands in Georgia to the desolate territory of Oklahoma in 1838. The discovery of gold in the Southeast had resulted in seizure of all lands occupied by indigenous tribes. Georgia government officials were quick to demand enforcement of the Indian Removal Act of 1830, which was designed to move all Native Americans from incorporated states to the unincorporated western territories.

Disease and starvation took the lives of at least 4,000 Cherokee during their arduous 1,200-mile trek and left hundreds of orphaned children in its wake.

Missionaries who set up orphanages and schools for the dislocated youths used the Cherokee Bible as a stepping-stone for "civilizing" the children into mainstream thought and behavior, and in the process nearly destroyed an ancient heritage. The Bible was in Cherokee, the only written language known to have been created by an individual who was himself illiterate. That person was Sequoyah, who created the remarkable syllabary between 1809 and 1821, shortly before the Trail of Tears. Today, the Cherokee people are the most numerous of all Native American tribes in the United States.

A caricature circa 1886 illustrating the governmental abuse of the Cherokee nation.

Apalachee chief
Gilmer Bennett
holding the quartz
cross discovered
in an Apalachee
gravesite during
excavations at
Mission San Luis.

in the area even before the mission was built.

To determine the composition of the cross, Tukufu met with Florida State University geologist Stephen Kish, who tested the artifact by shining a *polarized*, or optically filtered, light source through the relic. The illumination of the object proved it to be made of quartz crystal, a naturally occurring material unknown in Florida's geology. At the university's National High Magnetic Field Laboratory, scientist Dr. Michael Davidson explained to Tukufu that the highly refined fabrication of the crystal cross initially suggested that it was manufactured in a technically proficient European shop, but his opinion changed after examination through a powerful digital microscope.

Under extreme magnification, there was ample evidence of hand tooling in how the hole in the suspension loop was drilled, along with flaking marks on the edges of the crystal—the same marks a traditional *flint knapper*, or toolmaker, creates in shaping an arrowhead or other projectile point (see chapter 8). After speaking with archaeologist Dan Penton, an elder of the Native American Muscogee Nation of Florida, Tukufu was able to put the history and origin of the cross into perspective for Gilmer Bennett.

The Apalachee-crafted cross represented native beliefs in the ritual strength of crystal as a symbol of the great body of water that separates the upper world from the lower, and the

A close-up of the
remarkably pristine
quartz crystal cross
excavated from the
Mission San Luis
dig site.

cross shape itself as an emblem of the four cardinal directions of north, south, east, and west. Ritually important crystal was acquired through traditional trading with neighboring tribes who had access to natural mineral deposits outside of Florida. The iconic Christian cross was quite easily incorporated into traditional imagery, creating a dynamic symbolism far more powerful than even the Spaniards

Tukufu Zuberi and Gilmer Bennett inside Mission San Luis in Tallahassee, Florida.

could have imagined. In the end, Tukufu surmised that the crystal cross was undoubtedly interred with a highly respected individual of great ritual and social status in the Apalachee tribe, a symbol of two cultures that for two centuries found common ground and a peace that is both admirable and rare.

Queen Anne's War of 1701 signaled the end of the Apalachee way of life when English troops and their Creek Indian allies systematically destroyed Florida's missions. On July 31, 1704, the residents of Mission San Luis burned and abandoned the mission just days before a planned British attack. Throughout Florida, thousands of Apalachee were slaughtered or enslaved in the brutal onslaught, with many of the survivors fleeing westward to Alabama and then to Rapides Parish in French-owned Louisiana.

Land disputes and cultural hostilities in later years forced the few remaining Apalachee to slip quietly into the backwoods, denying their Native American heritage in a desperate effort to survive racial animosity. In the late 1820s, President Andrew Jackson believed the tribe to have vanished and dropped federal recognition, a decision that continues to plague current Apalachee tribe members. Although several hundred Apalachee are documented descendants of Florida's Native American people, state and federal bureaucracy continues to deny them official acknowledgment.

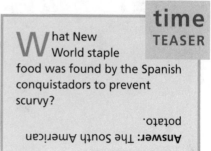

time
TEASER

What New World staple food was found by the Spanish conquistadors to prevent scurvy?

Answer: The South American potato.

DIY DETECTIVE

In 1994, Dr. Bob Brier, author of *The Murder of Tutankhamen* and one of the world's most renowned mummy researchers and experts, did something that no one has authentically done in over 2,000 years—he created an Egyptian-style mummy. Using a donated anonymous cadaver, Brier and his team meticulously recreated the exact process and conditions used by ancient Egyptian embalmers, including using bronze and copper knives, removing organs, and covering the body with the desiccating agent *natron* (a mixture akin to salt and baking soda). After thirty-five days, the now-dehydrated corpse was wrapped in white linen.

Six years later, after remaining in the controlled environment, Brier's mummy was perfectly preserved and bacteria free. It was an amazing achievement, one that you might think is totally antiquated. Not so. Did you know that you don't have to be a king or queen to preserve yourself for all eternity? There are in fact several methods you can investigate when planning your inevitable demise, the first of which is mummification.

In Salt Lake City, Utah, an organization called Summun (which is also a religion) has practiced modern mummification and transference since 1975 and is the only licensed organization able to provide that service. Through Summun's procedure, which is said to be "very thorough, detailed, yet gentle" and which involves plenty of fiberglass to prevent skin withering, your beauty can be eternally preserved for all future generations. You can select an artistically formed casket called a Mummiform that you can customize for yourself

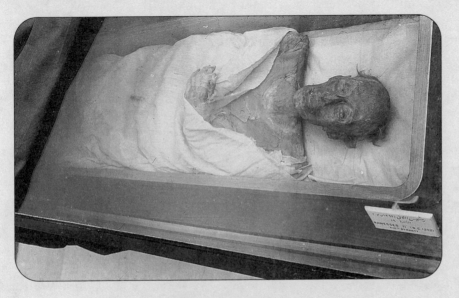

The remarkable mummy of legendary Pharaoh Ramses II, who lived to be approximately ninety. He was discovered in 1881 and remains on display in Cairo's Egyptian Museum.

or any of your beloved pets, or a simple Mummiform capsule. "Donations" for your mummification services alone start at $67,000 and go up from there, depending on your choice of Mummiform vessel, with your procedure taking a minimum of ninety days to complete. And in case you're wondering, having your cat eternalized will run you between $4,000 and $8,000, and for other animals, depending on their weight, it will run from $8,000 to over $128,000.

Of course, mummification isn't your only option. If you fancy yourself a gambler and prefer a shot at actually coming back to life, you might consider exploring the field of cryonics, which involves freezing a body in subzero temperatures in order to halt the postmortem process. This is done just after your heart ceases to beat—when you are considered dead yet still living biologically—in the hope that sometime in the future a cure for your illness or cause of death is discovered and you can, in theory, be reanimated.

If it sounds like science fiction, it is, especially considering that no human has actually ever been revived and the cryopreservation method is at best speculative. Still, you can choose to become a member of the Alcor Life Extension Foundation of Scottsdale, Arizona, which has been in business since 1972. Cryonics practices such as Alcor are controversial, with their attempts to preserve life often misinterpreted, but that doesn't mean

An impressive array of mummy sarcophagi in the Egyptian Museum.

folks aren't interested. It may get chilly over the decades, but ultimately, Alcor's futuristic endeavors give us an intriguing option when it comes to potentially getting a second chance at mortality.

CHAPTER SEVENTEEN
Flight, Fright, and Perilous Plights

G etting from one place to another in the most efficient manner has been an issue for humans since the first cavemen roamed the earth. Anything and everything has been used as a means of transporting people and supplies, from makeshift rucksacks to stretchers to horse-driven carts, bicycles, Studebakers, zeppelins, and the Concorde. And while transport is definitely key to our daily existence, it is never more important than when it applies to conflict—especially during wartime.

The most challenging concern for any nation at war is mobility, and many of the best efforts of invention have gone into developing extraordinary technologies for moving faster and slipping under the radar with impeccable stealth. Some mechanisms, such as tanks and submarines, were purposely created for warfare, while many others, such as trucks, steamships, and airplanes, were converted from civilian designs for specific military purposes. In this chapter you'll follow the History Detectives through novel adaptations of wartime travel, from the first motorcycles to go into action during World War I to the hair-raising flight of a brash billionaire and the harrowing last voyage of a nuclear submarine and its courageous crew.

The Riddle of the Historic Hog

There is probably no better known road-burning icon in the United States than the legendary Harley-Davidson motorcycle. With its distinctively syncopated exhaust rumble and retro appearance, Harley-Davidson flipped a decades-old "bad boy" image into one of the most prestigious brand names on the highway, attracting legions of diehard

enthusiasts with a taste for adventure and a penchant for racing with the wind. Tukufu Zuberi took a historical trip into the Harley mystique when Flemington, New Jersey, resident Frank Catena approached *History Detectives* with the mystery of an early 1900s Harley-Davidson that he had recently acquired from a Wisconsin man who had kept it tucked away in a barn since the 1940s.

The vintage Harley-Davidson that Frank Catena asked *History Detectives* to investigate.

While a restorable bike from the first years of Harley-Davidson's production line is quite a find, the truly unusual feature of this particular motorcycle is an image painted on its fuel tank—the Cross of Lorraine. Consisting of a distinctive vertical bar crossed by two smaller horizontal bars, the Cross of Lorraine served as a unifying symbol for the French military during the First World War, so the question facing Tukufu seemed obvious. With its early 1900s heritage, was it possible that this motorcycle played a part on the battlefields of France during World War I?

BORN TO BE WILD

Tukufu's first stop was the Harley-Davidson headquarters in Milwaukee, Wisconsin, to meet with Harley historian and bike restoration expert Bill

The curious Cross of Lorraine imprinted on the tank of Frank Catena's Harley.

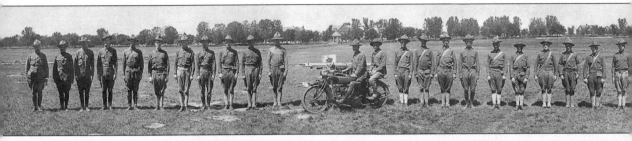

The Sanitary Company of the Fourth Nebraska National Guard proudly showcasing their World War I military service motorcycle circa 1917.

Rodencal, who confirmed that Harley-Davidson motorcycles had indeed played an important military role in the war effort, which was a significant vote of confidence in the quality of a company barely a decade old. In 1901, twenty-year-old Arthur Davidson joined forces with twenty-one-year-old William Harley in a ten- by fifteen-foot shed in Milwaukee to create a motorized bicycle. The intrepid duo took their cue from two different sources, the first a charcoal-fired, steam engine–powered bike built by Sylvester Roper in Massachusetts in 1868. Further inspiration came from German inventor Gottlieb Daimler's 1885 first effort at engineering a gasoline engine–driven bicycle. Four years later, Daimler built his first automobile and set the foundations for the famous Daimler-Benz auto manufacturing company.

In 1903, the year Harley-Davidson considers the birth of the company, the two founders rolled out three finished motorbikes. The new company officially broke ground on a new building in 1906 on the site of their current facility and produced 150 bikes the following year. Police departments immediately recognized the speed and maneuverability of Harley-Davidsons and began putting them into service as early as 1907 or 1908. With the increasingly successful use of motorcycles in law enforcement and the advent of World War I, the military also realized the tactical advantages of motorcycles in the field, and by 1917 nearly a third of Harley-Davidson's production went toward the war effort. In 1918, that number increased to half, and by the end of the war the armed forces had placed nearly 15,000 Harley-Davidsons into action in the European theater.

The endorsements of law enforcement and the military coupled with the sheer number of motorcycles they ordered helped establish the company's continuing status as a national icon. Upon closer inspection of Frank Catena's bike, Bill Rodencal quickly dispelled the notion that the old bike had played a role on the battlefields: he checked the identification number and determined that it was a 1914 model, long outdated by 1917 when the United States entered World War I. The fact that he had no idea why the Cross of Lorraine was on the tank only deepened the mystery.

LIVE TO RIDE, RIDE TO LIVE

To gather background on the Cross of Lorraine, Tukufu met with Dr. Kim Munholland, noted history professor at the University of Minnesota–Twin Cities, who has particular expertise in French history. Munholland explained that the symbol was taken up by Joan of Arc in her efforts to rally the French against English occupation in the fifteenth century and that it retained the same powerful patriotic significance during both World Wars. The double-barred cross first came into prominence as the emblem of Godfrey de Bouillon, the Duke of Lorraine, who gained fame as the first Christian ruler of Jerusalem during the Crusades in A.D. 1099.

General John J. Pershing receiving Tuberculosis Christmas Seals from a young health volunteer in 1921.

Making an observation that would change the direction of the investigation, Munholland also mentioned that the symbol was used in twentieth-century anti-tuberculosis campaigns. The Cross of Lorraine was chosen as the emblem of the National Association for the Study and Prevention of Tuberculosis, founded in 1904, after it was suggested as symbolic of the "crusade" against tuberculosis by Parisian Dr. Gilbert Sersiron at the first International Conference on Tuberculosis, held in Berlin in 1902. The Association has gone through several transformations over the decades, becoming the National Tuberculosis Association in 1918, the National Tuberculosis and Respiratory Disease Association in 1963, and the American Lung Association in 1973, with the Cross of Lorraine maintaining its distinction as a staunch symbol of the battle against deadly respiratory illnesses.

As a killer, tuberculosis had no equal during the nineteenth and early twentieth centuries, and it continues to affect an estimated twenty-three million people worldwide. Early on, the disease was referred to as "consumption" because it seemed to literally consume its victims, who often coughed up blood and sputum before succumbing to a slow, painful demise. Tuberculosis is fatal in more than 50 percent of untreated cases

A highly contagious worldwide scourge, tuberculosis was often treated in isolated care facilities. Above, cabins and tents at a tuberculosis camp in Illinois circa 1900. Below, a tuberculosis ward in Constantinople (modern-day Istanbul), Turkey, circa 1890.

and was one of the most dreaded illnesses on the planet. Given this new slant on the pervasiveness of tuberculosis and the significance of the Cross of Lorraine, Tukufu contacted the Wisconsin Historical Society in Madison and requested a check of early Harley-Davidson registration records. The historical group quickly discovered an intriguing link to Kim Munholland's observation. During the early 1900s, Harley-Davidson motorcycles were registered to state tuberculosis sanitoriums and to the Wisconsin Anti-Tuberculosis Association.

Back at Harley-Davidson headquarters, Tukufu put the puzzle pieces together with the help of company archivist Bill Jackson, who made the final connection to the Cross of Lorraine. As Tukufu would explain to bike owner Frank Catena, part of Harley-Davidson's commercial success stemmed from their willingness to put their products through real-world torture tests by supplying the armed forces and law enforcement with motorcycles; they reaped the rewards of practical feedback and the resulting publicity. Although Harley-Davidson didn't normally give bikes to non-profit organizations, the enormity of the tuberculosis crisis prompted them

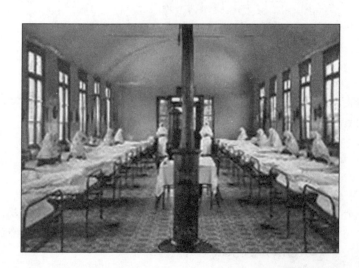

to donate motorcycles to the Wisconsin Anti-Tuberculosis Association so members could spread information about the disease and offer preventive measures to outlying rural communities. Frank Catena's 1914 Harley-Davidson was one of the bikes that scoured Wisconsin's back roads and helped turn the tide in the war on one of the deadliest epidemics in the United States. As a fitting end to this unforgettable *History Detectives* ride, Catena restored the old bike, bringing the engine back to life to once again roll along the highways of Wisconsin.

Hog Heaven

The creation of the first motorcycle in 1868 and its descendants during the early years of the 1900s attracted many of the best mechanical trendsetters on two wheels. In fact, one of the masterminds behind Harley-Davidson's successful 1903 engine design was Norwegian-born Ole Evinrude, who encouraged the young motorcycle makers to incorporate a few of his novel ideas into their de-

Tukufu Zuberi with a fully restored vintage 1914 Harley-Davidson.

signs. Evinrude himself went on to develop the first outboard boat engine in 1909 and spawned an industry of his own.

One of the most famous motorcycle makers in the U.S. market, the Indian Motorcycle Manufacturing Company, was created as the Hendee Manufacturing Company by George Hendee and Charles Hedstrom in 1901. The company changed its name to the Indian Motocycle Company in 1923—purposely dropping the "r" from *motorcycle*—and continued to be the most serious U.S. heavy cruiser competition for Harley-Davidson until 1953, when lagging sales forced the closure of the firm. The "Indian" motorcycle was revitalized in 1998 and struggled until 2003, when production once again halted. The Indian brand still attracts a legion of stalwart supporters and collectors, one of whom paid $93,600 at a 2007 auction for a rare customized 1929 Indian Scout with an original 1920s Crocker engine conversion kit. A year earlier, a 1934 Indian Sport Scout sold for $177,500.

In 1911, Tom and Bill Henderson created the Henderson Motorcycle, which featured a novel four-cylinder engine and which won a string of speed records and found a strong following with police agencies. Despite early successes, the Henderson Motorcycle Company was financially crippled by 1917 and was sold to Ignaz Schwinn, who in addition to owning the famous bicycle company

time TEASER

What is the current leading cause of death due to infectious disease?

Answer: Lower respiratory infections, primarily pneumonia.

also owned the Excelsior Motor Manufacturing and Supply Company, which manufactured the competing Excelsior motorcycle. Schwinn produced Henderson and Excelsior motorcycles until the onset of the Depression in 1931, when he discontinued the motorized divisions in favor of his wildly successful bicycle line.

As a collectible motorcycle, the Henderson holds its own, with a 1914 four-cylinder model selling in 2007 at a Half Moon Bay, California, auction for almost $94,000. The history behind that particular Henderson indicates that it was originally purchased by a Scotsman who took the bike with him into service during World War I. During the same auction, a 1926 Excelsior with original factory paint sold for $60,840. An amazing array of companies, such as Ace Motor Corporation, California Motorcycle Company, Cleveland, Crocker, Emblem, Marsh, Merkel, Pope, and Thor, took turns at scorching early twentieth-century racetracks and highways. The value of their original bikes continues to increase, as evidenced by the fact that one of the few existing Crocker originals sold in 2006 for a whopping $276,500. Although the list is far from complete, American motorcycles in all their high-speed glory played significant and innovative roles in permanently shifting the nation's perceptions of travel and adventure, lending credence to the Harley motto: "Live to Ride. Ride to Live."

time TEASER

What was the first motorcycle manufactured in the United States to win a race in excess of 100 miles per hour?

Answer: The 1921 Harley-Davidson.

Mysteries of the Coldest War

The conclusion of the Second World War brought an end to German and Japanese aggression and took the world into the long-running and equally frightening Cold War, which for five decades was fought with surveillance, propaganda, and the seemingly never-ending threat of unlimited firepower. There is ample evidence that the use of the atomic bombs on Japan in August of 1945 served not only to bring about a quick surrender, but also as a significant warning to the newly empowered Soviet Union. As a result, the race was on to foresee and forestall significant leads in the creation of increasingly sophisticated military threats, and the technology of spying and arms deployment encircled the globe from the dizzying heights of the stratosphere to the darkest depths of the world's oceans.

Fly Away Home

The mystery of one of the United States' least known epic flights landed on the desks of *History Detectives* when Shelly Monfort of Saratoga, California, claimed to own a piece of fabric from a U.S. Navy aircraft known as the NC-4. Doesn't ring a bell? It should. The NC-4 made the very first transatlantic fixed-wing flight when it was flown

The NC-4 in Ponta Delgado in the Azores circa 1919.

from New York to Newfoundland, and then on a 1,300-mile nonstop flight of fifteen hours to the Azores, and finally to Lisbon, Portugal. The journey began on May 8, 1919, and was completed on May 27, clocking an impressive twenty-seven hours of flying time. History Detective Elyse Luray determined that Monfort's fabric swatch is likely a souvenir from an overhaul of the NC-4 that occurred after the groundbreaking flight when the craft was refurbished for use as a recruiting tool during U.S. goodwill tours.

The NC-4, an enormous twin-winged seaplane, placed the pilots behind small windscreens in two open cockpits, largely exposed to the elements. Monfort's step-grandfather, Walter Hinton, was one of those courageous pilots and part of the six-man crew who made the historic flight. Hinton continued to make aviation history in the 1920s by exploring the Arctic by balloon and later making the first fixed-wing plane flight from North America to South America. The NC-4 is currently on display at the National Museum of Aviation History at the Naval Air Station in Pensacola, Florida.

Elyse Luray in front of the NC-4 with John Bayer, director of the NC-4 "First Cross" Organization, at the National Museum of Aviation History at the Naval Air Station in Pensacola, Florida.

The horrifying aftermath of the 9,700-pound atomic bomb that was dropped on Hiroshima, Japan, on August 6, 1945.

The History Detectives are no strangers to war artifacts, especially those involving new technologies of bygone eras. Wes Cowan conducted a fascinating examination of a fabric swatch from Professor Thaddeus Lowe's 1861 balloon *Enterprise*. In one of the first examples of aerial snooping, Lowe's Civil War–era hydrogen balloon monitored Confederate troop movements near the nation's capital (see chapter 4). Equally enthralling was Elyse Luray's investigation of a Civil War–era Confederate submarine that appeared to be a sister ship to the historic *H. L. Hunley*, the first submarine in history to destroy an enemy vessel in warfare.

Cold War technologies are often cloaked in secrecy, but that didn't stop two particular *History Detectives* investigations that exhibited more plot twists than a James Bond movie. Gwen Wright relied on her inexhaustible bag of sleuthing tricks to solve a mystery that plunged us fathoms below the surface of the Atlantic in an investigation of the demise of the USS *Thresher*. But first, we fly the not-so-friendly skies with Tukufu Zuberi on the aerial adventure of a prototype spy plane built and obliterated by the infamous Howard Hughes.

The Brash Billionaire Debacle

During World War II, high-flying reconnaissance aircraft served a vital function in tracking troop movements and monitoring enemy production facilities, and although the United States and its Canadian, Australian, and European allies joined with the Soviet Union to end German aggression, long-standing and bitter differences with the Soviet Bloc in ideology and postwar reconstruction intentions heightened the strategic need to develop improved observation aircraft. During the war, traditional fighter planes were stripped of weaponry and modified for operation at high altitudes for the express purpose of conducting photographic reconnaissance flights. Limitations on the altitude, range,

Tukufu Zuberi and Jim Kirkpatrick inspect the altimeter believed to have come from the wreckage of the XF-11.

and speed of modified warplanes triggered investigations into purpose-built spy planes, and the entrepreneurial Howard Hughes offered an alternative with the development of a craft dubbed the XF-11.

A close-up of the altimeter shows it to be virtually undamaged.

The story of this remarkable airplane came to *History Detectives* through Jim Kirkpatrick, whose father, Raymond Kirkpatrick, started as a mechanic for Hughes and eventually became one of his most trusted flight engineers. After his father's death, Jim Kirkpatrick was bequeathed an unusual relic of the XF-11's first test flight—an altimeter that his father claimed had been recovered from the ill-fated airplane's crash in 1946. This fascinating piece of aeronautical equipment and its unusual association with the eccentric billionaire inventor called for a full-blown *History Detectives* reconnaissance mission, one that required the skills of Tufuku Zuberi.

The XF-11 bore an unusual design, with twin engine booms, a centrally located cockpit *nacelle*, or housing, and a wingspan of over one

The second prototype of the XF-11 in successful flight with re-engineered single rotating propellers.

hundred feet. One of the first aircraft to incorporate a pressurized cockpit to compensate for the low oxygen environment of high-altitude flight, the XF-11 utilized dual counter-rotating propeller blades on each engine, which were intended to produce maximum thrust and fuel efficiency from a pair of proven twenty-eight-cylinder aircraft engines built by Pratt & Whitney.

The aircraft's design was inspired by the D-2 airplane originally conceived by Hughes as a fighter and later as a bomber during the first stages of World War II. Initially rejected by the military, Hughes built a prototype of the D-2 in secret that was similar in appearance to the highly successful P-38 *Lightning*—one of the most effective high-altitude U.S. fighter planes of World War II—with a significant variation in construction. The D-2 was built on an airframe of epoxy and heat-molded plywood using the very same technology that Hughes applied to its much more famous and much bigger brother, the Hercules H-4, famously known as the *Spruce Goose*.

DID YOU know

One of History Detective Elyse Luray's most curious investigations traced the background of a finely machined "pin within a pin" made by Milton Frank at a special Army operations unit at Maryland's Fort Detrick. As it turned out, the pin, which resembles a tiny drill bit, was designed as a suicide device for self-injected poison and was virtually identical to the pin concealed in a hollowed-out silver dollar found in the possession of U.S. pilot Francis Gary Powers after he was shot down on a surveillance mission over Russia on May 1, 1960, while flying a U-2 spy plane for the U.S. military.

After test flights in 1943, serious problems indicated that the D-2 would require significant design changes to sustain stable flight, but after several modifications were made and while still in the testing stages, the sole prototype of the D-2 was destroyed when a freak lightning strike hit its secret Mojave Desert hangar.

The widely ridiculed wood-framed H-4 Hercules developed by Hughes Aircraft, derisively nicknamed the *Spruce Goose.*

That the possible karmic message of that strike should have been heeded by a certain billionaire would soon become apparent. The D-2 concept was resurrected in 1944 and came to fruition as the infamous aluminum XF-11 that Howard Hughes flew on its maiden flight on July 7, 1946.

The first flight of the XF-11 was scheduled for a duration of fifteen to twenty minutes, but the enthusiastic pilot chose to ignore basic test procedures and pushed the aircraft to its limits; after all, it was his money,

Tukufu Zuberi comparing the array of instruments in the cockpit of the *Spruce Goose* with the altimeter belonging to Jim Kirkpatrick.

Infamously eccentric aviation pioneer and inventor Howard Hughes circa 1940.

his design, and *his* airplane. An hour and ten minutes into the flight, Hughes was blindsided by an oil leak in the right engine propeller control that kicked the rear propeller into reverse pitch, which had the unnerving effect of forcing the twin propellers to fly against each other. Barely in control and losing altitude quickly, Hughes attempted to guide the stricken craft toward an emergency landing at the Los Angeles Country Club but fell short and crashed into three homes in an upscale Beverly Hills neighborhood, crushing his collarbone, breaking six ribs, damaging his lungs, and causing third-degree burns to his arms and hands. The spectacular crash was masterfully recreated in the 2004 Oscar-nominated film *The Aviator*.

Although Tukufu's investigation of the altimeter's history provided little evidence of its origin other than a serial number and a number painted on the back like those often assigned to crash artifacts by investigators, his examination of crash site photographs proved that the XF-11's instrument panel had been largely undamaged. Tukufu also discovered that the same model of altimeter was used in the cockpit of the *Spruce Goose*, which is currently on display at the Evergreen Aviation and Space Museum in McMinnville, Oregon. The commonality of instrumentation on the *Spruce Goose* and the XF-11, as well as the memories of Raymond Kirkpatrick, who was on the scene at the ill-fated test and took part in the recovery of the wreckage, testified to the authenticity of the altimeter now belonging to his son Jim Kirkpatrick.

Howard Hughes eventually modified the design of the XF-11 by changing the dual counter-rotating propellers to a single prop for each engine and successfully flew a second prototype of the aircraft in 1947, but it proved to be too late and ultimately too expensive. The military chose a more frugal reconfiguration of the venerable B-29 bomber, designated the B-50 *Superfortress* (and later the RB-50B) as its primary long-range reconnaissance aircraft, and it continued in that role until 1955.

The XF-11 served as an inspiration for the creation of the celebrated U-2, which took to the air as the first successful purpose-built U.S. Air Force spy plane in 1955 and continues to serve as a counterpoint to the often overstated eccentricities of a brilliant aeronautical architect.

Tukufu's spy thriller certainly proved exciting, but what became of the brash billionaire who was the focus of the investigation? The injuries Howard Hughes suffered in the crash of the XF-11 resulted in a lifelong addiction to painkillers. Born into a life of wealth and handed the reins of business ventures begun by his father, Hughes developed a rebellious legacy of innovation and invention that was ultimately marred by addiction and untreated mental illness.

The scope of the billionaire's afflictions was clearly evident in 1966, when Hughes arrived in Las Vegas at the Desert Inn Hotel, where he intended to spend a couple of weeks. Instead, he remained in his room for four years. Unlike normal guests, Hughes refused to allow the room to be cleaned, and even worse, lined his walls with stacked jars filled with personal waste. Eviction threats were meaningless to the billionaire, who avoided conflict by simply purchasing the hotel. One of the richest men on earth, Hughes died on April 5, 1976, at the age of seventy from kidney failure brought on by the ravages of drug abuse and malnutrition.

Up, Up, and Away!

Amelia Earhart may be the best-known female aviator to conquer the skies, when she became the first female to fly solo across the Atlantic in 1932, but she had plenty of courageous company. At the outbreak of World War II in 1941, pilot Jacqueline Cochran submitted a proposal to prepare female pilots for wartime service to the U.S. Army Air Force that eventually came to the attention of renowned General Henry "Hap" Arnold. Initially resistant, Arnold invited Cochran to assemble a group of female pilots to study the successful British Air Transport Auxiliary, which already employed women pilots.

The result was the formation of the Women's Auxiliary Ferrying Squadron and the Women's Flying Training Detachment, which were combined into the Women Airforce Service Pilots (WASP) in July of 1943. Over 1,000 dedicated women flew for the U.S. military during the war years and were involved in delivering an estimated

Famed aviatrix Amelia Earhart circa 1928.

50 percent of the warplanes used in the field. The WASP program was designated a civil service branch and pilots were denied military status until the passage of the GI Bill Improvement Act in 1977, retroactively honoring the thirty-eight women who died in wartime flight activities.

Peter Stone holding up the documents left to him by his great-uncle Leonard Morgan.

Leonard Morgan, whose electrical diagrams triggered a *History Detectives* investigation.

An Unfathomable Mystery

While the U.S. Air Force was taking to the skies with the super-secret U-2 surveillance plane in 1955, the U.S. Navy was busy testing the equally clandestine USS *Nautilus*, the world's first nuclear-powered submarine. Highly innovative in its design and purpose, the *Nautilus* established the superiority of nuclear power over conventional diesel submarines with increased speed, silence, and submerged cruising range, which were successfully showcased by the first submerged voyage beneath the ice pack of the North Pole in 1959. Inspired by their successes, the Navy developed improvements in speed, stealth, maneuverability, and cruising depth with the USS *Thresher*—the first of a new class of nuclear submarines—which was commissioned into service on August 3, 1961.

The first years of the *Thresher's* operations were devoted to testing her many complex design systems. On April 10, 1963, she and her crew of 129 were conducting deep-diving exercises accompanied by the submarine rescue ship USS *Skylark* about 220 miles off the Massachusetts coast when increasingly garbled messages punctuated by static alerted the crew of the *Skylark* that something had gone very wrong with the *Thresher*. After hours of radio silence, it became hauntingly clear that the *Thresher* was lost.

The story of her tragic demise resurfaced when Peter Stone of Chicopee, Massachusetts, discovered in his basement a file of yellowing electrical diagrams that appear to be associated with the lost submarine. Stone related the discovery to History Detective Gwen Wright, explaining that his great-uncle

Leonard Morgan had worked for the Navy and that the documents were discovered after his death in 2005. According to Stone, Morgan was a man of few words who guardedly described his job with the Navy as that of an electrician. But the real question was, what was a mild-mannered Navy electrician doing with documents belonging to a top-secret nuclear project? This mysterious electrician and his documents piqued Gwen's curiosity, so she set off to explore one of the U.S. Navy's worst maritime disasters.

One of Leonard Morgan's diagrams of submarine electrical systems.

From the start, Gwen's investigation would prove frustrating. Inquiries through military channels produced only the terse response that the Navy declined to participate in the investigation, which set up an immediate roadblock to Gwen's research of Morgan's documents and naval duties. With that avenue thwarted, she met with nuclear submarine expert Hans Kristensen of the Nuclear Information Project at the Federation of American Scientists, a nuclear watchdog group, in an attempt to gather any background the organization might have. Although Kristensen had no knowledge of Morgan's involvement in the Navy's nuclear program, he suggested that the documents were electrical diagrams designed for crew training and were probably no longer classified.

Hoping that someone within another organization would know Leonard Morgan, Gwen focused her investigation on the *Thresher* Base, a submarine veterans organization and family support group chartered in 1989 to commemorate the 129 crewmen who had perished aboard the sub. That lead proved to be another blind alley, but Gwen gained a haunting personal perspective of the loss during a visit with Lori Arsenault, the daughter of Tilmon J. Arsenault, a chief engineer on the *Thresher's* ill-fated voyage. Lori was just eight years old when her family received the devastating

time
TEASER

In 1949 a pact was signed that created a military alliance between most of the countries of Western Europe and the United States. What was it?

Answer: The North Atlantic Treaty Organization (NATO).

news of the tragedy that threw their lives into turmoil. The *Thresher* Base was instrumental in bringing mutual support and encouragement to the families and shipmates of the lost crewmen. In the cyber age, many veterans' support organizations run Web sites that are available to families who have lost loved ones in military service, and specifically in disasters such as this one or the sinking of the USS *Indianapolis* (see chapter 20).

Gwen's understanding of the *Thresher* catastrophe came into sharper focus when she met a retired captain of the *Thresher* who had served aboard the vessel from 1960 to 1962. Captain John McNish lived with and served alongside most of the *Thresher's* crew during his distinguished career in the closely knit world of submariners, and he still grieves for lost friends and fellow sailors. McNish corroborated reports of naval and Congressional investigations Gwen found indicating that a pipe fitting had failed at a depth of about 1,000 feet, spraying seawater into the engine room and shorting out electrical systems, which resulted in the *scramming*, or shutting down, of the sub's nuclear reactor. Without power and unable to blow out ballast, the *Thresher* inexorably sank past its crush depth of about 1,500 feet and imploded under enormous water pressure. McNish also confirmed that Morgan's diagrams and drawings were designed to train crewmen, although he had no recollection of meeting the mysterious Leonard Morgan.

SEA HUNT

Although the Navy declined to participate in Gwen's investigation, the details of the accident are publicly documented. One source of information was Navy testimony given to the Joint Committee on Atomic Energy

The USS *Thresher*,
a U.S. nuclear submarine
commissioned in 1961.

DIY DETECTIVE

In an era of increasing concerns over national security, particularly after the horrific events of the terrorist attacks on September 11, 2001, the United States remains one of the few countries worldwide that maintains legislation to make formerly classified documents open to the public. The Freedom of Information Act, passed in 1966, significantly increased the transparency of federal records, and over the decades all fifty states have passed similar legislation. Despite these laws, however, many people are reluctant to make inquiries through either fear of retribution or an inherent belief that government records are none of their business.

While *classified* documents are out of reach due to their sensitivity, most records are available, and for U.S. citizens they are very much our business. Virtually every department in the U.S. government, from the CIA to the FBI to the Department of Energy maintains programs and Web sites that specifically address the Freedom of Information Act, with forms and instructions for making requests. There are usually nominal reproduction fees attached to specific requests, but fees can be waived under certain conditions described by each agency. In addition, the Reporters Committee for Freedom of the Press has a searchable index at www.rcfp.org/ogg/index.php that provides explanations of each state's open records laws. The same organization maintains another Web page at www.rcfp.org/foiact/index.html that provides an invaluable guide to obtaining information via the Freedom of Information Act.

A particularly helpful resource when making requests for specific information is the Student Press Law Center (www.splc.org/foiletter.asp), which provides an automated letter generator in which you can fill in the blanks and print out a professionally laid out records request letter to state agencies. It may take a little extra effort to determine the person or agency you'll need to contact for records and information, but the names of these contacts are available for those who are prepared to do their homework.

In addition, a large number of universities sponsor and maintain increasingly thorough libraries of declassified government documentation on the Internet, and many are freely accessible to the public. Using the term "university declassified documents" on any search engine will generate page after page of searchable material, hints, and tips on accessing electronic records. Bear in mind that there are far too many documents for them all to be available online, but the amount of material and documentation available is astonishing for any do-it-yourself history buff.

Gwen Wright meeting with retired Navy admiral Brad Mooney, former commander of the *Trieste II*, the deep-sea vessel that helped search for the *Thresher*.

in July of 1964. A review of engineering records indicated that an estimated 3,000 pipe joints on the submarine were subjected to full submergence water pressure, and that of those, 400 were substandard. It was also shown that the crew was unable to access equipment vital to stopping the flooding, and that the main ballast blow system failed to operate properly at the test depth, leading to ice formation in the lines and blockage of the blow rate. From a mechanical perspective, the *Thresher* was an accident waiting to happen—the intense water pressure of deep-sea trials was more than she could withstand.

Gwen continued her investigation by paying a visit to retired Navy admiral Brad Mooney, who was instrumental in the Navy's hunt for the lost *Thresher* by piloting the deep-sea search vessel *Trieste II* into depths of over 8,000 feet. Mooney's exhaustive search turned up the scattered and crushed remains of the *Thresher* and determined that the craft's nuclear reactor was fortunately intact. Regular monitoring by the Navy shows that the nuclear waste remains sealed, but it is still a continuing concern and a very real threat to the environment.

What really turned Gwen's case around was the revelation of a remarkable coincidence. When she showed Mooney the documents belonging to Leonard Morgan, the former admiral was astonished. Not only did he know about Morgan's diagrams and his work with the Navy,

DID YOU know

The Soviet submarine fleet lost the nuclear-powered K-141 *Kursk* on August 12, 2000, when a faulty torpedo exploded near the hull during battle exercises. Sadly, there is evidence in the form of goodbye letters to loved ones that nearly two dozen of her 118-man crew survived for several hours, and possibly days, after the sinking. The *Kursk* was raised in 2001 and all hands were recovered and interred in their homeland.

but he actually knew Morgan personally. As it turned out, Morgan had rented a room from Mooney's aunt for nearly twenty years while working on submarine electrical systems at the *Thresher's* birthplace at the Portsmouth Naval Shipyard. To Peter Stone's utter amazement, his great-uncle Leonard's description of his work as an "electrician" was a vast understatement of his position as a civilian electrical engineer for the Navy's highly innovative and top-secret nuclear submarine program.

VOYAGE TO THE BOTTOM OF THE SEA

Tragic as the *Thresher* disaster was, something positive did come out of it. Ceasing all submarine activity at depth for more than nine months, the Navy created an ongoing submarine safety program called SUBSAFE, which requires careful testing and certification of all materials and components that protect the integrity of deep-sea vessels. Since the implementation of SUBSAFE on December 20, 1963, no certified submarine has been lost. In the inherently dangerous and unforgiving environment of the deep ocean, it is devastating yet remarkable that only two U.S. submarines—the *Thresher* and the USS *Scorpion*—have been lost in the history of the nuclear program.

The *Thresher* was the victim of design flaws and careless maintenance, but the loss of the USS *Scorpion* in May of 1968 remains an unsolved puzzle. What little is known is that the *Scorpion* went out of communication and literally disappeared near the Azores, her wreckage undiscovered until five months later in over 10,000 feet of water. It's also documented that full SUBSAFE testing procedures were postponed *before* her disappearance, which may well have been a contributing factor to her tragic loss. In difficult exploration depths that exceed the *Thresher's* resting place by at least 2,000 feet, solid evidence of the *Scorpion's* demise remains elusive, even with the most sophisticated deep-diving apparatus the Navy possesses. Initial published reports pointed to pressure failures similar to those of the *Thresher*, while later reports suggest an internal explosion or a weapons malfunction that resulted in the *Scorpion* being hit by one of her own torpedoes. Despite expert opinions from the private sector and with the relatively limited military conclusion that the *Scorpion* was lost through accident rather than hostile action, the complete facts of her loss remain a mystery to this day.

CHAPTER EIGHTEEN

SIGNED, SEALED, AND DELIVERED

Whether we admit it or not, most of us have something we enjoy collecting, whether it be stamps, coins, rock and roll memorabilia, or even those funny kitchen towels with cows all over them. For some individuals, however, collecting artifacts and memorabilia is a serious business that generates millions of dollars. Autograph collecting is just one of many hobbies that has an ardent following, with people seeking a wide range of signatures on a variety of objects such as documents, photos, musical instruments, and all measure of sports equipment. For most collectors the thrill is in the chase, and once secured, a prize autograph is something they cherish. For both pros and amateurs, an authentic signature can be worth a bundle.

Unfortunately, just as more than a few savvy and highly talented forgers have polluted the art world, they've also taken advantage of the autograph marketplace and left their mark on the industry to the tune of millions of dollars. All four of our stalwart History Detectives are well versed in the matter of signature authentication, and as you'll find out in this chapter, there's much more to it than meets the eye, whether it's a ten-shilling note, a rumoured presidential visit, or the signature of one of baseball's greatest heroes.

The Riddle of the Ten-Shilling Note

If you're sitting in a bar with a group of friends and one of them asks you for your short snorter, what would you do? Would you slug down a shot of Jack Daniels? Would you order a plate of chicken wings? Would you sneeze? If it happens, you'd better reach for your wallet, or you'll owe all your buddies a round of drinks. So what exactly *is* a short snorter, you ask? The easiest explanation is that it's a piece of paper currency with a collection of signatures, usually from a group of individuals who are commemorating their friendship. During wartime, soldiers and military personnel often had chains of short snorters signed by their comrades, with each link consisting of a different country's currency. Those same signatures would also act as a record of those unfortunate soldiers who perished, while alternately giving reason for celebration for those who returned from battle unharmed.

A short snorter is also a drinking game or club whereby each member produces his or her bill, and the individual who has the fewest signatures must buy a round of drinks for everyone. No matter which way a short snorter was used, it ultimately served as a way for friends and soldiers to solidify their bonds in an intimate and sometimes very historic manner. Such was the case for History Detective Tukufu Zuberi, who set off to uncover what could prove to be an astonishing piece of World War II history.

The short snorter in question is a ten-shilling note that was purchased at an auction by New Yorker and World War II memorabilia collector Gary Schulze. If you were shown a typical short snorter, it's likely you wouldn't recognize any of the names, but this note is literally a Who's Who of World War II superstars. Writing

Gary Schulze displaying the prized "short snorter" he asked *History Detectives* to investigate.

The front and
back of Gary
Schulze's short
snorter.

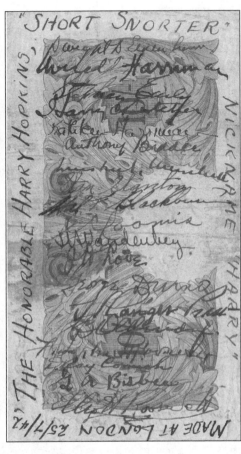

Presidential
advisor and
international
diplomat
Harry Hopkins.

on the bill indicates that the short snorter was started in London on July 25, 1942, and lists "The Honorable Harry Hopkins" at one end as well as his nickname, "Harry." Don't recognize the name? Well, how about Franklin Delano Roosevelt, Winston Churchill, Anthony Eden, George S. Patton Jr., Averill Harriman, Louis Mountbatten, and Dwight D. Eisenhower?

There are twenty-nine signatures on the note, including those of an impressive range of presidents, generals, admirals, press correspondents, and even Roosevelt's son, Colonel Elliot Roosevelt. Altogether, if proven authentic, Gary Schulze's extraordinary short snorter is the find of a lifetime. Accompanying the note was a picture of Harry Hopkins, a mysterious behind-the-scenes player who served as one of President Roosevelt's closest advisors and his unofficial emissary to both Communist leader Joseph Stalin and British prime minister Winston Churchill.

The impressive array of signatures on Gary Schulze's short snorter includes those of (clockwise from top left) Winston Churchill, Dwight D. Eisenhower, Franklin Delano Roosevelt, and George S. Patton.

Born in Sioux City, Iowa, in 1890, Hopkins was an impressive individual. Serving as Director of Civilian Relief for the Gulf Division of the Red Cross at the start of World War I, he eventually became general manager and president of the American Association of Social Workers. Later, Hopkins moved to New York and headed the New York Tuberculosis Association, after which he ran then Governor Roosevelt's Temporary Emergency Relief Administration during the early part of the Great Depression. An ardent fighter for relief organizations, Hopkins was a major proponent of Roosevelt's New Deal programs, including the Federal Emergency Relief Administration and the Works Progress Administration, among many others. If the short snorter did belong to Harry Hopkins, it played a part in one of the major turning points of World War II.

To begin his investigation, Tukufu met with former FBI document analyst and forensic scientist Gerald Richards, who felt it was best to take Tukufu to a bar to show him exactly what having a short snorter entailed. After both men took a drink, Tukufu produced a bill that Richards signed and returned to our happy detective, thereby beginning Tukufu's own personal short snorter and memento. In order to confirm the signatures on Gary Schulze's ten-shilling note, Richards turned to microscopic analysis. His first concern was how many different inks were used on the note, an issue that could trigger suspicion of forgery if only a few pens were used. In this instance, the inks appeared similar to the naked eye, but under close scrutiny they were all different. Further analysis of the more prominent signatures showed that they exhibited no sign of the hesitation marks

time TEASER

When and where did Winston Churchill and Franklin D. Roosevelt first meet?

Answer: August 9, 1941, on the deck of the HMS *Prince of Wales* near Newfoundland.

Former FBI document analyst Gerald Richards explaining the rules of the short snorter game to Tukufu Zuberi.

common to forgers, or of having been inserted at a later time. The flow of each signature was natural and was, by all appearances, authentic.

To learn more about Harry Hopkins and what was occurring around July 25, 1942, Tukufu met with war historian Warren Kimble, who was immediately taken by the significance of the date, which corresponded with a crucial World War II gathering. In 1942 Europe was in chaos, with Germany pummeling Britain with its infamous Blitz offensive, beginning its executions in concentration camps, and pushing into the Soviet Union with a force of over three million troops. Desperate for relief, the Allies sought help from the United States, which at that time didn't have the capacity for a massive invasion.

On July 25, a clandestine meeting was held in London between British and U.S. leaders and emissaries, who made the decision to attack the Germans in North Africa, a campaign dubbed *Operation Torch*. Harry Hopkins was among those leaders, but of the twenty-nine names on the short snorter, only seven signers were in attendance, a fact that only deepened the currency conundrum. At that point in the investigation, Tukufu paid a visit to the Library of Congress to confer with Dr. Daun Van Ee, an expert who specializes in British and American relations. In his opinion, there was one signature that held the key to solving the mystery,

Microscopic analysis of the inks used to create the signatures on the short snorter.

that of President Roosevelt, who signed the back side of the note just below U.S. Navy admiral Jesse Bartlett Oldendorf. The placement of both their signatures pointed to a time six months *after* the Operation Torch meeting.

As proof, Van Ee shared with Tukufu a thank-you letter that Roosevelt's naval aide wrote to Admiral Oldenfdorf after they met in Trinidad as Roosevelt and Hopkins were en route to yet another crucial secret Allied meeting in the Moroccan city of Casablanca. That meeting, which included Winston Churchill and U.S. Army general George S. Patton, took place in January 1943, six months after the Allies began their combined assault on North Africa with over 65,000 troops. The move ultimately thwarted the Axis powers by buying time for Allied troops to regroup for the European invasion to follow. The strategy worked, and in 1945 the Allies demanded the unconditional surrender of the Axis nations of Germany, Italy, and Japan. Through all of the political proceedings, Harry Hopkins worked his influence in the shadows of the world's most powerful leaders, bringing them together to make world-altering decisions. Gary Schulze's ten-shilling short snorter proved authentic, and marked not only two crucial moments in time, but the personal and international political bonds that even today remain unbreakable.

The Legend of the Strikeout King

In the days before mega-million dollar contracts, corporate meddling, and the repugnant influence of strength-enhancing drugs, professional baseball was a rough-and-tumble diversion that fielded some of the world's most inspiring athletes, who played with unsurpassed talent and the intimidating intensity of gladiators while surviving on a veritable shoestring budget. The most disturbing and prevalent aspect of the game during the last years of the nineteenth and first half of the twentieth centuries was that it reflected the social and cultural values of the era by splitting equally talented players into

Signatures of the Rich and Famous

Autographs of famous personalities are incredibly popular, and autograph seekers are some of the most relentless collectors out there, finding items that range in price from the $190 paid for a *Scarface* poster signed by Al Pacino to a signed letter from Abraham Lincoln that went for $748,000 in 1991.

Signatures of sports figures are of particular interest among collectors. Fellow baseball Hall of Famer Dizzy Dean once said of Satchel Paige: "He's a better pitcher than I ever hope to be. My fastball looks like a change of pace next to that pistol bullet he shoots at the plate." Both stars signed hundreds of baseballs, which have sold for $1,000 to $6,000 at auctions.

Even rarer balls, such as an autographed home-run baseball hit by Babe Ruth at the 1933 All Star Game, sold for a staggering $805,000 in 2006. An unusual example of a Babe Ruth signature that was written on a 1922 contract addendum limiting Ruth's late-night carousing during the season sold in 2007 for over $65,000.

Legendary baseball superstars Satchel Paige and Dizzy Dean.

the racially narrow-minded partitions of black and white.

Founded in 1871, the National Association of Professional Baseball Players is commonly considered to be the first professional league, and it became the foundation of the National League, formed in 1876. Although black players filtered into the first pro teams, often claiming to be Cuban or other "borderline" races, they were effectively banned from major play by 1887 through the blatantly racial biases of team owners, managers, and players. The ban dominated the sport until Jackie Robinson was signed on to the minor league Montreal Royals in 1946 and moved up to the majors with the Brooklyn Dodgers a year later. Until that groundbreaking change in policy, black players were confined to the successful National Colored Baseball League, formed in 1887. A handful of successive African American leagues kept fans enthralled until Robinson cracked the Major League color barrier and effectively ended the commercial viability of the last Negro National League.

History Detectives Tukufu Zuberi and Elyse Luray delved into the history of segregated pro baseball when Joe Miles of Kent, Washington, asked them to investigate a worn baseball that his father, Joe Miles Sr., had kept for decades. Although the specific details were lost to Miles Sr. as a result of the onset of Alzheimer's disease, the significance of the ball is its inscription. Dated July 12, 1944, Louisville, Kentucky, the ball bears the signature of Dizzy Dean, one of professional baseball's premier pitching stars from the 1930s to the 1940s. What Joe Miles believed was that it was used in a game Dean played alongside Negro League pitching phenomenon Satchel Paige and Joe Miles Sr., who was a U.S. serviceman at the time. The true curiosity is the date on the ball, which indicates that it was used a year before the end of World War II, when racial segregation was still rampant.

time
TEASER   During which major U.S. conflict did baseball become a common soldier's pastime?

Answer: The Civil War.

Among the sixteen million U.S. citizens who enlisted in the war were 4,000 minor league baseball players and 400 major leaguers, including Bob Feller, Joe Di Maggio, and Hank Greenberg. With so many ballplayers in the service and segregation still the norm for pro ball, how was it that a white player and a star of the Negro Leagues would become involved in a baseball game with a U.S. serviceman? It was a baffling mystery, one that for Tukufu and Elyse served up more than a few curve balls.

The 1944 baseball owned by Joe Miles Sr. that bears the alleged signature of pitcher Dizzy Dean.

BARNSTORMING BASEBALLERS

Jerome Hanna "Dizzy" Dean, a country boy from Lucas, Arkansas, played major league baseball for eleven consecutive seasons from 1930 to 1941 and returned for a final fling with the St. Louis Browns in 1947. During his career he established a reputation as one of the most feared pitchers and best-loved players in the nation's premier sport. But in the annual All-Star game of 1937, Dean suffered a broken toe when he was hit with a hard line drive, and while recovering from the injury he altered his pitching style, which many believed to be the cause of permanent damage to his throwing arm. By 1941 he was out of the game, and he slipped into a new career as a popular baseball announcer.

Leroy Robert "Satchel" Paige was one of the premier stars of the Negro Leagues and one of the best-known athletes to play ball in any league of the era. During the heyday of the Negro Leagues, Paige bounced from team to team depending on who was offering the highest pay, and he often farmed himself out as a "hired gun" for occasional single games for teams who hoped to capitalize on his fame. One of the characteristic activities of players in both white and black leagues was *barnstorming*, which involved big-name stars playing against each other or local teams in exhibition games for hometown crowds, and Satchel Paige was a master at creating his own all-star teams for just that purpose. Dean and Paige were known to be great admirers of each other and occasionally played together during those exhibitions. Still, it seemed unlikely that two of baseball's greatest stars would have met on the field with Joe Miles Sr., who had played only amateur ball in college and in the service.

The owner of the Dizzy Dean baseball, Joe Miles Sr., with his son, Joe Jr.

The year 1944 inscribed on the baseball belonging to Joe Miles Sr. certainly made the idea that Dizzy Dean had signed it during a baseball game seem far-fetched. During her research, Elyse found another serious flaw in the story when she had the baseball analyzed by Brian Marren of Mastronet Auctions, Incorporated, one of the premier sports memorabilia dealers in the country. According to Marren, the baseball itself is absolutely authentic, particularly in light of the label of the manufacturer, "Goldsmith," which merged with the MacGregor company in 1946. But comparisons of the signature with known Dizzy Dean autographs proved that the baseball star didn't sign the ball. Marren surmised that the ball might have been a stray foul ball signed by a fan to commemorate the game, but that was about as close as it got to Dizzy Dean himself.

Luckily, what Elyse and Tukufu discovered when researching newspaper articles sent the mystery out of the park. According to an article in Louisville's *Courier-Journal*, Satchel Paige traveled to Louisville to play an exhibition barnstorming game with the Louisville Black Colonels against a team of servicemen from Freeman Field in Indiana. That team, called the Freeman Field Blue Devils, was the very team Joe Miles Sr. played for during the war years. And better yet, the article noted that Dizzy Dean caught wind of the game and took the day off from his broadcasting duties to pitch several innings for the Blue Devils.

Although the autograph on the baseball wasn't put there by Dizzy Dean, the ball represents a remarkable moment in time when two of the greatest sports heroes of the 1940s met with heroic U.S. servicemen and made a little-known home run in history. Tukufu and Elyse's investigation originally aired during the summer of 2006. The retelling of this historic meeting stands as a permanent tribute to Joe Miles, Sr., who sadly passed on in the summer of 2007, a year after his historic baseball mystery was solved.

time
TEASER
What odd device did Babe Ruth use to keep his head cool during games?

Answer: He placed a cabbage leaf under his cap.

A Song in Her Heart

To say that California librarian Dr. Mayme Agnew Clayton was a typical collector of African American history memorabilia is a vast understatement. For over forty years Dr. Clayton collected more than 3.5 million artifacts, which constitute the largest privately held collection in the world. Her son, Avery, asked Gwen Wright to investigate one of those artifacts, a curious autograph book belonging to Nora Douglas Holt that features authentic signatures of Woodrow Wilson, Calvin Coolidge, Warren G. Harding, Theodore Dreiser, and Carl Van Vechten, among others. Who was Nora Holt and how did she acquire such an amazing book?

Gwen's research revealed that Holt was a famous composer, singer, and music critic who was the first African American woman to attend the Chicago Musical College and to earn a master's degree in music. In the 1920s, she also

Composer and singer Nora Holt.

played a big part in the explosion of creative talent that defined the Harlem Renaissance. Although the signatures range from 1921 to 1928, Gwen learned that on May 10, 1921, a party was held in Washington, D.C., that was attended by all of the political signators.

Nora's fifth husband, Joseph Ray, worked for Charles Schwab, a known autograph collector, who likely gave Nora the book as a wedding gift. Dreiser and Van Vechten were in her creative circle, and their signatures were added later. For more information about the Mayme A. Clayton Library and Museum, visit www.wsbrec.org. Or check out an extended interview with Avery Clayton at www.pbs.org.

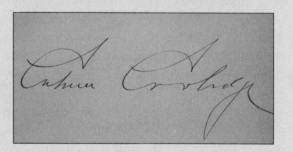

Celebrity autographs in Nora Holt's collection include those of writer Theodore Dreiser, President Calvin Coolidge, and Nora Holt herself.

The Write Stuff

Throughout the series, each of our four devoted History Detectives has conducted numerous investigations that required authentication of period papers and inks and a multitude of famous and infamous signatures. The Dizzy Dean baseball is a perfect example of what to analyze when confronted with a famous signature—especially a sports legend—because when it comes to sports memorabilia there's good reason for concern, given the amount of forgery inherent to the industry and the simple fact that people sometimes innocently mark objects for the sole purpose of remembering a spectacular event.

Fortunately, most of the *History Detectives* investigations involving autographs have turned up on the positive side, including Benjamin Dale's suffrage painting (see chapter 1), Artur Szyk's illustrations (see chapter 3), the Abraham Lincoln letter (see chapter 4), Nora Holt's autograph book, and all of the signatures on the World War II short snorter. And for everyone involved that was a coup. No matter whose signature we find, there's something inherently thrilling about discovering that it's the real deal, especially if the individual is a historic legend. Such was the case in a pair of *History Detectives* investigations that explored two individuals who couldn't be more different, but whose historical legacies are written in stone.

THE BAFFLING MORRISTOWN MONIKER

The first of these mysteries holds a special place of honor for everyone involved because it appeared in the very first episode of *History Detectives*. It posed a significant challenge for detectives Wes Cowan and Gwen Wright when they sought to explain how a presidential signature ended up in the guest register of the Morristown Independent Hose Company in Morristown, New Jersey. To begin the investigation they met with Fred Richards, president of the historic company, which was first brought together in 1834 and became the city's first official fire department in 1867.

When rummaging in the basement of the building,

The alleged signature of President Ulysses S. Grant in the guest register of the Morristown Independent Hose Company in Morristown, New Jersey.

Richards found a logbook containing a guest register and showed it to Morristown Public Library archivist Cheryl Turkington, who spotted the signature: "U.S. Grant, Galena, Illinois." Was it *really* President Grant's signature? Even more curious was the date on the page—July 4, 1876. If Grant's signature was proven authentic it would be a remarkable find, but the truly curious conundrum was, what was the president doing in Morristown on this important date, the centennial of the signing of the Declaration of Independence?

To answer the first of the two questions, Wes took the logbook to New York City to meet with Chris Coover, a renowned manuscript expert at Christie's auction house. Coover was quickly able to authenticate the paper as being correct to the era and then set about matching Grant's logbook signature to a genuine Grant signature. With its strong hand and distinct flourishes, there was no doubt that the signature belonged to the enigmatic president. However, excitement over the authentication was short-lived.

When Wes paid a visit to the New York Public Library, he found a *New York Times* article that confirmed that President Grant was in Washington, D.C., on July fourth, the same day he allegedly signed the logbook. So with an authentic signature but a date someone likely filled in after the fact, the question left to be answered was, when *did* Grant visit Morristown and for what purpose?

While Wes was in New York, Gwen pored over the Morristown Public Library archives with Cheryl Turkington, and while they did find a newspaper article mentioning a Centennial celebration at the firehouse, there was no mention of President Grant. Curiously, what initially drew Turkington's attention to Grant's signature was that Fred Richards had noticed the signature of Thomas Nast on the

Ulysses S. Grant, eighteenth president of the United States, circa 1865.

Famed political cartoonist Thomas Nast, who was an honorary member of the Morristown Independent Hose Company and a friend of Ulysses S. Grant.

time
TEASER

How many authenticated signatures of William Shakespeare are known to exist?

Answer: Six. One on a conveyance, one on a deposition, one on mortgage papers, and three in his will.

same page. Nast, a Morristown resident, was one of the most renowned political cartoonists of the day. A fervent Republican, he was the clue that broke the case wide open.

In 1873, Nast became an honorary member of the Hose Company, as did many wealthy men of the era who relished the thought of hanging out with tough firefighters and attending excellent parties. In the political arena Nast proved to be an excellent spin doctor for Grant, and as a result the two became good friends. As proof, the detectives found an article that noted that ex-president Ulysses S. Grant had dinner with Thomas Nast on May 8, 1877—almost a year after the logbook's date—indicating to the detectives that Grant had visited the firehouse and signed the logbook at the behest of his friend and political ally.

THE RIDDLE OF THE GOLDEN TICKET

Ed Goldberg displaying his mother's treasured baseball ticket allegedly signed by the great Lou Gehrig.

The tale of President Grant and the Morristown firehouse is typical of the twists and turns one might encounter when seeking to authenticate a signature and the circumstances surrounding its signing, and this certainly held true for Gwen when she investigated a curious ticket autographed by megastar baseball player Lou Gehrig—a ticket dated July 4, 1939. To Oregonian Ed Goldberg, the date was astonishing, as it marked Gehrig's final game with the New York Yankees, during which he declared to the heartbroken crowd that he considered himself "the luckiest man on the face of the earth." They were poignant words from a man who only two years later would succumb to Amyotrophic Lateral Sclerosis (ALS), now commonly known as Lou Gehrig's disease. Known as the "Iron Horse," Gehrig was one of the greatest players ever to grace a baseball diamond, playing 2,130 consecutive games with a humility that's rarely seen today.

Ed Goldberg found the ticket in his mother's high school yearbook and recalled her telling him that she would ditch school and head to Yankee Stadium to watch Gehrig play. While Goldberg recognized

DIY DETECTIVE

If you're in the business of autograph collecting or are interested in getting started, your number-one priority is education. The more you know and the more questions you ask before making a purchase, the better off you'll be when it comes to making an informed decision on whether or not a putter signed by Tiger Woods is up to par. Researching the various operations run by the FBI and books written about their successes is also helpful in determining the types of things forgers are doing to create their works, how they're distributed, and especially how they operate on the Internet.

Operation Bullpen was an FBI undertaking that began in the Bureau's Chicago division during the mid-1990s and focused on the sports and celebrity memorabilia industries. The results of their investigation sent shockwaves across the nation. Operation Bullpen broke up fifteen large forgery rings and convicted over sixty highly talented and deceptive criminals.

One of the Bureau's most famous exposures was San Diego sports memorabilia dealer Wayne Bray and his primary forger, Greg Marino, whose entire family went down when Bray turned on them. So profoundly talented were Bray and especially Marino that they developed dipping and shellacking processes that aged baseballs so convincingly that experts would authenticate them to the 1940s. The balls even smelled old. Amazing as it may sound, Bray and his cohorts forged memorabilia—

covering everyone from Babe Ruth to Marilyn Monroe—and polluted the market across the nation to the tune of over $100 million.

One of the benefits of Operation Bullpen was heightened awareness of the extreme measures forgers are prepared to employ in producing convincing fakes. There are a great many reputable dealers and auction houses out there, and they're more careful than ever to verify the validity of their wares with the aid of highly trained appraisers who are well versed in the fine art of authentication. Today, the autograph and memorabilia markets are going strong, as prices for one-of-a-kind pieces continue to rise, although industry experts advise that serious collectors avoid mass-produced signings and limited-edition memorabilia as investments.

Immersing yourself in the finer points of autograph collecting is your best bet, and that means consulting industry-respected price guides and researching specific athletes and celebrities to determine their representation, whether their signatures are limited, and prices of authentic items that have recently sold. As an overriding rule, don't be fooled by prices that seem too good to be true, and always remember that certificates of authenticity aren't actual guarantees. Reputable dealers and auction houses are very careful to protect their reputations and integrity by providing 100 percent guarantees. For more information, visit *History Detectives* at www.pbs.org.

AMERICAN LEAGUE
BASEBALL CLUB
OF NEW YORK
RAIN
CHECK
Game No. 34
L
01663
STADIUM $1.10
Est. Price $1.00 Total
Tax Paid .10
If 4½ innings are not played this Check may be exchanged for any other game this season.

Ed Goldberg's historic
ticket from July 4,
1939, marking Lou
Gehrig's final game.

that the date on the ticket had been handwritten by his mother, he wanted to learn if Gehrig's signature and the ticket were authentic.

To begin her investigation, Gwen sought the sports memorabilia expertise of fellow History Detective Elyse Luray, who confirmed that the ticket was correct to the period, but the signature didn't quite match known Lou Gehrig autographs. Continuing her research, Gwen visited the National Baseball Hall of Fame and Museum in Cooperstown, New York. Goldberg's ticket showed that it was for game thirty-four at Yankee Stadium, the date of which could prove confusing, given scheduling changes due to bad weather. Fortunately, Gwen was able to work with researcher Bill Francis, and together they consulted *Spalding's Official Baseball Guide* to determine that the ticket was indeed for the July 4, 1939, game, when the Yankees played the Washington Senators.

With that information, Gwen consulted Lou Gehrig biographer Jonathan Eig, who produced a cache of personal correspondence from Gehrig to his doctors. The last letter was dated two weeks after Gehrig retired from baseball. Even more intriguing was the fact that Gehrig's wife, Eleanor, communicated with one of Gehrig's physicians, encouraging him to hide the truth about the seriousness of the disease from her husband so as to protect him. Ironically, it appears that Gehrig played along to protect his wife. To put the finishing touches on her investigation, Gwen met with renowned professional autograph authenticator James Spence, who had over 1,500 authentic and forged Gehrig autographs to consult for comparison.

The back side of
Ed Goldberg's ticket
bearing the alleged
signature of Lou
Gehrig.

The 1925 opening
ceremonies at
New York's famed
Yankee Stadium.

Several examples showed that a stamp of Gehrig's signature was created when he became too ill to sign, while others showed that oftentimes individuals connected to the Yankees organization signed autographs on a player's behalf. But when Spence took a hard look at the signature on Ed Goldberg's golden ticket, he immediately knew who had signed it. Meeting with Goldberg, Gwen revealed that his ticket had been signed by none other than Gehrig's wife, Eleanor Twitchell Gehrig. It was likely that Goldberg's mother had sent the ticket to Mrs. Gehrig, who had been kind enough to accommodate an ardent fan. To this day, it remains a mystery as to whether or not Lou Gehrig knew he was dying when he gave what many consider to be the most amazing speech in baseball history, but in the larger scheme of things, that matters little, because the legacy of the Iron Horse marches on in the heart of every ball player and every individual inspired to battle a still incurable disease.

time
TEASER

Who actually invented baseball and when was it invented?

Answer: Abner Doubleday is commonly credited, but there is evidence that Alexander Cartwright created the game and wrote the first rules in 1845.

CHAPTER NINETEEN

Dubious Dwellings

When it comes to structures that have tantalizing tales attached to them, investigators are often faced with the challenge of having to include in their research oral accounts of conspiracies that are not very well documented. By their very nature, the events surrounding such dwellings are typically sensationalized and leave a flurry of legends and questionable accounts in their wake. All of this may be fascinating, but would *you* really want to live in a house with a lurid past?

In this chapter we delve into several high-profile events that left permanent marks in the history books. The first of these occurrences is the Salem witch trials, a period of Puritan hysteria that while natural in origin was rife with supernatural accusation. The second event we'll explore marks a tragic time in U.S. history with a war that culminated in the assassination of one of the nation's most beloved leaders. Despite occurring centuries apart, these two remarkable events have something in common—both involve unusual homes that were investigated by *History Detectives*. We'll also introduce you to the science of core-sample analysis, which can help determine the age of structures hundreds of years old and may even help scientists disover the most ancient lifeforms on Earth.

In researching historical structures, there are plenty of tools investigators and scientists can use when attempting to uncover the truth about what really goes on behind closed doors, and for History Detective Gwen Wright, those resources came into play when investigating an accused witch's haunts and a presidential assassination conspiracy.

The Curse of the Wicked Witch

E ssex County in Massachusetts is no stranger to the alleged practice of witchcraft, an evil undertaking that enveloped its straitlaced citizenry during the late seventeenth century. One home in particular bears a strong connection to a suspected witch, and it was just that history that led Deane and Joan Kemper to pull up their West Coast roots and purchase the house. A plaque over their front door claims the home was built in 1685 by Benjamin Abbot, who accused his neighbor Martha Carrier of being a witch. Was it possible that Abbot built his home on what was once land that belonged to the Carrier family? If an individual was accused of witchcraft, was their accuser entitled to their property?

Gwen Wright had a seriously bewitching mystery on her hands when she arrived to investigate the Kempers' home, an investigation that would require more focus than hocus-pocus. But first things first. To understand

The Essex County home of Deane and Joan Kemper, a structure investigated by *History Detectives* for allegedly having connections to accused witch Martha Carrier.

The plaque hanging above the Kempers' front door.

the climate and sentiment of New England in the late seventeenth century, and what might have provoked Benjamin Abbot, among others, into accusing Martha Carrier of witchcraft, one must delve into one of the most complex and fascinating chapters in American history—the Salem witch trials.

CASTING SPELLS AND ASPERSIONS

So who was afraid of the big bad witch? In the spring and summer of 1692, everyone in Salem Village was, and it's safe to say no one living today would wish to go back in time to take part in the unbelievable hysteria and death that hovered over a lethal cauldron of political, cultural, economic, spiritual, and ideological turmoil. To say that the Salem witch trials were sensational is a massive understatement. Guided by strict Puritan beliefs and triggered by Puritan minister Cotton Mather's widely read 1688 book *Memorable Providences*, which discussed witchcraft and possessions, a group of impressionable young girls—whether they knew it or not—set about destroying a village and everyone in it.

What is now Danvers, Massachusetts, was once Salem Village, a town of 25,000 inhabitants. The initial problem began with nine-year-old Betty Parris, who was the daughter of Reverend Samuel Parris, and her eleven-year-old cousin Abigail Williams. When Parris took up his position as Salem's minister, he and his family brought with them a West African slave named Tituba, who allegedly told the girls enchanting folktales involving voodoo and witchcraft.

After a time, the girls began exhibiting bizarre behavior, which snowballed amid a circle of young girls; their contortions, rantings, and delusions sent accusations flying. On the whole their stories were remarkably similar, as they banded together to accuse a

Puritan minister Cotton Mather, author of the 1688 book *Memorable Providences*, which some speculate fueled the witchcraft hysteria of 1692.

wide range of citizens—from beggar Sarah Good to former Salem minister George Burroughs—of being witches.

The hysteria that permeated Salem Village spread like wildfire, as the girls and members of the staunch Puritan population began accusing anyone they chose. In effect, a mere dislike of someone or any political motive or social warring between two families could easily have been the underlying cause of someone's accusations. No one will ever know for certain what caused the hysteria, but by June of that year, Bridget Bishop had the distinction of being the first witch to be hanged at Gallows Hill. And that was just the beginning. It's estimated that between 100 and 200 individuals (including children) were accused

and jailed for witchcraft during that manic year, most of them women. And while the majority escaped execution, a handful—including Martha Carrier—did not.

Illustrations from the late 1800s depicting the hysteria and brutality of the Salem witch trials.

By today's standards, the trials were an abomination. So rabid was the bloodlust of the villagers, judges, and politicians of the day that unsubstantiated evidence allowed in the courtroom included hearsay, gossip, and even bodily searches for the "marks" of witches. In addition, two other outlandish assertions could also be admitted as evidence. If someone allegedly saw the apparition of an accused witch, it was considered

CONFESSION OF SALEM JURORS, &c.

From Calef's "Salem Witchcraft." Page 294.

" Some that had been of several Juries, have given forth a paper, signed with their own hands, in these words:

" WE whose names are under written, being in the year 1692, called to serve as jurors in court at *Salem* on trial of many ; who were by some suspected guilty of doing acts of witchcraft upon the bodies of sundry persons.

" We confess that we ourselves were not capable to understand, nor able to withstand the mysterious delusions of the powers of darkness, and prince of the air ; but were, for want of knowledge in ourselves, and better information from others, prevailed with to take up with such evidence against the accused, as on further consideration, and better information, we justly fear, was insufficient for the touching the lives of any : Deut. xvii. 6., whereby we fear we have been instrumental with others, though ignorantly and unwittingly, to bring upon ourselves and this people of the Lord, the guilt of innocent blood ; which sin the Lord saith in scripture, he would not pardon : 2 Kings xxiv. 4 ; that is, we suppose in regard of his temporal judgment. We do therefore hereby signify to all in general (and to the surviving sufferers in special) our deep sense of, and sorrow for our errors, in acting on such evidence to the condemning of any person.

" And do hereby declare that we justly fear that we were sadly deluded and mistaken, for which we are much disquieted and distressed in our minds ; and do therefore humbly beg forgiveness, first of God for Christ's sake for this our error ; and pray that God would not impute the guilt of it to ourselves nor others ; and we also pray that we may be considered candidly, and aright by the living sufferers as being then under the power of a strong and general delusion, utterly unacquainted with, and not experienced in matters of that nature.

"We do heartily ask forgiveness of you all, whom we have justly offended, and do declare according to our present minds, we would none of us do such things again on such grounds for the whole world ; praying you to accept of this in way of satisfaction for our offence ; and that you would bless the inheritance of the Lord, that he may be entreated for the land.

An excerpt from an apology issued by several Salem witchcraft trial jurors after the hysteria of 1692.

"spectral evidence." The power of a witch's touch, which was said to halt the afflictions of a possessed girl, was also tested and allowed in court. It was the modern-day equivalent of taking as gospel the rantings of a complete lunatic.

In the end, over twenty poor souls perished as a result of witchcraft hysteria. Five men and fourteen women met their fate at the gallows, and Giles Corey (who refused to be tried) was cruelly and slowly pressed to death with stones upon his chest after enduring their crushing weight for two days. Still others died in prison awaiting their trials. By the following year, higher political officials and common sense finally kicked in to put an end to the insanity. But it was, unfortunately, much too late for Martha Carrier.

HAGS AND NAGS

Founded in 1799, the Peabody Essex Museum in Salem proved to be an invaluable resource for Gwen, as she was able to peruse the original transcripts from the witch trials. A document dated May 31, 1692, chronicled Martha Carrier's trial, during which she was accused by not one, but over a dozen different people who were questioned, including two of her own children. Among her accusers were youngster Abigail Williams, who claimed that "Goody Carrier" had hurt her, and Benjamin Abbot, whose deposition proved particularly intriguing. In it, Abbot stated that "having some land granted to me near to Good Man Carrier's land, and when this land came to be laid out, Good Wife Carrier was very angry, and she caused a pain in my foot and a pain in my side exceedingly tormented." In addition, another villager named Alan Toothaker claimed he heard Martha say that "Benjamin Abbot would wish he had not meddled with that land so near our house." By all accounts, it would seem Martha was an easy target for witchery because she had a land grievance with Abbot. But does that prove that Abbot, being one of many accusers, was entitled to her land?

From historical documentation, it's clear that life for Martha Carrier was very challenging, especially given her quarrel with Abbot, but there was more to the story. The Puritans of the late seventeenth century were basically English Protestants who favored more religious rigidity than was dictated by Queen Elizabeth's Protestant reformation. The Puritan way of life was simple and morally rigorous, so the real question is, what else could Martha have possibly done to incite public animosity? Further archive research at Salem's Town Hall gave Gwen her answer. In March of 1674, Martha wed Thomas Morgan (aka Carrier). The marriage may not have been an issue, but the fact that she gave birth to their first child a mere two months later likely spun more than few morally stringent Puritans on their heads.

Unfortunately, things didn't get any better, as the villagers apparently tried to oust Martha and her family for allegedly spreading smallpox. Those accusations, coupled with the "wicked carelessness" of her having conceived a child out of wedlock were enough to convince the community that Martha was the next Typhoid Mary. Puritans of the day felt strongly that plagues were punishment from God, and given that thirteen villagers—including Martha's father and two brothers—died of smallpox the following year, it seems clear that Martha Carrier was easy prey when it came to hanging witches.

Armed with the tragic tale of Martha Carrier and her feud with Benjamin Abbot, Gwen needed to take a closer look at the Kempers' house. If it had belonged to the Carriers, it had to have been built before 1692. The plaque above the door reads 1685, but that date came about as a result of oral history and could be inaccurate. In

Gwen Wright examining the interior ceiling and beams of the Kempers' home.

time TEASER

Thomas Cranmer, the Archbishop of Canterbury, was burned at the stake in 1556 by Queen Mary I, commonly known as "Bloody Mary." What was Cranmer's offense?

Answer: Cranmer was convicted of heresy for being a Protestant.

order to date the house, Gwen had to ascertain which was the oldest room among several rooms that had obviously been added over the years. Two of the ground-floor rooms might have been part of the original house, but Gwen surmised that the first room she explored was likely built later for storage purposes. An examination of the parlor showed that it was constructed with a wattle and daub mixture of mud, straw, and sand used to fill wood seams, which was common to late 1600s building practices. Even so, it was unlikely that an opulent parlor would have been the first room built. Gwen then focused on the hall, which showed promise, save for a huge nine-foot-long fireplace that was more typical of an eighteenth-century home.

A Tree Grows in Essex

In order to establish the age of the Kempers' home, Gwen wanted to take advantage of a highly specialized testing procedure called *dendrochronology*, which can help estimate the dating of certain events by sampling and analyzing the growth of tree rings. It's a complex but fascinating and relatively accurate scientific methodology, for which Gwen enlisted the help of renowned expert Dr. Michael Worthington of the Oxford Dendrochronology Laboratory in London, who traveled to Massachusetts to perform the necessary tests. Worthington first examined the timber used in the ground-floor construction and decided to collect six to ten samples from the three main rooms. Testing involved drilling into the wood with a hollow corer to obtain samples roughly the size of a typical cigar. Worthington would later sand the face of the wood down with a belt sander until it was polished to a mirror finish to reveal the growth rings. Dendrochronology can actually date timber to the year it was felled and shed light on the types of tools used to shape the wood.

In many cases, by studying measurements and cross matching other samples of the tree ring growth, scientists can often determine not only the year the tree was felled but the specific season. Trees growing in temperate climates produce annual rings, and by analyzing the rings Worthington tracked unique sequences and compared the samples to other centuries-old timber samples from Massachusetts. His conclusions proved to be the case breaker for Gwen and her witchhouse mystery.

Confident of her findings, Gwen was able to reveal to Deane and Joan Kemper the origins of their bewitching abode. Michael Worthington's dendrochronology testing provided several astonishing revelations. The plaque above their front door states that Benjamin Abbot built the house in 1685, which was obviously not the case. The timber from their dining room area had been felled during the winter of 1710 and 1711. The home was originally a one-room structure that included the hall, and more than likely, it was Abbot's son and heir, Benjamin Jr., who built the home in 1711, six years after his father had passed on in 1705. Chances are that the plaque was added much later, perhaps as an enticement to tourists.

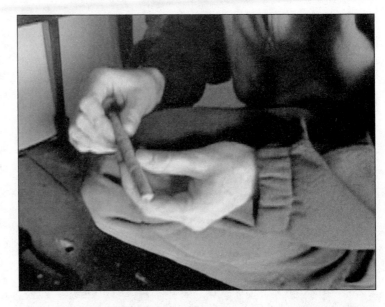

One of the cigar-sized samples Dr. Michael Worthington collected from the Kempers' home.

The simple but somber headstone marking the final resting place of accused witch Martha Carrier.

Home Sweet Home

The science of dendrochronology played a crucial role in the study of a log cabin that was symbolic of a popular public perception of seventh U.S. president Andrew "Old Hickory" Jackson as a pioneering frontiersman of humble origins. Jackson purchased the 640-acre Hermitage plantation near Nashville, Tennessee, in 1804 and soon after added 360 adjoining acres to the farm. Jackson's first home on Hermitage was an existing, architecturally sound two-story cabin filled with fashionable furnishings, and it was from this residence that Old Hickory began making a name in Tennessee politics.

Although Jackson indeed came from an unpresuming background, he went on to become a prosperous lawyer, farmer, merchant, soldier, and politician. He completed construction of the expansive brick-built Hermitage Mansion between 1819 and 1821. After moving into the mansion, Jackson downsized the cabin to a single story and used it as slave quarters. Even after Jackson's death in 1845, the cabin functioned as slave housing until the end of the Civil War. Dendrochronology tests performed on the cabin in 2001 indicated that it was constructed of tulip poplar that had been felled sometime between 1798 and 1800.

Andrew Jackson's cabin at the Hermitage plantation.

While the discovery was a shock to the Kempers, Gwen's companion for her return journey was even more of a surprise. Accompanying Gwen was Diane Fowles—a tenth-generation descendant of accused witch Martha Carrier. Even today it's impossible to say what really caused the hysteria of 1692. Historians and scholars have proposed everything from delinquent teenagers rebelling against Puritanism to natural psychoses, and even a form of poisoning caused by fungus-infested rye crops—a phenomenon that has also been used to explain *lycanthropy*, or werewolves. But one thing is for certain. Martha Carrier met her demise on August 16, 1692, at the hands of an angry crowd, and her words speak for themselves: "I am wronged. It is a shameful thing that you should mind these folks that are out of their wits."

Waterworld

The dendrochronology testing Gwen employed in solving the Essex house mystery is a scientific dating method that has certainly proven its worth, but it's not the only technique to serve the investigative community admirably. The little-known science of ice core technology is similar in practice to dendrochronology, and by employing it scientists have made remarkable strides across unknown territory.

In the twenty-first century it seems un-fathomable that there are still areas of the planet that are untouched by mankind, but such an amazing place does exist on the world's fifth-largest continent—an area covered almost entirely by ice and plagued by the most extreme weather on Earth.

Antarctica, whose name is derived from the Greek word *antarkitos*, meaning "opposite to the north," is the Earth's southernmost continent, one void of human populations and home to a handful of plant and animal life genetically built to withstand temperatures as low as −130° Fahrenheit. It's a secretive and inhospitable land that only the toughest human could possibly withstand and for only a short period of time. In the last decade, however, Antarctica has given up one of her long-held secrets—a remarkable discovery that sheds new light on not only our planet, but others as well. Though it had been speculated upon since the 1960s, it wasn't until 1996 that Russian and British scientists confirmed the existence of a sub-glacial body of water approximately the size of Lake Ontario that is said to be the last remaining untouched freshwater lake on the planet. It's called Lake Vostok, and the truly astonishing thing about it, in addition to its size, is that its water contains microbial life. The presence of microbes in this lake, which is similar to Jupiter's ice-covered moon, Europa, bolsters the argument that there may be a similar kind of life on Europa.

Lake Vostok is just one of over seventy lakes that have been documented under the Antarctic ice sheet, but its size of over 10,000 square kilometers, and especially its depth (over 500 meters at its deepest), coupled with the fact that it has been unspoiled by humanity and Earth's

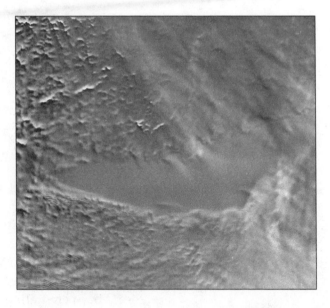

A satellite view of Antarctica's Lake Vostok, one of Earth's last untouched bodies of fresh water. Scientists surmise it may contain ancient life forms.

DID YOU **know**

More than a few intrepid explorers lost their lives attempting to discover the North and South poles. In 1911, the Antarctic race for the South Pole was on between Norwegian explorer Roald Amundsen and Englishman Robert Falcon Scott. On October 19, Amundsen began his trek, arriving at the pole first on December 14. Scott reached the pole around January 17, 1912, only to find that Amundsen had been there thirty-five days earlier. Scott and his comrades suffered terribly on the return journey. Sadly, he and the last of his three surviving expedition members died a mere eleven miles from their supply depot.

biosphere, make it truly unique. Amazing as it may sound, it's estimated that the lake is between 500,000 and a million years old, and that beneath its three-kilometer-thick icecap, the water remains in liquid form. The information that has already been gathered and the potential for obtaining future data from a superoxygenated lake that could actually contain ancient microbial and ecological data is a scientist's dream. Of course, reaching the liquid water has proven to be a technological nightmare.

Established directly above Lake Vostok is Russia's Vostok station, where an international scientific team is working to study and take samples of the lake—that is, the part they can reach. Lake Vostok embodies the perfect scientific and technological conundrum. Ice core technology is philosophically similar to dendrochronology in that it involves drilling into the ice to retrieve cylindrical-shaped samples that can then be measured and analyzed to uncover various facts about climate and life in the lake. This type of testing began in 1998, but an inherent problem with the process is that penetrating the lake would likely contaminate it with biological materials from the instrumentation. At present, drilling has ceased approximately 130 meters above the water, but in the last two years, plans have been made to build and test a robotic mechanism, a submersible "hydrobot" capable of penetrating the ice and merging into Vostok without contaminating it. When technology does finally catch up to the scientific endeavor, it's certain that the secrets of Lake Vostok will one day be revealed—and they'll likely prove to be out of this world.

The Abraham Lincoln Mysteries

When you think of famous national figures, who immediately springs to mind? George Washington? Amelia Earhart? Martin Luther King? When it comes right down to it, there are few individuals who are able to achieve phenomenal success in their lives, but without question, President Abraham Lincoln did just that. During his lifetime, the Kentucky-born Lincoln renewed a nation's hope that the sanctity of life far outweighed the contentious beliefs of a war-torn country. The immortal words he spoke in his 1863 Emancipation Proclamation set into motion the eventual hard-won freedom of slaves, while also hastening an end to the bloodiest conflict ever fought on U.S. soil.

time
TEASER   Legend has it that Abraham Lincoln was challenged to a duel by James Shields in 1842, but Shields capitulated soon after learning of Lincoln's choice of weapons. What were they?

Answer: Broadswords.

An early 1900s illustration depicting Abraham Lincoln's assassination on April 14, 1865.

A photo of President Abraham Lincoln from his last official photo session in February of 1865, just two months prior to his assassination.

Lincoln had been president a mere five months when on April 12, 1861, Confederate forces in Charleston, South Carolina, opened fire on Fort Sumter and began the Civil War (see chapter 4). As the first Republican leader of a racially divided nation, Lincoln did his best to assuage seething political tension. Arguably the most famous and impassioned speech he gave was his Gettysburg Address, which began: "Fourscore and seven years ago our fathers brought forth on this continent a new nation, conceived in liberty, and dedicated to the proposition that all men are created equal." They were powerful, immortal words that continue to ring true for every generation to this day.

As a humble and homegrown politician, Lincoln would be re-elected in 1864, but his second term was short-lived. On April 9, 1865, General Robert E. Lee surrendered to Ulysses S. Grant in Appomattox, Virginia, bringing an end to the Civil War. Five days later, Lincoln was shot in the head by John Wilkes Booth during a performance at Ford's Theatre in Washington, D.C. The president died the following day. That such a man should meet his end at the hand of an assassin is still inconceivable to most, but not entirely unexpected. Treacherous individuals such as Booth have been in abundance throughout history, each of them creating an abyss of grief, hatred, and persistent conspiracy theories.

A bird's-eye view of Abraham Lincoln's funeral procession down Pennsylvania Avenue in Washington, D.C., four days after his assassination.

Even today, there are plenty of rumors, studies, and debates surrounding Lincoln's murder, ranging from then Vice President Andrew Johnson being linked to Booth, to the Confederacy planning his death, and even the Freemasons or the Catholic Church having something to do with it. You might think we know all that can be known about John Wilkes Booth, but that wasn't the case when Gwen Wright took on a mystery involving a potentially conspiratorial abode.

THE HOUSE IN GREENWICH VILLAGE

What would you do if you heard that your beloved domicile had played a part in a presidential assassination? Would you be intrigued? Horrified? Or would you call *History Detectives*? That was the dilemma facing New Yorker Jean Dierking, who fortunately chose the latter option and invited Gwen Wright into her home to investigate its allegedly sordid past. Over the years, Dierking had heard that the planning of Abraham Lincoln's assassination had taken place in her building, which if true would prove to be a remarkable situation, given that as an actor, John Wilkes Booth was primarily based in Washington, D.C. The overriding question to this mystery was, what would Booth have been doing in Greenwich Village at 45 Grove Street?

Gwen began her investigation by examining Dierking's building to see if the date of its construction was within the correct time frame. It was a plain Federal-style structure with an inset, arched doorway, a small porch, and lintels above the windows. Its ornamentation consisted primarily of bricks set in an alternating long and short pattern known as Flemish bond. In Gwen's estimation, the building was likely from the late 1820s to around

1830, but to be certain she needed to research the history of the building at the New York City Landmarks Preservation Commission. What she found was a Greenwich Village Historic District report that revealed the building was once one of the largest and finest Federal mansions in the area. In 1851, however, it was sold and reclassified as a commercial property, most likely for renting rooms.

Gwen's next search for a link between John Wilkes Booth and 45 Grove Street proved intriguing. What she learned from her

The Federal-style home at 45 Grove Street in New York that Gwen Wright investigated for *History Detectives*.

Columbia University colleague, Eric Foner, was that New York's racial climate during the Civil War would have made it easy for Booth to find Southern sympathizers for his cause. She also discovered that in November 1864, six months prior to Lincoln's slaying, Booth and his brothers Junius Brutus and Edwin, a renowned Shakespearean actor, had performed in a special production of *Julius Caesar* at New York's Winter Garden Theatre. Also acting in the performance was Samuel K. Chester—a boyhood friend of John Wilkes Booth—who happened to live at 45 Grove Street.

Jean Dierking at the entrance to 45 Grove Street.

A portrait of Abraham Lincoln assassin John Wilkes Booth, taken during the 1860s.

With the knowledge that Samuel K. Chester resided in Greenwich Village, Gwen traveled to the National Archives in Maryland to research records from Lincoln's assassination investigation. Among the original handwritten documents from 1865, she found a statement from Chester that confirmed that he and Booth were long-time friends, and that in late 1864 Booth paid him a visit. After a night of considerable drinking, the distracted Booth took a walk with Chester and attempted to enlist his help in a conspiracy plot to kidnap Lincoln and other governmental heads and take them to Richmond in an effort to bring victory to the Confederacy. When Chester adamantly refused, Booth went so far as to offer him $3,000 to $4,000, and even threatened him with his loaded Derringer— the same type of weapon he used to shoot the president.

Chester's statement went on to say that he and Booth later exchanged letters, and that a week before Lincoln's assassination Booth once again visited him in New York. During that visit, Booth made clear to Chester that his conspiracy plan had dissolved and that he'd abandoned the entire sordid affair. His words, however, belied his true intentions, for on the evening of April 14, 1865, Booth entered Ford's Theatre

Ford's Theatre, in Washington, D.C., in April of 1865.

during a performance of *Our American Cousin* and shot Abraham Lincoln in the head. He then jumped to the stage, breaking his left leg in the process, and managed to escape, eluding authorities until April 26, when he was besieged in a Virginia tobacco barn until finally being shot dead by Union soldiers.

Centuries later, Jean Dierking could rest easy knowing that her home on 45 Grove Street hadn't been used to plan one of the United States' most famous and darkest conspiracies. Her Federal abode, however, had housed a thespian who did his best to discourage a would-be assassin from acting on an insane endeavor. Samuel K. Chester was never named as one of the conspirators of Lincoln's assassination, but the same can't be said for a Maryland woman named Mary Surratt.

MARY, MARY, QUITE CONTRARY

Gwen's investigation of the Greenwich Village home proved it wasn't used for the planning of Lincoln's assassination, but this invites the question, where *did* the planning take place? Part of the answer has to do with a seemingly respectable woman and her association with John Wilkes Booth. The name Mary Surratt isn't a household word, but it should be, considering that she was not only deeply involved in the slaying of President Lincoln, but was the first woman hanged by the U.S. government.

What is known about the former Mary Jenkins is that in 1840 she married John Surratt, and they had three children. By 1852, John had bought several hundred acres of land in Maryland that would eventually become Surrattsville and that included a post office, a tavern, a polling station, and the Surratt family home. The area quickly became a local hangout for everyone from farmers to politicians, and the tavern is said to have served as a safe haven for individuals who were part of the Confederate underground. In 1862, John Surratt died, leaving Mary to

The Pirate and Ocean Born Mary

In 1720, an Irish couple named James and Elizabeth Wilson sailed across the Atlantic Ocean bound for New Hampshire. Unfortunately, their ship was attacked by pirates the same day Elizabeth gave birth to their daughter. The leader of the rogues, Captain Don Pedro, heard the baby's cries and upon seeing her decided that if the couple named the infant Mary, after his mother, the passengers would be unharmed. Pedro gave Mary a beautiful green silk brocade as fabric for her future wedding dress and sailed away.

Twenty-two years later, Mary wed James Wallace in her green silk dress; she went on to have five children and was eventually widowed. It's said that the piratical Don Pedro retired to Henniker, New Hampshire, and eventually wed Mary, who died in 1814. Legend has it that her ghost still haunts their Henniker mansion. Is the legend true? Mary Wallace was indeed born at sea and a pirate did spare the crew of her vessel. And yes, her wedding gown was the same green silk. But truth be told, Mary would have been in her seventies and Don Pedro in his nineties had they actually married. The Ocean Born Mary House they never lived in is a popular Henniker tourist attraction.

contend with massive debt compounded by the turmoil of the Civil War. The tavern and the home were rented out, and she took up residence in Washington, D.C., to run her own boardinghouse. So how exactly did this woman become involved in the Lincoln conspiracy?

The Surratt family quite clearly were Southern sympathizers. Both of Mary's sons, John and John Harrison, joined the Confederate Army, and it was while working as a secret agent that John allegedly became acquainted with John Wilkes Booth. Involved in Booth's original plan to kidnap Lincoln was Lewis Paine (also known as Lewis Powell), David Herold, George Atzerodt, and John Surratt, but when the plan was foiled by a change in Lincoln's schedule, Booth opted for more drastic measures. It's unclear as to whether or not he ever rented a room from Mary Surratt, but he was a frequent guest and it's likely that plans were discussed there.

Mary Surratt, one of the convicted co-conspirators in the plot to assassinate President Abraham Lincoln.

After Booth shot Lincoln, he escaped and met up with David Herold, stopping at Mary's tavern in Surrattsville, which she'd leased to John M. Lloyd. Two days after President Lincoln perished, Mary was arrested and taken to the Old Capitol Prison. On May 9, 1865, the conspiracy trial commenced, and the star witness against Surratt was John Lloyd, who testified that Mary had certain items—including a field glass and firearms—available for Booth and Herold when they passed through. Likewise, one of Mary's boardinghouse tenants, Louis Weichmann, revealed that Mary had many conversations with the other conspirators, including Booth, and that on the night of the fatal shooting, she traveled to the tavern with a package and met privately with the assassin. In the end, the Fates had a brutal demise in store for Mary Surratt. She was found guilty by the military commission and sentenced to death—but she wouldn't stand on the gallows alone.

Mary's son John managed to escape the hangman, but Paine, Atzerodt, and Herold, who'd given himself up at the tobacco barn when hiding with Booth, were hanged alongside Mary Surratt on July 7, 1865, in front of an enthusiastic audience, who actually had tickets for the execution. The four bodies were buried in shallow graves next to the gallows and remained there for several years until being released to their families. Of course, as with many such deaths, there are the inevitable ghost stories that take on a life of their own.

Mary Surratt maintained her innocence in the Lincoln conspiracy until her dying breath, and her ghost is apparently none too pleased with her demise. Legend has it that she is haunting several locations, including the site of the gallows (the Washington Arsenal Prison), where Fort McNair currently stands, as well as her former Maryland home and tavern and her Washington boardinghouse, where many folks have allegedly seen her apparition floating about within the buildings.

Mary Surratt and her convicted co-conspirators Lewis Paine, David Herold, and George Atzerodt meet the Grim Reaper at the gallows on July 7, 1865.

Some people even contend that the ghost of John Wilkes Booth haunts an area near Ford's Theatre, but the 1975 book *The Reincarnation of John Wilkes Booth* portrays an even more outrageous claim. Written by hypnotist Dr. Dell Leonardi, the book includes conversations with a man bearing the pseudonym "Wesley" who claims to have once been the infamous assassin. The wild story alleges that Booth wasn't killed by Union soldiers in 1865 but lived out his life without further incident or identification.

A View to a Kill

Gwen Wright's investigation of Samuel K. Chester's abode and the examination of John Wilkes Booth brings into sharper focus the treachery of past and present-day assassination. Every country in the world

DID YOU know

In 1876, a gang of grave robbers attempted to steal Abraham Lincoln's body and hold it for ransom. In 1900, Lincoln's oldest son, Robert, decided to build a safer, more permanent tomb. The following year, a site was constructed with an enormous cage buried ten feet down. Lincoln's casket was placed inside the cage, and the entire site was ultimately encased in tons of cement.

Bad to the Bone

Sometimes a house inherits the reputation of its evil owner. During the 1820s, in Reliance, Maryland, the infamous Johnson-Cannon Gang wreaked havoc on free blacks by kidnapping them and selling them back into slavery. Led by the ruthless Patty Cannon, the gang allegedly operated from a house near Wilson's Crossroads now belonging to Jack and Rose Messick. Gwen Wright and Elyse Luray investigated the house to determine if the historical marker in the front yard was legitimately placed. Their research uncovered depositions from 1829 that indicated Cannon killed several children and had other bodies buried on her property. But is it the same house? Patty Cannon did indeed purchase the land from her son-in-law Joseph Johnson, but her house, where so much evil took place, was several hundred yards from the Messick's, and was torn down in 1948.

When investigating the infamous Patty Cannon house, *History Detectives* proved that historical markers aren't always what they appear to be.

has its dark past, those times in history that painfully reveal the depravity of the human soul, whether as a result of desperation, ideation, delusion, misconception, or just plain evil. It may come as a shock to realize how many important leaders over the centuries have met their fate at the hands of men and women whose beliefs were in sharp contrast to the good of a nation, its citizens, or various individuals or organizations.

When it comes to assassination, there are untold numbers of people who have met their demise by a wide range of unseemly methods, but when world and political leaders are the intended target, the phenomenon often becomes an epic tale of Shakespearean proportion. Some of the most famous and infamous movers and shakers in history have been assassinated, a word derived from the Arabic word *hashshashin*, after a secret order of Muslims at the time of the Crusades. Long before the Crusades, however, the Roman Empire, one of the greatest civilizations the world has ever known, had a long and tumultuous history of disposing of its own leaders.

Pompey the Great, a distinguished military leader and the man responsible for wiping out Mediterranean Sea piracy in 67 B.C. (a bold campaign that rid the area of pirates for over 400 years) was stabbed and decapitated in Egypt in 48 B.C. His archrival Julius Caesar, the general and dictator known for his conquest of Gaul and Britain and his scandalous dalliance with Egypt's queen Cleopatra, was brutally murdered by a group of Roman senators on the Ides of March in 44 B.C. The next year, renowned Roman orator Cicero was

DIY DETECTIVE

For many individuals, one of the rewards for putting in long hours dealing with the humdrum routine of daily life is the opportunity to take a well-deserved road trip. This can be a great opportunity to explore historical sites, and many of them may be closer than you think. The National Park Service maintains informative Web sites that highlight hundreds of historically important locations. You can get started by going to www.nps.gov, where you'll find an interactive map on the home page that provides links to national parks and historical locations in each state. The Park Service also maintains a Web page just for kids at www.nps.gov/history/kids.htm, with links to youth-oriented archaeology, historical landmarks, and stories of many of the nation's early leaders and heroes. These sites are a great way to research landmarks, because as *History Detectives* learned when investigating the notorious Patty Cannon, historical landmarks can sometimes be deceiving.

One of the most interesting Web sites for historical exploration is the National Historical Landmarks Program at www.nps.gov/history/nhl. There are countless historical sites throughout the nation, but those that have meaning to all U.S. citizens make up the list of National Historic Landmarks. These include places where major events occurred, such as battlefields, locations where prominent people lived, places that characterize early colonial ways of life, and notable archaeological locations. Currently there are just under 2,500 sites listed on the registry, with more than half of those in private ownership. Access to privately held locations is often limited, but the list of public sites is enormous and well worth investigating. With the amazing range of travel information available on the Internet, getting away from it all for a few weeks or just a quick weekend can be a historical adventure that you can share with the entire family.

decapitated, followed in A.D. 41 by the assassination of depraved despot Emperor Caligula.

Hundreds of infamous assassinations followed over the centuries, including that of King Gustav III of Sweden in 1792, Russian emperor Alexander II in 1881, Archduke Franz Ferdinand of Austria and Hungary and the Archduchess Sophie in 1914, Czar Nicholas II and his entire family in 1918, India's Mahatma Gandhi in 1948 and Prime Minister Indira Gandhi in 1984, Egyptian president Anwar Sadat in 1981, and Israel's prime minister Yitzhak Rabin in 1995. Japan has also lost its share of leaders, with five prime ministers assassinated from 1878 to 1932. Even

The John F. Kennedy motorcade in Dallas, Texas, just prior to his assassination on November 22, 1963.

the iconic Pope John Paul II became a target in 1981, though the pontiff—perhaps by the grace of God—was one of the lucky few to survive.

The United States has suffered its own share of murderous intent. From 1865 to 1963, four U.S. presidents were assassinated while in office, including Abraham Lincoln, James Garfield, John F. Kennedy, and William McKinley (see chapter 11). Andrew Jackson, Theodore Roosevelt, Franklin D. Roosevelt, Harry Truman, Gerald Ford, and Ronald Reagan were fortunate to have escaped assassination attempts, but other prominent figures, such as Robert F. Kennedy, Medgar Evers, Malcolm X, Martin Luther King, and San Francisco mayor George Moscone were not.

CHAPTER TWENTY

World at War

Every generation of the past nine decades has been deeply affected by the world wars. The stories and artifacts of those eras remain in our minds as we attempt to analyze and decipher all the images, events, battles, and oral histories we have heard from a multitude of sources both public and private. Perhaps the most poignant of these stories involve items that have been handed down from one family member to another, in which case the mystery surrounding those artifacts becomes deeply personal.

In this chapter we focus on several investigations brought to *History Detectives* by the families of fallen soldiers. The sinking of the USS *Indianapolis* is well documented, but what isn't well known is the story of Arthur Michno, a brave young sailor who was aboard the *Indy* when she went down. His tale sent History Detective Wes Cowan on a poignant journey into one of the worst naval disasters in U.S. history. Equally touching is Tukufu Zuberi's investigation of a pair of alleged U-boat propellers, and Gwen Wright's revelations of the horrors of chemical warfare. Each of these investigative odysseys marked a moment in time—one that had it not been for the determination of several families might never have emerged from the shadows of the world's greatest generations.

Trouble at Sea

In the 1975 blockbuster film *Jaws*, there was one scene that stood out above all others, and it had nothing to do with a great white chomping on an unsuspecting coed. Instead, the scene occurred just prior to a major attack by a very angry and vindictive shark, when the astonishingly phlegmatic Captain Quint, brilliantly played by Robert Shaw, told the haunting tale of having been on the USS *Indianapolis* at the time of its sinking on July 30, 1945. So convincingly impassioned was his telling of the unimaginable experience of waiting for rescue amid endless hungry sharks that you felt as if you were there bobbing right next to him, floating in the cold, dark depths.

More than likely, the story of the USS *Indianapolis* was lost on younger viewers who didn't realize that the event was not only terrifying—it was true. En route from Guam to the Leyte Gulf in the Philippines, the *Indy* had just completed a very special and top-secret mission when she was torpedoed by the Japanese submarine *I-58* and sank in a mere twelve minutes. Out of a crew of 1,196, nearly 300 men perished when the *Indy* sank and over 900 ended up in the water, praying for a swift rescue. Their prayers weren't answered.

Day after day, the sailors struggled to remain afloat, with no rations and nothing but a few life vests and the clothes on their backs. Then came the sharks, and it was at that very moment that the true meaning of survival

An official U.S.
Navy photo of the
USS *Indianapolis*
circa 1937.

became crystal clear. Four long days later, a PV-1 submarine hunter, flying a routine patrol, spotted the survivors and sounded the alarm that the *Indy* had met a terrible fate. By the time help arrived, the sailors had been in the ocean nearly five days, with only 317 surviving the ordeal. To call them heroes doesn't do justice to the extraordinary courage these men displayed.

The front page of the *Washington Post* on August 15, 1945, when tragic news of the *Indy's* sinking was released to the world.

BOMBS AWAY

The *Indy's* mission ultimately speaks to a great loss that for its own reasons triggered the beginning of the end of World War II. On July 26, 1945, the *Indy* arrived at the Northern Mariana island of Tinian after a fast ten-day trip from San Francisco. Her highly classified cargo included essential components of the first atomic bomb. Transported in sections via the *Indy* and several military air transports, two bombs were fully assembled at Tinian. The first, a 9,700-pound bomb nicknamed "Little Boy," was carried by the B-29 *Enola Gay* and dropped on the Japanese city of Hiroshima on August 6. Three days later, a 10,000-pound bomb nicknamed "Fat Man," was dropped on Nagasaki by the B-29 *Bockscar*. The combined devastating force of the two bombs was the equivalent of nearly 36,000 tons of TNT.

With a population of around 255,000 at the time of the attack, it's estimated that over 140,000 people in Hiroshima died during and several months following the bombing. An additional 40,000 perished in Nagasaki. The human tragedy of the atomic disasters was the extreme outcome of a war in which tensions ran high and attacks such as that on the *Indy* were executed with brutal force. History Detective Wes Cowan's investigation of artifacts related to the USS *Indianapolis* sent him on a journey that honored not one, but every sailor who served on a ship during wartime missions. Many survived their ordeal and many more did not.

time
TEASER

During World War II, six people were killed by an enemy bomb within the continental United States. Where did it happen?

Answer: Just outside Bly, Oregon. On May 5, 1945, a woman and five children discovered a Japanese bomb carried into the country by balloon. It went off when they attempted to move it.

An ominous image of the atomic bomb mushroom cloud rising over Nagasaki on August 9, 1945.

One of those unlucky men aboard the *Indy* was Seaman Second Class Arthur R. Michno, and it was his family who approached *History Detectives* with an intriguing assortment of items he left at home in April 1945 just prior to embarking on that fateful mission. Michno's nephew, Larry Klubert, shared with Wes the items, which included a heavy metal fragment, a Japanese identification plaque, and a pair of uniform patches, all of which he was told might have come from a devastating kamikaze attack on the *Indy* on March 31, 1945, in the Battle of Okinawa four months before she was sunk.

In order to authenticate Arthur Michno's artifacts, Wes needed to visit several military experts. His first stop was the Naval Historical Center in Washington, D.C., to consult historian Jack Green, who reiterated the importance of the Battle of Okinawa and the Imperial Army's success in using kamikaze planes to forestall the imminent U.S. invasion of Japan. Green's analysis of the uniform patches with their anchor and chrysanthemum insignias indicated that they were from the Japanese Imperial Navy. The yellow on one patch indicated that it was worn by a petty officer in the seaman's branch. The green coloring on the second patch showed that its wearer was a seaman first class in aviation maintenance.

Research in the center's archives confirmed that the kamikaze that attacked the *Indy* was a single-seat Japanese Imperial Army Nakajima Ki-43 fighter, which the Japanese dubbed *Hayabusa* and the Allies called the "Oscar." The fact that this was an army plane made clear that Michno's two naval patches didn't belong to the kamikaze pilot. But what about the Japanese identification plaque? A meeting with Japanese aircraft expert Todd Peterson enlightened Wes as to the aluminum plaque's possible origin: it was probably attached to an oil or fuel

time
TEASER

The first bomb dropped by the Allies on Berlin during World War II resulted in an unusual casualty. What was it?

Answer: The only elephant at the Zoologizer Garten Berlin was killed by the blast.

pressure regulator from an Imperial Army aircraft. Peterson also pointed out that it was common for servicemen to collect and trade any plaques with Japanese writing on them as souvenirs, which very often were sent home to the States. That left the mysterious chunk of metal, which Wes had tested by chemist Jim Holcombe at the University of Texas at Austin. Scrapings from the metal were analyzed using a high-tech inductively coupled plasma time-of-flight mass spectrometer, which heats the sample and allows an elemental analysis of the resulting ions.

Michno's metal chunk was composed primarily of pure nickel, a substance the Japanese didn't have access to in mass quantities. For comparison, Holcombe also tested a known sample from the kamikaze that hit the *Indy*, and it showed the high quantity of aluminum one would expect from a Japanese plane. With his scientific avenues exhausted, Wes concluded that chances were slim the artifacts came from the *Indy*'s kamikaze attack; they were likely souvenirs that Arthur Michno had collected elsewhere. But what about Michno himself? What actually happened during the kamikaze attack and during the *Indy*'s unfortunate sinking?

In Plane Sight

For a very special interview, Wes went to the National Museum of the Pacific War in Fredericksburg, Texas, to meet with *Indy* survivor L. D. Cox, who was only nineteen when the great ship met her demise. (His full interview can be viewed at www.pbs.org.) Cox was also on board during the Okinawa battle when the *Indy* was hit by the kamikaze. He was eating breakfast when the alarm sounded to man battle stations, and by the time he reached mid-ship, he caught a glimpse of a shadowy plane headed straight for them. When the Japanese fighter hit, Cox was blown into the air as the plane violently smashed into the *Indy*'s decks and flood compartments while also dislodging a pair of the ship's propellers. Nine sailors lost their lives during the attack, which temporarily immobilized the 9,800-ton heavy cruiser.

Arthur Michno's World War II Pacific Theater artifacts, including a pair of Japanese uniform patches, a mysterious chunk of metal, and an identification plaque.

Wes Cowan meeting with USS *Indianapolis* survivor L. D. Cox.

After the attack, Cox picked up a piece of debris from the enemy plane and kept it as a souvenir. He later donated it to the Pacific War Museum. It was the same aluminum fragment that Wes used for comparison when chemically testing Arthur Michno's metal fragment. Even more astounding is Cox's recollection of what happened the night the *Indy* was sunk months later. Cox was on the bridge preparing to go on watch when a horrible explosion occurred, followed by more explosions and Captain Charles Butler McVay's order for his crew to abandon ship. What Cox and his crewmates didn't know was that Japanese submarine commander Mochitsura Hashimoto's first torpedo had hit the *Indy*'s bow, with subsequent hits near the ship's midsection of the starboard side. Unfortunately, this set off a fuel tank and a powder magazine, which caused the *Indy* to literally split and quickly begin her descent to a watery grave. Cox jumped over the main deck and swam as fast as he could away from the ship to escape the imminent suction the *Indy* would produce when sinking.

As Cox tells it, during the first few hours in the cold, dark water many of his mates began suffering from dehydration and hallucinations. Not long after, the sharks appeared—dozens of them—and, ruthless in their attacks, they "struck like lightening," pulling sailors underwater, never to be seen again.

USS *Indianapolis* Seaman Second Class Arthur R. Michno, one of the brave crewman who was lost when the *Indy* went down.

L. D. Cox was one of the brave and fortunate sailors who epitomize the very heart of human existence and the will to survive. Hearing all that Cox had endured, Wes had but one final question to ask on behalf of Larry Klubert, something that would mean more to Klubert and his family than any genuine artifact or souvenir. Producing a picture of Arthur Michno, Wes asked L. D. Cox if he recognized him, a memory that would pay ultimate tribute to a fallen sailor. With a twinkle in his eye and a wonderful smile, Cox did indeed recognize Arthur Michno, a seventeen-year-old Ohio sailor and unsung war hero.

The Kaleidoscope of War

Both world wars shaped the face of world politics and geography, but they also continue to influence the lives of the families of each individual who puts his or her life in harm's way. The History Detective's unique approach of bringing the enormous scale of global conflict into humanized perspective by pursuing the legacies of unassuming individuals has been highlighted in episodes from several points of view. Gwen Wright's investigation

A Rain of Locusts

During all of the campaigns fought by the United States during World War II, no fighting force generated more fear and loathing than the suicide pilots of the Japanese military who purposely crashed into Allied vessels. Although the Japanese didn't use the term during World War II, the *kamikaze*, commonly translated as "divine wind," forced the development of new Allied battle tactics to shoot down the aggressive aircraft before they could come within striking distance. Even so, nearly 3,000 kamikazes reached their targets, sinking dozens of ships and damaging hundreds more, including those of the United States, Great Britain, and Australia.

In Japan, enthusiastic young patriots enlisted in droves to learn just enough piloting skills to make what would be their only combat flight. Indeed, there were many more volunteers than planes. Some who were not assigned aircraft zealously crammed into cockpits along with the pilots to give encouragement and participate in the glory of the ultimate sacrifice.

The USS *Missouri* being attacked by a kamikaze pilot on April 11, 1945. The plane struck the side of the ship below decks, causing minimal damage and no casualties.

of a Texas POW camp that housed German prisoners brought World War II home to U.S. soil. The same can be said for Elyse Luray's mystery surrounding a WWII landing-craft tank. Likewise, Wes Cowan's tale of a shotgun purportedly belonging to Hermann Göering, although proven unlikely, sheds light on the inevitable pilfering of confiscated goods by victorious armies no matter what their nationality. And then there was the Manhattan Project letter, which Wes discovered to be not only authentic but very telling. Ultimately, there were two other very personal *History Detectives* investigations that illuminated the devastating technologies of a world at war and at the same time brought a sense of pride and closure to the descendants of two brave men. We'll take a look at their very separate but equally poignant tales.

THE PERPLEXING PROPELLER MYSTERY

During World War II, the Atlantic Ocean was the scene of hundreds of sneak attacks by German submarines bent on disrupting the steady flow of shipping between the United States and Europe, but not everyone is aware that some of the final attacks of the war occurred just a few miles off the coast of New England in U.S. waters. During the first years of the war, hundreds of stealthy German submarines called *Unterseeboots,* or U-boats, attacked Allied shipping virtually at will, but later British advances in radar and magnetic detection as well as the cracking of German communication codes and the technical ability to trace radio signals to their sources triggered an onslaught of successful retaliations by sea and air that shattered the German submarine fleet.

Toward the end of the war, U-boat activity was reduced to a relative handful of solitary missions. The story of one such mission came to light after brothers Bob and Paul Westerlund of Brockton, Massachusetts,

DID YOU know

Many survivors' organizations maintain Internet sites dedicated to the fallen heroes of the U.S. Navy. The USS *Indianapolis* has such a site, which, as well as recording information and tributes, documents efforts to clear the *Indy*'s captain, Charles Butler McVay III, of any dereliction of duty in the ship's sinking. In-depth coverage includes McVay's historic court-martial and the remarkable story of Mochitsura Hashimoto, the commander of the submarine that sunk the *Indianapolis*. In later years, in a remarkable turn of events, Hashimoto himself joined in the effort to clear McVay's name. To learn more about the *Indy*, visit www.ussindianapolis.org.

approached History Detective Tukufu Zuberi with the mystery of a pair of propellers said to have been salvaged from the wreckage of a German submarine, possibly from the very U-boat responsible for sinking their father's ship, the USS *Eagle 56*, on April 23, 1945, in the waters off the coast of Maine. Tukufu quickly learned that the Westerlunds were no strangers to the nature of war mysteries.

Brothers Bob and Paul Westerlund, who enlisted the help of *History Detectives* to find out what really happened to the USS *Eagle 56* in 1945.

The U.S. Navy's official report was that the USS *Eagle 56*, a World War I– era patrol craft, was towing targets for aircraft bombing practice when a boiler exploded, taking the ship down and leaving just thirteen survivors of her crew of sixty-seven. Among the dead was thirty-two-year-old seaman Ivar Westerlund. Many of the survivors disagreed with the report, claiming that they had clearly seen the conning tower of a submarine painted with the German insignia of a red horse trotting on a yellow shield moments after their ship exploded, but the Navy stuck to the official version for decades.

The Westerlund family never accepted the official report, and in 1998, Bob and Paul related the story to attorney Paul Lawton, who was struck by the tragedy of the loss and subsequent cover-up. After digging through declassified records, interviewing survivors, and involving Navy archivist Bernard Cavalcante, who resurrected long-buried Navy documentation, it finally emerged that the *Eagle* had unquestionably been hit by a torpedo launched from a German submarine, the *U-853*. The Navy responded by revising the official account, and in June of 2001, each member of the *Eagle*'s crew was awarded the Purple Heart in an emotional ceremony for the few remaining survivors and the families of the victims.

One of a pair of propellers that allegedly came from the German submarine *U-853*.

A close-up of the identification number stamped into the propellers.

No one knows exactly why the Navy covered up the reality of that fateful day, but many theorize that there was a fear of panicking the public with the knowledge that the enemy was lurking so close to U.S. shores. There's also the possibility that the Navy was attempting to mislead the German high command by reporting the sinking as an accident and avoiding publicized knowledge of U-boat activity in the area, which would put German submarines on high alert and make them even more cautious and elusive than usual.

The propellers the Westerlunds asked Tukufu to investigate lay on the grounds of the Castle Hill Inn near the coastline of Newport, Rhode Island, and Tukufu learned from the inn's owner that they were purchased in 1953 from a salvager who had long since disappeared. With photographs in hand, Tukufu met with Keith Grill, exhibition curator at the Chicago Museum of Science and Industry, where one of the few remaining intact U-boats captured during the war is on display. Grill confirmed that the propellers had indeed been designed for a German submarine.

Bernard Cavalcante, the archivist who helped the Westerlunds discover the history of the *Eagle*, soon put Tukufu in touch with German naval historian Jürgen Rohwer to research the propeller identification numbers, and with his response the final piece of the puzzle of the Westerlunds' mystery fell into place. The propellers were matched to the German submarine *U-853* that sank their father's ship. After decades of misinformation and uncertainty, and finally through their own determination and the efforts and resources of archivists, historians, and Tukufu Zuberi, the Westerlunds could finally see and feel a tangible part of the cold machinery of war that had taken their father to a hero's watery grave.

The German *U-853* was commanded by German Oberleutnant Helmut Frömsdorf, who was thought to be just twenty-three years old during his final mission to the North American seaboard to report on weather conditions and attack targets of opportunity. After sinking the USS *Eagle 56*, the *U-853* crept southward along the coastline in an elusive cat-and-mouse game with the U.S. naval forces that hunted her. To avoid detection by increasingly sophisticated Allied surveillance, the *U-853* remained out of radio communication with the German command and, in a cruel twist of irony, missed a fateful message.

Just seven days after the sinking of the *Eagle*, Adolf Hitler committed suicide in his Berlin bunker headquarters, and on May 4, Hitler's successor, Admiral Karl Donitz, issued orders effective the following day, to cease fire and surrender—a broadcast the *U-853* never received. On that day, May 5, the U-boat encountered the coal freighter *Black Point* near Point

Ivar Westerlund, one of the heroic crewmen who lost his life aboard the USS *Eagle 56* in 1945.

Crowds gather around a stranded German U-boat on an English beach at the close of World War I.

Crewmen of the USS *Moberly* monitor a pattern of depth-charge explosions that contributed to the destruction of German submarine *U-853*.

Judith, Rhode Island, on a voyage to Boston, and at about 5:40 P.M. the sub fired a torpedo squarely into her stern. Within fifteen minutes, the *Black Point* rolled over and sank beneath the waves.

The lookout at Point Judith lighthouse saw the attack and sent word to U.S. Navy headquarters, which quickly dispatched the destroyer *Ericcson*, the destroyer escorts *Amick* and *Atherton*, and the frigate USS *Moberly*, which were all part of a task force operating in the region. The ships made for the area where their commanders believed the *U-853* would seek shelter in undersea formations, and established a line abreast about 3,000 yards apart to sweep the depths with sonar. At around 10:30 P.M., the Navy vessels located the U-boat and began dropping volley after volley of depth charges and underwater explosives known as *hedgehogs*. Within fifteen minutes, oil and debris began floating to the surface.

The wary warships continued a relentless bombardment until noon the following day, when continually surfacing remains made it clear that the *U-853* was finished, along with her fifty-five-man crew, who inescapably perished in the wreckage. Navy divers soon confirmed the kill and in the recovered debris found a commander's cap that undoubtedly belonged to Helmut Frömsdorf. It remained in the possession of an unidentified crew member until it was donated to the Destroyer Escort Historical Foundation in 1999. It is currently on display aboard the USS *Slater*, which is moored in Albany, New York.

The *U-853* lay undisturbed seven miles from Block Island near Rhode Island in 130 feet of water until recreational divers discovered her location in 1953. Salvagers followed shortly after and dismantled accessible sections for resale, among which were

Prisoners at War

Eastern State Penitentiary in Philadelphia is one of the city's most imposing structures and was the largest building in the United States when it was constructed in 1829. One of the more unusual tales in the history of the prison is that it was also home to a unique rehabilitation plan that encouraged paroled prisoners to join the armed forces at the height of U.S. involvement in World War I. When President Woodrow Wilson declared war on Germany on April 6, 1917, the Army consisted of about 17,000 men, but Wilson initially declared that the nation would need a million men to fight. The solution to the manpower shortage was the May 18 implementation of the Selective Service Act. According to the original Selective Service classifications, felons were considered undesirable, but after the requirements of the war effort increased and many more men were needed, exceptions were made.

The Eastern State Penitentiary plaque commemorating paroled inmates who served in the armed forces during World War I.

At the request of Elizabeth McKenty, Wes Cowan and Tukufu Zuberi took on the investigation of a plaque inside the prison that listed prisoner identification numbers that corresponded to the names of former convicts who became soldiers. Ultimately, they learned that Elizabeth's great-grandfather, prison warden Robert J. McKenty, arranged for close to 300 paroled prisoners to fight for their country and argued for full pardons for the many former felons who distinguished themselves in battle.

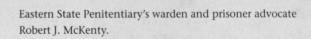

Eastern State Penitentiary's warden and prisoner advocate Robert J. McKenty.

time
TEASER

Which notorious World War II figure edited newspapers during World War I?

Answer: Benito Mussolini, who edited the socialist newspaper *Avanti* for several years before founding the paper *Il Popolo d'Italia* (The People of Italy) in 1914.

the propellers that found their way to the Castle Hill Inn. What remains of the hull of the *U-853* is still a popular site for divers and a grim reminder of the lives lost through the technology of one of the war's most dangerous and elusive weapons.

THE CASE OF THE CURIOUS CHART

Imagine for a moment that you're far from home, involved in a life-and-death struggle with unknown and unseen enemies on foreign soil. You've heard artillery fire and nearby explosions, and you are huddled in fear in the soft earth when suddenly the whine of a shell passes overhead. It lands nearby and you wait for the boom but hear only a dull pop. Is it a dud? Suddenly you hear screams and cries of horror and someone yells, "Gas!" You fumble in panic for the mask hanging from your chest and pull it over your head with frantic, trembling hands. You struggle to breathe in the claustrophobic confines of the shrouded hood, and through the thick misty panes you see men gasping for air, clutching their throats, writhing in the mud and muck to a horrible and agonizing end.

This was the harsh reality for over a million soldiers who suffered from the deadly fumes and injuries of gas warfare during World War I, in an era that saw unprecedented use of deadly chemical agents. Detective Gwen Wright opened an investigation after Michelle Theriot contacted *History Detectives* about a document that had belonged to her grandfather Everett Daniel Theriot and was discovered after his passing in 1992. The docu-

Michelle Theriot, whose grandfather Everett Theriot, fought on the battlefields of France during World War I.

ment is a sheet of paper about seventeen by twenty-two inches in size, and dated 1918. Printed on one side is a map of French regions including the Moselle River, and on the reverse side is a chart of chemical weapons and their characteristics. What was this puzzling paper all about, and how did it relate to Everett Theriot?

When meeting with Michelle in Baton Rouge, Louisiana, Gwen learned that Everett Theriot was in the U.S. Army Corps of Engineers during World War I and had taken photographs of fellow soldiers in France, but his specific activities during the conflict were a mystery. More than anything, Michelle wanted to learn more about her beloved grandfather, what he did during the war, where he'd served, and if in fact he had been exposed to chemical attacks. Examination of Theriot's photographs showed several men outfitted in battle gear with gas mask packs hanging from their necks, a sure sign they were prepared for one the worst fates the war had to offer.

Gwen began her investigation at the National Archives in College Park, Maryland, by researching Everett Theriot's military records and found that he was assigned to Company C of the 508th Engineers, stationed at St. Mihiel, France, during the pivotal battle fought there in 1918 from September 15 to 18. She also learned that he and the unit he commanded were given the task of repairing roads after they came under German bombardment. Mitch Yockelson, a historian and World War I expert, met Gwen at the archives to review Theriot's chart and confirm the role of the Army Corps of Engineers at St. Mihiel. According to Yockelson, the map side of the chart was there more by chance than purpose. The map had simply been recycled for the purpose of printing the chart with important information a soldier might need to survive a chemical attack.

At the U.S. Army War College in Pennsylvania, Gwen conferred with Dr. Douglas V. Johnson II, a professor of National Security Affairs at the Strategic Studies Institute, who confirmed Mitch Yockelson's findings and

World War I soldier and hero Everett Theriot, who served as a member of the 508th Engineers.

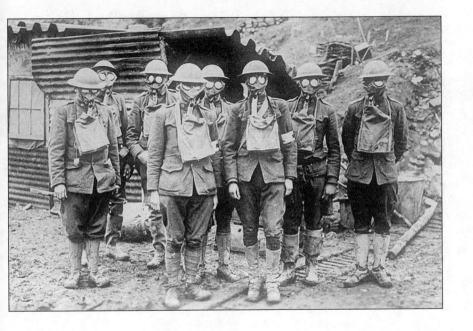

A group of World War I soldiers preparing themselves for a possible chemical warfare attack.

The chemical warfare document Michelle Theriot found amid her grandfather's belongings after his passing in 1992. This side shows various gas projectiles the Germans employed during World War I.

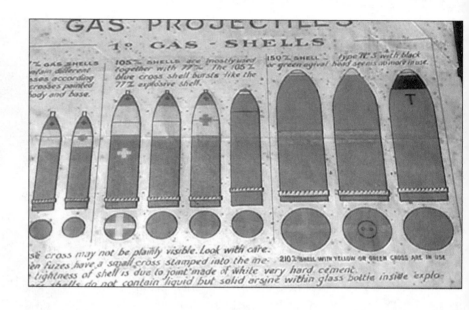

The other side of Everett Theriot's chemical warfare map shows a map of the Moselle River region of France.

pointed out that the awkward wording on the chemical chart was probably written by an English-speaking Frenchman, indicating that the chart was likely printed as a French assistance to Allied troops. According to Johnson, U.S. soldiers were "woefully unprepared" for gas warfare.

Until the United States entered into the conflict on April 6, 1917, industrialized warfare was an unknown concept to U.S. military tacticians, and training for chemical attacks was virtually nonexistent. Most soldiers wouldn't see a chemical chart such as Everett Theriot's until just before they marched into battle. Although chemical warfare caused fewer deaths than artillery fire, the damage and injury were catastrophic and sufficient to take men out of the fight—which was precisely its intent. As Johnson explained, from a military perspective it makes just as much sense to wound a man who then requires two people to take him from the field and five more to aid in his recovery as it does to simply kill him.

Dr. Johnson then invited Gwen to try on a World War I–era gas mask, and even in the obvious safety of a peaceful environment the experience triggered a claustrophobic sense of panic and breathing difficulty that left her visibly shaken. With this new and frightening perspective on the realities thousands of soldiers faced and the background she had gathered on Everett Theriot at the battle of St. Mihiel, Gwen returned to Baton Rouge to convey her findings. Michelle Theriot was overcome with emotional pride and shock that her grandfather may well have come under the fire of a gas attack through his direct involvement with the battle of St. Mihiel. According to National Archive records, Everett Theriot's company was moved to avoid a gas attack and artillery fire, which left their camp uninhabitable.

The records made clear that Everett Theriot received a government pension after the war. These pensions were given only to the severely wounded or those who suffered from gas exposure. Theriot lived to the ripe old age of ninety-six and was far more fortunate than the hundreds of thousands of European soldiers and the estimated 58,000 U.S. casualties who fell victim to a chemical nightmare so repugnant that the Geneva Convention condemned and outlawed its use in 1925. To his granddaughter, the news of his wartime plight proved highly emotional, but it paled in comparison to his survival instinct and courage, both of which confirmed how heroic a man he really was.

LEARN TO ADJUST YOUR RESPIRATOR
CORRECT and **QUICK**
Don't breathe while doing it. and this won't happen to you.

A cautionary poster designed for troops facing the threat of World War I chemical warfare.

Michelle Theriot paying her respects at her grandfather's final resting place.

DIY DETECTIVE

The idea that historical figures and fame are inherently linked is pervasive, particularly in a society where celebrity status garners so much public attention. Historical documentaries and books don't tell us everything about the past, but fortunately, the *History Detectives* crew are masters at uncovering amazing stories of ordinary people who provide links that lead us to fascinating perspectives on historical moments.

War casualties and veterans such as Arthur Michno of the USS *Indianapolis*, Seaman Ivar Westerlund of the USS *Eagle 56*, and Army engineer Everett Theriot were men who did what they needed to do, yet their lives and stories have a profound and lasting effect on their descendants and the rest of us who caught a glimpse of history from their unassuming roles. Likewise, trailblazers such as Groote Manuel (chapter 12), the Dutch slave who wanted nothing more than the freedom to support his family, and Alice Paul and Lucy Burns (chapter 1), who argued for women's rights, had no expectations of becoming even a minor blip on our historical radar.

No doubt all of them would be astonished to know that a small piece of their lives would someday captivate a national audience.

We sometimes tend to forget that this is the reality of existence—that our lives and experiences, no matter how simple or unassuming, do count and will make a difference to our own descendants, whether that's the next generation or a dozen generations into the future. A sadder reality is that people pass away, too often taking unrecorded histories, legends, and legacies with them. We have often seen the History Detectives struggle with discovering the truth in the neglected margins of history that include slave backgrounds, ethnic communities, the impoverished, and social situations deemed unfit to record. Particularly in those margins, the slightest shred of evidence can make the difference between bringing closure and light to the past and facing confusion and a stark historical uncertainty.

Capturing the oral histories and living memories of our elders is a necessity that will help preserve their legacies and invariably prove to be a gift to our children and their own children, and it's as easy as making a few phone calls and visits to rela-

take copious notes, and you might also consider tape recording or videotaping them. Also bear in mind that you'll likely get more accurate responses by asking specific questions rather than general ones.

For instance, instead of asking someone what their childhood was like, ask them about their favorite toy or if they remember their first grade-school crush. In the same vein, inquiring what someone's first thoughts were when they heard that Pearl Harbor was bombed will likely generate a much more vivid memory than asking

tives and friends in order to interview them. To get you on on the right track, there are a multitude of Web sites that have primers on gathering oral histories and are well worth pursuing. To get started, check out www.ancestry.com and www.rootsweb.ancestry.com.

Before chatting with someone about the past, it's helpful to do as much background research as possible. If you have any idea of where an individual or family grew up or the time frame they lived in, peruse old newspapers, encyclopedias, or history books and formulate a set of inquiries. During interviews you definitely want to

what they did during the war, or the even more vague question: "Did anything interesting ever happen during your life?" If you take the time to learn a few memory joggers, you'll often get surprising responses.

As illustrated by the images on these pages, the vast majority of us spring from humble roots of diverse ethnicities and backgrounds. The hopes, dreams, travails, and triumphs of family generations are seldom recorded in history books, and it's often only through the research of oral histories that we can assemble the pieces that form the mosaic of our past.

EPISODE GUIDE

Investigations covered in this book are referenced by a page number in parentheses at the end of their description.

SEASON ONE (2003)

EPISODE ONE

Old Fire Station
Premiered: Season One, Episode 101
The Detectives: Wes Cowan and Gwen Wright
The Place: Morristown, New Jersey
The Case: Detectives investigate a logbook allegedly signed by President Ulysses S. Grant on America's centennial. The book was found at Morristown's historic Independent Hose Company, and the detectives must work to determine if Grant's signature is authentic, if he really visited the firehouse, and the circumstances that might have brought him there. (312)

Pebble in the Sand
Premiered: Season One, Episode 101
The Detective: Elyse Luray
The Place: Mantoloking, New Jersey
The Case: Detective Elyse Luray meets with a New Jersey woman who made an unusual discovery when beachcombing along the Jersey shoreline. What she found was a pebble with sculpted human features. Elyse must determine the artifact's age and its possible Native American origin. Can she find the answer, or will this mystery be left unsolved? (248)

Pop Lloyd Baseball Stadium
Premiered: Season One, Episode 101;
Repeated: Season Two, Episode 210
The Detectives: Gwen Wright and Tukufu Zuberi
The Place: Atlantic City, New Jersey
The Case: In an investigation where baseball and politics intersect, the detectives are asked to find out why an Atlantic City baseball stadium was named for famed Negro Leagues shortstop Henry "Pop" Lloyd during an era rife with intense racial segregation. Was naming the stadium after a revered baseballer truly an honorific, or was a different kind of game being played on the political field? (31)

EPISODE TWO

Bonnie and Clyde Bullets
Premiered: Season One, Episode 102;
Repeated: Season Two, Episode 208
The Detectives: Wes Cowan and Tukufu Zuberi
The Place: Brodhead, Wisconsin
The Case: Wes Cowan and Tukufu Zuberi investigate five .45 caliber bullets owned by a woman in a small Wisconsin town. Could these examples of 1930s forensic evidence be responsible for the demise of notorious outlaws Bonnie Parker and Clyde Barrow, and if so, who fired the fatal shots? (213)

Sears Home
Premiered: Season One, Episode 102
The Detective: Gwen Wright
The Place: Akron, Ohio
The Case: A couple in Ohio want to know if their home in historic Firestone Park has the unusual distinction of being a do-it-yourself kit home ordered through the Sears catalog. Gwen Wright investigates the mail-order home phenomenon and the history of Sears Roebuck and Harvey Firestone. (65)

Movie Palace
Premiered: Season One, Episode 102
The Detectives: Elyse Luray and Gwen Wright
The Place: Baraboo, Wisconsin
The Case: In this theatrical foray, the detectives are asked to investigate the exquisite Al Ringling Theater in Wisconsin. They attempt to determine if the theater, an architectural masterpiece designed in the style of the great French opera houses, could have been one of the nation's first great movie palaces.

EPISODE THREE

Witch's House
Premiered: Season One, Episode 103;
Repeated: Season Two, Episode 207
The Detective: Gwen Wright
The Place: Essex County, Massachusetts
The Case: In the summer of 1692, Salem Village was stricken with a severe case of witchcraft hysteria. Now, a couple in Essex County wants to know if their home once belonged to accused witch Martha Carrier. The high-tech science of dendrochronology comes into play during this bewitching investigation, which yields surprising results. (319)

Whaling Ship
Premiered: Season One, Episode 103
The Detectives: Wes Cowan and Tukufu Zuberi
The Place: Mystic, Connecticut
The Case: A Connecticut sea captain wants to know if the *Charles W. Morgan*, a whaling ship docked in Mystic Seaport, has connections to the Underground Railroad. Did the ship really play a part in securing freedom for African Americans during the mid-1800s?

Jigsaw Puzzle
Premiered: Season One, Episode 103
The Detectives: Wes Cowan and Elyse Luray
The Place: Worcester, Massachusetts
The Case: A man in Massachusetts owns a quirky antique jigsaw puzzle from the latter part of the nineteenth

century, depicting women playing rough contact sports. Wes Cowan and Elyse Luray attempt to determine the origin of this curious puzzle and if it was possible that women really were playing rugby or football in 1894.

EPISODE FOUR

Independence Trumpet

Premiered: Season One, Episode 104
The Detectives: Elyse Luray and Tukufu Zuberi
The Place: Bucks County, Pennsylvania
The Case: A man in Pennsylvania asked *History Detectives* to help shed light on an unusual type of trumpet he found under a table at an antiques fair. Is it possible that the instrument played a crucial part in the Revolutionary War? And if so, who owned it and what was it used for? (168)

George Washington Portrait

Premiered: Season One, Episode 104; Repeated: Season Two, Episode 208; Season Three, Episode 305
The Detective: Wes Cowan
The Place: Frederick County, Maryland
The Case: A Maryland man owns an unusual drawing of George Washington allegedly sketched by renowned portrait artist Gilbert Stuart. In an unpredictable investigation, Wes Cowan's research reveals astonishing facts about art forgery and a hidden secret that stuns two families. (33)

Patty Cannon House

Premiered: Season One, Episode 104
The Detectives: Elyse Luray and Gwen Wright
The Place: Reliance, Maryland
The Case: Detectives investigate a Maryland family's home to determine if the historical marker in their front yard is legitimately placed, or if ruthless kidnapper and slave trader Patty Cannon lived in their home. Does the house have a lurid past, or is the marker a case of mistaken identity? (336)

EPISODE FIVE

General Lee Farewell Address

Premiered: Season One, Episode 105
The Detectives: Wes Cowan and Elyse Luray
The Place: Beech Island, South Carolina
The Case: Members of the Beech Island Agricultural Club made an astonishing discovery—a signed copy of one of the most famous documents in Civil War history. Wes Cowan and Elyse Luray must determine whether the document, Confederate general Robert E. Lee's "General Order #9," is an authentic copy composed during the surrender of his troops in 1865.

Natchez House

Premiered: Season One, Episode 105
The Detective: Tukufu Zuberi
The Place: Natchez, Mississippi
The Case: On the "Spanish Esplanade" overlooking the Mississippi River stands a magnificent home that was built by an African American man who arrived in the United States on a slave ship in the 1820s. Tukufu Zuberi examines the fascinating history of this man and how he became one of the most successful businessmen in Natchez.

Napoleon's Sword

Premiered: Season One, Episode 105
The Detectives: Wes Cowan and Tukufu Zuberi
The Place: St. Martinville, Louisiana
The Case: A Louisiana family call upon *History Detectives* to investigate a stunning sword owned by their family for generations. The sword initially belonged to their ancestor Jean Julien Rousseau, who allegedly received it in gratitude for protecting Napoleon's flag during the 1809 battle for Austria.

EPISODE SIX

Chinese Poems

Premiered: Season One, Episode 106; Repeated: Season Two, Episode 207

The Detectives: Wes Cowan and Gwen Wright
The Place: San Francisco, California
The Case: Detectives delve into the sad history of Angel Island, the infamous San Francisco immigration station that is estimated to have detained up to 200,000 Chinese immigrants between 1910 and 1940. A woman wants to confirm that her ancestors had been at the station and if so, if they had written any of the profound poems on the walls of the barracks. (183)

John Brown's Letters

Premiered: Season One, Episode 106
The Detective: Tukufu Zuberi
The Place: Sacramento, California
The Case: Tukufu Zuberi explores the life and legacy of renowned abolitionist John Brown and his daughter Sarah. Remarkably, a woman in California discovered a box of Brown's letters in her grandmother's garage, and it's up to Tukufu to prove whether or not she is one of Brown's descendants. (195)

Japanese House

Premiered: Season One, Episode 106
The Detective: Gwen Wright
The Place: Gilroy, California
The Case: In a case that focuses on the 1939 San Francisco World's Fair and World War II Japanese internment, a couple in rural northern California is anxious to know the origins of their authentic Japanese house and the circumstances surrounding its history and construction just prior to the bombing of Pearl Harbor in 1941. (76)

EPISODE SEVEN

Pirate Spyglass

Premiered: Season One, Episode 107
The Detectives: Wes Cowan and Tukufu Zuberi
The Place: Texas City, Texas
The Case: Detectives explore the world of early nineteenth-century piracy and the career of renowned French pirate, privateer, and war hero Jean Lafitte. The in-

vestigation centers on a unique spyglass, allegedly owned by Lafitte, that is part of a collection at a Texas library. Is it the real deal, or just another pirate legend? (241)

Mexican Currency

Premiered: Season One, Episode 107
The Detective: Elyse Luray
The Place: San Antonio, Texas
The Case: The owner of a San Antonio printing company wants to know if the Mexican currency he discovered in his great-grandfather's belongings have a direct link to Pancho Villa and leaders of the Mexican Revolution, and if his company actually produced currency to support the revolution. (147)

Railroad Station

Premiered: Season One, Episode 107
The Detectives: Gwen Wright and Tukufu Zuberi
The Place: Dallas, Texas
The Case: A local historian asks *History Detectives* to research a small train depot that he believes was the first railroad station in Texas. Is this the little depot that put Dallas on the map, or just another pit stop along the road of forgotten history?

EPISODE EIGHT

Ventriloquist's Dummy

Premiered: Season One, Episode 108; Repeated: Season Two, Episode 207
The Detective: Tukufu Zuberi
The Place: Brooklyn, New York
The Case: Tukufu Zuberi investigates talented African American ventriloquist John W. Cooper. Contacted by Cooper's daughter, Tukufu searches to answer the question of how Cooper was able to get his big break in vaudeville, and whether or not his dummy, Sam Jackson, could have been created by Theodore Mack. (19)

Home of Lincoln Assassination Plot

Premiered: Season One, Episode 108; Repeated: Season Two, Episode 206
The Detective: Gwen Wright

The Place: Greenwich Village, New York
The Case: A woman in New York wants to verify the rumors surrounding her building. According to local legend, assassin John Wilkes Booth was said to have planned Abraham Lincoln's murder in her Federal-style home. Are the rumors true? A shocking conclusion provides new insight into a very high-profile murder. (330)

Boardinghouse Flag

Premiered: Season One, Episode 108
The Detectives: Wes Cowan and Elyse Luray
The Place: Staten Island, New York
The Case: The Staten Island Historical Society owns a Civil War–era flag that, according to legend, was hurriedly sewn in order to replace a Confederate flag hanging from a New York boardinghouse. Did the flag really save the structure from being burned to the ground as a result of persecution by Union sympathizers?

EPISODE NINE

Revolutionary War Poem

Premiered: Season One, Episode 109; Repeated: Season Two, Episode 208; Season Three, Episode 305
The Detectives: Elyse Luray and Gwen Wright
The Place: Salem, Oregon
The Case: When rifling though an antique trunk filled with books, an Oregon man found a poem by Daniel Goodhue, allegedly written while Goodhue was incarcerated during the Revolutionary War. Is the poem authentic? What were the circumstances of his imprisonment? And what became of Daniel Goodhue?

Mark Twain's Watch

Premiered: Season One, Episode 109
The Detective: Wes Cowan
The Place: Portland, Oregon
The Case: A man in Oregon owns a watch allegedly given to his great-

grandfather Captain John Commingers Ainsworth by legendary author Mark Twain. Wes Cowan delves into the lives of both men and searches for a possible point of intersection. Did the author and one of the founding fathers of Portland really know each other well enough to exchange gifts? (90)

Dutch Colonial Home

Premiered: Season One, Episode 109
The Detective: Elyse Luray
The Place: Fort Yamhill, Oregon
The Case: In 1856, the U.S. Army built Fort Yamhill in Oregon and appointed as its head officer Lieutenant Phillip Sheridan, who would later become one of the Civil War's most famed generals. Now, an Oregon woman who has a connection to one of the builders of the home wants to know why the fort was built on this site.

EPISODE TEN

Flintlock Rifle

Premiered: Season One, Episode 110
The Detectives: Wes Cowan and Elyse Luray
The Place: Bucks County, Pennsylvania
The Case: A descendant of the notorious outlaws known as the Doan Gang asks *History Detectives* to investigate a flintlock rifle that was said to have been used in a legendary shootout in 1783 near the end of the American Revolution. Did it really belong to one of these loyalist sympathizers? (221)

Prison Plaque

Premiered: Season One, Episode 110; Repeated: Season Two, Episode 211
The Detectives: Wes Cowan and Tukufu Zuberi
The Place: Philadelphia, Pennsylvania
The Case: Inside the Eastern State Penitentiary is a plaque commemorating a group of men who served in World War I. Who were these brave men and what did prison warden Robert McKenty have to do with their enlistment? (351)

Lafayette China
Premiered: Season One, Episode 110
The Detectives: Elyse Luray and Gwen Wright
The Place: Philadelphia, Pennsylvania
The Case: Philadelphia's Powel House is a gorgeous eighteenth-century townhouse where elite socialites Samuel and Elizabeth Powel lived and entertained important figures of the day. One of the landmark's board members wants to know if a porcelain china set was given to Elizabeth by the French Marquis de Lafayette.

SEASON TWO (2004)

EPISODE ONE

Civil War Submarine
Premiered: Season Two, Episode 201
The Detective: Elyse Luray
The Place: New Orleans, Louisiana
The Case: Amid the bustling French Quarter of New Orleans sits a historic relic of the Civil War—a Confederate submarine. A Louisiana man believes his ancestor might have built it. Elyse Luray investigates whether or not the sub was built from scratch, and who might have come in contact with it.

Red Cloud's Peace Pipe
Premiered: Season Two, Episode 201
The Detective: Wes Cowan
The Place: Livermore, California
The Case: Dr. James Irwin served as an Indian agent for the Oglala Sioux tribe during the mid-1800s. His descendants own a peace pipe allegedly given to him as a gift by renowned Oglala warrior Chief Red Cloud, and they want to know if the pipe is authentic and learn why an Indian chief would show such admiration for an Indian agent. (131)

Thomas Edison's House
Premiered: Season Two, Episode 201;
Repeated: Season Three, Episode 308
The Detective: Gwen Wright

The Place: Union, New Jersey
The Case: Did Thomas Alva Edison's ingenuity spread as far as designing and constructing a home made entirely of concrete? This is the question a New Jersey man asks of Gwen Wright, who investigates the inventor's career and his penchant for taking on seemingly impossible tasks. Did Edison really build this curious concrete creation, and if he didn't, who did? (74)

EPISODE TWO

Early Monopoly
Premiered: Season Two, Episode 202
The Detective: Elyse Luray
The Place: Arden, Delaware
The Case: A Delaware man owns an old board game that uncannily resembles modern-day Monopoly. The only hitch is that his game was invented two decades before Parker Brothers put their version on the market. Who invented this obvious precursor? Was its inception purely for entertainment purposes or was it a political statement? (114)

Internment Artwork
Premiered: Season Two, Episode 202;
Repeated: Season Three, Episode 307
The Detective: Tukufu Zuberi
The Place: San Francisco, California
The Case: Tukufu Zuberi takes an emotional look at the dark side of American history, focusing on the Japanese internment camps of the 1940s and an unknown artist whose paintings—drawn on the back of an internment notice—depict his sad incarceration. A San Francisco archivist found the lost paintings and he wants to know who the artist is and what became of him. (200)

Lewis and Clark Cane
Premiered: Season Two, Episode 202
The Detectives: Wes Cowan and Tukufu Zuberi
The Place: Richfield, Minnesota

The Case: An unusual cane becomes the focus of this investigation. The cane belongs to Patrick McClellan, a descendant of Robert McClellan, and according to family legend, it was given to Robert by Meriwether Lewis and William Clark. Is the cane authentic, and if so, what was Robert's connection to the famed explorers?

EPISODE THREE

WWII Landing Craft
Premiered: Season Two, Episode 203
The Detective: Elyse Luray
The Place: Bayfield, Wisconsin
The Case: The remote northern town of Bayfield, Wisconsin, has an unusual piece of history floating in its harbor. A Bayfield man wants to know whether or not the landing-craft tank called the *Outer Island*—now used for dredging and hauling rocks—played a role in the invasion of Normandy during World War II.

Anti-Slavery Flag
Premiered: Season Two, Episode 203
The Detectives: Wes Cowan and Tukufu Zuberi
The Place: Rockford, Michigan
The Case: When two Michigan brothers went through an antique family trunk, they came across an old sheet. Was it actually used as bedding, or is it possible that it helped contribute to the end of slavery in the United States?

Mail-Order Brides
Premiered: Season Two, Episode 203
The Detective: Tukufu Zuberi
The Place: Los Angeles, California
The Case: A California collector owns an unusual quartet of photos of Victorian women. The reverse side of each photo reveals the woman's personal information and the details of any inheritance she was to receive. Who were these women and why would they give out such intimate information? Could they have been the victims of a scam artist?

EPISODE FOUR

King Kong Camera
Premiered: Season Two, Episode 204
The Detectives: Wes Cowan and Elyse Luray
The Place: Lake Bay, Washington
The Case: A Washington man purchased a classic professional movie camera at an auction in England. He believes that the camera could have been owned by cinematographer Eddie Linden. Detectives investigate Linden, the Mitchell Standard camera, and the exciting prospect that it was used in the filming of the 1933 blockbuster *King Kong*. (251)

Hollywood: Warner's Lighter
Premiered: Season Two, Episode 204
The Detective: Elyse Luray
The Place: Los Angeles, California
The Case: When shopping at a flea market a California man came across a sleek brass lighter. On one side is engraved the name "Ufatone" and on the other side, the name "Harry Warner." Elyse Luray investigates the lighter and the intriguing question of how the Nazi propaganda machine and one of Hollywood's major power players might have intersected. (262)

First Movie Studio
Premiered: Season Two, Episode 204
The Detective: Gwen Wright
The Place: Los Angeles, California
The Case: A woman residing in Lincoln Heights, California, wants to confirm a local legend that her neighborhood park was once the site of the first motion picture studio in Los Angeles. Is it possible that a park ten miles southwest of Hollywood could have set the stage for the entire film industry?

EPISODE FIVE

Dueling Pistols
Premiered: Season Two, Episode 205
The Detective: Elyse Luray
The Place: San Francisco, California

The Case: On the morning of September 13, 1859, U.S. senator David Broderick and California Supreme Court judge David Terry engaged in a legendary duel in which Broderick was killed. Today, a bank in San Francisco owns a pair of ornate antique pistols that are rumored to have been used in the duel.

Nesbit Portrait
Premiered: Season Two, Episode 205;
Repeated: Season Three, Episode 311
The Detectives: Elyse Luray and Tukufu Zuberi
The Place: New Jersey
The Case: A stunning Howard Chandler Christy painting of a beautiful woman seated in a chair prompts an investigation into the world of early twentieth-century art, modeling, and a shocking 1906 murder dubbed the "trial of the century." A New Jersey woman believes the portrait showcases socialite Evelyn Nesbit. Is the woman in the painting a scandalous supermodel or someone equally surprising? (41)

Little Big Horn Bayonet
Premiered: Season Two, Episode 205
The Detective: Wes Cowan
The Place: Cookstown, New Jersey
The Case: The family home of a Civil War–era soldier holds a surprising secret. Recent renovations revealed an old bayonet hidden in the attic rafters. Wes Cowan investigates the claim that the bayonet was recovered at the Battle of Little Big Horn and had once belonged to General George Armstrong Custer.

EPISODE SIX

The Preston Brooks Riding Crop
Premiered: Season Two, Episode 206
The Detective: Tukufu Zuberi
The Place: Long Island, New York
The Case: A Long Island man owns a beautiful old riding crop he claims was given to one of his ancestors by Jefferson Davis, president of the Confeder-

acy. Tukufu Zuberi investigates the claim that the crop was presented as a congratulatory gift after a notorious altercation in the U.S. Senate that many regard as a significant contribution to the movement toward secession.

Home of Lincoln Assassination Plot
See Season One, Episode 108

Revolutionary War Cannon
Premiered: Season Two, Episode 206;
Repeated: Season Three, Episode 305
The Detective: Elyse Luray
The Place: Boston, Massachusetts
The Case: A Boston woman believes a cannon stored in a National Parks facility might be the same one that members of the Boston Militia stole from the Boston Armory and hid on her ancestor's land just before the Revolutionary War. Elyse Luray investigates the claim and discovers an intriguing link to colonial preparation for war with Britain. (162)

EPISODE SEVEN

Ventriloquist's Dummy
See Season One, Episode 108

Witch's House
See Season One, Episode 103

Chinese Poems
See Season One, Episode 106

EPISODE EIGHT

Bonnie and Clyde Bullets
See Season One, Episode 102

Revolutionary War Poem
See Season One, Episode 109

George Washington Portrait
See Season One, Episode 104

EPISODE NINE

Lost Gold Ship
Premiered: Season Two, Episode 209
The Detective: Elyse Luray
The Place: Southeast Alaska

The Case: Elyse Luray leads a team of scientists to Alaska's Katalla River to investigate the wreckage of a ship alleged to be the Gold Rush steamer SS *Portland*. An Alaska environmentalist who found the wreck is anxious to learn if his discovery is indeed the *Portland,* which sank during a storm in 1910. If proven authentic it would be a remarkable landmark. Could it be that the lost *Portland* has finally been found? (243)

John Hunt Morgan Saddle
Premiered: Season Two, Episode 209
The Detective: Wes Cowan
The Place: Paris, Kentucky
The Case: In 1863, a group of Confederate cavaliers took part in a bold military move they hoped would change the course of the Civil War. Their leader was guerilla general John Hunt Morgan. Over two centuries later, a man in Kentucky owns a saddle he believes Morgan used during his 1863 rampage.

Cesar Chavez Banner
Premiered: Season Two, Episode 209
The Detective: Gwen Wright
The Place: San Francisco, California
The Case: In 1966, a group of Mexican and Mexican American farm workers led by Cesar Chavez engaged in a 350-mile march from the town of Delano to California's state capitol in Sacramento. Gwen Wright investigates a banner that might have been used during that historic protest.

EPISODE TEN

Pretty Boy Floyd's Gun
Premiered: Season Two, Episode 210
The Detective: Wes Cowan
The Place: La Verne, California
The Case: In an investigation that ends with a "bang," Wes Cowan researches the exploits of infamous public-enemy era gangster Charles Arthur "Pretty Boy" Floyd. The focus of this mystery is a vintage Colt automatic handgun that a California man's family legend indicates was given to

his uncle by Floyd during a 1930s altercation in Bolivar, Missouri. (220)

Pop Lloyd Baseball Stadium
See Season One, Episode 101

Continental Army Muster Roll
Premiered: Season Two, Episode 210
The Detective: Tukufu Zuberi
The Place: Las Vegas, Nevada
The Case: A collector of African American memorabilia owns an old Continental Army muster roll issued in 1780. Among the sixteen men listed is "Paul Cuffee." Tukufu Zuberi examines the remarkable life of an African American man who became a whaling captain, a shipbuilder, and an advocate of the "back to Africa" movement during the Revolutionary War era.

EPISODE ELEVEN

Charlie Parker's Saxophone
Premiered: Season Two, Episode 211
The Detectives: Wes Cowan and Gwen Wright
The Place: Oakland, California
The Case: Detectives research the personal life and professional career of one of history's most gifted jazz musicians—Charlie Parker. Presented with a stunning alto saxophone owned by the daughter of jazz musician Bill Hood, detectives must determine if the sax once belonged to Parker and if he actually pawned it and gave the ticket to his friend Bill Hood. (26)

Prison Plaque
See Season One, Episode 110

Koranic Schoolbook
Premiered: Season Two, Episode 211
The Detective: Gwen Wright
The Place: Mulvane, Kansas
The Case: The descendants of Mary Steele own a beautifully written schoolbook containing complex mathematics, affirmations, and passages from the Koran. The Koranic passages themselves might not be surprising, except for the fact that the date on the book is

1800. Gwen Wright explores how a progressive Kentucky frontierswoman came to know the Koran.

EPISODE TWELVE

Body in the Basement
Premiered: Season Two, Episode 212
The Detective: Gwen Wright
The Place: Annapolis, Maryland
The Case: At a dig site in Anne Arundel County in Maryland, members of the Lost Towns Project were excavating a colonial site when they came across something unexpected—skeletal remains. In a mystery reminiscent of a *CSI* episode, renowned forensic anthropologist Dr. Doug Owsley helps determine who the individual was and how the death might have occurred. (267)

Newport U-boat
Premiered: Season Two, Episode 212
The Detective: Tukufu Zuberi
The Place: Newport, Rhode Island
The Case: Two brothers enlist the help of Tukufu Zuberi in revealing the mystery behind a pair of German U-boat propellers they believe came from the submarine that was responsible for sinking the USS *Eagle 56* in 1945—a tragedy in which their father perished. Did the *Eagle 56* really sink as a result of a boiler explosion, or did an alleged cover-up result in the victim's families never learning what really happened that fateful day? (346)

Shippen Golf Club
Premiered: Season Two, Episode 212
The Detectives: Elyse Luray and Gwen Wright
The Place: Scotch Plains, New Jersey
The Case: Approached by the grandson of famed golfer John Shippen, the History Detectives examine an aged golf club that may have belonged to Shippen, the first African American to compete in the U.S. Open golf tournament in 1896. Did racial prejudice of the era result in the renowned sporting event being canceled? (182)

SEASON THREE (2005)

EPISODE ONE

Lindbergh Engine
Premiered: Season Three, Episode 301; Season Four, Episode 405
The Detective: Tukufu Zuberi
The Place: Parsippany, New Jersey
The Case: Two brothers want to determine if their uncle was involved in building the airplane engine that powered Charles Lindbergh's famous transatlantic crossing in May 1927 in the *Spirit of St. Louis*. Is it possible that their uncle holds that amazing distinction? (183)

Poison Pin
Premiered: Season Three, Episode 301
The Detective: Elyse Luray
The Place: Kansas City, Missouri
The Case: In Missouri, a man who creates miniatures made an intriguing purchase at an auction. Wrapped in a newspaper dated 1960, he found two peculiar pins that had been machined so they could contain some kind of liquid. Elyse Luray investigates this Cold War drama that could link the pin's design to downed U-2 spy plane pilot Francis Gary Powers. (292)

Geronimo Photograph
Premiered: Season Three, Episode 301
The Detective: Gwen Wright
The Place: New Mexico
The Case: A Kentucky woman whose heritage goes back to the 1870s, when her great-great-grandfather was lieutenant governor of the still-untamed New Mexico territory, hopes *History Detectives* can shed light on her treasured keepsake—a beautiful antique photograph of an Indian warrior on horseback that could be famed Apache leader Geronimo. (126)

EPISODE TWO

Black Star Line
Premiered: Season Three, Episode 302; Repeated: Season Four, Episode 408
The Detectives: Elyse Luray and Tukufu Zuberi
The Place: Williamston, North Carolina
The Case: A North Carolina woman found a pair of Black Star Line stock certificates that had been purchased by her great-grandfather in 1919. She wants to know why her ancestor purchased so many shares, and learn more about the unique efforts of renowned African American equal rights activist and Black Star owner Marcus Garvey. (206)

Mouse Toy
Premiered: Season Three, Episode 302; Repeated: Season Four, Episode 404
The Detective: Wes Cowan
The Place: San Francisco, California
The Case: Popular history has it that Mickey Mouse was born from a drawing sketched on a napkin by Walt Disney during a train ride from New York to Los Angeles in 1928. Wes Cowan investigates a claim made by a San Francisco toy collector who believes his small mouse figurine could turn the legend of Mickey on its ears. (115)

Texas POW Camp
Premiered: Season Three, Episode 302
The Detective: Gwen Wright
The Place: Hearne, Texas
The Case: A woman in Texas heard rumors that during World War II there was a German POW camp located just outside Hearne, Texas. The land on which the camp allegedly stood is said to have been owned by her family. Gwen Wright investigates the history of POW camps in the United States and sheds light on an obscure episode of wartime Nazism in America.

EPISODE THREE

Szyk Pictures
Premiered: Season Three, Episode 303
The Detective: Elyse Luray
The Place: Glendale, California
The Case: A Polish American art collector purchased four striking drawings after finding them at an online auction, and he believes that the drawings could be the work of Arthur Szyk, America's most influential political cartoonist during World War II. Elyse must determine if the paintings are authentic, and why they depict Russian soldiers. (44)

Civil War Balloon
Premiered: Season Three, Episode 303; Repeated: Season Five, Episode 506
The Detective: Wes Cowan
The Place: Midland, Michigan
The Case: A Michigan collector believes he owns a fragment of American aviation history. At first glance, the object appears to be a simple piece of frayed material in a frame, but on the back of the frame are the words: "A piece of Prof. Lowe's Aeronautical balloon, *Enterprise*." Wes Cowan turns up some surprising facts when investigating Professor Thaddeus Lowe and his innovative hydrogen balloons. (54)

WWI Chemical Warfare Map
Premiered: Season Three, Episode 303
The Detective: Gwen Wright
The Place: Baton Rouge, Louisiana
The Case: After her grandfather's passing, a woman in Louisiana found a curious map of a battlefield in France that also has a chemical weapons chart printed on the reverse side. Gwen Wright researches Everett Daniel Theriot, a man who served as an engineer under General Pershing during World War I, and reveals the harrowing experiences of soldiers exposed to the horrors of chemical warfare. (352)

EPISODE FOUR

Cherokee Bible
Premiered: Season Three, Episode 304
The Detectives: Elyse Luray and Gwen Wright
The Place: Austin, Texas
The Case: At the request of a Texas woman of Cherokee descent, Elyse Luray and Gwen Wright investigate a mysterious bible she inherited from

her father that is printed in the Cherokee language. Could this unusual relic be intrinsically linked to the infamous relocation of the Cherokee people, known as the Trail of Tears? (277)

Slave Banjo
Premiered: Season Three, Episode 304
The Detectives: Wes Cowan and Tukufu Zuberi
The Place: Baltimore, Maryland
The Case: Wes Cowan and Tukufu Zuberi investigate a worn banjo that was purchased by a Maryland man at an auction. A tattered note inside the instrument says the banjo dates to the mid-1800s and was bought from a former slave in Bethel, Ohio, by an abolitionist family. Could this be one of the earliest intact slave banjos ever discovered? (23)

United Empire Loyalist
Premiered: Season Three, Episode 304
The Detective: Tukufu Zuberi
The Place: Northridge, California
The Case: A California college dean is intrigued by a family tree she inherited from a deceased aunt. Alongside several names are the words "United Empire Loyalist." Tukufu Zuberi launches a genealogical investigation in the hopes of finding a fascinating link to colonial loyalists who fought for Britain during the American Revolution. (188)

EPISODE FIVE

George Washington Portrait
See Season One, Episode 104

Revolutionary War Cannon
See Season Two, Episode 206

Revolutionary War Poem
See Season One, Episode 109

EPISODE SIX

Car Tape Deck
Premiered: Season Three, Episode 306;
Repeated: Season Four, Episode 404
The Detective: Tukufu Zuberi

The Place: Opelika, Alabama
The Case: An Alabama man thinks he may have inherited the first commercially produced automobile tape player in the United States. Even more fascinating is the possibility that the technology to produce this early tape player was stolen from the Nazis in a secret mission during the closing days of World War II.

Snowshoe's Mailbag
Premiered: Season Three, Episode 306
The Detective: Wes Cowan
The Place: Modesto, California
The Case: While browsing through a Montana antiques store, a man discovered an unusual leather satchel with an identifying tag that reads: "Shoe Thompson." Wes Cowan investigates the satchel to determine if it could have belonged to John "Snowshoe" Thompson—a man who risked life and limb to deliver mail across the Sierra Mountains starting in 1856. (14)

Birth Control Box
Premiered: Season Three, Episode 306
The Detectives: Elyse Luray and Tukufu Zuberi
The Place: Statesboro, Georgia
The Case: A Missouri woman inherited a number of items that had been in her family for over 130 years, including an unusual wooden dovetailed box. The label affixed to the inside of the box contains the date 1894, and the name "Gray's Recurrent Syringe." Is it possible the box once contained what might have been a cleverly disguised birth control device?

EPISODE SEVEN

Doc Holliday's Watch
Premiered: Season Three, Episode 307;
Repeated: Season Four, Episode 408
The Detective: Wes Cowan
The Place: Tombstone, Arizona
The Case: Several years ago, a pawn shop clerk in Tulsa, Oklahoma, met a customer who claimed to be a descendant of infamous Old West gunfighter John Henry "Doc" Holliday. Detective Wes Cowan dons a ten-gallon hat and takes his investigation to the OK Corral to determine if the customer's pawned antique watch could have belonged to Holliday.

Civil War Soldier Photo
Premiered: Season Three, Episode 307
The Detective: Elyse Luray
The Place: Shreveport, Louisiana
The Case: Elyse Luray investigates the unusual contention of a Louisiana collector who owns a Civil War photograph of a fine-boned, slight-figured soldier. The soldier is simply identified as a member of the Second Louisiana Infantry—but could the soldier actually be a woman in disguise?

Internment Artwork
See Season Two, Episode 202

EPISODE EIGHT

Göering Gun
Premiered: Season Three, Episode 308;
Repeated: Season Four, Episode 406
The Detective: Wes Cowan
The Place: Lewiston, New York
The Case: In the dying days of the Third Reich, Hermann Göering, the former head of the mighty German Luftwaffe, was holed up in his castle in the German countryside. A notorious art collector, he possessed thousands of artifacts, many of which were looted at the time of his arrest in 1945. A New York collector believes a shotgun he purchased at auction could be one of those items.

Calf Creek Arrow
Premiered: Season Three, Episode 308;
Repeated: Season Four, Episode 408
The Detective: Elyse Luray
The Place: Tulsa, Oklahoma
The Case: While foraging in a dry riverbed along the Arkansas River an amateur fossil hunter in Oklahoma discovered an unusually well preserved

bison skull. Lodged in the bone was a handmade projectile point he believes dates back to around 3000 B.C. Employing some of the most advanced scientific technologies currently available, Elyse Luray investigates the skull—and her results are nothing short of astonishing. (118)

Thomas Edison's House
See Season Two, Episode 201

EPISODE NINE

Coney Island Lions
Premiered: Season Three, Episode 309
The Detectives: Gwen Wright and junior detective Sade Falebita
The Place: Coney Island, New York
The Case: A New York collector purchased a pair of giant zinc lion paws from the estate sale of Frederick Fried, a renowned collector of amusement park memorabilia. Along with a junior detective, Gwen Wright examines the history of the paws and their association with Steeplechase Park, the wildly popular amusement park created by George C. Tilyou in Coney Island. (105)

Lee Family Doll
Premiered: Season Three, Episode 309
The Detectives: Tukufu Zuberi and junior detective Graham Sweeney
The Place: Brookeville, Maryland
The Case: A retired school principal owns a beautiful, very rare nineteenth-century "Greiner" doll that may have a unique history. Partnered with a junior detective, Tukufu Zuberi investigates the claim that the doll once belonged to a former slave of legendary Confederate general Robert E. Lee.

Broadway Ballet Shoes
Premiered: Season Three, Episode 309
The Detectives: Elyse Luray and junior detective Mariel O'Connell
The Place: Long Island, New York
The Case: A young ballet dancer learned from her grandmother that

her ancestor once made ballet shoes for many of the top dancers in the 1920s and 1930s, including legendary Ziegfeld Follies star Marilyn Miller. Elyse Luray enlists the help of the youngster when she investigates the innovative cobbler, his shoe patent, and the assertion that he could have served as mentor to renowned shoe designer Salvatore Capezio. (100)

EPISODE TEN

Jim Thorpe Ticket
Premiered: Season Three, Episode 310
The Detective: Wes Cowan
The Place: Jamestown, New York
The Case: After a New York man purchased an antique book at an auction, he found that the book contained a pair of sports tickets from 1927, for a basketball game featuring Jim Thorpe. Wes Cowan investigates the tickets and the legendary Native American athlete who was known for his 1912 Olympic gold medals and Herculean strength as a football and baseball player. Are the tickets authentic? And did Thorpe *really* play professional basketball?

Leisurama Homes
Premiered: Season Three, Episode 310
The Detective: Gwen Wright
The Place: Lauderhill, Florida
The Case: The grandson of Andrew Geller, the designer of the quintessential 1960s Leisurama homes, is trying to find out if his grandfather's legendary homes still exist in Lauderhill, Florida. Gwen Wright investigates the Leisurama legacy and Geller's link to the infamous 1959 "Kitchen Debate" between U.S. vice president Richard Nixon and Soviet premier Nikita Khrushchev. (70)

Land Grant
Premiered: Season Three, Episode 310
The Detective: Tukufu Zuberi
The Place: Fairfax, Virginia

The Case: A Virginia historian and collector invites *History Detectives* to examine a fragment of aged parchment that if proven to be authentic might be one of the first documentations of early land ownership among free slaves in Dutch Colonial America. Was former slave Groote Manuel granted land in 1667, and if so, what were the circumstances that led to his good fortune? In a remarkable twist, could the answer lie with one of Manuel's descendants? (207)

EPISODE ELEVEN

Home for Unwed Mothers
Premiered: Season Three, Episode 311
The Detective: Gwen Wright
The Place: Kansas City, Missouri
The Case: In one of the most unique investigations ever conducted by *History Detectives*, a Kansas City woman wants to find her birth family and learn the circumstances of her birth and adoption. The only reminder she has of her birthplace is a tiny Medal of the Immaculate Conception that was attached to her diaper when she was presented to her adoptive parents. Will she learn where she born? And more importantly, will this investigation lead to her reuniting with her birth family? (176)

Long Expedition
Premiered: Season Three, Episode 311
The Detective: Wes Cowan
The Place: Omaha, Nebraska
The Case: A group of archaeologists discover a tract of farmland along the Missouri River that appears to contain evidence of an encampment from the 1819 "Long Expedition." Wes Cowan travels to the site and investigates this little-known but significant episode in American history that shed light on the biological diversity of Nebraska during the 1820s.

Nesbit Portrait
See Season Two, Episode 205

SEASON FOUR (2006)

EPISODE ONE

Chisholm Trail
Premiered: Season Four, Episode 401
The Detective: Elyse Luray
The Place: Donna, Texas
The Case: In the decades following the Civil War, more than six million cattle were herded from Texas to the railhead in Kansas along the Chisholm Trail. A woman in the southern town of Donna, Texas, wants to know if the small town was actually part of the famous trail.

Houdini Poster
Premiered: Season Four, Episode 401
The Detective: Gwen Wright
The Place: New York City
The Case: In an appearance worthy of Houdini, a Chicago roofer replacing roof insulation in a 1920s bungalow realized that the old material he was ripping down contained scores of vintage posters for a Harry Houdini show at the Shubert Princess Theater in 1926. Could such rare and random theater posters be authentic? And why did they advertise Houdini's attempts at debunking spiritual mediums? (69)

McKinley Casket Flag
Premiered: Season Four, Episode 401;
Repeated: Season Five, Episode 509
The Detective: Wes Cowan
The Place: Cincinnati, Ohio
The Case: A Washington man has a flag which he claims once draped the casket of President William McKinley, who was assassinated in 1901. Could this forty-five-star flag really have been given to his great-grandfather Charles Kennedy? And if so, what was Kennedy's possible connection to the U.S. president? (189)

EPISODE TWO

Wartime Baseball
Premiered: Season Four, Episode 402

The Detectives: Elyse Luray and Tukufu Zuberi
The Place: Kent, Washington
The Case: A Washington man approached *History Detectives* with an interesting piece of sports memorabilia owned by his father—a baseball bearing the autograph of baseball icon Dizzy Dean. The ball is dated July 12, 1944, and he believes that his father played catcher in a wartime baseball game that brought together two legendary pitchers—Dizzy Dean and Negro League star Satchel Paige. (307)

Confederate Eyeglass
Premiered: Season Four, Episode 402
The Detectives: Wes Cowan and Elyse Luray
The Place: Terre Haute, Indiana
The Case: A couple in Indiana owns a tiny brass eyeglass called a *stanhope* that, when peered through, reveals an image of Confederate president Jefferson Davis. Elyse Luray and Wes Cowan investigate the miniature "Davis" eyeglass to determine whether it's a clandestine wartime adornment that was worn by Confederate supporters.

The Howard Hughes Invention
Premiered: Season Four, Episode 402
The Detective: Gwen Wright
The Place: San Jose, California
The Case: At the start of the twentieth century, at an oil well in Texas, a crew of workers watched in awe as Howard Hughes Sr. showed off his new invention: a twin-cone drill bit that would allow oilmen around the world to tap into previously unreachable oil reserves. But was it in fact Hughes who invented this now common device or did the honor belong to someone else?

EPISODE THREE

Vicksburg Map
Premiered: Season Four, Episode 403
The Detective: Tukufu Zuberi
The Place: Tucson, Arizona

The Case: A man in Tucson owns an astonishing artifact—a map of the infamous Battle of Vicksburg that he inherited from his great-grandfather. The Vicksburg conflagration was vital to the North's command and ultimate success in the Civil War. Tukufu Zuberi investigates the authenticity of the hand-drawn map of battle positions, and the circumstances of the Union soldier who claimed to have drawn it. Will his conclusions prove astonishing to Civil War experts? (57)

Coca-Cola Trade Card
Premiered: Season Four, Episode 403
The Detective: Elyse Luray
The Place: Parkersburg, West Virginia
The Case: A West Virginia man owns what could be an extraordinary and very valuable piece of memorabilia—a pocket-sized card dated 1886 advertising a strange-sounding beverage. Could this 1886 card be a unique piece of early Coca-Cola advertising?

Lawrence Billy Club
Premiered: Season Four, Episode 403
The Detective: Wes Cowan
The Place: Methuen, Massachusetts
The Case: In January of 1912, tens of thousands of immigrant workers participated in the highly volatile Bread and Roses strike at the textile factories in Lawrence, Massachusetts. A Massachusetts man inherited a billy club with an inscription that reads "Lawrence Strike." Could this lethal-looking truncheon have been used in the contentious affair?

EPISODE FOUR

Calhoun Books
Premiered: Season Four, Episode 404
The Detective: Gwen Wright
The Place: Spartanburg, South Carolina
The Case: A South Carolina man owns a beautiful eight-volume set of Edward Gibbon's famous *History of the Decline and Fall of the Roman Empire*, which he

acquired at a local library sale in the town of Edgefield. The volumes are inscribed with the signature of John C. Calhoun, the famed intellectual architect of the Confederacy, but are they authentic?

Car Tape Deck
See Season Three, Episode 306

Mouse Toy
See Season Three, Episode 302

EPISODE FIVE

USS *Indianapolis*
Premiered: Season Four, Episode 405; Repeated: Season Five, Episode 508
The Detective: Wes Cowan
The Place: Cleveland, Ohio
The Case: Wes Cowan investigates four souvenirs, including a pair of Japanese naval patches, a Japanese plaque, and a chunk of metal, owned by a man who believes the artifacts were collected by his uncle, Arthur Michno, who perished on the USS *Indianapolis* on July 30, 1945, after the ship delivered components of the atomic bombs used on Hiroshima and Nagasaki. Could the artifacts be remnants of one of Japan's infamous kamikaze attacks? And is there a remote possibility that one of the *Indy*'s survivors recognizes Seaman Second Class Arthur Michno? (340)

Highlander Badge
Premiered: Season Four, Episode 405
The Detective: Elyse Luray
The Place: Augusta, Georgia
The Case: While scuba diving in the Savannah River, a Georgia man uncovered a mysterious metal badge. With the number 71 inscribed in Latin, and with imprints of a thistle and a crown, it looks like a Regimental military badge. Elyse Luray enlists the help of top forensic scientists to determine if an amateur treasure diver really has turned up an authentic Revolutionary War artifact. (156)

Lindbergh Engine
See Season Three, Episode 301

EPISODE SIX

Chinese Opium Scale
Premiered: Season Four, Episode 406
The Detective: Elyse Luray
The Place: Butte, Montana
The Case: In the 1960s, a woman in Montana purchased what looks like an old miniature fiddle case in the Montana mining town of Butte. Was the case really intended to hold a fiddle, or could it have been designed to hold a scale used for weighing opium in an Old West Chinese community?

Silent Film Reel
Premiered: Season Four, Episode 406
The Detective: Gwen Wright
The Place: Elsmere, Kentucky
The Case: A Kentucky man was searching through his grandfather's attic when he stumbled upon a short piece of film from the Silent Era in a canister marked "Dangerous Hour with Eddie Polo." Anxious to find out how his grandfather came to own the film, he enlists the help of Gwen Wright, who investigates the curious circumstances surrounding what could be a very rare piece of cinematic history. (259)

Göering Gun
See Season Three, Episode 308

EPISODE SEVEN

Survivor Camera
Premiered: Season Four, Episode 407
The Detective: Wes Cowan
The Place: Boynton Beach, Florida
The Case: Wes Cowan investigates a man named Adolf Fingrut, who left an antique camera to his niece after his passing. Fingrut escaped the death camps of the Holocaust, but it's unclear how he was able to survive, and what part his camera might have played in his escaping one of the most

harrowing ordeals in world history. Or was it an entirely different circumstance that saved Fingrut's life? (12)

Alcoholics Anonymous Letter
Premiered: Season Four, Episode 407
The Detective: Gwen Wright
The Place: Laurel, Maryland
The Case: Gwen Wright delves into the history of Alcoholics Anonymous and one of the organization's co-founders, Bill Wilson. A letter owned by a Maryland man acknowledges his grandfather's support for A.A., and was written to his grandmother after his grandfather's passing. Why was this supposedly sober attorney praised by Bill Wilson, and how did they come to meet?

Mystery Crystal Cross
Premiered: Season Four, Episode 407
The Detective: Tukufu Zuberi
The Place: Tallahassee, Florida
The Case: In an intriguing geological and spiritual mystery, Tukufu Zuberi meets the current chief of the Apalachee Tribe, who has a crystal cross that was discovered at an archaeological dig at Mission San Luis in Florida. Is it possible that the iconic cross could have been made centuries ago by the chief's ancestors? (274)

EPISODE EIGHT

Calf Creek Arrow
See Season Three, Episode 308

Doc Holliday's Watch
See Season Three, Episode 307

Black Star Line
See Season Three, Episode 302

EPISODE NINE

Civil War POW Photos
Premiered: Season Four, Episode 409
The Detective: Wes Cowan
The Place: Florida
The Case: A Florida man owns an extraordinary set of photographs thought

to have been taken with a homemade camera made by his great-great-grandfather Robert M. Smith, a lieutenant in the Union Army during the Civil War. Wes Cowan takes up the investigation with the help of an expert who creates a camera with the same materials Smith allegedly used to build his. Adding to the mystery is the fact that at the time, Smith was imprisoned at a Confederate POW camp. (2)

Grace Kelly Car
Premiered: Season Four, Episode 409
The Detective: Elyse Luray
The Place: Los Angeles, California
The Case: In the 1955 Hitchcock film *To Catch a Thief,* Grace Kelly has a classic romantic interlude with Cary Grant in one of the most elegant cars ever produced—a Sunbeam Alpine convertible. A Los Angeles man owns a Sunbeam Alpine, and he believes it could be the same car used during *Thief's* filming on the French Riviera. Elyse Luray investigates what could be a very valuable piece of movie memorabilia.

Harley-Davidson Motorcycle
Premiered: Season Four, Episode 409
The Detective: Tukufu Zuberi
The Place: Flemington, New Jersey
The Case: In a wild investigation, Tukufu Zuberi investigates a beautiful vintage 1914 Harley-Davidson motorcycle owned by a man in New Jersey. Curiously, the tank of the bike bears the iconic French symbol the Cross of Lorraine, leading Tukufu to wonder if the bike saw service on the battlefields of France during World War I. Was the bike really used in Europe, or did it serve a very different purpose in the United States? (283)

EPISODE TEN

Lou Gehrig Autograph
Premiered: Season Four, Episode 410
The Detective: Gwen Wright
The Place: Portland, Oregon

The Case: It's not often that someone finds a ticket to one of the most historic baseball games in history, but an Oregon man believes that's exactly what he has. Found in his mother's high school yearbook, the ticket bears the alleged autograph of baseball legend Lou Gehrig. Was the ticket actually signed by Gehrig on July 4, 1939, the day he announced his retirement and in a poignant speech declared himself "the luckiest man on the face of the earth?" (314)

Cleveland Electric Car
Premiered: Season Four, Episode 410
The Detective: Wes Cowan
The Place: Cleveland, Ohio
The Case: In an investigation rife with political intrigue, Wes Cowan meets an Ohio man who has a passion for trains and has long wondered about what happened to the once extensive electric trolley car network in Cleveland. Did the cars simply go out of style, or was there a much darker political reason for the lines being discontinued?

Philadelphia Freedom Paper
Premiered: Season Four, Episode 410
The Detective: Tukufu Zuberi
The Place: The Bronx, New York
The Case: A New York collector with a longtime interest in African American history purchased an intriguing document at a flea market that he believes to be a "freedom paper" for an African American man named John Jubilee Jackson. Tukufu Zuberi examines what this unique document might have meant to a slave in pre–Civil War Virginia.

EPISODE ELEVEN

Superman Sketch
Premiered: Season Four, Episode 411
The Detective: Wes Cowan
The Place: Toledo, Ohio
The Case: A woman in Ohio offered up an intriguing challenge to detective

Wes Cowan in the form of a hand-drawn sketch of Superman signed by the Man of Steel's creators, Jerry Siegel and Joe Schuster. Wes investigates the drawing's authenticity and how the woman's late father might have crossed paths with the legendary artists during the early 1940s. (93)

Lost Musical Treasure
Premiered: Season Four, Episode 411
The Detective: Tukufu Zuberi
The Place: Port Washington, Wisconsin
The Case: Nearly seventy-five years after the demise of Paramount Records, a Wisconsin man challenged *History Detectives* to examine a pair of metal "masters" that were used to press shellac records during the 1920s and 1930s. Tukufu Zuberi investigates whether the masters represent surviving fragments of a lost moment in American musical history.

Rebel Whiskey Flask
Premiered: Season Four, Episode 411
The Detective: Gwen Wright
The Place: Washington, Pennsylvania
The Case: The year was 1794, and trouble was brewing in western Pennsylvania, where thousands of protestors dared to fight back against the newly established U.S. government because of the tax placed on whiskey. A New Jersey woman called upon Gwen Wright to determine whether a glass whiskey flask that was found underneath her family's cabin is a relic from what came to be known as the 1794 Whiskey Rebellion. (73)

SEASON FIVE (2007)

EPISODE ONE

3-D Cuban Missile Crisis
Premiered: Season Five, Episode 501
The Detective: Wes Cowan
The Place: Portland, Oregon

The Case: A woman in Oregon has a 3-D projection view screen that may have helped save the Free World. Wes Cowan investigates the device, which was allegedly used to show President John F. Kennedy the aerial spy photos that helped him resolve the Cuban Missile Crisis.

Amos 'n' Andy Record
Premiered: Season Five, Episode 501
The Detective: Tukufu Zuberi
The Place: Lakeland, Florida
The Case: A man in Florida owns an aluminum record with the words "Amos & Andy" handwritten on its label. Could this be an actual recording of one of their radio broadcasts from the 1930s? Tukufu Zuberi investigates the possibility that the record is an early recording from one of the most infamous and racially misguided radio programs in U.S. history.

Women's Suffrage Painting
Premiered: Season Five, Episode 501
The Detective: Gwen Wright
The Place: League City, Texas
The Case: Over twenty years ago, a woman in Texas purchased a beautiful watercolor painting at a garage sale in Galveston. The image is of a trumpeting herald on a horse, and the wording on the image reads: "Official Program Woman Suffrage Procession, Washington D.C. March 3, 1913." Gwen Wright investigates the authenticity of the painting and the role it might have played in helping American women secure the right to vote. (7)

EPISODE TWO

Continental Currency
Premiered: Season Five, Episode 502
The Detective: Gwen Wright
The Place: Omaha, Nebraska
The Case: A family in Nebraska made a puzzling discovery between the pages of a book. What they found was a six-dollar bill dated February 17, 1776, that was allegedly produced by

the "United Colonies." Gwen Wright examines the history of Continental Currency and investigates whether this bill is real—or *real* fakery. (139)

Short Snorter
Premiered: Season Five, Episode 502
The Detective: Tukufu Zuberi
The Place: New York City
The Case: A World War II memorabilia collector owns what could be the ultimate autograph hunter's dream. Tukufu Zuberi investigates a British ten-shilling note dated July 25, 1942, that once belonged to a man named Harry Hopkins. Called a "short snorter," the note is signed by almost every luminary on the Allied side of World War II, from George S. Patton to Winston Churchill and Franklin D. Roosevelt. Is the bill authentic, and who was Harry Hopkins? (303)

Liberty Bell Pin
Premiered: Season Five, Episode 502
The Detective: Elyse Luray
The Place: Charlotte, North Carolina
The Case: A woman in North Carolina owns an unassuming pin that, according to her family's lore, is made of metal drawn from the Liberty Bell. Elyse Luray investigates whether or not part of America's most iconic symbol was melted down and turned into a pin, given to a man who was instrumental in bringing the Liberty Bell to an Atlanta exposition in 1895. (163)

EPISODE THREE

Jefferson Pledge
Premiered: Season Five, Episode 503
The Detective: Wes Cowan
The Place: Washington, D.C.
The Case: An archivist discovered what may be a monumental piece of history—a list of signatures from public figures of the early 1800s, including President Thomas Jefferson, offering their own money for a seemingly humble proposal. Did the development of the nation's public education system

begin with this long-forgotten document?

Dempsey Fight Bell
Premiered: Season Five, Episode 503
The Detective: Tukufu Zuberi
The Place: Reno, Nevada
The Case: A man in Nevada asks *History Detectives* to investigate a bell that is mounted on the wall of his favorite bar. Tukufu Zuberi examines the possibility that this bell could have been was used at ringside during a 1919 heavyweight title fight between Jack Dempsey and Jess Willard.

GAR Photograph
Premiered: Season Five, Episode 503
The Detective: Elyse Luray
The Place: Etters, Pennsylvania
The Case: A Civil War enthusiast owns a striking vintage photograph that depicts a group of older men in full dress uniform. What makes the photo so unusual is that included in the group are three African Americans. In an investigation with an astonishing genealogical conclusion, Elyse Luray examines the remarkable fraternal post–Civil War order known as the Grand Army of the Republic, an organization that crossed racial boundaries and united and supported the survivors of America's most traumatic internal conflict. (49)

EPISODE FOUR

Atocha Spanish Silver
Premiered: Season Five, Episode 504
The Detective: Tukufu Zuberi
The Place: Cedartown, Georgia
The Case: On July 20, 1985, one of the greatest maritime treasure discoveries in history was made off the Florida Keys, when the wreck of the Spanish ship the *Nuestra Señora de Atocha* was found by legendary treasure hunter Mel Fisher. As payment for his salvaging efforts on the *Atocha*, Fisher's nephew received a silver ingot, and he wants to know what the strange markings on the

bar indicate and why it's five pounds heavier than most of the other recovered ingots. (231)

The Lucy Parsons Book
Premiered: Season Five, Episode 504
The Detective: Elyse Luray
The Place: New Haven, Connecticut
The Case: Amid the stacks at the Wesleyan University Library, a student has found a book emblazoned with the name and address of legendary anarchist Lucy Parsons. Police had supposedly raided her home and confiscated all of her subversive literature in the early 1920s. Is it possible that the once-feared Parsons had actually owned this politically radical book? (15)

Ernie Pyle's Typewriter
Premiered: Season Five, Episode 504
The Detective: Wes Cowan
The Place: Portland, Oregon
The Case: A man in Oregon owns a typewriter that he believes once belonged to America's most beloved WWII battlefront correspondent, Ernie Pyle. Wes Cowan investigates the vintage Corona 3 typewriter and the life and wartime career of Pyle, and his unfortunate demise on April 18, 1945, at the hands of a sniper. (83)

EPISODE FIVE

Great Mexican War Poster
Premiered: Season Five, Episode 505
The Detective: Wes Cowen
The Place: San Francisco, California
The Case: While searching through his basement, a California man discovered a huge poster announcing a film about the "Great Mexican War," made by an obscure cinematographer named Charles Pryor. Wes Cowan investigates the tantalizing possibility that Pryor was an eyewitness chronicler of the Mexican Revolution.

Nora Holt Autograph Book
Premiered: Season Five, Episode 505
The Detective: Gwen Wright

The Place: Los Angeles, California
The Case: Upon his mother's passing, a man in California inherited her astonishing collection of African American memorabilia assembled over a forty-year period—over 3.5 million artifacts. Amid the collection is a curious small green leather autograph book that belonged to Nora Holt. Gwen Wright investigates Holt's career and why this Harlem Renaissance luminary owned a book bearing the signatures of presidents and renowned artists and writers. (311)

Muhlenberg Robe
Premiered: Season Five, Episode 505
The Detective: Elyse Luray
The Place: Philadelphia, Pennsylvania
The Case: According to a Revolutionary War legend, Lutheran pastor Peter Muhlenberg turned his pulpit into a recruiting station for revolutionary fighters in 1776. During a fiery sermon, he tore his robe from his shoulders to reveal a uniform and rallied 300 able-bodied congregants to the patriotic cause. Elyse Luray examines a robe at the Lutheran Theological Seminary in Philadelphia to learn if it's really the garment that bore witness to this event.

EPISODE SIX

NC-4: First Across the Atlantic
Premiered: Season Five, Episode 506
The Detective: Elyse Luray
The Place: Saratoga, California
The Case: In 1919, almost ten years before Charles Lindbergh's famous solo flight across the Atlantic, the NC-4 was the first aircraft to make the transatlantic journey. Elyse Luray investigates a claim made by a woman in California, who inherited a small square of canvaslike fabric that she believes came from the plane that made the historic flight. (289)

The Howard Hughes Crash
Premiered: Season Five, Episode 506

The Detective: Tukufu Zuberi
The Place: Laramie, Wyoming
The Case: On July 7, 1946, Howard Hughes piloted the first flight of his XF-11, designed to be the highest, fastest spy plane of its time. An hour and ten minutes into the flight, Hughes crashed into a Beverly Hills neighborhood. Tukufu Zuberi examines an altimeter that a man in Wyoming believes was retrieved from the wrecked airplane by his father, who was a mechanic for Hughes Aircraft. (291)

Civil War Balloon
See Season Three, Episode 303

EPISODE SEVEN

Red Cloud Letter
Premiered: Season Five, Episode 507
The Detective: Gwen Wright
The Place: Chappell, Nebraska
The Case: A man from Nebraska obtained a curious letter from his grandfather, who had spent time on South Dakota's Pine Ridge Reservation during the early part of the twentieth century. The letter is from Mount Rushmore sculptor Gutzon Borglum to a Lakota Sioux leader named James Red Cloud, a descendant of Chief Red Cloud. Gwen Wright investigates the unusual friendship between the two men during the period that the monument was being built on Sioux land.

1932 Ford Roadster
Premiered: Season Five, Episode 507
The Detective: Tukufu Zuberi
The Place: Benicia, California
The Case: A man in California owns a 1932 Ford roadster that originally had an engine too powerful for normal driving and wondered if his car was used for dry-lake racing—a sport that had its heyday in Southern California in the 1930s and 1940s. Tukufu Zuberi goes for a wild ride in this investigation, and works to determine whether or not this old hot rod is actually a historic race car.

Cast Iron Eagle

Premiered: Season Five, Episode 507
The Detective: Wes Cowan
The Place: Sussex, New Jersey
The Case: One of the main attractions at the family-run Space Farms Zoo and Museum in New Jersey is a majestic, twelve-foot-high cast iron eagle that is mounted on an orb in the center of the park. Wes Cowan investigates the family legend that the eagle had once perched atop a clock tower at Grand Central Station in Manhattan.

EPISODE EIGHT

Lincoln Letter

Premiered: Season Five, Episode 508
The Detective: Elyse Luray
The Place: Tampa, Florida
The Case: When a Florida firefighter purchased a stack of photos at a yard sale, he was surprised to find a letter dated August 2, 1858. The signature on the letter? "A. Lincoln." With what could prove to an extremely rare historical treasure, Elyse Luray investigates the authenticity of the letter, the political subterfuge occurring at the time, and the potential secret strategy that Abraham Lincoln may have been employing to win political power. (55)

Quaker Map

Premiered: Season Five, Episode 508
The Detective: Gwen Wright
The Place: Bradley Beach, New Jersey
The Case: A hand-drawn map that a woman in New Jersey purchased at a garage sale for forty-five dollars depicts in crude strokes the geography of southern Ohio during the mid-nineteenth century. The map's key states: "Those marked thus are meetings of friends." Does the map indicate Quaker meeting houses, and could it be linked to the legendary Underground Railroad?

USS *Indianapolis*

See Season Four, Episode 405

EPISODE NINE

Bill Pickett Saddle

Premiered: Season Five, Episode 509
The Detective: Tukufu Zuberi
The Place: Staten Island, New York
The Case: A woman in New York owns a well-worn saddle with the name "Bill Pickett" burned into it, and she believes it was once owned by the legendary African American cowboy and Wild West show and film star. Could this saddle have once belonged to a son of slave parents who rose to entertain kings and dignitaries with his innovative rodeo skills?

McKinley Casket Flag

See Season Four, Episode 401

Hitler Films

Premiered: Season Five, Episode 509
The Detective: Gwen Wright
The Place: Staten Island, New York
The Case: A man in New York recently found several film canisters he believes may contain German home movies of Nazi officials and possibly even Adolf Hitler. Hidden away for decades, the films were liberated by U.S. serviceman Walter Ladziak in the bombed-out ruins of a German opera house in 1945. Could they be authentic? Gwen Wright examines the origin of the films, what they were meant for, and how they were first discovered by Walter Ladziak. (10)

EPISODE TEN

USS *Thresher*

Premiered: Season Five, Episode 510
The Detective: Gwen Wright
The Place: Chicopee, Massachusetts
The Case: Gwen Wright investigates a stack of technical drawings and engineering documents that a man in Massachusetts found in his deceased great-uncle's basement. Details indicate that the documents describe the electrical systems of the nuclear submarine USS *Thresher*, an attack-class vessel that had been the pride of the U.S. Navy during the Cold War, and which sank in 1963 with the loss of all hands. (296)

Pete Gray Cartoon

Premiered: Season Five, Episode 510
The Detective: Elyse Luray
The Place: Brooklyn, New York
The Case: A comic book collector in New York owns several storyboards from a cartoon comic strip dating to the immediate post–World War II period that showcases the story of Pete Gray, the first one-armed major league baseball player, who later became an icon for disabled WWII veterans. Elyse Luray examines these unsigned drawings from the "Golden Age" of comics to determine whether they tell the tale of a real-life superhero.

Manhattan Project Letter

Premiered: Season Five, Episode 510
The Detective: Wes Cowan
The Place: Manhattan, New York
The Case: Two researchers from the Gilder Lehrman Institute of American History in New York approached *History Detectives* with an assortment of typed and handwritten documents that appear to be connected with the top-secret Manhattan Project, which developed America's first nuclear bombs during World War II. Wes Cowan investigates whether the documents were a plea to the U.S. government for reduced secrecy regarding nuclear affairs in the scientific community once hostilities had ended.

DVD PURCHASE

If you're interested in purchasing *History Detectives* episodes, please visit the *History Detectives* Web site at www.pbs.org and click on the link for *History Detectives* or Shop PBS.

PHOTOGRAPHY CREDITS

Unless otherwise specified, copyright on the works reproduced lies with the respective photographers, illustrators, agencies, and museums. Despite extensive research, it has not always been possible to establish copyright ownership. Where this is the case, we would appreciate notification.

PREFACE

History Detectives: xii, xiii, xiv, xv

CHAPTER 1

SNAPSHOTS IN TIME

Courtesy of the Douglas County Historical Society: page 14 left.

Courtesy of Geoffrey Feazell: page 6 bottom.

Courtesy of the Fingerhood family: page 13 all.

Courtesy of Laura Greiner: page 8.

History Detectives: pages 1, 5 all, 6 top, 14 right, 15, 17.

History Detectives via public domain: page 3.

CHAPTER 2

ENTERTAINMENT IN THE SHADOWS

Courtesy of Dave Brown: page 24 all.

History Detectives: pages 18, 21 all, 22, 26, 31 left.

History Detectives via public domain: page 31 right.

Courtesy of Joan Maynard: page 19.

The New York World-Telegram and the Sun Newspaper Photograph Collection courtesy of the Library of Congress, James J. Kriegsmann, photographer: page 27.

CHAPTER 3

LIFE IMITATES ART

History Detectives: pages 34, 36 top, 39, 43.

History Detectives via public domain: pages 36 bottom, 42 top right, bottom, 44 left.

Library of Congress: pages *vii*, 32, 33, 41, 42 top left, middle, middle, 44 right, 47.

Courtesy of Adam Lubas: page 46 all.

CHAPTER 4

AN UNCIVIL WAR

Courtesy of George Geder: pages 49, 51 all.

Courtesy of Fred Gumbart: page 58.

History Detectives: pages 52, 56, 57.

Library of Congress: pages 48, 55.

CHAPTER 5

IF WALLS COULD TALK

Courtesy AP Photo: page 71.

History Detectives: pages 65, 70, 73 bottom, 75, 76, 78, 80.

Courtesy of the Jake Gorst Collection: pages 72, 73 top.

Library of Congress: pages 64, 66, 69 right, 74.

The McManus-Young Collection courtesy of the Library of Congress: page 69 left.

CHAPTER 6

AMERICAN ICONS

Courtesy of AP Images: page 85 bottom.

Courtesy of the Ernest Hemingway Collection, at the John F. Kennedy Presidential Library and Museum, Boston: page 86.

Courtesy of Diane VanSkiver Gagel: page 94 top.

History Detectives: pages 81, 83, 91 bottom, 92 bottom, 93, 94 bottom all, 95, 96.

History Detectives via public domain: page 90.

Library of Congress: pages 92 top, 98 all.

Courtesy of the Lilly Library, Indiana University, Bloomington, Indiana: pages 84, 85 top, 89.

National Park Service: page 87.

Courtesy of the Oregon Historical Society: page 91 top.

The U.S. News & World Report Magazine Photograph Collection courtesy of the Library of Congress: page 82.

CHAPTER 7

CHILD'S PLAY

Courtesy of Sudee Campbell: page 104 all.

Courtesy of Charles Denson: pages 110, 111 top.

The George Grantham Bain Collection courtesy of the Library of Congress: page 102.

History Detectives: pages 100 left, 103 bottom, 105, 106, 111 bottom, 116.

History Detectives via public domain: page 109 bottom.

Library of Congress: pages 107 all, 109 top.

Courtesy of the O'Connell family: page 100 right.

Courtesy of Carol Sherman: pages *viii* top, 99, 101.

United States Patent and Trademark Office: pages 103 top, 114.

CHAPTER 8

WHISPERS IN THE MIST

Courtesy of the Academy of Natural Sciences, Philadelphia: page 133.

Courtesy of the C. Silkeborg Museum, Denmark: page 124.

The Edward S. Curtis Collection courtesy of the Library of Congress: pages *viii* bottom, 130 bottom.

Courtesy of Velma Falconer: page 128.

History Detectives: pages 119 all, 120, 126, 131 top.

Courtesy of Dr. Floyd Johnson: page 123.

Library of Congress: pages 127, 131 bottom, 132.

The National Photo Company Collection courtesy of the Library of Congress: page 135.

Courtesy of the Sam Noble Oklahoma Museum of Natural History, University of Oklahoma: pages 117, 118.

Courtesy of the Woolaroc Museum, Bartlesville, Oklahoma: page 130 top.

CHAPTER 9

DOLLARS AND SENSE

Courtesy of the Clarke Printing Company, San Antonio, Texas: page 150.

The George Grantham Bain Collection courtesy of the Library of Congress: pages 144, 151 top.

Courtesy of Paulette Hammerstrom: page 139 top.

History Detectives: pages 138, 149 top, middle, 151 bottom.

History Detectives via public domain: pages 148 all, 149 bottom.

Library of Congress: pages 140, 146.

Courtesy of the University of Notre Dame, Special Collections Department: pages 139 bottom, 141, 143 all, 145.

Courtesy of Westside Coins, Portland, Oregon: pages 137, 152, 153.

CHAPTER 10

LET FREEDOM RING

Courtesy of Chris Gates (http://www.chrisgates.net): pages 156 right, 163 bottom left.

History Detectives: pages 156 left, 157, 160 all, 163 top left, top right, bottom right, 164 top, 165, 167, 172.

Library of Congress: pages 155, 166, 170 bottom.

National Park Service: page 164 bottom.

The Roger Fenton Crimean War Photograph Collection courtesy of the Library of Congress: page 159.

Courtesy of Sotheby's New York: page 173.

Courtesy of Howard Szmolko: pages 154, 168 all, 170 top.

CHAPTER 11

FAMILY TIES

History Detectives: pages 175, 178 all, 179, 180 bottom, 183 all, 184 all, 185 top, 187 all, 189 top left, top right, bottom left, bottom right, 190, 193 all.

History Detectives via public domain: page 180 top.

Courtesy of Dodie Jacobi: pages 176 all, 177 all.

Library of Congress: page 192 all.

Courtesy of the National Library of Medicine: pages 185 bottom, 186, 188.

U.S. Coast Guard: page 181.

Courtesy of the William McKinley Presidential Library & Museum, Canton, Ohio: page 189 middle right.

CHAPTER 12
THE QUEST FOR EQUALITY

Courtesy of Rachael Clifford: page 206 top right, bottom.

Courtesy of Lori Deal: pages 197 all, 199 middle, bottom.

The Farm Security Administration, Office of War Information Collection courtesy of the Library of Congress: page 202 bottom.

The George Grantham Bain Collection courtesy of the Library of Congress: page 206 top left.

History Detectives: pages 198 bottom right, 203 bottom, 207 top, 210 bottom.

Library of Congress: pages *ix* bottom, 195, 196, 198 top, 200, 202, 203 top.

Courtesy of Mark Mitchell: pages 207 bottom, 210 top.

Courtesy of the Saratoga Historical Foundation: pages 198 bottom left, 199 top.

Courtesy of George Tamura: pages 194, 202 top, 204 all, 205 all.

CHAPTER 13
ARMED AND DANGEROUS

The Farm Security Administration, Office of War Information Photograph Collection courtesy of the Library of Congress: page 227 top.

Federal Bureau of Investigation: pages 217, 222, 227 bottom, 229 bottom.

Courtesy of Cassandra Goss: page 214 all.

History Detectives: pages 212, 213 all, 218 bottom, 219 all, 220 top, 221, 224, 225, 226.

Courtesy of Richard Kee: page 220 bottom.

The National Archives: page 223.

The New York World-Telegram and the Sun Newspaper Photograph Collection courtesy of the Library of Congress: pages 215, 229 top.

Courtesy of the Southwest Historical Society: page 218 top.

CHAPTER 14
THE TREASURE TROVE

History Detectives: pages 231, 232, 234 all, 236 all, 241, 243, 244 bottom, 245 all, 247 bottom, 248, 249.

Library of Congress: pages 230, 238, 239, 240, 246, 247 top.

Courtesy of the Mariner's Museum: page 242.

NASA: page 237.

Courtesy of the Oregon Historical Society: page 244 top.

Courtesy of Chuck Sotzin: page 235.

CHAPTER 15
THAT'S ENTERTAINMENT

Courtesy of Robert Gallant: page 262.

The George Grantham Bain Collection courtesy of the Library of Congress: page 260.

Courtesy of Ray Harryhausen: page 255.

History Detectives: pages 250, 251, 253 all, 254 all, 256, 259 bottom, 261 all, 263 bottom.

Library of Congress: pages 252, 257, 258, 263 top.

The National Photo Company Collection courtesy of the Library of Congress: page 259 top.

CHAPTER 16
SKELETONS IN THE CLOSET

Courtesy of the Anne Arundel County Lost Towns Project: pages 266, 267, 268 top, 270.

The G. Eric and Edith Matson Photograph Collection courtesy of the Library of Congress: pages 280, 281.

History Detectives: pages 268 bottom, 269 all, 271, 277 top, 278 top, 279.

Library of Congress: pages 275, 277 bottom.

The Metropolitan Museum of Art, Rogers Fund, 1929 by exchange (29.3.2) Image@The Metropolitan Museum of Art: page 273.

Courtesy of Mission San Luis: *ix* top, pages 276, 278 bottom.

The University of Glasgow courtesy of the National Library of Medicine: page 272.

CHAPTER 17
FLIGHT, FRIGHT, AND PERILOUS PLIGHTS

The Abdul-Hamid II Collection courtesy of the Library of Congress: page 286 bottom.

Courtesy of the Federal Aviation Administration: page 293 top.

The George Grantham Bain Collection courtesy of the Library of Congress: pages 286 top, 289 top.

History Detectives: pages 283 all, 287, 289 bottom, 291 top, 293 bottom, 296 top, 300.

Courtesy of Jim Kirkpatrick: page 291 bottom.

Library of Congress: pages 282, 284, 285, 292, 294, 295.

Courtesy of Peter Stone: pages 296 bottom, 297.

Official U.S. Army photograph courtesy of the Library of Congress: page 290.

Official U.S. Navy photograph from the collections of the Naval Historical Center: page 298.

CHAPTER 18

SIGNED, SEALED, AND DELIVERED

The Carl Van Vechten Photograph Collection courtesy of the Library of Congress: page 311 top.

The George Grantham Bain Collection courtesy of the Library of Congress: page 317.

History Detectives: pages 303, 306 all, 311 bottom all, 312, 314, 316 all.

Library of Congress: pages 313 all.

Courtesy of Joe Miles Jr.: pages *x* top, 302 (baseball), 309, 310.

Courtesy of the Photographic Archives, Ekstrom Library, University of Louisville: page 308.

Courtesy of Gary Schulze: pages 304 all, 305 all.

Courtesy of Rick Sutherland: page 302 (baseball bat).

CHAPTER 19

DUBIOUS DWELLINGS

Photo © 2007 Henri D. Grissino-Mayer, University of Tennessee: page 324.

History Detectives: pages 319, 320 top, 323, 325 all, 331 all, 336.

Library of Congress: pages 320 bottom, 321 all, 322, 329 all, 330, 332 all, 335, 338.

Courtesy of the Mary Surratt Museum: page 334.

NASA/Goddard Space Flight Center Scientific Visualization Studio: page 327.

National Park Service: pages 318, 326.

CHAPTER 20

WORLD AT WAR

The Edward S. Curtis Collection courtesy of the Library of Congress: page 357 top.

The Farm Security Administration, Office of War Information Photograph Collection courtesy of the Library of Congress: page 356 all.

The Frank and Frances Carpenter Collection courtesy of the Library of Congress: page 357 middle.

The G. Eric and Edith Matson Photograph Collection courtesy of the Library of Congress: page 357 bottom.

History Detectives: pages *x* bottom, 343 all, 344 top, 347, 348 all, 351 top, 352, 354 all, 355 bottom.

Courtesy of Larry Klubert: page 344 bottom.

Library of Congress: pages 341, 349 bottom, 355 top.

Courtesy of the McKenty family: page 351 bottom.

National Photo Company Collection courtesy of the Library of Congress: page 353 bottom.

Courtesy of Michelle Theriot: page 353 top.

Official U.S. Army Air Force photograph courtesy of the Library of Congress: page 342.

U.S. Coast Guard: page 350.

Courtesy of the U.S. Naval Historical Center: page 345.

Official U.S. Navy photograph from the collections of the Naval Historical Center: pages 339, 340.

Courtesy of the Westerlund family: page 349 top.

INDEX